POPULAR PROTEST AND
POLITICAL CULTURE IN
MODERN CHINA

POLITICS IN ASIA AND THE PACIFIC
Interdisciplinary Perspectives

Haruhiro Fukui
Series Editor

Popular Protest and Political Culture in Modern China, Second Edition,
edited by Jeffrey N. Wasserstrom and Elizabeth J. Perry

Southeast Asia in the New International Era, Second Edition,
Clark D. Neher

China Under Reform, Lowell Dittmer

Global Television and the Politics of the Seoul Olympics,
James F. Larson and Heung-Soo Park

Japan's Foreign Aid: Power and Policy in a New Era,
edited by Bruce M. Koppel and Robert M. Orr, Jr.

FORTHCOMING

Japan's Land Policy and Its Global Impact, Shigeko N. Fukai

Mass Politics in the PRC: State and Society in Contemporary China,
Alan P.L. Liu

Comparative Politics of Asia, Sue Ellen M. Charlton

Second Edition

POPULAR PROTEST AND POLITICAL CULTURE IN MODERN CHINA

EDITED BY

Jeffrey N. Wasserstrom
INDIANA UNIVERSITY

Elizabeth J. Perry
UNIVERSITY OF CALIFORNIA–BERKELEY

Westview Press
BOULDER · SAN FRANCISCO · OXFORD

Politics in Asia and the Pacific: Interdisciplinary Perspectives

Copyright © 1992, 1994 by Westview Press, Inc.

Published in 1994 in the United States of America by Westview Press, Inc., 5500 Central
Avenue, Boulder, Colorado 80301-2877, and in the United Kingdom by Westview Press, 36
Lonsdale Road, Summertown, Oxford OX2 7EW

Library of Congress Cataloging-in-Publication Data
Popular protest and political culture in modern China / edited by
Jeffrey N. Wasserstrom, Elizabeth J. Perry. — 2nd ed.
    p.   cm. — (Politics in Asia and the Pacific)
    Includes index.
    ISBN 0-8133-2042-9 (HC). — ISBN 0-8133-2043-7 (paperback)
    1. China—History—Tiananmen Square Incident, 1989.   2. Political
culture—China.   I. Wasserstrom, Jeffrey N.   II. Perry, Elizabeth
J.   III. Series.
DS779.32.P67   1994
951.05'8—dc20
                                                                     94-19867
                                                                       CIP

Printed and bound in the United States of America

The paper used in this publication meets the requirements
of the American National Standard for Permanence of Paper
for Printed Library Materials Z39.48-1984.

10   9   8   7   6   5   4   3   2

*This volume is dedicated to the unsung heroes
and forgotten martyrs of 1989—the farmers, teachers, workers,
entrepreneurs, policemen, smugglers, officials, and soldiers
who risked their careers and personal safety
to help students and other protesters escape arrest,
and the city dwellers of all classes
who died in the streets of Chengdu
and other places far from Tiananmen Square.*

CONTENTS

PREFACE TO THE
SECOND EDITION

When Susan McEachern of Westview Press asked if we might be interested in preparing a revised and expanded edition of *Popular Protest and Political Culture in Modern China,* we were happy for an obvious reason: Her request indicated that people were buying and (presumably) reading the first edition. We were also pleased for another reason: Ever since the book had gone to press, we had been troubled by a nagging sense that there were a number of ways in which it could have been a more satisfying volume. Because of our belief that it was important to say certain kinds of things about the cultural dynamics and historical resonances of contemporary Chinese politics while the images left by the intense media coverage of the protest and repression centering in and around Tiananmen Square were still fresh in the minds of our readers, the first edition had been put together quite quickly. For the most part we were happy with the results, and we remain convinced that (on balance) it was a good decision to get the collection into print when we did, since many of the essays offered perspectives on the events of 1989 in China that were different in important ways from those provided by most of the other early works on the subject. Nonetheless, we were happy to be given the opportunity to rethink the structure and contents of the book in an effort to make it more effective as a work of scholarship and more useful as a teaching tool.

The main aspect of the first edition that dissatisfied us from the start was the absence of Chinese voices. We were also concerned that since Daniel Chirot was the only contributor whose work typically focuses on countries other than China, his comparative chapter might appear somehow out of place. By the time we actually started working on this revised edition, our list of areas that might be worth tinkering with had grown considerably, thanks to the useful comments we had received from a variety of colleagues who had either written reviews of the book or communicated with us in a less formal fashion about their experiences using the volume in the classroom. It would have been impossible to act upon every suggestion, since the chapters that some colleagues said should be left out of future editions were precisely the ones that others praised most fervently. Nonetheless, we have taken many of their suggestions to heart, and as a result the new edition is different from its predecessor in several ways.

Here it seems worthwhile to describe briefly the four main changes we have made and to offer a short explanation of why we decided not to follow up on some of the other specific suggestions made by colleagues, including that of providing more coverage of three important topics that received comparatively little attention in the first edition: power struggles within the Communist Party leadership, the role that gender plays in political struggles other than student movements, and expressions of dissent (past and present) that have been based in villages rather than in cities. First, the changes to be found in this edition:

1. "Learning from 1989" is no longer used as a subtitle for the collection. According to one reviewer, even though many of the chapters were clearly written with the events of 1989 in mind, when taken as a whole, the first edition came across as a more general introduction to contemporary China than the subtitle would lead one to expect. Because the present edition includes two new essays ("Discos and Dictatorship" by Tony Saich and "The Politics of Popular Music in Post-Tiananmen China" by Andrew F. Jones) that focus on developments that have occurred since 1989, the subtitle would be even more misleading now.

2. The new edition includes three new chapters that help resolve the issues that concerned us most about the first edition. Namely, the new edition contains two important contributions by Chinese scholars who participated in and observed the events of 1989 as well as a new essay by historical sociologist Craig Calhoun, best known for his work as a social theorist and for his discussions of countries other than China. Calhoun was an eyewitness to the occupation of Tiananmen Square, and the chapter he contributes focuses on twentieth-century Chinese events. Nevertheless, because of his interest in theoretical issues that have tended to attract comparatively little interest in the Chinese-studies community (at least until quite recently), the inclusion of Calhoun's piece has made Chirot's insightful discussion of Eastern European events in 1989 seem less isolated and more a part of the whole.

3. Unlike the first edition, this one is divided into topical sections, each of which contains two or three chapters on a common theme. This change was designed primarily to facilitate the book's use in a variety of classroom settings. The needs of teachers and students were also at the front of our minds when we decided to begin these sections with brief introductions that draw connections between the chapters and provide suggestions for supplementary readings (see "A Note to Teachers" for more information).

4. This edition does not include three of the essays that appeared in the original version of the book. The decision to drop these chapters was not a reflection of any change in our opinion about the high quality of the work done by the scholars involved, as our references to their work

in the suggested readings sections of this edition indicate. Rather, our motivation for the deletions was inspired by an interest in making the book more cohesive as an integrated whole. In addition, some of the chapters in question either did not fit into the format of the new edition or had proved difficult to use in undergraduate classroom settings.

Now, a few comments about why we decided not to provide more coverage of elite (power) politics, (nonstudent-movement) sexual politics, and rural politics. We initially looked for pieces already in print that both addressed these issues and would fit in with the basic structure of our volume, and in a couple of cases we even went as far as attempting to persuade scholars (whose work we admired) to write new essays that would serve this need. For various reasons, however, none of these efforts panned out. In retrospect, this is probably for the best—had we included a single chapter on topics as important as these, we would have run the risk of treating them in an artificial or superficial fashion. What we decided, therefore, was to handle the situation by paying particular attention to those subjects in the sections of the new edition that suggest supplementary readings to be used in conjunction with this book but to include only new chapters that flesh out the topics already covered in the first edition. The second edition is thus more focused than the first: It is designed primarily as an introduction to the cultural dimensions of urban politics, and we do not try to hide the fact that most chapters focus on the protest activities and mentalities of China's *zhishi fenzi* (a term for "intellectuals" that includes university students). Ideally, as we suggest in "A Note to Teachers," instructors will pair it with other readings that shed light on important subjects that we do not address.

One additional feature of the first edition has *not* been changed, despite the criticisms we have heard from some colleagues: We continue to insist that the shortcomings as well as the virtues of the protesters of 1989 deserve to be highlighted. Although it is often said that history is kindest to winners (in part because it is they who often live to tell the tale or who end up with the power to control what appears in print), there is always a temptation to present the activities of noble losers in a hagiographic fashion. As much as we admire the bravery of many of those who took part in the occupation of Tiananmen Square, and as distasteful as we find the official CCP version of the crackdown that presents the protests as the work of "black hands" and "counterrevolutionary rioters," we remain convinced that it is necessary to find a way to mix criticism with admiration when discussing the social movement of 1989. Better yet, it is time to find some way to conceptualize and discuss China's dilemmas in terms that go beyond simplistic dichotomies; the temptation to think only in terms of praise and blame, backwardness and modernization, revolution and counterrevolution, and other generally unproductive binary oppositions has infused and constrained discussions of Chinese history and politics, both inside and outside of China, for far too long. This, it seems to us, is one of the arguments Liu Xiaobo makes in the passionate and provocative essay that he wrote for this edition.

The chapters retained from the first edition have not been changed in significant ways. It would have been tempting to give the authors of these chapters the opportunity to modify their arguments in light of the considerable scholarship that has appeared since the first edition went to press—or at the very least to allow them to update their footnotes to refer to the most interesting of recent works on related topics. In the end, however, we decided that—for both logistical and intellectual reasons—it would be more interesting to reprint them in their original form and to make only minor editorial (and mostly cosmetic) modifications (although one of us has used our editorial prerogative to add a new postscript to the piece on "History, Myth, and the Tales of Tiananmen"). Thus, the chapters from the first edition continue to illustrate early attempts by culture-minded China specialists to rethink their basic assumptions concerning history and politics in the immediate aftermath of the traumas of 1989. Recent developments in Chinese political culture are explicitly dealt with in several of the new chapters contributed to this volume, and references to some of the most important works on relevant subjects that have been published since the first edition of this book went to press can be found in the suggested readings provided both in "A Note to Teachers" and in the introductions to the volume's topical sections.

Jeffrey N. Wasserstrom
Elizabeth J. Perry

ACKNOWLEDGMENTS

The editors express appreciation to Anne E. Bock for expert assistance in preparing many of the chapters for electronic typesetting and improving some of the prose. We would also like to thank Peter Erickson (who carefully translated the chapter by Liu Xiaobo) and the following people at Westview Press: Susan McEachern, who helped us in innumerable ways with both the original manuscript and this second edition; Michelle Asakawa, who has patiently shepherded us through the process of preparing this edition for publication; and the copy editors, Alice Colwell and John Wilson, who helped us refine the writing in both editions. Jeffrey Wasserstrom is grateful to the following institutions for providing him with research funds and other forms of assistance: the National Academy of Education, the Spencer Foundation, the National Endowment for the Humanities, the Pacific Cultural Foundation, and Indiana University. Elizabeth Perry would like to thank the Henry M. Jackson School of International Studies, the Political Science Department and Institute of East Asian Studies at the University of California–Berkeley, and the National Endowment for the Humanities.

J.N.W.
E.J.P.

A NOTE TO TEACHERS

The first edition of this volume was intended for classroom use, and since its appearance in 1992 we either have assigned it ourselves or heard of it being assigned as required reading for a variety of courses, ranging from general introductory surveys of modern Chinese history to specialized classes that deal exclusively with conflicting interpretations of the events of 1989 to comparative seminars that focus on theories of revolutionary change. One of our main goals in putting together the second edition was to make the book a more effective and attractive pedagogic tool for the teachers of these and other related courses. As we pointed out in the Preface, some chapters were deleted and new ones were added to some degree with this aim in mind, but perhaps the most significant changes relating to classroom use in this volume are those that have affected the format of the book. Whereas the first edition simply presented a series of chapters on different specific topics, this new edition is broken up into thematic parts, each of which begins with a brief introduction and an annotated list of readings that we felt might be useful to assign in conjunction with this book. The main purpose of this note is simply to explain the reasoning behind the construction of these lists, to describe our vision of how these lists might best be used, and then finally to draw attention to some supplementary works that, for one reason or another, did not seem appropriate to list in the introduction to any particular thematic part.

First, we have not included the lists of recommended materials as an attempt to present a canon of the "most important" works on particular subjects. Instead, the supplementary readings are intended to draw attention to thought-provoking texts by scholars (and in some cases journalists, novelists, poets, filmmakers, or artists) whose arguments reinforce those presented here, differ from them in interesting ways, or explore specific issues that the contributors to this volume do not address directly. The lists are meant to be suggestive rather than comprehensive, and we admit that they are idiosyncratic. When compiling the lists, we have tried to avoid the temptation to simply pull out a few of the main works cited by various contributors in their chapters, since it is easy enough for the reader to figure out whom particular authors are looking to for evidence and inspiration. Of course, some of the texts on our lists are cited in various chapters of the book; but in the introductions to each part we also have drawn attention to works that either were ignored by contributors or appeared after their chapters were completed.

How instructors will use our lists will depend largely on the types of classes and level of students they teach. With this in mind, we have divided each list into four categories: works on contemporary (or what is sometimes called "post-Mao") China; works on Chinese history; studies of other countries or theoretical pieces that do not focus on any particular nation; and primary sources (for example, films, a book of reproductions of propaganda posters, and more conventional types of literary texts). We have tried to make sure that each list draws attention to at least some works that are short, readily available, and straightforward enough to assign in introductory courses. While our emphasis throughout is on article-length pieces, we also include references to monographs and (in a few cases) even unpublished dissertations that we thought might make useful reading for advanced-undergraduate and graduate students preparing papers or in-class presentations. Almost all the books listed are available in paperback editions.

Finally, we should mention the omission from the lists of several types of works that some instructors might find very helpful to pair with this book but that contain arguments or information that have relevance for all of the thematic parts of this volume rather than for any particular one. This is true, for example, of most of the best general introductory texts to modern Chinese history or politics, such as Frederic Wakeman Jr.'s *The Fall of Imperial China* (New York: Free Press, 1975), a social historical survey of the events leading up to 1911; Jonathan Spence's *The Search for Modern China* (New York: Norton, 1992), which covers the period from circa 1644 to 1989; Lucien Bianco's *Origins of the Chinese Revolution* (Stanford: Stanford University Press, 1966), which remains the best concise and accessible introduction to the Chinese Communist Party's rise to power; Maurice Meisner's *Mao's China and After* (New York: Free Press, 1986), which chronicles the history of the People's Republic of China; Lowell Dittmer's *China's Continuous Revolution* (Berkeley: University of California Press, 1987), which highlights the importance of ideology and culture in the development of the People's Republic of China; Roderick MacFarquhar, ed., *The Politics of China: 1949–1989* (Cambridge: Cambridge University Press, 1994), which contains chapters on key themes in contemporary politics; and James R. Townsend and Brantly Womack's *Politics in China* (Boston: Little, Brown, 1986), which provides an intelligent structural-functional analysis of the workings of the contemporary Chinese political system. These works should prove particularly useful in undergraduate courses. For graduate seminars, texts that provide general comparative, theoretical, or historiographic frameworks that help place the chapters in this volume in perspective include Paul Cohen's *Discovering History in China: American Historical Writing on the Recent Chinese Past* (New York: Columbia University Press, 1984), Daniel Chirot's *The Crisis of Leninism and the Decline of the Left: The Revolutions of 1989* (Seattle: University of Washington Press, 1991), and assorted volumes of *The Cambridge History of China* (Cambridge: Cambridge University Press, various years). In addition, because our volume focuses on urban China, undergraduate and graduate students alike might benefit from reading it in conjunction with a work on Chinese village life that highlights the interplay between culture and politics, such as Anita Chan, Richard Madsen, and Jonathan Unger's *Chen Village Under Mao and Deng* (Berkeley: University of California Press, 1992).

Three other types of books that we do not cite in the lists provided in the introductions to the specific thematic parts are collections of essays on 1989 that are similar to this one, works composed largely of translations of documents from the 1989 social movement, and eyewitness accounts both of the protest and the repression by people who were in Beijing or other parts of China at the time. Of the many conference volumes and other types of essay collections that have appeared, the following are some of the ones that might be most interesting to pair with ours: Roger Des Forges et al., eds., *Chinese Democracy and the Crisis of 1989: Chinese and American Reflections* (Albany: SUNY Press, 1993); Arthur Rosenbaum, ed., *State and Society in China: The Consequences of Reform* (Boulder: Westview Press, 1992); George Hicks, ed., *The Broken Mirror: China After Tiananmen* (Chicago: St. James Press, 1990); and Tony Saich, ed., *The Chinese People's Movement: Perspectives on Spring 1989* (Armonk, N.Y.: M. E. Sharpe, 1990). Some of the most useful document collections include Suzanne Ogden et al., eds., *China's Search for Democracy: The Student and Mass Movement of 1989* (Armonk, N.Y.: M. E. Sharpe, 1992); Michel Oksenberg et al., eds., *Beijing Spring, 1989: Confrontation and Conflict, The Basic Documents* (Armonk, N.Y.: M. E. Sharpe, 1990); and Han Minzhu, ed., *Cries for Democracy* (Princeton: Princeton University Press, 1990). A few of the more thoughtful firsthand narratives include Lee Feigon, *China Rising: The Meaning of Tiananmen* (Chicago: Ivan R. Dee, 1990); Scott Simmie and Bob Nixon, *Tiananmen Square* (Seattle: University of Washington Press, 1989); Jonathan Unger, ed., *The Pro-Democracy Protests in China: Reports from the Provinces* (Armonk, N.Y.: M. E. Sharpe, 1991); and George Black and Robin Munro, *Black Hands of Beijing* (New York: John Wiley, 1993).

INTRODUCTION:
CHINESE POLITICAL CULTURE
REVISITED

Elizabeth J. Perry

Since its inception following World War II, the field of contemporary Chinese studies has been confronted by a series of extraordinary events. The first generation of specialists, schooled in a classical sinological tradition that stressed China's unique cultural continuity, was immediately challenged by what seemed—at least on the face of it—a major rupture with the past: the Communist Revolution of 1949. Not surprisingly, these specialists' efforts to explain this momentous aberration defined the initial contours of contemporary Chinese studies. Although scholarly opinion on the nature of the revolution was deeply divided, the debate centered on the extent to which the ideology and practice of Chinese communism could be said to reflect indigenous cultural influences, as opposed to a wholesale importation of the Soviet model.[1]

Once they had recovered from the initial shock of "losing" China, many analysts chose to take comfort in their sinology, emphasizing a peculiar political tradition intelligible only to the classically trained specialist. As C. P. Fitzgerald summarized this position, "The Chinese conceptions which underlie the theory of government are unique; unlike any others, and evolved in China. The roots are deep and nourished in a soil alien to the West; the flower is therefore also strange, and hard to recognize."[2] Superficial revolutionary changes were believed to belie a deeper continuity: "The Chinese Communists, embracing a world authoritarian doctrine in place of one local to China, have enlarged the arena in which old Chinese ideas can once more be put into practice, in more modern guise, expanded to the new scale, but fundamentally the same ideas which inspired the builders of the Han Empire and the restorers of the T'ang."[3]

Although never fully resolved (as academic arguments seldom are), the controversy surrounding the origins of Chinese communism abated as the storm of revolutionary struggle was overtaken by the calm of regime consolidation. A second generation of specialists set about the sober task of documenting the development of Chinese communism, which seemed increasingly to resemble its Soviet precursor in many respects.[4] Whether wedded to a totalitarian model or to a more pluralist perspective, this new generation of China scholars—now increasingly trained as social scientists rather than as historians—identified the Chinese Communist model's numerous similarities to Soviet and East European counterparts.[5]

However, just as the comparative communism perspective was gaining popularity, along came the Great Proletarian Cultural Revolution of 1966–1969. Faced with the challenge of explaining this unexpected event, those in the contemporary Chinese studies field again were caught up in controversy. China's dramatic break with Soviet-style communism—exemplified in Mao's Cultural Revolution—aroused renewed interest and disagreement over the continuing importance of indigenous political traditions. However, unlike the first generation of scholarly debate on the Communist Revolution of 1949, the new round of controversy was debated instead by scholars whose training and academic self-identity derived from the burgeoning field of political science. Drawing on recent trends in their discipline, these political scientists viewed the Cultural Revolution as a problem in "political development." Wedded to central precepts of the modernization paradigm, they stressed the role of "political culture"[6] in fashioning China's unorthodox and uncertain developmental path.

Modernization theorists emphasized the close relationship of political culture to "political socialization" (that is, "the process whereby political values and attitudes are inculcated") and "secularization" (that is, "the process whereby men become increasingly rational, analytical, and empirical in their political action").[7] In the case of China, distinctive patterns of childrearing and schooling (or "socialization") were blamed for the seeming irrationalities (or lack of "secularization") characteristic of Red Guard excesses during the Cultural Revolution. By this account, the Cultural Revolution constituted a crisis in political development whose origins could be traced back to peculiarities of Chinese culture—particularly as embodied in conflictual authority relations.[8]

Although strongly influenced by prevailing political science fashion, advocates of a political culture approach within the Chinese studies field also departed methodologically from mainstream currents in their discipline. Most analysts of political culture, dovetailing their studies with the behavioral revolution then sweeping the U.S. social sciences, pursued their projects through statistical interpretations of large-scale attitude surveys.[9] By contrast, students of Chinese political culture—denied access to field research in mainland China—resorted to a much less rigorous brand of methodology. Personal impressions (presented as psychocultural analysis) were combined with small-scale surveys of unrepresentative samples in Taiwan and Hong Kong, as well as schematic references to philosophical texts and historical events, so as to cobble together a portrait of Chinese political culture that proved unconvincing to many in the sinological and social science camps alike.[10] As a result, the concept of political culture developed a rather unsavory reputation among China specialists. Moreover, as fascination with attitude surveys waned within the political science profession at large, the study of political culture was largely abandoned by other wings of the discipline as well.

The simultaneous fading both of the Chinese Cultural Revolution and of the disciplinary interest in political culture drew scholars of contemporary China back to more prosaic styles of comparative analysis. Elite policymaking—whether approached in terms of factionalism, bureaucratic politics, or ideology—dominated the field.[11] In addition, those who deigned to search below the commanding heights of the political system for the activities of ordinary peasants and workers generally did so from a "structuralist" rather than a "culturalist" point of view.[12] Moreover, as post-Mao China embarked upon a reform program that resembled ongoing experiments in Eastern Europe and the Soviet Union, comparisons with other Communist systems regained currency.[13]

The Challenge of 1989

Recently, students of contemporary China have been confronted again by a crisis in understanding prompted by a popular protest that defied the best predictions of specialists in the field. The unrest of 1989, during which protesters in Beijing and other major cities throughout China took to the streets to demand both an end to official corruption and a guarantee of greater political freedom, shook the very foundations of Communist Party rule. With the help of the capabilities of modern communications technologies, these same events also sent shock waves around the world. The occupation of Tiananmen Square, the confrontation between a lone protester and a row of government tanks, the erection of a "Goddess of Democracy" statue, and the June Fourth Massacre in which soldiers of the People's Liberation Army turned their weapons upon unarmed citizens—images such as these appeared immediately on television newscasts in countries across the globe, alternately inspiring and horrifying audiences and changing forever the way they thought about China.

The events of the 1989 protest and its subsequent repression had an equally profound impact upon those who study China for a living. Once again, the academic world was forced to question many of its most basic premises about contemporary Chinese society and politics. The present volume is an attempt to take stock of some of the reconsiderations to which the 1989 movement gave rise. As was the case with the Communist Revolution of 1949 and *every* the Cultural Revolution of 1966–1969, the uprising of 1989 and its aftermath *20 yrs.* have generated more controversy than consensus. Thus, the chapters that follow will not present a unitary interpretation. Rather, they introduce some of the ways in which leading scholars from different disciplines, with different areas of expertise and different methodologies, have started to place the recent events into perspective. All of the chapters are meant to offer insights into distinctive features of the 1989 movement and its consequences as well as to stimulate new thinking about contemporary China in general. Taken as a whole, the essays suggest some of the directions in which recent developments have already begun to alter the analysis of Chinese popular protest.

Despite the diversity of these contributions, they share a fascination with political culture, although the authors tend to shy away from that particular term, tainted as it is with unpleasant memories of past usage. As they did in the debates that followed earlier crises in the unfolding of the Chinese Revolution, scholars are again looking to indigenous precedents to answer why the outcome in Beijing differed so radically from that in Budapest, Bucharest, or Berlin. In so doing, they join a "culture craze" *(wenhua re)* that has swept both Chinese and Western academic circles in recent years.[14]

The New Political Culture

Is this culturalist trend nothing more than a temporary (and perhaps misguided) phase, soon to be replaced by a more sober return to elitist and structuralist modes of analysis? As adherents of the neoculturalist perspective, we let our defense rest upon the belief that this approach differs significantly from previous efforts to explain Chinese protest in cultural terms and that it offers a more credible, and thus longer-lived, means of interpreting political change.

Whereas earlier cultural initiatives were promoted variously by historians steeped in sinology or by political scientists seeking to link up with the latest disciplinary fad, the current turn to culture has attracted historians and social scientists alike. Happily, recent years have seen a blurring of the sharp division between history and the social sciences that emerged with the second generation of contemporary China specialists. Gone are the days when the year 1949 demarcated a strict disciplinary boundary that was to be trespassed only at some risk to one's professional standing.[15] Constructive interaction between history and the social sciences has moderated the eccentricities of antiquarianism, on the one hand, and paradigm faddism, on the other, to which each of these branches of learning—if left to its own devices—was often prone.

Another advantage enjoyed by scholars today is the greater maturity and sophistication of both historical and contemporary studies. Thanks to a generous infusion of new talent into the China field, we have all learned a good deal about the *complexities* of Chinese society and politics—past and present. Our picture of "traditional" culture is a more refined one (with greater appreciation of temporal and regional variation) than was available to preceding generations.[16] Furthermore, our understanding of the current scene also has been much advanced by the access to fieldwork and other previously unobtainable sources that has enlivened the past decade of research.[17]

One result of this new accumulation of knowledge is an aversion to static or monochromic portraits of Chinese culture. Differences in time period, social status, and geographical location were, we now realize, characterized by important distinctions in belief and behavior. As a consequence, the challenge to the student of contemporary Chinese popular protest is to discover which of a *multitude* of available cultural repertoires is being drawn upon. Moreover, recognition of the fluidity and flexibility of cultural practice alerts the analyst to the possibility of innovation and originality. Rather than seeing Chinese politics as forever condemned to a treadmill of repetitive patterns, we look instead for creative deviation and breakthrough. Such transformations in political culture, one hastens to add, are not necessarily in the direction of greater "secularization." One finds little evidence, in China or elsewhere in the world, of a process whereby "traditional" orientations inexorably give way to more "rational" modes of thinking.[18] The dichotomous mentality underlying modernization theory, it turns out, is a poor guide to the complexities of political change in the real world.

But whether one is more impressed with continuity or with transformation (a matter on which the contributors to this volume differ among themselves), political culture is seen as an arena of *conflict* as well as consensus—rooted in, yet not reducible to, the social context.[19] Thus, in place of socialization (which was credited in modernization theory with creating value consensus),[20] neoculturalist approaches emphasize the importance of symbolism, language, and ritual. Such "discourses," if we may employ that overworked term, are viewed as loci of confrontation and contestation among social actors. Accordingly, the connection between political culture and social context is seen as intimate, indeed inseparable. As Lynn Hunt, a pioneer in the analysis of the political culture of the French Revolution, has written:

> Revolutionary political culture cannot be deduced from social structures, social conflicts, or the social identity of revolutionaries. Political practices were not simply the expression of "underlying" economic and social interests. . . . This is not to say, however, that the Revolution was only intellectual or that politics had primacy over society rather than vice versa. The revolution in politics was an explosive interaction between ideas and reality, between intention and circumstance, between collective practices and social context. If revolutionary politics cannot be deduced from the social identity of the revolutionaries, then neither can it be divorced from it: the Revolution was made by people, and some people were more attracted than others to the politics of revolution. A better metaphor for the relationship between society and politics [than the metaphor of levels] is the knot or the Mobius strip, because the two sides were inextricably intertwined, with no "above" and "below."[21]

By providing "equal time" for cultural practice and social structure, refusing to elevate either of them to the level of an "independent variable," the neoculturalist perspective strives for a comprehensive understanding of political change. It is this feature of the approach, we believe, that will rescue it from the short-lived fates suffered by previous culturalist efforts.

A political culture approach predicts neither that China will remain forever unchanged nor that China is headed down the road of convergence (either with the liberal West or with other formerly Communist societies in Eastern Europe). It does claim, however, that change will inevitably draw heavily on established cultural repertoires. To make sense of popular protest will therefore require serious attention to the language, symbolism, and ritual of both resistance and repression.[22] And these, in turn, can be deciphered only in historical context—as meanings established over generations of political practice. Of course, no society is immune from outside influence; patterns of change in China are inevitably shaped by (and themselves shape) developments elsewhere around the world. Yet the interpretation of foreign models will proceed in Chinese terms—variegated and variable as we now know these to be.

The chapters that follow examine the relationship between the events of 1989 and changing Chinese repertoires of resistance and repression. Preliminary as this excursion into neoculturalist analysis is, we hope that it will stimulate more sophisticated, similar endeavors in the future. Recent reexaminations of the French Revolution demonstrate just how fruitful the approach can be.[23] In stressing the diversity of the cultural material from which both revolutionaries and authorities fashion their beliefs and behaviors, we aim toward a more refined understanding of the links to tradition than was evident in scholarship on the Communist Revolution of 1949 and the Cultural Revolution of 1966–1969.

The Protest of 1989 and Chinese Political Culture

In Part 1 of this volume, the contributing historians lay out some guiding frameworks. The multiplicity of political legacies that confronted both reformers and protesters in 1989 is the subject of Ernest Young's contribution. As Young points out, contemporary Chinese are heirs to several very different anciens regimes: the imperial reign of the Qing dynasty (1644–1911), the chaotic warlord interregnum (1911–1927), the Nationalist rule of the Kuomintang (1927–1949), and communism under Chairman Mao (1949–1976). The often contradictory nature of these various traditions has resulted in an identity crisis for Deng Xiaoping's post-Mao reforms; confusion has surrounded the whole question of which aspects of the past are to be altered. Although anxious to demonstrate a transformative break with the conservative Qing, for example, reformers have been equally anxious to avoid the radical excesses of Maoism. Such dilemmas have led to a confusing political discourse on the part of authorities and dissenters alike. Thanks to "the multitude of ghosts that China's modern history has conjured up," reformers turn into repressors and democrats into elitists. Young asserts that we are dealing in 1989 "not only with the persistence of an attitude or with the consequences of an unchanging Chinese political culture, but also with a cumulative effect. Every generation's repetition of the rationale for postponing democracy produces a changing meaning, as well."

This theme of change within repetition is further pursued by Joseph Esherick and Jeffrey Wasserstrom, who view the events of 1989 as "an exercise in political theater." Student protesters, even when improvising, worked from familiar "scripts" of state rituals and protest repertoires—some of which dated back for millennia and others of which were of relatively recent vintage. The centrality of ritual in imperial China was joined by new forms of popular protest at the turn of this century to render political theater a dominant mode of political expression. Efforts by the Communist state to tame this behavior into ritualized mass campaigns were not entirely successful, as both the Cultural Revolution and the protests of 1989 make clear. Yet, according to Esherick and Wasserstrom, Chinese street theater is politically limited. Unlike in Eastern Europe, where democratic institutions played a critical role in translating street theater into programs for political change, in China a weak civil society has undermined the development of pluralist politics.

In Part 2, Craig Calhoun, Lee Feigon, and I explore the bases of participation in the social movement of 1989. In my chapter, I stress the extent to which student protesters were fettered by tradition. In their subservient style of remonstrance, their search for political patrons, and above all their elitist moralism, students evidenced patterns of belief and behavior befitting the heirs of Confucianism. Picking up on the theatrical metaphor of Esherick and Wasserstrom, I emphasize the limited cast of characters included in the 1989 performance. Students reserved for themselves the starring roles, relegating workers, peasants, and entrepreneurs to the sidelines. The explanation for this undemocratic style is, I suggest, structural: Institutionalized links between students and state officials continued to limit alliances of intellectuals with other social groups.

The inegalitarian inclinations of student protesters is further explored in Part 2 in Lee Feigon's discussion of gender. Despite the prominence of Chai Ling and some other women leaders, males dominated the upper echelons of the 1989 protest movement. Moreover, neither men nor women showed a serious commitment to overcoming gender-based inequality. According to Feigon, women were prone to accept a state-defined image of femininity that accentuated differences with men and confined women to less public roles. Even the Goddess of Democracy, although ostensibly a challenge to state authority, "demonstrated the hollowness of this conception of feminine strength and of the dependence of the student movement on the Chinese government." On the question of gender, as on the issues of democracy and economic reform, students were strongly influenced by state authority and logic.

In contrast to this emphasis on the limitations of student radicalism, Craig Calhoun highlights the protesters' "capacity for heroism." Calhoun reminds us that social movements involve a constant construction and reconstruction of political identities. Over the course of the protest movement itself, "the basic self-identification of the protesting students in Tiananmen Square—and not just their intellectual self-categorization but their lived identity—was transformed, and at least for a time radicalized, by six weeks of activism." Self-interest was replaced by a willingness to sacrifice for the Chinese people as a whole. Historical tales of martyrdom became exemplars for contemporary acts of bravery that could not be explained in terms of class position or concrete material interests: "That so many rose to the challenge of their own ideals was crucial to giving the events of 1989 their enduring significance."

In Part 3, two analysts examine the place of art and music in the construction of new Chinese political identities. Tsao Tsing-yuan's firsthand account of the making of the "goddess of democracy" stresses the eclecticism of the sculptors who created the statue that came to symbolize the aspirations of the protest movement. Striving for "a new work of universal appeal," the young artists at the Central Academy for Fine Arts borrowed freely from foreign precedents. Like Calhoun, Tsao underscores the selfless devotion of these students whose creation "was as close to a true collaborative work as any project of this kind can be."

Sculpture was not the only cultural vehicle for political protest in 1989. As Andrew Jones explains in Part 3, popular music also assumed an unprecedented importance: "rock bands performed for hunger-striking students on the square, and satires of government corruption set to popular melodies were regularly broadcast over makeshift public address systems throughout Beijing." In the wake of the suppression of the protest movement, however, the politics of popular music have changed. Despite an increase in the number of rock bands, their political criticism has diminished significantly. In contrast to the universalism of the Tiananmen era, today's musicians strive for "a distinctly Chinese sensibility" and advocate "a nativist return to traditional roots." Moreover, their search for commercial success has resulted in a gradual abandonment of an oppositional cultural politics in favor of what Jones dubs "commodity nativism."

In Part 4, the contributing authors focus more intensively on the changing roles of intellectuals in contemporary China. Vera Schwarcz contrasts the protagonists of the drama of Tiananmen with earlier student movements. Superficial similarities between the events of 1989 and the May Fourth Movement of 1919, she argues, obscure a more disturbing parallel with the Cultural Revolution. Although quick to commemorate their link to May Fourth, many Chinese intellectuals overlooked the more painful lesson of the Cultural Revolution: Student idealism could be abused in the context of crowd politics. Like the Red Guards of the 1960s, students in 1989 were, according to Schwarcz, "swallowed by the language of political revolution." Exhilarated with the heady taste of protest, they failed "to take notice of the heavy burden of the past that hung over the sea of red flags in Tiananmen Square."

Timothy Cheek further pursues the restraints on contemporary intellectuals, noting that most Chinese intellectuals have yet to make the transition from "priests" serving the interests of the state to independent professionals. Operating under a "social contract" that affords opportunities for public service and scholarship in exchange for obedience to the state, many intellectuals still cleave to their "old mandarin function." Cheek suggests that the events of 1989 may have worked to accelerate "the movement from priest-rentiers serving the cosmic state (Confucian or Leninist) to professionals salaried in a bourgeois society." But he concludes that this process is as yet not far advanced, a situation that helps to explain why China's popular protests did not result in the dramatic regime changes witnessed in Eastern Europe.

In contrast to Cheek's emphasis in Part 4 on stability, Stephen MacKinnon sees considerable evidence of dramatic transformation. Noting that "it is hard to overestimate the effect in political terms of American media penetration of Chinese cities," he stresses the importance of the press—both American and Chinese—in promoting political change. MacKinnon draws parallels between journalism in the 1980s and in the 1930s–1940s (on the eve of revolution). In both periods, he sees journalists as committed "to a higher kind of loyalty: to truth outside the state." Despite the effectiveness of Communist Party controls today, MacKinnon looks forward by the end of the century to "the leading contribution of both media to the creation of a civil society in China."

According to Daniel Chirot, it was just such a process that ultimately brought down the Communist states of Eastern Europe. Part 5 contributors explore the relationship between regime stability and popular legitimacy. As important as economic problems were to the demise of communism in Eastern Europe, Chirot argues that "utter moral rot" was the essential cause of the collapse. Once the utopian ideology of the Party had been discredited, charges of immorality fueled the public alienation. Central to this development was the growth of a civil society, where intellectuals and other urbanites wrote and talked about alternatives to the corrupt rule of the Party-state. Looking ahead, Chirot predicts that "more than ever, the fundamental causes of revolutionary instability will be moral. The urban middle and professional classes, the intellectuals and those to whom they most directly appeal, will set the tone of political change."

Tony Saich delineates a series of changes in state-society relations in post-1989 China that "make the practice of rule much more difficult." Highlighting a decline in the state patronage system analyzed by Cheek, Saich sees among Chinese intellectuals the emergence of a "more critically minded" form of expression. From films and songs to jokes and hair styles, Party credibility is being undermined by an alternative public discourse outside the bounds of state control. The result, Saich concludes, is that "the Party-state is denied legitimacy by much of its urban population." Yet the prognosis is not necessarily an immediate collapse of the system, as occurred in Eastern Europe. In place of the state's moral authority, a "free-for-all urban society" in China has undermined interpersonal relationships and led to a moral vacuum.

The relative weakness of Chinese urbanites has prompted many analysts to discount the likelihood of fundamental political transformation in the near future. In Part 6, Jeffrey Wasserstrom and Liu Xiaobo consider efforts by Western observers and Chinese participants to make historical sense of 1989. As Wasserstrom observes, Western interpretations have tended to present the events of 1989 as tragedy—a noble quest doomed to failure. Controversy has surrounded the question of who the protagonists were (the students or Deng Xiaoping and Zhao Ziyang) and why they failed (whether because of circumstances beyond their control or because of their own shortcomings). Chinese accounts, by contrast, have often portrayed the uprising of 1989 as romance—a conflict between good and evil that results in the exaltation of the hero. Here again there have been disagreements over the identity of the protagonists (with Hu Yaobang, student martyrs, or People's Liberation Army (PLA) soldiers variously assuming this role in different versions) and over the meaning of their struggle. For his own part, Wasserstrom favors a tragic narrative that sees the uprising of 1989 "as related to but also significantly different from earlier PRC struggles." He concludes that "to leave open the possibility that the events of 1989 may have fundamentally altered Chinese political arrangements, and perhaps even Chinese political culture itself, is to suggest that those who died on June 4 may not have sacrificed their lives in vain."

The meaning of sacrifice is further explored in the concluding contribution by Liu Xiaobo, a central figure in the events of 1989. Like Chirot and Saich, Liu speaks of a weakening of legitimacy—but he sees this trend as largely confined to intellectuals; among ordinary people, Deng Xiaoping's reforms built "deep popular support and a solid, practical legitimacy." Like Calhoun, Liu stresses the tendency of a protest movement to take on a life of its own: "As soon as the kindling of revolution is lit, it burns, the fire rapidly becoming flames that reach to heaven." But he views this process of radicalization as the ultimate undoing of the movement: "The illusion created by the dynamism of the moment caused us to ignore the horrible consequences which would result from the continual escalation of the movement." Liu interprets the psychology of sacrifice and martyrdom that took hold during the protest as a reflection of the success of Communist Party education and as antithetical to the process of democratization. Echoing the theatrical metaphor that frames this volume, he confesses: "I don't know if we university students and intellectuals who played the role of revolutionary saints and democratic stars for two months can reasonably, calmly, justly and realistically reevaluate what we did and thought in 1989. . . . If we can, then the blood of June Fourth will not have flowed in vain—it will still be thicker than water. If we can't, then the blood of June Fourth will at most be able to nurture those shameless bloodsuckers."

Conclusion

The year 1989 will undoubtedly go down as a watershed in modern world history. Fittingly, the bicentennial of the French Revolution was marked by protests across the globe raising many of the same demands that we associate with the storming of the Bastille. In Eastern Europe these protests brought about stunning political change, whereas in China the uprising was brutally suppressed. Yet the French precedent cautions against too early or too easy an assessment of the ultimate results. Now, two hundred years after the fact, scholarly reappraisals of the French Revolution are revealing a far more complicated—if no less consequential—event than previously recognized. Central to this reconsideration is an appreciation of the significance of political culture.[24] As liberating as the French Revolution was, it was also limited by the rhetoric and rituals of the past.

Comparisons with France thus offer both inspiration and admonition to the student of contemporary China. We must be alert to the heavy hand of history—including its unattractive as well as its appealing features—while remaining open to the possibility of real change. Cultural traditions provide raw materials for political action but not in any formulaic fashion. As French historian Keith Baker puts it, "Political culture is a historical creation, subject to constant elaboration and development through the activities of the individuals and groups whose purposes it defines. As it sustains and gives meaning to political activity, so is it itself shaped and transformed in the course of that activity."[25]

That Chinese political culture gives shape to recognizable but flexible patterns of protest can be seen by comparison with Taiwan, another Chinese society recently rocked by popular unrest. In March 1990, a massive, week-long student sit-in occupied the Chiang Kaishek Memorial grounds in the center of Taipei. Their demands (for dissolution of the National Assembly and direct elections of the President) were different, but the style of protest was remarkably reminiscent of the previous year's student movement on the mainland. The Chinese protesters in Taiwan donned the same white headbands, broadcast the same rock music, and undertook a similarly dramatic hunger strike as their counterparts had done in Beijing. One Taipei student captured the special attention of the media precisely because of her striking resemblance to Chai Ling, the woman activist of Tiananmen fame. Yet there were important departures, as well. In place of the foreign-inspired Goddess of Democracy that loomed over Tiananmen Square, the Taiwan students erected a huge papier-mache lily, a native plant symbolic of both purity and independence. And although Taipei protesters imitated the Beijing exemplar in establishing a picket line to separate themselves from ordinary citizens, the students actually welcomed members of the labor movement, the farmers' movement, the women's movement, and environmental and homeless advocates inside the cordon.[26] Thanks to the socioeconomic changes of recent years, the distinctions between urban intellectuals and other social groups had become much less pronounced in Taiwan than was the situation on the opposite side of the Taiwan Straits.

The importance of innovation within tradition forms the central theme of this volume. The authors present popular protest as anchored in, yet not immobilized by, longstanding cultural practice. In analyzing the sources of change, moreover, we acknowledge the inextricable and interactive connections among society, economy, polity, and culture. While this new political culture approach is still in its infancy in the contemporary Chinese studies field, its application to the study of political change elsewhere in the world is well established. Our hope is that the further development of this perspective among China scholars may improve our understanding of Chinese popular protest so that future uprisings will find us better prepared than was the case in 1949, 1969, or 1989.

Notes

1. Contributions to this early debate included John King Fairbank, *The United States and China* (Cambridge: Harvard University Press, 1948); Karl A. Wittfogel, "The Influence of Leninism-Stalinism on China," *Annals*, vol. 277 (September 1951), pp. 22–34;

Wittfogel, *Oriental Despotism* (New Haven: Yale University Press, 1957); Wittfogel, "The Legend of 'Maoism,'" *China Quarterly*, no. 1 (January–March 1960), pp. 72–86, and no. 2 (April–June 1960), pp. 16–31; Benjamin Schwartz, "The Legend of the 'Legend of Maoism,'" *China Quarterly*, no. 2 (April–June 1960), pp. 35–42; and Joseph R. Levenson, *Confucian China and Its Modern Fate* (3 vols.) (Berkeley: University of California Press, 1958–1965).

2. C. P. Fitzgerald, *The Birth of Communist China* (Harmondsworth, Middlesex, England: Penguin, 1964), p. 20.

3. Ibid., p. 42.

4. Examples of the comparative communism approach are found in Donald W. Treadgold, ed., *Soviet and Chinese Communism: Similarities and Differences* (Seattle: University of Washington Press, 1967); and Chalmers Johnson, ed., *Change in Communist Systems* (Stanford: Stanford University Press, 1970). See also Thomas P. Bernstein, "Leadership and Mass Mobilisation in the Soviet and Chinese Collectivisation Campaigns of 1929–1930 and 1955–1956: A Comparison," *China Quarterly*, no. 31 (July–September 1967), pp. 1–42.

5. For recent critiques of both the totalitarian and pluralist perspectives, see Vivienne Shue, *The Reach of the State: Sketches of the Chinese Body Politic* (Stanford: Stanford University Press, 1988), chapter 1; and Andrew G. Walder, *Communist Neo-Traditionalism: Work and Authority in Chinese Industry* (Berkeley: University of California Press, 1986), chapter 1.

6. The standard definition of political culture as "attitudes, beliefs, values and skills which are current in an entire population, as well as those special propensities and patterns which may be found within separate parts of that population" appears in Gabriel A. Almond and G. Bingham Powell, Jr., *Comparative Politics: A Developmental Approach* (Boston: Little, Brown, 1966), p. 23.

7. Ibid.

8. The main statements of this position were Lucian W. Pye, *The Spirit of Chinese Politics* (Cambridge: MIT Press, 1968); and Richard Solomon, *Mao's Revolution and Chinese Political Culture* (Berkeley: University of California Press, 1971). More recently, Pye's *The Dynamics of Chinese Politics* (Cambridge: Oelgeschlager, Gunn and Hain, 1981) and *The Mandarin and the Cadre* (Ann Arbor: University of Michigan Center for Chinese Studies, 1988) present updated versions of this line of analysis.

9. The standard was set by Gabriel A. Almond and Sidney Verba's comparative study of the United States, Great Britain, Germany, Italy, and Mexico: *The Civic Culture: Political Attitudes and Democracy in Five Nations* (Boston: Little, Brown, 1965).

10. For a critique from the sinological point of view, see Frederick W. Mote's review of Solomon's book in the *Journal of Asian Studies;* for a social science critique, see Richard Kagan and Norma Diamond, "Father, Son, and Holy Ghost: Pye, Solomon, and the 'Spirit of Chinese Politics,'" *Bulletin of Concerned Asian Scholars*, vol. 5, no. 1 (July 1973), pp. 62–68. Another critical review is John Gittings, "Bringing Up the Red Guards," *New York Review of Books* (December 16, 1971), pp. 13–17.

11. On factions, see Andrew J. Nathan, "A Factional Model of Chinese Politics," *China Quarterly*, no. 53 (January–March 1973), pp. 34–66; and the critique by Tang Tsou, "Prolegomenon to the Study of Informal Groups in CCP Politics," *China Quarterly*, no. 65 (January–March 1976), pp. 98–113. Also William L. Parish, "Factions in Chinese Military Politics," *China Quarterly*, no. 56 (October–December 1973), pp. 667–699. On bureaucratic politics, see David M. Lampton, *The Politics of Medicine in China: The Policy Process, 1949–1977* (Boulder: Westview Press, 1977); and Kenneth Lieberthal and Michel Oksenberg, *Policy Making in China: Leaders, Structures, and Processes* (Princeton: Princeton University Press, 1988). On ideology, see Dorothy Solinger, ed., *Three Visions of Chinese So-*

cialism (Boulder: Westview Press, 1984); and Harry Harding, *Organizing China: The Problem of Bureaucracy, 1949–1976* (Stanford: Stanford University Press, 1981).

12. William L. Parish and Martin King Whyte, *Village and Family in Contemporary China* (Chicago: University of Chicago Press, 1978); and Martin King Whyte and William L. Parish, *Urban Life in Contemporary China* (Chicago: University of Chicago Press, 1984); Walder, *Communist Neo-Traditionalism;* Jean Oi, *State and Peasant in Contemporary China: The Political Economy of Village Government* (Berkeley: University of California Press, 1989); John P. Burns, *Political Participation in Rural China* (Berkeley: University of California Press, 1988); David Zweig, *Agrarian Radicalism in China* (Cambridge: Harvard University Press, 1989). Notable exceptions to the structuralist mainstream are Richard Madsen, *Morality and Politics in a Chinese Village* (Berkeley: University of California Press, 1984); Perry Link, Richard Madsen, and Paul G. Pickowicz, eds., *Unofficial China: Popular Culture and Thought in the People's Republic* (Boulder: Westview Press, 1989); and Helen F. Siu, "Recycling Tradition: Culture, History, and Political Economy in the Chrysanthemum Festivals of South China," *Comparative Studies in Society and History,* vol. 32, no. 4 (October 1990), pp. 765–795.

13. Elizabeth J. Perry and Christine Wong, eds., *The Political Economy of Reform in Post-Mao China* (Cambridge: Harvard University Press, 1985); Victor Nee and David Stark, *Remaking the Economic Institutions of Socialism: China and Eastern Europe* (Stanford: Stanford University Press, 1989).

14. On the Chinese side, the film "River Elegy" (*He shang*) was one influential manifestation of this trend. (For further discussion, see especially the chapters by Calhoun, Jones, and Saich.) See also Xiao Gongqin, *Rujia sixiang de kunjing* (The Confucian dilemma) (Chengdu: Sichuan People's Press, 1986). On the Western side, influential works range from E. P. Thompson, *The Making of the English Working Class* (Harmondsworth, Middlesex, England: Penguin, 1963), to Pierre Bourdieu, *Language and Symbolic Power* (Cambridge: Harvard University Press, 1991).

15. Important examples of recent works that defy the traditional dividing line are political scientist David Strand's *Rickshaw Beijing* (Berkeley: University of California Press, 1989) and historian Philip C. C. Huang's *The Peasant Family and Rural Development in the Yangzi Delta, 1350–1988* (Stanford: Stanford University Press, 1990).

16. Paul A. Cohen, *Discovering History in China: American Historical Writings on the Recent Chinese Past* (New York: Columbia University Press, 1984) discusses these developments. See also David Johnson, Andrew J. Nathan, and Evelyn S. Rawski, eds., *Popular Culture in Late Imperial China* (Berkeley: University of California Press, 1985).

17. For an overview of the contemporary field, see Michel Oksenberg, "The Literature on Post-1949 China: An Interpretive Essay," in Roderick MacFarquhar, ed., *The Cambridge History of China,* vol. XIV (Cambridge: Cambridge University Press, 1985).

18. In Almond and Powell, *Comparative Politics,* pp. 24–25, cultural secularization is described as "the process whereby traditional orientations give way to more dynamic decision-making processes involving the gathering of information, the evaluation of information, the laying out of alternative courses of action, the selection of a course of action from among these possible courses, and the means whereby one tests whether or not a given course of action is producing the consequences which were intended." One need look only as far as the Islamic Revolution in Iran or the fierce ethnic conflicts now raging across much of Eastern Europe to grasp the obvious point that political change may not lead to cultural secularization.

19. This point is made in Lynn Hunt, "Political Culture and the French Revolution," *States and Social Structures Newsletter,* no. 11 (Fall 1989), p. 2. See also Lynn Hunt, ed., *The New Cultural History* (Berkeley: University of California Press, 1989).

20. This view was of course heavily influenced by the work of sociologist Talcott

Parsons. For a critique of Parsons, see especially Alvin Gouldner, *The Coming Crisis of Western Sociology* (New York: Basic Books, 1970).

21. Lynn Hunt, *Politics, Culture, and Class in the French Revolution* (Berkeley: University of California Press, 1984), pp. 12–13.

22. Whereas the "new social history" has tended to stress the popular resistance side of the equation, studies by political scientists and anthropologists have often focused on the state's use of symbolic power to maintain legitimacy. See, for example, Murray Edelman, *The Symbolic Use of Politics* (Urbana: University of Illinois Press, 1964); Clifford Geertz, *Negara: The Theatre State in Nineteenth-Century Bali* (Princeton: Princeton University Press, 1980); Raymond Cohen, *Theatre of Power* (New York: Longman, 1987); and David I. Kertzer, *Ritual, Politics, and Power* (New Haven: Yale University Press, 1988). For those who want a general sense of the ways in which students of modern China have come to terms with both sides of this equation, two of the best places to start are Joseph W. Esherick and Mary B. Rankin, "Introduction," in idem., eds., *Chinese Local Elites and Patterns of Dominance* (Berkeley: University of California Press, 1990), pp. 1–24; and Daniel Little, *Understanding Peasant China: Case Studies in the Philosophy of Social Science* (New Haven: Yale University Press, 1989). In discussing the work of various China specialists, as well as leading scholars of Southeast Asian protest such as James Scott and Hue-Tam Ho Tai, Little uses the term "political culture" much as it is used in this essay. See especially Little, *Understanding Peasant China*, pp. 183–184.

23. See especially Keith Michael Baker, ed., *The Political Culture of the Old Regime* (Oxford: Pergamon, 1987); Colin Lucas, ed., *The Political Culture of the French Revolution* (Oxford: Pergamon, 1988); and Francois Furet and Mona Ozouf, eds., *The Transformation of Political Culture, 1789–1848* (Oxford: Pergamon, 1989).

24. Ibid.

25. Baker, "Introduction," *Political Culture*, p. xii. It is worth noting in passing that scholars working in various parts of the world have begun using the term "political culture" in the sense Baker describes. This is true, for example, within Latin American studies, a field that (like Chinese studies) was once heavily influenced by the Almond and Verba approach, as well as other related theories that stressed deeply ingrained national predispositions toward certain types of political behavior. Recent and forthcoming studies of Latin America that stress themes related to those addressed in this volume (and use the term "political culture" in a similar fashion) include Gilbert Joseph and Daniel Nugent, eds., *Everyday Forms of State Formation: Revolution and the Negotiation of Rule in Modern Mexico* (Durham: Duke University Press, 1994); and Peter Guardino, *Peasants, Politics, and the Formation of Mexico's National State: Guerrero, 1800–1857* (Stanford: Stanford University Press, forthcoming), the author of which explicitly associates his use of the term "political culture" with Keith Baker's approach. See also the discussion of political culture in Jeffrey L. Gould, *To Lead as Equals: Rural Protest and Political Consciousness in Chinandega, Nicaragua, 1912–1979* (Chapel Hill: University of North Carolina Press), pp. 188–189, which stresses the need to pay close attention to the complex ways that elite and popular cultural traditions intersect with and diverge from each other.

26. He Jinshan, Guan Hongzhi, Zhang Lijia, and Guo Chengqi, *Taibei xueyun* (The Taipei student movement) (Taipei: China Times Press, 1990), pp. 18, 32, 46, and 94–95.

Part One

GENERAL FRAMEWORKS

The two chapters in this thematic part were written by historians who share both an interest in the symbolic dimensions of Chinese politics and a common concern with the central role that appeals to the past can play in contemporary struggles for power. In their efforts to place the rhetoric and actions of 1989 in perspective, the authors introduce many historical events (such as the May Fourth Movement of 1919) and theoretical concepts (such as the notion of "civil society") that will figure prominently in later chapters by other contributors. The chapters in Part 1 also provide concrete illustrations that help to flesh out several of the general points raised in the preceding Introduction, including the suggestion that China specialists can learn a great deal from the approach to the study of political culture adopted by historians of the French Revolution. Young's discussion of the extent to which revolutionaries define their cause in opposition to an image of the "ancien régime" that they themselves have helped to craft fits in well with the arguments presented in some of the works on 1789 mentioned below in our list of supplementary materials, and the same is true of Esherick and Wasserstrom's discussion of political theater and political ritual.

Recommended Supplementary Materials for Classroom Use

Scholarship on China: Contemporary Politics

Bergere, Marie-Claire. "Tiananmen 1989: Background and Consequences." In Marta Dassu and Tony Saich, eds., *The Reform Decade in China: From Hope to Dismay.* London: Kegan Paul International, 1990, pp. 132–150. A brief summary of the social, cultural, economic, and political factors leading up to the protest and repression of 1989, by one of France's pre-eminent China specialists.

Pieke, Frank. "The Ordinary and the Extraordinary: An Anthropological Analysis of

Chinese Life and Protest in the Reform Era" (doctoral dissertation, University of California, Berkeley, 1991). A detailed participant-observer account, which emphasizes
the ritualized aspects of mass action and the connections between patterns of protest
and patterns of daily life.

Pye, Lucian. "Tiananmen and Chinese Political Culture: The Escalation of Confrontation from Moralizing to Rage." *Asian Survey*, vol. 30, no. 4 (1990), pp. 331–347. An
assessment of the events leading up to the massacre of early June, by a leading China
specialist whose approach to political culture is quite different than that which informs this volume (see the preceding Introduction).

Wagner, Rudolph. "Political Institutions, Discourse, and Imagination in China at
Tiananmen." In Jon Manor, ed., *Rethinking Third World Politics*. London: Longman,
1991, pp. 121–144. A study of the symbolic dimensions of the events of 1989 by one of
Germany's leading China specialists; parts of it complement the arguments presented here.

Zweig, David. "Peasants and Politics." *World Policy Journal* (Fall 1989), pp. 633–645.
Zweig analyzes the impact that the urban protests of 1989 had on the inhabitants of
the Chinese countryside and rural responses to the massacre.

Scholarship on China: Historical Perspectives

Huang, Philip C. C., et al. *Symposium "Public Sphere"/"Civil Society" in China?* A special
issue of *Modern China*, vol. 19, no. 2 (1993). A series of interconnected essays by six
social scientists and historians, each of whom advances a different view concerning
the perils and possibilities of using the terms in question as lenses through which to
examine China's past and present.

Israel, John. "Reflections on 'Reflections on the Modern Chinese Student Movement.'"
In the first edition of Wasserstrom and Perry, *Popular Protest and Political Culture in
Modern China*. Boulder: Westview Press, 1992, pp. 85–108. An analysis of China's
long tradition of campus activism; ends with comments that place 1989 within the
broad historical framework provided by the main body of the essay.

MacFarquhar, Roderick. "Epilogue: The Onus of Unity." In Roderick MacFarquhar and
John K. Fairbank, eds., *The Cambridge History of China, Volume 15: The People's Republic
of China, Part 2*. Cambridge: Cambridge University Press, 1991, pp. 875–881. A concise effort to place the events of 1989 into a broad historical perspective, in which
MacFarquhar focuses on the emphasis Chinese political leaders of different eras have
placed on the need for national unity; he also highlights the contrasting leadership
styles of Mao Zedong and Deng Xiaoping.

Madsen, Richard. "The Countryside Under Communism." In Roderick MacFarquhar
and John K. Fairbank, eds., *The Cambridge History of China, Volume 15: The People's
Republic of China, Part 2*. Cambridge: Cambridge University Press, 1991, pp. 619–681.
Madsen surveys aspects of rural life, including the nature of village rituals, that have
and have not changed since 1949; the work of a sociologist deeply concerned with
cultural issues.

Nathan, Andrew J. *Chinese Democracy*. New York: Knopf, 1985. A survey of democratic
thought and action from the late nineteenth century up through the Democracy Wall
protests of the late 1970s.

Comparative Works and Case Studies of Other Countries

Davis, Natalie. *Society and Culture in Early Modern France*. Stanford: Stanford University
Press, 1975. A collection of essays by a leading figure associated with both the development of the "new" social history and the "new" cultural history; many of the pieces

focus on the ritualized and theatrical aspects of riots and other types of collective action.

Furet, François, Keith Michael Baker, and Colin Lucas, eds. *The French Revolution and the Creation of Modern Political Culture,* Three Volumes. Oxford: Pergamon Press, 1987, 1988, and 1989. A collection of topical essays on everything from the changing meanings of specific terms (such as "ancien régime" and "revolution") to the evolution of key institutions (such as the National Assembly); the collection includes chapters by each of the co-editors and many other leading scholars of the French Revolution.

Hunt, Lynn. "The Sacred in the French Revolution." In Jeffrey Alexander, ed., *Durkheimian Sociology: Cultural Studies.* Cambridge: Cambridge University Press, 1988, pp. 25–43. A concise survey of the symbolic struggles and ritual acts that accompanied and helped shape the course of the French Revolution.

Lukes, Steven. "Political Ritual and Social Integration." *Sociology,* vol. 9, no. 2 (1975), pp. 289–308. A critical review of the literature on official ceremonials, which stresses the similarities between these events and acts of social protest.

Thompson, E. P. "Patrician Society, Plebeian Culture." *Journal of Social History,* vol. 7, no. 4 (1974), pp. 382–405. Thompson discusses the efficacy and limitations of the hegemony of the eighteenth-century British gentry, which depended heavily upon theatrical displays of benevolence but was continually being challenged by a "countertheatre of threat and sedition."

Primary Sources

Barmé, Geremie, and Linda Jaivin, eds. *New Ghosts, Old Dreams: Chinese Rebel Voices* (New York: Times Books, 1992), Section II: "Bindings," pp. 117–212. A selection of works of fiction and essays by Chinese dissidents, past and present, who highlight the negative impact that a variety of cultural practices and structures (ranging from the binding of women's feet in earlier times, to contemporary political arrangements that constrain individual creativity) have had on the people of China.

Mao Zedong. "Report on an Investigation of the Peasant Movement in Hunan." In *Selected Works of Mao Tse-tung* (Beijing: Foreign Languages Press, 1967), vol. 1, pp. 42–47. Along with presenting a passionate defense of a specific uprising, Mao's essay paints a vivid picture of the oppressive nature of village life in pre-Communist China.

Su Xiaokang et al. *Deathsong of the River: A Reader's Guide to the Chinese TV Series Heshang.* Ithaca: Cornell East Asia Series, 1991, edited by Richard W. Bodman and Pin P. Wan. The complete script of the influential miniseries of the late 1980s, which uses a variety of symbolic devices to suggest that many features of the *ancien régime* that the Communist Party claimed to have defeated in 1949 continue to plague contemporary China.

1

IMAGINING THE ANCIEN RÉGIME IN THE DENG ERA

Ernest P. Young

Revolutionaries hasten to break eggs in order to make fresh omelets, we are told, whereas reformers favor less strenuous recipes for change, by which the ingredients are more gently and gradually introduced. The distinction strongly colors our ideas of political or social reform. It is with such vocabulary that we have marked the great turn taken by China after the death of Mao Zedong: from continuing the revolution to reformist modernization. Although both Mao and Deng Xiaoping have aspired to change China profoundly, under Deng the methods would minimize violence and hew to a practical gradualism, in contrast to the headlong ruthlessness of Mao's transformational mobilizations. One of the jarring aspects, then, of the brutal suppression of the Chinese protests of 1989 is the incongruity between the reformist character of Deng Xiaoping's regime since 1978 and its most unreformist attack on people who at least potentially were among reform's most enthusiastic constituents. In other words, why was the very embodiment of China's opening up, both to the outside and with respect to domestic economic and social organization, acting in a way that was so pernicious for the long-run success and development of those reforms? Why was the key player in the retreat from radicalism acting so recklessly? How could such a reformer be such a repressor?

The simplest explanation may be the best. One can argue that Deng's first priority had always been power and the perpetuation of the system that seemed to grant that power. He was willing to reform so far, but no further, and he always stopped when the reforms began to threaten the autocracy. According to this argument, Deng has always been a pragmatist who would use ideological claims to gain support for his programs but never let ideology get in the way of a practical concern with maintaining existing power relations. This kind of argument carries a good deal of weight because spring 1989 was not, after all, the first time since Deng's ascendancy that a liberal oppositional voice had been silenced.

Despite its attractions and a degree of fundamental validity, this explanation is problematic in two ways. First, it is so general that it applies to the behavior of political leaderships in many times and places. Second, it underestimates the continuing importance of ideological concerns within the Chinese Communist Party (CCP). The search for finer explanations must, therefore, go on. One useful way to particularize an analysis of June 4, 1989, is to locate the Deng era within China's broader modern experience.

I follow here the lead of Paul Cohen. He has argued that Deng Xiaoping's modernization program can be understood as the continuation of "a kind of mainstream Chinese reformism" that reaches back in the modern era to the Self-Strengtheners of the late nineteenth century.[1] Cohen wishes to persuade us that the regimes of the Empress Dowager Cixi (for the years 1898–1900), of President Yuan Shikai, and of President Chiang Kaishek in the Nanjing era were reformist in many of the same ways that Deng's has been. Deng's version of modernization, he says, has shared more, though certainly not everything, with those unlikely predecessors than with the socially transformational or politically redistributive impulses of the Taiping rebels (1850–1864), the 1898 reform movement, the 1911 revolution, or the PRC in the early 1950s (not to mention the Maoist era of the Great Leap Forward and the Cultural Revolution). The bent of his argument is not to affirm Deng's reformist credentials, about which there would be little disagreement. Rather, he tries to establish and define the reformist character of the programs of Cixi, Yuan Shikai, and Chiang Kaishek, so that placing Deng in their line of succession becomes plausible.

Having shown how autocrats of earlier decades shared the reformism of Deng, Cohen then turns around and notes how Deng shares their authoritarianism: "The fact is, Deng's reforms are guided by a very potent ideology—we may call it an ideology of 'authoritarian modernization'—and it is precisely this ideology that Deng shares with his non-Communist predecessors."[2] Although he recognizes the vast differences in international and domestic circumstances between pre-1949 China and that of the 1980s, Cohen was moved by his analysis to a degree of skepticism about the future of reform under Deng. In a 1988 publication, he argued the need for "institutionalized arrangements for genuine power sharing" and saw no sign that Deng and colleagues were "prepared to countenance such a far-reaching move."[3] These remarks were underscored by events the following year.

Defining Deng's Ancien Régime

I should like to try a related but somewhat different approach to the relevance of China's history to Deng's reforms and to his decision to repress the protests of 1989. I hope it is an approach that illuminates not only Deng's behavior but also to some degree the character of the protest movement. The starting point is the question of the identity of the ancien régime.

We are accustomed to revolutions having an ancien régime. In fact, we cannot conceive of a revolution without one: If it were missing, a revolution would have to invent one. Indeed, anciens régimes to a considerable extent *are* invented as part of the revolutionary process. The historical image of the ancien régime is part of the ideology of the revolution and defines, by contrasts and opposites, the revolutionary program. Our favoring the French term over ordinary English signals the abstractness of the idea.

The French Revolution has provided us with the term, which was first invested with its modern meaning during the last decades of the eighteenth century. William Doyle, author of a short monograph devoted to the role of the concept in the revolution, stresses its originality, noting that "there had been no anciens régimes under the Ancien Régime."[4] Diego Venturino, who has written a chapter on the topic for a recent multivolume work on the political culture of the French Revolution, echoes this point in the very title he gives his piece: "La naissance de l'Ancien Régime" (The birth of the Ancien Régime).[5] Doyle and Venturino also stress the term's broad reference to all aspects of the old order (political, social, spiritual), and its dynamic, defining relationship to the revolution. Above all, they argue, it was an ideological construct, albeit a flexible one. Crystallizing out of the theme of reforming old abuses, the notion of an ancien régime came to refer to the past as a whole. It summoned up a vision of the past (privileged, feudal, chaotic, despotic, and so on) in the form of a legitimating antithesis to the revolutionary present. The ancien régime bequeathed manners and customs (*moeurs*) whose persistence explained delays and difficulties in realizing revolutionary purposes. Ultimately, Venturino writes, "the 'ancien régime' became a personage; an actor with personal character, a will, a role to fill; the negative pole in all events of the moment; in other words, the enemy."[6]

Probably less from imitation than from parallel impulses, modern revolutionaries everywhere, including those in China, have fashioned their own, appropriate "ancien régime." Revolutionaries characteristically construct an image of a rather static and unattractive society, ascribe it to their predecessor regime, and commit themselves to changing it. That the image in each case is invented does not mean that the picture of the former regime is simply or wholly false. It generally borrows heavily from experience. Yet it is not limited to experience and is crucially shaped by dreams and aspirations, as well as the need to justify.

Major reform programs, like revolutions, also have anciens régimes. An intrinsic part of a reform program is a conception of the entity that requires correcting and against which the reform movement defines itself. At least so it is in the contemporary Chinese case. Perhaps the Deng regime, as a reform movement arising within a far-from-extinct revolutionary tradition, is unusually alert to the problem of defining its ancien régime.

When we look at texts coming out of Deng's China for clues as to conceptions of the appropriate ancien régime, we seem to find a rather complicated answer. The candidates for what has been the relevant ancien régime for the Deng Xiaoping era are disturbingly numerous and various. They include the Maoist era, the Nanjing government under the Kuomintang (KMT), the warlord phenomenon, and the Qing. The last term opens out into broader conceptions of Confucian society and feudalism. The Maoist era and the Qing are particularly formidable historical images in the reformist imagination.

So in Deng's China the identification or definition of the ancien régime has involved the selection from among several eras, each with its own image. The meanings of the reform programs of the different layers of anciens régimes have been quite various, causing reformers some confusion about exactly what they were supposed to be reforming. As a result, the reform impetus has had, I would argue, a severe identity crisis. Inside this identity problem may lie clues to the repression of 1989.

Although the problem became more acute in Deng's era, it was not brand new. The problem's reflection—or its other face—can be seen in the CCP leadership's uncertainty regarding China's position in some schedule of historical change, a variability that goes well back into the Maoist era. The early redefinitions of China's status could be explained in terms of forward movement: from "New Democracy" in the 1940s and early 1950s (completing the tasks left unfinished by the bourgeoisie and extirpating feudalism) to building socialism in the middle of the 1950s. Suddenly in the late 1950s China was not only working on a very advanced version of socialism but was edging into communism, with all that such a transition implied about what needed to be reformed. This vision was soon abandoned, and in the 1960s the Chinese were warned by their supreme leader that the country was slipping backward toward capitalism—which involved yet another conception about the appropriate objects (and methods) of reform.

By the mid-1980s, a different leadership discovered that China was only in the preliminary stage of socialism. The notion drew sarcastic comment during the 1989 protests: "What was denounced as capitalistic yesterday could well be regarded as socialist today. Socialism, after several decades, has not yet entered its advanced stage; on the contrary, it has reverted to its elementary stage."[7]. As the conception of reform again shifted after June 1989, the CCP has moved away from the idea of locating China's current development at so modest a stage.[8]

Each of these shifts, back and forth along some line of developmental progress, has implied a different choice of a relevant ancien régime. Perhaps one should say, especially with regard to the Deng era, that there is an attempt to have at hand several possibilities at once and to weave them into a single picture. The result is rent with contradictions. Let us explore the main elements of the Deng-era portrayal.

The top layer of anciens régimes has been the almost two decades of Mao Zedong's transformational regime—the Great Leap Forward, the Cultural Revolution, and all their works. It was the most important politically in the initial phase of the Deng reform era. In the Dengist view, by trying to transform China at breakneck speed into a socially and spiritually socialist, even communist, order, Mao had brought only ruin and chaos to the country. By no means incidentally, he had also inflicted great injury to its political and intellectual elite. The ideological purposes in the portrayal of this ancien régime were evident in the flattening out of the Maoist era, for example, in the notion of a ten-year Cultural Revolution ("the ten dark years"), homogenizing the considerable variability of policy in the last ten years of Mao's life.[9]

In this dimension—the undoing of the ancien régime of Mao Zedong—the Deng reforms had a markedly conservative coloring. That is, a major component of the reform program was dismantling institutions and programs intended to be socially transformative and putting in their place arrangements meant to restore some status quo ante (whatever their actual effects). There was a vigorous discrediting of the radical rhetoric of the Maoist era and a more modest effort to reduce the size of Mao himself.

Although Dengists have criticized the Maoist period for its lack of procedural regularity—administrative and legal—its lack of liberal political institutions is precisely an area that has *not* received much attention from Deng's regime. A sustained effort to correct China's lack of democratic institutions would have placed the Deng reform era in a relationship of relative radicalism with respect to Mao's politics, but we have not seen more than glimpses of such moves, and those short-lived. (It has been this neglect, of course, that has spawned a liberal opposition.)

In short, the Mao era has been a crucial ancien régime—the primary rationale for the Deng ascendancy. Nevertheless, there has not been a complete negation of it, as the continued use of the phrase "Mao Zedong Thought" to refer to the ideology of the CCP attests. Since June 1989, furthermore, there has been increased resort to Mao's sanctifying spirit to prop up a regime in trouble.

The politics of Deng's regime has evoked other anciens régimes as well. Brief mention may be made of the next two layers. Despite the political need to soft-pedal criticisms that might impede a deal with Taiwan, the notion that the PRC is based on a rectification of the failings of the KMT has remained relevant to political discourse. The protesters of 1989 readily picked up on the idea in order to highlight the corruption of the Deng administration. The same official malfeasance that had discredited the Nanjing government was now, astonishingly, a feature of the Communist Party.[10] On this point, Deng had to agree, for who would dispute the proposition that any respectable Chinese government had to represent the negation of this picture of the Nationalist ancien régime? One sign of just how potent criticisms of KMT-like misconduct are in contemporary China became clear during the months that followed the crackdown of June 1989. In this period, the Deng regime made few public attempts to redress most of the grievances the students had articulated, but it did launch a new drive against official corruption.

Deng and his hard-line supporters have also emphasized another feature of the Nanjing government since June 4: the KMT's alleged subordination to foreign power. In his much-quoted June 9, 1989, remarks to military commanders in Beijing explaining the necessity of the crackdown on "counter-revolutionary" forces, Deng warned against China's becoming "a bourgeois republic subordinated to the West" (*xifang fuyonghua de zichan jieji gong-heguo*).[11] This was for Deng a stick to be used against the protesters. In various ways, as these examples show, the ancien régime of Chiang Kaishek remained a part of the definition of Deng's reform goals. Chen Xitong's June 30, 1989, "Report to the National People's Congress," perhaps the single most important comprehensive defense of the government's actions, provided numerous illustrations of this point. Not only does the report provide details concerning the alleged efforts Western forces made to "bring China under the rule of international monopoly capital" in 1989, it also argues that remnant supporters of the KMT and agents from Taiwan played a role in instigating the protests.[12]

The image of the warlord era as the pinnacle of twentieth-century disorder in China has also lived on as a standard for guiding policy. A reform program must check extreme decentralization or the creation of baronies. And it must retain the subordination of military to civilian authority. It was part of the charge against Mao that he had risked these dangers. As with every leader since the 1920s, Deng's responsibilities include repressing any sign of resurgent warlordism.

The most insistent, compelling alternative to the Maoist ancien régime for defining Dengist politics has been the Qing and the society associated with it. The Qing as a specific period and political phenomenon is actually too limited for what is involved in the portrayal of this ancien régime. "Feudal society" is the catchphrase, and the concept is as elastic as "traditional society" in Western parlance. In this usage, "feudal" is a pejorative masquerading as an analytic term, but one that evokes an array of linked characteristics drawn from particular conceptions of Chinese history. Among its notable features are a despotic monarchy, a creaky but oppressive bureaucratic administration, an exploitative landlord class, a stagnant economy, and a trod-upon peasantry, restive but culturally benighted. From a twentieth-century, Marxist-influenced perspective, "feudal" has carried with it the judgment of "backward."

The Chinese term that we translate as "feudal" (*fengjian*) did not fully acquire the pejorative meaning just described until a couple of decades into the twentieth century. However, the idea of a backward society inherited from China's long imperial experience was already being articulated by the end of the nineteenth century and quickly became general among the educated classes. Early twentieth-century Westernizing reform programs were constructed around some version of this idea, which served as the necessary ancien régime for reform or revolution. The political dimension of the old order was the first object of change. Social features were soon being added to the picture.

The first point about this ancien régime of the Qing, of "feudal society," that I wish to stress in its relation to understanding the Deng era is its contrast with the ancien régime of Maoism. With respect to feudalism, the Deng regime has conceived of itself not as rescuing China from the reckless schemes of change associated with Mao but as transforming by modernization a backward and inhibiting part of China's ancient inheritance. We see here a tension between gradualism and transformationalism that has marked the Deng era.

A second notable point about Deng's relation to this much older ancien régime is that he ascribes to it great continuing influence. Not only did his revolutionary and reformist predecessors fail to extirpate it, they were fatally undermined or contaminated by the ancien régime, so that their modernizing efforts foundered or were misdirected. Remarkably, Mao Zedong is no exception. Apparently Deng's own reforms are quite far from the desired goal of overcoming the power of feudal remnants in contemporary China. "Feudal society" is a truly old ancien régime, but it seems to be still a formidable one.

In this view of China's situation, how does one explain the persistence of feudal society after numerous reform regimes, revolutionary movements, and campaigns for social transformation? There has been no single answer, of course, but the key seems to lie in the Chinese peasantry. Karl Marx had laid down the theory in *The Eighteenth Brumaire of Louis Bonaparte*, which has enjoyed a revival in China. The argument is that the social circumstances of peasant life are conducive to ignorance and superstition—a backwardness that retards social progress for everyone. Peasant society is consequently fertile ground for both political despotism and mindless radicalism.

In this view, Mao's style of rule and his radical politics were a product of China's feudal backwardness. The argument was alluded to in the CCP's formal reinterpretation of its history in 1981.[13] It has been made explicit by a number of commentators, including Mao's chief Chinese biographer, Li Rui, who attributes Mao's autocracy and his policies in the Great Leap and the Cultural Revolution to his "neglecting the grim task of rooting out pernicious feudal influences," which have their ground in "a closed-door small-scale peasant economy and the system of feudalism, patriarchialism and despotism."[14] Apparently destroying the landlord class was not enough. Li Rui traces Mao's radicalism to "an ocean of peasant small-scale producers."[15] Maos greatest contribution, then—in fashioning a rural strategy for coming to power—becomes at the same time the reason for the greatest errors of his rule. Immersion in the peasantry had imbued the Party with feudalism.

To this picture we might add that all this was made concrete in the numerous cadres of rural background who, by joining the Red Army during the revolution, eventually acquired power over urban populations. The urban folk saw themselves as more advanced culturally. Clashes between urbanites and their new peasant overlords were common. Hence personal experience gave concrete support to the theoretical point about damage from the feudal virus and about the peasantry as its most persistent carrier.[16]

Anciens Régimes and
the Roots of Dissent and Repression

What is the relevance of all this to what happened in China in spring 1989? Deng was defending his regime against many layers of problems—or so he would certainly see it. All those anciens régimes, with their unresolved issues, meant challenges on many fronts. The demonstrators, in this view, were unwitting Maoists, whom the authorities felt justified in describing as new Red Guards determined to take China into another Cultural Revolution, a

line of argument Esherick and Wasserstrom discuss and critique in Chapter
2.[17] At the same time the frequent invocation of the danger of civil war drew
its resonances not only from the Cultural Revolution but also from the warlord period. I have already mentioned the concern that the more radical
Westernization ("bourgeois liberalization") allegedly espoused by the protesters would render China a "bourgeois republic subordinated to the West."
The reference to the Nationalist regime is apparent.

The bedrock argument against liberalization of politics, or power-sharing,
has remained China's backwardness—the persistence of "feudal society" in
the late twentieth century. As a *People's Daily* writer said in July 1989:

> Our country's socialism . . . is still economically and culturally rather backward;
> history has bequeathed us very little democratic tradition; the influence of feudal
> thought is very profound; and many people have only a dim consciousness of de-
> mocracy and legality; this sort of basic national condition has determined that the
> construction of a socialist democratic politics can only be a gradual process of
> step-by-step accumulation.[18]

His conclusion, citing Deng Xiaoping: Elections that included the whole population would produce chaos and civil war. One might paraphrase by saying
that the 1989 protest movement had to be resisted because the Qing was not
yet all gone.

Would it be going too far to say that Deng and his fellow gerontocrats felt
embattled in part because of the confusing but reinforcing multiplicity of
threats that the protests seemed to pose? Of course all these points were serving rhetorical needs and immediate purposes. Nonetheless, one still has to
account for the rhetorical choices being made, and these kinds of choices provide clues to important thought processes.

In any case, this view of the world was certainly confusing, as became clear
during the initial attempts the regime's defenders made to mount a persuasive propaganda campaign that would explain what had happened. How
was it that in some people's minds "bourgeois liberalization" had sup-
planted the "four cardinal principles" (in brief, socialist ideology and party
rule)? According to an early apologist named Lu Zhichao, in its keenness to
refute leftism (that is, in reforming the Maoist ancien régime), the Chinese
government overdid it and aroused doubts about socialism itself. Further, in
the regime's drive to expand the economy (that is, overcoming the backwardness inherited from "feudal society"), it created and even rewarded interests
contradictory to socialism. By opening China up to extensive contact with
the outside world, Deng encouraged the comparison of China with advanced
countries, so that the forty-year history of the PRC came to be seen by some
as a total failure. The administration needed instead to spread awareness of
the Chinese past (back to the Qing and other anciens régimes) and an accompanying sense of historical progress.[19]

Subsequent apologists for the regime have tried to clarify the issues. As
Wasserstrom details in the Afterword, the authorities have sponsored a variety of collections of essays and documents that try to justify and explain the
repression of 1989. In these works, authors set out to explain such things as

what exactly the term *bourgeois liberalization* means, how precisely the West planned to turn China into a dependent state, and so forth. Nonetheless, these books do not resolve the questions that Lu's article raises. The reader is still left wanting to ask the Dengist ideologues which ancien régime creates the real problem and how exactly so many kinds of vestiges of the past have remained alive. They say that Maoism was a product of contamination from the old "feudal society" and thus impeded progress away from feudalism. Yet they also hold that Mao was criticized too much, so that people underestimated the progress that China has actually made from feudalism. When explaining why China should not liberalize politically, they say that the population is not ready. China is too backward for democracy, which would only bring breakdown. When explaining why liberal ideas have spread and produced a movement, they say that China's great strides under socialism—including with Mao—have not been sufficiently credited.

Protesters and the Anciens Régimes

The students and intellectuals involved in the 1989 protests, though they arrived at some different conclusions, shared in this discourse. Their beliefs regarding certain things—for example, the speed with which China should work to reform its political system—were undeniably quite different from those of the authorities they challenged. Nonetheless, the protesters shared many of the same assumptions and often invoked the same kinds of symbols as those whose power they sought to undermine. Feigon's exploration of gender (Chapter 5), Perry's discussion of social elitism within the movement (Chapter 3), and Liu's critique of the rhetoric of "Revolution" (Chapter 14) illustrate this point. So too does a closer look at the way protesters conceived of the anciens régimes that stood in the way of true revolutionary change. Like the Deng regime, dissenting students and intellectuals saw China plagued by multiple vestiges of the past, and (as with the authorities) their rhetorical stances may be interpreted in light of this vision of overlapping anciens régimes.

Just as Deng's side castigated the protesters for exposing China to the dangers of revived Maoism, the protesters accused Deng of "errors of a gravity no less than [those committed in] the 'Cultural Revolution.'"[20] In their "May 16th Declaration" in support of the protests, a group of leading dissident intellectuals also invoked the specter of the "ten bad years" and warned the authorities that to suppress the demonstrations would be to repeat one of the mistakes of the infamous Gang of Four.[21] Two months later, Yan Jiaqi, a leading dissident who had emerged from within Deng's reform movement and one of the signers of the declaration, called the crackdown of early June "far more cruel than the Cultural Revolution."[22] Despite the displays of Mao icons by some marchers—the meanings of which Esherick and Wasserstrom treat in the next chapter—protesters' references to the Maoist legacy usually had the same negative overtones as did the Dengist interpretation.

Although one cannot attribute to the protesters anything close to a unitary view, the prominence of the idea of a continuing influence from "feudal society" also stands out. The ancien régime of the Qing, in other words, was highly visible in the protesters' pronouncements, both rhetorically and analytically. Deng Xiaoping was likened to the Empress Dowager Cixi, "directing government from behind a screen."[23] The image of a monarchical Deng regime occurred frequently, one observer noting that "it has been 76 years since the demise of the Qing government. But China still has an emperor without a crown on his head. He is an old and muddleheaded dictator."[24] One finds the same assertions about the CCP's having been imbued with peasant feudalism, as an explanation not just of Maoism but also of Deng's autocracy.[25] The whole issue of China's achievements was stated most poignantly in a Beijing University poster of early May: "A century has gone by since the Reform Movement of 1898, and it seems we are still stuck at the starting line, trying to change our old ways and make our country strong."[26]

Surprisingly, the similarities between the Dengist analysis and that of the protesters concerning the continuing relevance of the Qing extend to an uncertainty about how to evaluate China's progress out of feudal society and the consequences for democracy. Early in the movement, one poster compared the government's excuse for not implementing democracy—that is, the people's backwardness—with Chiang Kaishek's rationale for political tutelage. Was it possible that the PRC had not improved on the Nanjing regime? Or, as the question was phrased on another poster, "How can it be that forty years of Communist rule have produced a citizenship that is not even fit for a democratic society?" We have observed the contortions of Deng apologists in dealing with this point. In this case, the poster-writer makes his or her own U-turn and accepts the idea that most Chinese could not properly adjust to democracy. The prescription is that only city folk, intellectuals, and Communist Party members should enjoy democratic privileges for the moment.[27] The young student leader Wuer Kaixi made a parallel point after the June events: that in an evolution toward democracy, peasants would not play a decisive role.[28]

I sense throughout the movement's wall posters, manifestos, and statements a searching on the part of the protesters for the relevant ancien régime. Was China's problem residual Maoism in the Deng order? Or in some curious way (implied by the Mao placards and in references to the relative purity and commitment of Mao and his era) was it not enough Maoism?[29] Was it the persistence or revival of a KMT legacy of official corruption? Was it a continuing feudalism in the Party? Or was the issue that defined the ancien régime for the protesters really the Deng reforms themselves (the matters of inflation and vice would be elements of analysis here)?[30] When students compared their protests to the May Fourth Movement of 1919 (an event that Calhoun and Schwarcz treat in detail in Chapter 4 and Chapter 8, respectively), was their main point that the "feudal" modes of thought against which intellectuals of seventy years before had railed were still alive and well in the PRC? Was it that CCP officials were modern-day equivalents of the repressive warlords who had ruled China in 1919?[31] There is no reason that there should be a clear choice among these possibilities. Because both the warlord and Nanjing regimes had suppressed popular movements in their day, for example, there is no reason why the authors of the May 16th Declaration cited above should not have reminded their audience that the actions of these former rulers as well as those of the Gang of Four had been "recorded in China's history as pages of shame."[32] Nonetheless, further attempts to figure out how much emphasis protesters put on the unresolved problems left over from particular anciens régimes would be useful, as they could provide us with clues about the direction and possible future courses of the movement.

Democratic Impulses and Authoritarian Solutions: An Enduring Theme

In his studies of the idea of democracy in twentieth-century China, Andrew Nathan has tied the preference for authoritarian solutions to the perception of China as backward.[33] Successive generations of reformers and revolutionaries have drawn back at the edge of political democracy, as they calculated the risk of social disorder in any precipitate institutionalization of popular control of government. Liang Qichao, an early advocate of parliamentary government for China, became convinced in the first years of the century that the Chinese were not ready and must be prepared during an era of "enlightened despotism."[34] Even the optimistic Sun Yatsen endorsed a program of stages by which representative government would be introduced after a successful revolution—the early, predemocratic portions of which turned out to be almost indefinitely extendable, in the actual practice of KMT rule. In the 1980s, from Zhao Ziyang's circle emerged the notion of the "new authoritarianism" so reminiscent of Liang Qichao's conception.[35] The repetition of schemes to postpone democracy have been accompanied by repetition of the concerns about the unreadiness of the population. The image of the Chinese people as a sheet of loose sand—unable on their own responsibility to form a coherent citizenry—was shared by Yuan Shikai, Sun Yatsen, and Deng Xiaoping. Each believed that China would not easily entertain democratic politics.

Mao Zedong was among those who often dissented from the common view of the political backwardness of the Chinese majority. "The masses are more progressive than we are."[36] The implications that he drew for politics, however, were hardly liberal. Then intellectuals of the 1980s closed the circle by attributing Mao's illiberalism to the backwardness of the peasantry.[37]

My argument is broadly congruent with Nathan's analysis. My focus on the multiplicity of anciens régimes would lead me to add that by 1989 one is dealing not only with the persistence of an attitude or with the consequences of an at best slowly changing Chinese political culture but also with a cumulative effect. Every generation's repetition of the rationale for postponing democracy produces a changing meaning as well. Each round of authoritarianism produces a new image of what the consequences of backwardness are, of what the problems are for any reformer who would break fully out of China's "feudal" inheritance.

Could the reformer Deng Xiaoping be also the cruel tyrant of June 4, 1989, because of the multitude of ghosts that China's modern history has conjured up? Deng was faced with the uncompleted tasks of each previous reform and revolutionary movement. Their failures were examples of paths that should not be taken. And yet the protests were seen as pushing the regime to repeat old errors. As a challenge to Deng's authority, the movement was cast as an agent, no matter how unwitting, of revived Maoism, the foreign dependency of the KMT, the chaos of warlordism. It wished, in Deng's view, to force a precipitate jump into democracy, which threatened to release the large "feudal" residuum in the Chinese population. Faced with too confusing an array of anciens régimes, Deng ferociously defended the status quo. But there cannot be reform without forward motion. "Authoritarian modernization," what Paul Cohen describes as China's reformist mainstream, is in crisis.

Notes

1. Paul Cohen, "The Post-Mao Reforms in Historical Perspective," *Journal of Asian Studies*, 47, 3 (1988), pp. 518–540, esp. 533.

2. Ibid., p. 535.

3. Ibid., pp. 536–537.

4. William Doyle, *The Ancien Régime* (New York: Humanities Press, 1986); and "Presentation," in Colin Lucas, ed., *The French Revolution and the Creation of Modern Political Culture*, vol. 2, *The Political Culture of the French Revolution* (New York: Pergamon, 1988), pp. 3–9, quote taken from p. 6.

5. Diego Venturino, "La naissance de l'Ancien Régime," in Lucas, *Political Culture of the French Revolution*, pp. 11–40.

6. Venturino, "La naissance," pp. 18, 26–27.

7. Han Minzhu, ed., *Cries for Democracy* (Princeton: Princeton University Press, 1990), p. 153.

8. For example, a post–June 4 *People's Daily* article contained the following statements: "The building of socialism in China has taken no more than 40 years" and "China has been victoriously advancing along the socialist course for 40 years." Lu Zhichao, "Lun sixiang jiben yuanze yu zichan jieji ziyouhua" (On the opposition between the four cardinal principles and bourgeois liberalization), *Renmin ribao* (People's daily), November 1, 1989, pp. 1 and 8. The late 1989 formula held that China was fully socialist, not just at a preliminary stage. Only the level of prosperity was still elementary, and even that was not so low either.

9. The theme of marked changes in policy and power balances among the leadership in these years appears in Lowell Dittmer, "Mao Zedong and the Dilemma of Revolutionary Gerontocracy," in Angus McIntyre, ed., *Aging and Political Leadership* (Albany: SUNY Press, 1988), pp. 151–180; and Frederick C. Teiwes, "Mao and His Lieutenants," *Australian Journal of Chinese Affairs*, vol. 19–20 (1988), pp. 1–80.

10. Han, *Cries*, p. 164.

11. The original version of this famous June 9 speech has been reprinted, in complete or excerpted form, to serve as the first document or preface for many official texts dealing with 1989. See, for example, Sichuan ribao bianchuan bu (Sichuan News Editorial

Department), eds., *Xuechao, dongluan, baoluan* (Student storm, turmoil, revolt) (Chengdu: Sichuan People's Press, 1989), pp. 1–6; and Zhonggong Zhongyang Xuanchuanbu (CCP Central Propaganda Department), eds., *Jianyue yonghu dangzhongyang juece pingxi fangeming baoluan* (Firmly support the central government's decision to put down the counterrevolutionary upheaval) (Beijing: People's Press, 1989), pp. 1–2. An English-language version appeared in *Beijing Review*, July 10–16,1989, pp. 18–21; this is reprinted with some explanatory notes, in Cheng Chu-yuan, *Behind the Tiananmen Massacre* (Boulder: Westview, 1990), pp. 226–230.

12. A translation of the full text of Chen's "Report" appears in Yi Mu and Mark Thompson, *Crisis at Tiananmen* (San Francisco: China Books, 1989), pp. 194–233, see esp. pp. 195 and 223.

13. Helmut Martin, *Cult and Canon: The Origins and Development of State Maoism* (Armonk, N.Y.: M. E. Sharpe, 1982), pp. 205–207.

14. Li Rui, "Study of Mao Zedong Thought Examined," *Renmin ribao*, March 28, 1988, p. 5.

15. Ibid.

16. One student wall poster charged that 75 percent of Party members had no more than an elementary school education; Han, *Cries*, p. 43. Apparently the poster-writer felt no need to explain why this fact was a criticism of the Party. Fox Butterfield conveys this outlook by describing an urbanite's resentment at the power over his career of a cadre of rural background; see his *China: Alive in the Bitter Sea* (New York: Times Books, 1982), pp. 286–287.

17. Along with the sources Esherick and Wasserstrom cite, see the comments attributed to Li Peng and Deng Xiaoping in Mu Wang, "The Actual Facts About the Power Struggle Within the Highest Leadership Stratum of Zhongnanhai," *Jing bao*, June 12, 1989, translated in Foreign Broadcast Information Service: China (hereafter, FBISCHI), 89-110, pp. 22–32; and Chen Fangen, "Deng Xiaoping's Instructions on Beijing Incident," *Guang jiao jing*, April 16, 1990, translated in FBIS-CHI-90-076, pp. 7–9.

18. Zhang Lin, "What Kind of Democracy Do We Need?" *Renmin ribao*, July 21, 1989, p. 6.

19. Lu, "On Conflict Between the Four Cardinal Principles and Bourgeois Liberalism," pp. 18–24.

20. Han, *Cries*, pp. 53 and 352.

21. The declaration is translated in Yi and Thompson, *Crisis*, pp. 163–166.

22. Wuer Kaixi and Yan Jiaqi, "Deng Will Have Thousands of People Killed," *Der Spiegel*, July 10, 1989, translated in FBIS-CHI-89-131, pp. 25–28.

23. Han, *Cries*, pp. 141–142.

24. Yan Jiaqi et al., "May 17th Declaration," *Ming bao*, May 18, 1989, translated in FBIS-CHI-89-095, pp. 47–48, and Yi and Thompson, *Crisis*, pp. 166–167.

25. Han, *Cries*, pp. 136 and 285.

26. Ibid., p. 170.

27. Ibid., pp. 33–35.

28. Wuer Kaixi and Yan Jiaqi, "Deng," p. 27.

29. See Michael Weisskopf, "Nostalgia for Mao Signals Discontent Amung Chinese," *Washington Post*, July 22, 1989, p. A14, and the discussion in Chapter 2 of this book.

30. An important discussion of the role of the reforms as a contributing factor to the protests is Huang Yasheng, "The Origins of the Pro-Democracy Movement: A Tale of Two Reforms," *Fletcher Forum of World Affairs*, 14, 1 (1990), pp. 30–39.

31. Student attempts to present themselves as inheritors of the May Fourth legacy are discussed at length in Wasserstrom's Afterword.

32. Yi and Thompson, *Crisis*, p. 164.

33. Andrew Nathan, *Chinese Democracy* (Berkeley: University of California Press, 1985); and Nathan, *China's Crisis: Dilemmas of Reform and the Prospects for Democracy* (New York: Columbia University Press, 1990).

34. Nathan, like others writing about Liang Qichao, makes much of Liang's critical evaluation in 1903 of the cultural and political level of overseas Chinese, even in the free environment afforded them in the United States, and of Liang's inference that Chinese generally needed authoritarian rule. See, for example, *Chinese Democracy*, p. 60. Kenneth Scott Wong argues in a recent unpublished paper, "Liang Qichao and the Chinese of America: A Re-evaluation of His 1903 Travels in the New World," that there were a variety of inconsistencies, errors, and omissions in Liang's discussion of Chinese in the United States. Wong raises the question whether Liang fashioned his remarks on overseas Chinese to suit an argument that had its origins in other concerns.

35. For a critical discussion of this concept and its prominence in 1989, see Anita Chan and Jonathan Unger, "China After Tiananmen: It's a Whole New Class Struggle," *Nation*, January 22, 1990, pp. 79–81.

36. When citing this remark, which sums up a major theme in Mao's thinking, Nathan states that this side to Mao "spawned the democratic challenge" of the late 1970s. But he goes on to say that other and more profound sides to Mao—and to the Chinese tradition—fed into the suppression of that movement. *Chinese Democracy*, pp. 74 and 101.

37. Nathan puts it this way: "The consensus [among writers in all fields in the 1980s] has been that the cultural revolution was made possible by the peasant mentality of utopianism, egalitarianism, and authoritarianism shared by both Mao and the Chinese people." *China's Crisis*, p. 125. Similarly, in a study of Party analyses in the first years of the Deng era regarding the origins of Mao's personal dictatorship, Lawrence Sullivan finds a key element in these official explanations to be "the population's cultural and ideological backwardness"—including superstitious beliefs and a "peasant mentality." "The Analysis of 'Despotism' in the CCP, 1978–1982," *Asian Survey*, 27, 7 (1987), pp. 800–821.

2

ACTING OUT DEMOCRACY:
POLITICAL THEATER
IN MODERN CHINA

Joseph W. Esherick and Jeffrey N. Wasserstrom

For two and a half months in spring 1989, China's student actors dominated the world stage of modern telecommunications. Their massive demonstrations, the hunger strike during Mikhail Gorbachev's visit, and the dramatic appearance of the statue of the goddess of democracy captured the attention of an audience that spanned the globe. When we began work on this essay early in 1990, the movement and its bloody suppression had already produced an enormous body of literature—from eyewitness accounts by journalists and special issues of scholarly journals to pictorial histories and documentary collections—tracing the development of China's crisis. This flood of

This piece first appeared in the *Journal of Asian Studies*, 49, 4 (1990), pp. 835–865; it is reprinted here with the permission of the Association for Asian Studies. As befits an essay that continually crosses disciplinary lines between history and anthropology, this chapter is based upon firsthand observation as well as written and pictorial sources. Joseph Esherick was in Xian, Jinan, and northern Shaanxi in spring 1989, and Jeffrey Wasserstrom was in Shanghai during the protests of December 1986. Where no additional citation is given, information on these times and places comes from personal observation or discussion with participants.

The authors would like to thank the following people for sharing thoughts, criticisms, recollections, and unpublished papers: Jeffrey Cody, Dru Gladney, James Hevia, David Jordan, Barry Naughton, Michel Oksenberg, Elizabeth Perry, Frank Pieke, Henry Rosemont, Jr., Clark Sorenson, Frederic Wakeman, Jr., and two anonymous readers. Audiences at the University of Washington, the University of California, San Diego, and the University of Oregon provided helpful comments on an earlier version of this chapter. Grants from the Committee on Scholarly Communication with the PRC and Fulbright-Hayes supported the authors' research in China; grants from the University of Kentucky and the National Academy of Education made the writing and revising of this chapter possible.

material, which now includes important analytical works and textbook chapters as well, has continued during the past twelve months, but the problem that originally inspired us to write this essay remains.[1] As valuable as much of the available scholarship is—and some of it (including the other chapters in this volume) is valuable indeed—we still lack a convincing general framework that places the Chinese events within the context of China's modern political evolution and also provides a way to compare China's experience to that of Eastern Europe. Such an interpretation should help us understand why massive public demonstrations spurred the evolution toward democratic governance in Eastern Europe (a process Daniel Chirot traces in Chapter 11), but led only to the massacre of June 3–4 and the present era of political repression in China.

None of the most frequently mentioned characterizations of the movement seems truly adequate. For example, in the Chinese leadership's attempts to link the protesters with one or another of the anciens régimes, as Ernest Young delineates in the previous chapter, it has portrayed both the 1989 movement and its predecessor of 1986–1987 as manifestations of "bourgeois liberalism" or as acts of *luan* (chaos) reminiscent of the Red Guards in the Cultural Revolution or as some combination of the two. But if the 1989 protests were the result of "bourgeois" contamination, why was the most prominent anthem of the demonstrators *The Internationale,* and why did some students and workers carry pictures of early leaders of the CCP?

Official characterizations of recent protests as acts of *luan* are also unsatisfying to say the least. Protesters unquestionably committed disorderly acts in both 1986 and 1989. Nonetheless, most foreign observers were impressed by the discipline and orderliness of the students.[2] The prominence of march monitors, the security forces that maintained order in Tiananmen Square, the student "arrest" of youths for defacing a portrait of Mao—these activities hardly suggest an atmosphere of *luan.*

Depictions of the protesters of the late 1980s as contemporary Red Guards or remnant supporters of the Gang of Four are even more seriously flawed. There were certainly continuities between the 1960s and the 1980s in terms of protest tactics and symbols (e.g., the insistence upon free passage to Beijing, the pasting up of posters, the use of portraits of Mao in marches). This is hardly surprising because some of the young teachers who advised the students of 1986 and 1989 were former Red Guards, as were several leading dissident figures such as Su Xiaokang (whose work and influence Calhoun discusses at some length in Chapter 4). Nevertheless, the complete lack of anti-Western rhetoric or devotional loyalty to any living CCP leader by the students of the late 1980s makes analogies with the Red Guards extremely tenuous, as do the generally negative references to the Cultural Revolution in protesters' posters.[3] Even some of the tactical and symbolic continuities between the late 1960s and the late 1980s noted above are more ambiguous than they at first appear. The Mao portraits carried by demonstrators in 1989 are a case in point. They may have reminded some onlookers of the Red Guards, but various kinds of evidence suggest that the main Mao being honored in 1989 was not the demigod of the Cultural Revolution but the selfless hero of the pre-1949 years and the early days of the PRC. This was certainly the implication of comments heard on the streets, which favorably contrasted Mao's behavior toward his own children during the 1950s with the nepotistic tendencies of contemporary leaders.[4] Because some of the protesters of 1989 carried posters of Zhou Enlai (who is revered in part for his opposition to the Gang of Four) whereas others carried posters that showed Mao flanked by his erstwhile second in command, Liu Shaoqi (who became the chief target of Red Guard fury), portrayals of the recent demonstrations as a revival of Cultural Revolution extremism seem still more unconvincing.[5]

The analyses offered by Western social scientists, foreign journalists, and Chinese dissidents, though considerably more persuasive than the official CCP line, are also problematic. Many, especially the professional Pekingologists of political science, stress the role that power struggles between Li Peng and Zhao Ziyang played in shaping the 1989 events.[6] There is no doubt that internal divisions paralyzed the party leadership in April and May, preventing an effective response to the demonstrators. But at the start of the movement, one of the protesters' most common abusive rhymes in Beijing and Tianjin was "Ziyang, Ziyang, xinge buliang" (Zhao Ziyang, Zhao Ziyang, you are not a good man) and as late as May 19 (long after the Voice of America and BBC broadcasts had been focusing on the Li-Zhao conflict) the protesters' posters and slogans in Xian still had two central targets: Deng Xiaoping and Zhao Ziyang. Corruption in Zhao's immediate family made him so unpopular that it is impossible to see him successfully manipulating the movement for his own ends. Indeed, like Hu Yaobang before him, Zhao Ziyang became a hero only after (and to a large degree because) he was ousted from power by the alliance of hard-liners and party elders around Deng.

The Western press and Chinese dissidents abroad usually characterize the events of China's spring as a "democracy movement." There is no question that *minzhu* was frequently invoked in the protesters' banners and slogans, but it would be hasty to associate *minzhu* (literally, rule of the people) with any conventional Western notion of democracy. Consider, for example, Wuer Kaixi's words in the televised dialogue with Li Peng on May 18. Early in the meeting, Wuer Kaixi explained what it would take to get students to leave Tiananmen Square: "If one fasting classmate refuses to leave the square, the other thousands of fasting students on the square will not leave." He was explicit about the principle behind this decision: "On the square, it is not a matter of the minority obeying the majority, but of 99.9 per cent obeying 0.1 per cent."[7] This may have been good politics—and Wuer Kaixi certainly made powerful theater—but it was not democracy.

The hunger-striking students in Tiananmen Square had adopted a position designed to preserve their unity and enhance their leverage with the government. But in elevating the principle of unity above that of majority rule, they were acting within the tradition of popular rule (*minzhu*) thinking in modern China. When Sun Yatsen assumed the presidency of the Republic of China in January 1912, his message to the revolutionary paper *Minlibao* was a simple slogan (in English): "'Unity' is our watchword"[8]—not "democracy" or "republicanism," but "unity." Closer to the present, the dissident magazine

Enlightenment wrote in 1979 of the miraculous effects that the "fire" of democracy would have on the Chinese people:

> The fire will enable people completely to shake off brutality and hatred, and there will be no quarrel among them. They will share the same views and principles and have identical ideals. In lofty and harmonious unity they will produce, live, think, pioneer, and explore together. With these dynamic forces they will enrich their social life and cultivate their big earth.[9]

Although Western democratic notions are normally linked to pluralism and the free competition of divergent ideas, *minzhu* in China is here linked to a vision in which people will "share the same views" and have "identical ideals." It is thus difficult to analyze the events of China's 1989 spring as a "democratic movement" in the pluralist sense of the term.[10]

Nor do the words and deeds of the protesters of 1986–1987 or 1989 fit easily with more radical Western ideas of direct or participatory democracy. In many cases the students seem to have read the *min* in *minzhu* in a limited sense to refer not to the populace at large but mainly or exclusively to the educated elite of which they are part. This elitist reading of *minzhu* was clear in the wall posters that appeared in Shanghai in December 1986, many of which took their lead from the speeches Fang Lizhi gave at the city's Tongji University earlier that year. The main theme of these posters, as in many of Fang's lectures and writings, was not that the CCP should be more responsive to the ideas of China's masses but rather that it should allow the intelligentsia a greater voice in national affairs.[11] This elitist strain carried over into student tactics in 1986: At one point, when Shanghai workers came out to support their protesting "younger brothers," the students told them to go home.

The situation in 1989 was somewhat different, for at times students actively sought (and received) the support of groups not connected to the intelligentsia. Nonetheless, as Chapters 3 and 5 stress, some educated youths and older intellectuals continued to see democratic reforms in elitist, inegalitarian terms. For example, two foreign observers found Fujian students deeply disturbed by the suggestion that general elections would have to include the participation of the peasantry.[12] Other reports highlight student distrust of the *laobaixing,* or untutored masses (a distrust symbolized by the groups of students who roped themselves off from bystanders during some marches); the intelligentsia's lack of concern for the needs of workers and peasants; and the appeal that ideas associated with the "new authoritarianism" had within protest circles in 1989.[13] Western critics and Chinese dissidents alike have also taken leaders of the movement to task for behaving in nondemocratic and elitist ways, both at the time of the occupation of Tiananmen Square and during the formation of new protest leagues in exile.[14]

The preceding comments do not mean that there was nothing "democratic" about the movement. Clearly, there was a great deal about the protests—the calls for freedom of speech, the demands for popular input into the way China is governed—that Westerners associate with the term "democracy." We do not wish to imply that Chinese are somehow incapable of understanding or acting upon Western concepts of democracy. Nor do we wish to imply that a Chinese movement must meet a stringent set of contemporary Western standards to earn the accolade "democracy movement." After all, as Donald Price has observed, we consider many Western states to have been "democratic" long before they reached the stage of universal suffrage.[15] The point we do wish to stress is simply that, given the various contours of meaning the term *minzhu* had in 1989, labeling the protests a "democracy movement" does not take us very far in our efforts to make sense of them. In some cases, in fact, it obfuscates more than it clarifies.

China's Spring as Political Theater

It would seem that a more productive way to understand the events of April–June 1989 is to view them as an exercise in political theater. Scholars as diverse as E. P. Thompson and Clifford Geertz, working on political systems as dissimilar as eighteenth-century England and nineteenth-century Bali, have demonstrated the value of interpreting politics in theatrical terms, that is, as symbol-laden performances whose efficacy lies largely in their power to move specific audiences.[16] This approach would seem ideally suited for analysis of the Chinese protests of 1989. As essentially nonviolent demonstrations that posed no direct physical or economic threat to China's rulers, the protests derived their power almost exclusively from their potency as performances that could symbolically undermine the regime's legitimacy and move members of larger and economically more vital classes to action.

A number of the more insightful analysts of the Chinese protests of 1989 have already highlighted the importance of symbolism and role-playing. Frank Pieke has analyzed the "ritualized" quality of protest actions in one essay and has highlighted the significance of audience participation in the Chinese marches in another piece. Perry Link has compared the petitioning at Tiananmen Square to "morally charged Beijing opera." In a related vein, Dru Gladney and Lucian Pye have interpreted the symbolic implications of a variety of student actions and texts, and David Strand has used theatrical metaphors to capture the mood and explain the impact of student demonstrations in Beijing since 1919.[17] Our goal is to expand upon these themes and to place the events of 1989 in a larger historical and theoretical context. In particular, it seems important to examine the relationship between political theater and ritual—a more tightly prescribed form of cultural performance that was so vital to the governance of imperial China.

What, then, was the political theater of 1989? First, it was street theater: untitled, improvisational, with constantly changing casts. Though fluid in form, it nevertheless followed what Charles Tilly calls a historically established "repertoire" of collective action.[18] This means that even when they improvised, protesters worked from familiar "scripts" that gave them a shared sense of how to behave during a given action, when and where to march, how to express their demands, and so forth. Some of these scripts originated in the distant past, emerging out of traditions of remonstrance and petition stretching back for millennia. More were derived (consciously or unconsciously) from the steady stream of student-led mass movements that have taken place since 1919. Thus, for example, in 1989 when youths carrying banners emblazoned with the names of their alma maters paraded from school to school and called on students at other institutions to join their fight to *jiuguo* (save the nation), they were following closely in the footsteps of participants of the May Fourth Movement and other protesters of the Republican era (1911–1949).[19]

State rituals and official ceremonies supplied other potential scripts. The April 22 funeral march in memory of Hu Yaobang was a classic example of students usurping a state ritual, improvising upon an official script to make it serve subversive ends.[20] Chinese funerals (especially those of wealthy or politically important figures) have always been key moments for public ritual.[21] As newspaper accounts of early twentieth-century funeral processions show, these ceremonies were an important opportunity for elite families to display their status, with musicians and hired mourners joining family and friends, carefully ordered by age, gender, and social status, in a symbolic representation of the proper social order.[22] In the People's Republic, memorial services for important political leaders are a critical political moment, and the composition of funeral committees is carefully scrutinized for clues to changing political alignments.[23] Here is a political ritual with all the liminality that Victor Turner's conception requires: transitional between two preferably stable political states and thus highly dangerous.[24]

The particular danger in the case of political funerals arises from the possibility that unauthorized people will usurp the ritual and rewrite the script into political theater of their own. The most famous previous example of this was in fact not quite a funeral but the Qingming remembrance that followed soon after the death of Zhou Enlai in 1976. It produced the first "Tiananmen incident," in which thousands of Beijing residents used the opportunity to pay their respects to Zhou and in the process level a wide variety of direct and indirect attacks on the Gang of Four.[25] Critical to the nature of such ceremonies is that the authorities cannot prohibit them: They are politically required rituals of respect for revolutionary heroes. But when students usurp the ritual, they can turn it into political theater. Thus the funeral march becomes a demonstration. Though they march behind memorial wreaths to the deceased and carry their official school banners, they also chant slogans and hoist signs with their own political messages.

Marches of this sort inevitably lead to the central square of the city. That square normally faces the seat of government authority, which is also likely to be the venue for an official memorial service. At this point, the demonstration becomes a petition movement. The most dramatic was the petition of 1989 presented by three students kneeling on the steps of the Great Hall of the People. The symbolism of this petition was important, for it demanded an explanation of the background to Hu Yaobang's resignation as general secretary of the Party in 1987. This demand focused attention on the fact that the party leaders who were orchestrating the official ceremonies inside the

Great Hall were precisely the same men who had removed Hu Yaobang from power. Thus, the street theater unmasked the hypocrisy of the official ritual and revealed the students on the streets to be the true heirs to the legacy of Hu Yaobang. In the end, the officially required ritual becomes the mechanism for attacking the authorities.[26]

Once the public stage has been captured, the street actors are all the more free to write their own script. In Beijing they proved extraordinarily creative, successfully upstaging two more state rituals: On the seventieth anniversary of the May Fourth Movement, the party's formal commemorations paled before the students' protest marches; and later that month the welcoming rally students held for Gorbachev—complete with signs bearing slogans in Russian and Chinese—stole the thunder from the official ceremonies of the summit. One reason for the success of these protests, and for the relative weakness of the official rituals they mocked, came from their respective settings. Throughout much of May, students were in full control of Beijing's symbolic center, Tiananmen Square. The government was forced to hold its gatherings in less public and less powerful venues—the Great Hall of the People on May 4, the airport to welcome Gorbachev.

The group hunger strike launched in Beijing in mid-May, which was replicated in several other cities within days, was another stroke of creative genius. Although dissident officials in imperial times sometimes refused food to show their displeasure with a ruler and protesters of the Republican era and Cultural Revolution period occasionally used hunger strikes as a tactic, this kind of group fast was not a central element of the Chinese student protest repertoire until the influential one performed in Hunan in 1980. Its use in 1989, by students who compared their strike to those of dissidents in other nations, showed how internationalized models for dissent had become.[27]

The placement of the statue of the goddess of democracy in Tiananmen Square—directly between two sacred symbols of the Communist regime, a giant portrait of Mao and the Monument to the People's Heroes—was another powerful piece of theater, as Tsao Tsing-yuan's essay (Chapter 6) shows. Though Western journalists often treated this twenty-eight-foot icon as a simple copy of the Statue of Liberty and the Chinese government insisted that this was so, the goddess was in reality a more complex symbol combining Western and Chinese motifs, some employed reverently, some ironically. Some features of the goddess did resemble the Statue of Liberty (an exact replica of which was carried through Shanghai in mid-May), but others called to mind traditional boddhisattva and even socialist-realist sculptures of revolutionary heroes found in Tiananmen Square. It was also reminiscent of the giant white statues of Mao that were carried through the square during National Day parades of the 1960s. A potent pastiche of imported and native symbolism, the goddess statue appeared on the square just as the movement was flagging, bringing new crowds of supporters and onlookers to the area.[28]

Street theater of this sort is also dangerous, however, because it is impossible to control the cast. As noted above, students tried at times to keep the *laobaixing* at arm's length, but this was not always possible, and in many cases organizers anxious to swell the number of protesters encouraged bystanders from all walks of life to join the crowd. Inevitably, this attracted members of the floating population of youths who had been in and out of trouble with the state apparatus. Mistreated by police or public security men in the past, many bore grudges they were anxious to settle. It appears that these young men were responsible for some of the violence that broke out as early as April 22 in Xian and Changsha and on June 3 in Beijing.

Once we recognize the movement as an instance of political theater, it becomes tempting to rate the performances. One of the best acts was put on by Wuer Kaixi in the dialogue with Li Peng. The costuming was important: He appeared in his hospital pajamas. He upstaged the premier by interrupting him at the very start. Later in the session, he dramatically pulled out a tube inserted through his nose (for oxygen?) in order to make a point. Especially for young people in the nationwide television audience, it was an extraordinarily powerful performance.

For older viewers, however, perhaps the most riveting act was performed by the Chinese Central Television (CCTV) news announcer Xue Fei as he read the official martial law announcement on May 20. Again, costuming was important: He wore all black, the suit rumored to have been borrowed for the occasion. And he read the announcement from beginning to end without ever lifting his eyes from the page, in a perfect imitation of the tone reserved for funeral eulogies. Xue Fei's performance was a scene witnessed, understood, and remembered by virtually every television viewer in the country.

In any performance, the audience is critical. In street theater, audience participation becomes part of the drama, and this was certainly true in Beijing and other cities in 1989.[29] First, citizens lined the parade route to applaud the student demonstrators. Then, there were banners announcing support and stands set up to provide food and drink. By the end, the nonstudent crowds had been fully drawn into the act, as the citizens of Beijing came out in force to block the army's entrance after the declaration of martial law.

Television provided a powerful new dimension to the movement's audience appeal. Most obviously, with the world press gathered for the Gorbachev visit, the demonstrators gained a global audience. That audience certainly helped dissuade the leadership from an early use of force against their critics. But the domestic television audience was at least as important. Through television, by mid-May Chinese across the country could directly witness the scale of the massive demonstrations in Beijing, and that knowledge emboldened the young people who launched their own protest marches in cities all across China. Furthermore, the Beijing demonstrators were keenly aware of the power of this new medium, as they showed through their demand for a live broadcast of their dialogue with the government. As a political mode, theater is only as powerful as the audience that it can move; and this theater certainly inspired and energized hundreds of millions of people in China and across the world.

As ritual and theater, the actions of the demonstrators naturally call forth certain responses from the authorities, and the efficacy of official performance is substantially dependent on how well they play these roles.[30] The party leadership's failure to acknowledge in any way the petition of the

students kneeling on the steps of the Great Hall was a major violation of ritual, and it significantly increased public anger against official arrogance.[31]
This is important because ritually correct responses to earlier student petitions—such as those submitted in 1918 (the year before the May Fourth
Movement) and 1931 (when Japan invaded Manchuria) by youths angered at
the way Chinese authorities were handling relations with Japan—had helped
to defuse potentially volatile situations.[32]

The refusal to acknowledge the student petition in April was but the first
of a series of unskillful official performances. When Li Peng was forced to
join the televised dialogue with the student leaders, for example, he was
clearly unsuited for his role and very uncomfortable in it—and predictably
he played it very badly. Later, the visit of Li, Zhao Ziyang, and other party
leaders to the hospitalized hunger strikers was another ritually required act
of compassion, this one performed somewhat more adroitly. The loyalist rallies the Party organized in the suburbs of Beijing during the week before the
massacre were remarkable, but far less effective, acts of official theater: Participants told Western journalists that officials had instructed them to take
part, and televised coverage of the events showed a mixture of bored, un-
happy, and embarrassed faces.[33] Even the tanks of June 4 can be seen as
a kind of theater. One does not choose tanks for their efficacy in crowd
control—this was a performance designed to show irresistible power.

For official theater, however, nothing was more important than the ritual
biaotai that followed the movement's suppression. These public statements of
one's position (and here the only permissible position was one in favor of the
regime) began with provincial leaders, regional military commands, and
functional ministries of the national government. Broadcast on the national
news and reported in the press, they announced the speed with which the
constituent parts of the state apparatus fell in behind the new central Party
leadership. These *biaotai* of Party and military elites were followed by similar
performances in schools, factories, research institutes, and administrative
bodies across the nation as virtually every urban citizen was required to account for his or her actions since April and publicly announce solidarity with
the new hard-line policies. Such rituals were a special form of performance
(*biaoyan*). The participants were clearly *acting*—most were not sincere—and
everyone knew it. They recited memorized scripts, with key phrases lifted
from articles and editorials in the *People's Daily*. Because few believed the
words they were uttering, most of the *biaotai* were bad theater. But the
regime's unremittent insistence on their performance testifies to the importance of such theater in the Chinese political system.

It should be noted that politically sensitive members of the Chinese public
recognize the practices described above as a form of theater. In their view,
politics is a performance, and public political acts are often interpreted in
that way. Thus, for example, a typical reaction to Li Peng's speech announcing martial law was to evaluate it as a performance, and the reviews were
uniformly bad: Words were mispronounced, the tone was too shrill, and so
on. As one Beijing intellectual put it: "He should have been wearing a patch
of white above his nose"—the standard makeup of the buffoon in Beijing

opera. Protesters at times presented Li as the clown or villain in propaganda presentations based on traditional theatrical forms. One Beijing street performance (transmitted to a large crowd by way of an improvised sound system), for instance, combined comic cross talk with operatic motifs to portray the attempts of a courtesan (representing Li Peng) to flatter, appease, and thereby gain the protection of an old man (representing Deng Xiaoping). The symbolism of the piece was clear to the crowd, who showed its appreciation for this mockery of China's two top leaders by laughing uproariously.[34]

Metaphors from the world of the theater are so much a part of the language of politics in modern China (as elsewhere) that protesters and observers continually adopted theatrical turns of speech. When protesters attacked Li Peng and Deng Xiaoping, the slogans they used included "Li Peng xiatai!" (Li Peng, get off the stage!) and "Xiaoping, Xiaoping, kuaixie xiatai" (Deng Xiaoping, Deng Xiaoping, hurry up and get off the stage).[35] Whenever previously little known actors play a major political role, there is discussion of who their *houtai* (backstage managers) might be. And after the Tiananmen incident, there was significant debate as to whether or not it should be termed a "tragedy."[36] But the sense in which the Chinese people see all this as performance was most powerfully suggested by a wise old peasant from northern Shaanxi who, when asked the difference between Mao Zedong and Deng Xiaoping, simply laughed and said, "They were just singing opposing operas [*chang duitai xi*]!"

Ritual and Theater

Our discussion to this point has used two terms to describe public political performances: "ritual" and "political theater." These terms, as we define them here, refer to two distinctive genres of action, though the line demarking the two is not always clear, as many acts include both ritualistic and theatrical elements.[37] Before exploring the gray area where the forms overlap, we must distinguish the two ideal types, because the differing degrees to which a polity depends upon and leaves legitimate space for one or the other genre of activity have profound implications for the nature of politics in that system. Thus, the ritual-infused politics of imperial China was qualitatively different from China's twentieth-century politics, with its distinctive political theater.

There are almost as many definitions of ritual as there are anthropologists. Defined most loosely, the term refers to virtually any "rule-governed" or "communicative" activity, in which case everything from strictly ordered coronations to highly improvisational demonstrations would qualify as political rituals.[38] We will use the term in a narrower sense here. Borrowing heavily from Clifford Geertz's work, we will define rituals as "traditionally prescribed cultural performances that serve as models *of* and models *for* what people believe."[39]

Such a definition conforms well with the Confucian sense of *li*, a term frequently translated as "ritual." *Li* serves to support and reinforce the existing

status quo, bringing order to a community, reaffirming the distinctions between and bonds connecting its individual members, and generally giving
people a shared sense of how to behave correctly in a wide range of circumstances. Taking our lead from Confucius and his followers, we will highlight
this system-maintenance function of ritual, a function also stressed by Emile
Durkheim and his followers.[40]

We must also, however, take account of recent critics of the functionalist
approach to rituals, which in the words of one writer treats the acts simply as
"a sort of all-purpose social glue."[41] Again building upon the work of Geertz,
we will highlight the symbolic nature of rituals as acts with hidden meanings
that need to be decoded.[42] And following Victor Turner, we will stress the
processual and dynamic nature of rituals.[43] According to Turner, though rituals serve to confirm existing hierarchical relations, these relationships are frequently suspended or temporarily overturned during the ritual *process*. This
creates a volatile and potentially dangerous situation: There is always the
chance that (as with Hu Yaobang's funeral) people will capitalize upon the
instability or liminality of the process and subvert it to other ends.

To put Turner's point another way, there is always the chance that people
will turn a ritual performance into an act of political theater. Central to the
notion of ritual, in our sense of the word, is the idea that only careful adherence to a traditionally prescribed format will ensure the efficacy of the performance.[44] With any significant departure from a traditional script, any break
with what James L. Watson calls "orthopraxy," a ritual ceases to be ritual.
Ritual thus gives relatively limited play to the creative powers of script-
writers or actors, and as soon as participants break away from traditional
structures, their actions become theatrical. Theater, by nature, is more liberated from the rigid constraints of tradition and provides autonomous space
for the creativity of playwrights, directors, and actors. This gives theater a
critical power never possessed by ritual: It can expose the follies of tradition
(or the follies of abandoning tradition), mock social elites, or reveal the pain
and suffering of everyday life.[45]

Although he is talking about *aesthetic* theater (the formal dramas of the
stage), Turner makes additional distinctions between theater and ritual that
are relevant to our more metaphorical use of the term.[46] One such distinction,
particularly important in the Chinese context, has to do with role-playing
and the audience. Role-playing is central to all ritual, and Chinese ritual is
particularly concerned to fix each individual in his or her proper social role.
Participation is by invitation only, each participant assigned a specified role.
Rituals separate people into superior and inferior, elder and younger, male
and female. In short, according to the *Li Ji* (Classic of ritual), "without [ritu-
als] there would be no means of distinguishing the positions of ruler and subject, superior and inferior, old and young."[47] But paired with this role for
ritual was another role that Confucians gave to music: Music unites. Thus the
Li Ji notes that the *li* "make for difference and distinction," but "music makes
for common union."[48] It does so because it creates an undifferentiated audience, and that is what theater does as well. As one leading dramatic theorist

writes: "Theater comes into existence when a separation occurs between audience and performers."[49] The homogeneity of the audience should not be overstressed because different members of the audience may identify with different characters or respond to different themes. But in general the relatively undifferentiated audience in theater (as opposed to the carefully stratified *participants* in ritual) enjoy a shared experience and may be drawn toward a common identity. At the very least, the audience, in its anonymity, is freed to interpret the drama and identify with particular roles as it wishes. This is quite different from ritual, which, by involving all the "audience" forces each participant into a prescribed role, and a particular place in the sociopolitical structure.

Theater, then, is a cultural performance before a mass audience. *Political theater* is theater that expresses beliefs about the proper distribution and disposition of power (defined broadly, or in a "Foucauldian" sense) and other scarce resources. Unlike political rituals, which in our limited definition always perform a hegemonic function of confirming power relations, political theater often challenges or subverts the authority (or in E. P. Thompson's phrase "twists the tail") of ruling elites.[50]

Although political theater can be (and often is) counterhegemonic, it is by no means always so. Groups within the ruling elite can use political theater to defend their position against attacks from below or to maximize their power vis-à-vis other elite groups. The rowdy London street parades by eighteenth-century supporters of the new Hanoverian regime, which were staged to offset Jacobin mockeries of George I; the gatherings held by U.S. political parties or civic groups to show support for presidential candidates or honor national holidays; and the patriotic mass rally German students organized for Otto Bismarck in 1895 to mark the Iron Chancellor's eightieth birthday—these are but a few examples of acts of political theater that uphold rather than challenge the hegemony of ruling institutions or elites.[51]

Having distinguished ritual from theater, we must now note what the two forms have in common. Perhaps the most fundamental similarity between them is that both ritual and theater are performed for social effect. Language and symbols are used not primarily to convey truths but to produce effects—on the participants or the audience or the gods. This is "pragmatic speech," whose function is to *move*, not to inform. One sees this most clearly in linguistics, in what J. L. Austin has called the "performative utterances" of ritual. In a marriage ceremony, the "I do" is not a report on one's mental act of acceptance; the words *in themselves* complete the act.[52] As such, it is not meaningful to debate the truth value of such utterances: All that counts is that uttering the words had the prescribed effect of completing the marriage ceremony. Similarly, in the Chinese ritual discourse, it would be quite inappropriate to take literally the polite refusal of a gift or the confession of unworthiness when offered a position.[53] These polite phrases are not spoken to express one's true intentions or feelings, and a literal reading of the words uttered in such cases would cause a complete misinterpretation of the ritual. It is the *symbolic effect* of the words, in the context of the total verbal and nonverbal *performance*, that really counts: The words and actions convey a posture of humility, of thanks, and of respect for the other party in the social transaction.[54]

These simple points are important for interpreting events in China, for we will understand the protesters' actions better if we focus on their symbolic meanings and intended effects than if we scrutinize their words in search of some coherent political program. The slogans, big-character posters, pamphlets, open letters, and speeches of the protesters were replete with emotive statements of commitment and dissent. They were proclamations of personal positions, moral statements of resolve. They announced the role a participant was committed to play in the emerging political drama; they rarely put forward an analysis of the failings of the Chinese political system, much less a concrete program for political change. But this was natural, for theirs was a performance designed to impress and move an audience, not an essay or lecture designed to inform.

To say this is certainly not to suggest that the movement was *merely* play-acting. In the post-Reagan era, there are grave risks in writing of politics as performance. One can easily be misunderstood as suggesting that it is all fakery: artificial props, carefully staged events, all medium and no substantive message. That is not our intent. Our point is rather that it makes a good deal more sense to analyze performed actions and utterances not for their truth value but for their symbolic meaning. For example, on April 21 and again on April 27, many students at Beijing universities wrote out last testaments (*yiyan* or *yishu*). They proclaimed their willingness to die for democracy, freedom, their homeland; they said good-bye to their parents and begged their forgiveness and understanding.[55] It makes little sense to ask whether these students really knew what "freedom" and "democracy" meant, and still less sense to ask whether they were truly prepared to die for their beliefs. These last testaments were powerful public statements of great symbolic meaning. They revealed a fundamental alienation from the regime and a willingness to make great (perhaps even the ultimate) sacrifice for an alternative political future.

Ritual and theater have more in common than their involving symbolic action. There is also a great deal of borrowing of scripts between ritual and theatrical performances, in part because the roots of the two cultural forms are so closely intertwined. Most aesthetic theater grew originally out of ritual performance: Greek tragedy from the dithyramb sung around the alter of Dionysus, medieval European passion plays from the Catholic mass, acrobatics and magic acts from shamanistic practices.[56] The earliest forms of Chinese drama likewise had their roots in sacrificial rites.[57] The bond between Chinese opera and ritual performance is evident in everything from the use of Mulian plays in conjunction with funeral rites to the traditions of staging theatrical performances to entertain the gods.[58]

Political theater also borrows heavily from ritual scripts, though often inverting the meaning of these scripts. In sixteenth-century France, religious rioters frequently mocked their opponents' most sacred rites in acts of political theater: Protestant paraders would force a priest to burn his vestments;

Catholics would parody Protestant prayers by transposing the words "devil" and "God."[59] Twentieth-century U.S. antiwar demonstrators have similarly found a variety of ways of turning ritual occasions into theatrical ones (by holding marches on holidays designed to honor the military) and ritual objects (flags, draft cards, army fatigues) into theatrical props.[60]

The transmission of texts between ritual and political theater is by no means always unidirectional: Some ritual performances have their roots in what Turner calls "social dramas."[61] This is not surprising, as one function of rituals is to heal wounds between groups by symbolically reenacting instances of social conflicts (ranging from wars and feuds to shouting matches and bitterly contested elections) and then concluding with a symbolic reintegration of the community.[62] Thus some rituals simultaneously commemorate and deradicalize subversive acts of political theater. Recent work on the French Revolution by scholars such as Mona Ozouf suggests that the Jacobins and others were interested in creating new festivals precisely in order to "represent radical aspirations, while at the same time curbing them."[63] As Lynn Hunt argues, French festivals of the decade after 1789, combining symbolic reenactments of attacks on the ancien régime with ritualized pledges of loyalty to the new order, both "recognized" and "partially defused" the revolutionary potential of the populace.[64]

The mutual borrowing of scripts between political theater and ritual gives the relationship between the forms what one theorist calls a "braided" quality: The two strands continually overlap and reemerge, alternately taking precedence over each other.[65] One of the best illustrations of how this kind of relationship works has direct relevance for understanding the events of 1989: the transformations of the May Fourth Movement from ritual to theater and back. When students took to the streets in 1919 to protest imperialist threats from abroad and warlord corruption at home, they established the classic script for student political theater. Subsequently, both the Kuomintang and the CCP have tried to use the political theater of the May Fourth Movement as the basis for new rituals of conciliation. Though the two parties have commemorated May Fourth differently, both have sought to turn the May Fourth anniversary into a safe revolutionary festival.[66] The script begins with a replay of the conflict of 1919, usually through speeches describing and praising the actions of former student protesters. The ritual then moves into a healing phase, in which official speakers emphasize that there is no longer a division between the interests of the nation's rulers and its youth because the present regime is carrying on in the May Fourth tradition. These speakers claim that the duty of contemporary students is to prove their patriotism by working hard to help the party build a new China rather than by protesting, and the members of the audience (often students) show their acceptance of this interpretation by clapping, shouting loyalist slogans, and singing loyalist songs.

These official attempts to "recognize" and "defuse" the revolutionary potential of students in this fashion have never been wholly successful, as educated youths have repeatedly managed to transform May Fourth rituals back into May Fourth theater. They have done this by emphasizing the reenactment aspect of the official ritual yet denying the reconciliatory phase. In 1947 under the Kuomintang, for example, some Shanghai students chose to engage in anti-KMT propaganda work rather than attend official commemoration activities. But the most dramatic case of subversion occurred in 1989, when Beijing students upstaged the Communist Party's festival to literally retrace the steps of their predecessors of seventy years before. What made this piece of street theater so subversive was its implication (clearly spelled out in banners and slogans) that the ideals of the May Fourth Movement (which the CCP claimed to represent) remained unfulfilled and needed to be fought for on the streets. (For more discussion of the May Fourth commemorations of 1989, see Chapter 8.)

Despite these symbolic links between ritual and theater, it remains important to distinguish between the two and to note when one or the other predominates within a specific political system. It is particularly important for our purposes because the impact of street theater is in part determined by the degree to which political theater is seen as having a legitimate connection to governance. To illustrate this point, we must briefly review the roles of ritual and theater in Chinese politics, past and present.

Political Ritual in Imperial China

Few cultures have given ritual as crucial a role in governance as did China. Confucius argued that "If [a ruler] could for one day 'himself submit to ritual,' everyone under Heaven would respond to his goodness."[67] As Confucianism emerged as a distinct school of thought in ancient China, this notion of rule by ritual became central to its teaching. As various scholars have noted, the administrative weakness of the imperial state, the comparatively small size of its formal bureaucracy, combined with the Confucian disdain for rule by regulations and coercive punishments to make ritual indispensable for the maintenance of social order.[68] Confucian ritual was primarily a secular ritual, but for Confucius, as Herbert Fingarette has put it, the secular was sacred.[69] Elaborate ceremonies governed all social relationships and guaranteed that the human society would operate in harmony with the cosmic order. A central concern of political philosophers was defining, categorizing, and describing the correct practice of the *li* associated with relationships among heaven, the emperor, officials, and members of the populace at large.

Imperial ritual, the highest genre of *li*, was overwhelmingly confined to the palace and the special temples for imperial sacrifices near the capital. Within the walls of the Forbidden City, the rituals were extraordinarily elaborate (one thinks of the opening scene of the movie *The Last Emperor*). The places, costumes, gestures, and words of the participants were all carefully choreographed to display the ordered hierarchy of the court and bureaucracy and the emperor's unique role connecting human society to the greater cosmos. But high walls and imperial guards excluded the general public from any participation, and the carefully prescribed roles of the participants excluded all possibility for political theater.[70]

behind palace walls

The most notable exceptions to the patterns of imperial confinement were the hunts and southern tours of the Kangxi and Qianlong emperors of the Qing. The emperors were greeted by vast crowds as forerunners assembled all officials, as well as local gentry and commoners, to kneel and greet the imperial arrival and departure. But the emperor traveled in an enclosed sedan chair or barge, before which the people were to prostrate themselves, so that even on tour, the pattern of imperial seclusion was not entirely abandoned. The Kangxi emperor occasionally used his tours and hunts to meet ordinary peasants and inquire of their crops and especially of any oppression by local officials. But the extraordinary nature of these contacts is suggested in a Jesuit account, according to which the peasants "were all eager to see his Majesty, who instead of concealing himself gave everyone the liberty of coming near him." Such Jesuit sources are important because the official record is silent on contacts of this sort between the emperor and the people—which itself suggests the ritually problematic nature of such contact.[71]

Official ritual tended to imitate the imperial. Officials were, to paraphrase Alexander Woodside, "spiritual micro-monarchs."[72] They replicated the imperial sacrifice to the Altar of the Soil and Grain and led worship at the Confucian temple. Day-to-day ritual was largely confined to the tribunal or to the private ritual of visits with local notables or other bureaucrats. Officials on tour were proceeded by criers and banners ordering silence and reverence, and, again, the public bowed before them. The arrival and departure of officials did at least provide the ritual (at these liminal moments) of a procession, and these rituals could provide opportunities for the public to express their regret over the departure of a popular official (or opposition to the arrival of an unpopular one).[73] But in general *participatory* political rituals, of the sort that are most easily transformed into political theater, were absent from the official vision of how politics should operate. Instead, there were rigidly stratified hierarchic forms in which the ritual leader (emperor, official, or kin-group patriarch) confronted a mute audience that in many cases (because prostrate) never even saw the ceremonial head.[74]

The contrast to European royal and civic ritual is striking. From the fourteenth century, the royal entry to a city was one of the most important forms of ritual procession. But on entering a city, the monarch would be met (confronted?) by the city's armed militia, handed the keys to the city (an act of fealty, but also a gesture to a guest), and welcomed with street pageants symbolically portraying the virtues the citizenry expected of its ruler.[75] In some German cities jealous of their civic autonomy, the burghers' welcome of their prince or bishop could turn into an armed show of force in which townspeople confronted their sovereign as a rival.[76] But everywhere these ceremonies provided an opportunity for the corporate bodies of urban life (universities, guilds, parliaments or senates, clergy, militia, lawyers, merchants, and tradespeople) to organize and openly announce their place in the public order. As a consequence, even monarchical rituals "tended to describe the essence of national kingship in such a way as to exalt civic virtues and encourage the preservation of urban liberties."[77] All the more was this true of civic rituals on such feast days as Corpus Christi, when the autonomous strength of the corporate groups that made up European civil society was regularly given ritual legitimacy and public display.[78]

One notable feature of Chinese political rituals is the general absence of public speaking. There were, of course, the *xiangyue*, the public lectures on the Sacred Edict. But all accounts agree that this form quickly atrophied in the Qing and never caught on in Chinese culture.[79] China lacked the rhetorical tradition of Greek and Roman forums or of many nonliterate societies. Confucius was suspicious of men with "clever words" (who he believed were seldom men of "humanity"), and Confucian bureaucrats clearly preferred the authority of the written word.[80] Orthodox religious ritual provided no rhetorical models: China had no congregational religion with regular weekly sermons. Consequently, in the very limited civil society of guilds (*huiguan*) that grew up in late imperial China, there were neither the ecclesiastic nor the Roman republican models for public meetings and speeches that one sees in merchants' and artisans' guilds in Europe.

In short, rhetoric and expressions of public opinion—even expressions that supported rather than challenged the status quo—had little place in official Chinese politics. This can be seen by the distinction China's classical philosophers drew between rule by *li* (ritual, traditional practices, correct actions that are carried out spontaneously, almost instinctively, simply because they are "right," not because they are proved to be so) and rule by *fa* (laws and statutes that are obeyed to gain reward or avoid punishment). Neither the idealistic Confucians who considered governance by *li* the only moral form of rule nor the pessimists who argued that the only stable political systems were those that relied heavily upon governance by *fa* devoted much attention to strategies that do not fall into either of these categories.[81] The possibility of using persuasion, organized displays of popular opinion, rhetoric, and other theatrical methods that are neither *li* nor *fa* to maintain control is seldom addressed by either Confucians or Legalists, though a concern with rhetoric is central to classical Western political philosophy.[82] Even the simple act of gathering together to discuss political issues was frequently seen as subversive and thus an act to be controlled by *fa*, as the repeated edicts limiting the activities of academies issued during the Ming dynasty illustrate.[83]

The one legitimate political activity that provided an opening for political theater was the right to petition officials for the redress of grievances. In ancient China a "complaint drum" (*dengwen gu*) was supposedly placed before a ruler's palace to summon attendants to hear a grievance. The drum continued in use in imperial times, and the Qing placed it just southwest of Tiananmen. Nonetheless, the Qing code was interpreted in such a way as to discourage strongly such direct appeals to Beijing, and most petitions were presented to local authorities.[84] Naturally, the right to petition led frequently to a political theater of mass demonstrations, which might develop into riots or even rebellions.[85] A late nineteenth-century account of such a petition movement evokes images of modern protest repertoires:

> I once saw a procession of country people visit the yamens of the city mandarins.
> . . . Shops were shut and perfect stillness reigned as twenty thousand strong, they

wended their way through the streets, with banners flying, each at the head of a company and each inscribed with the name of the temple where the company held its meetings. "What is the meaning of this demonstration?" I inquired. "We are going to reduce taxes," was the laconic answer.[86]

Such mass petition movements were surely unusual, but the script was well enough known to be replicated when necessary. Furthermore, a significant feature of the Chinese case was the replication of the bureaucratic hierarchy in the world of the gods. Consequently, gods were petitioned—and far more frequently than officials. Thus religious ritual could serve, in Emily Ahern's words, as a "learning game," teaching ordinary Chinese "how to analyze (and so manipulate) the political system that governed them."[87]

Petitions provided one small avenue of public access into the otherwise closed realm of legitimate politics in imperial China. But the state dealt harshly with any attempt to use petitions for more than personal grievances. They were not to be an excuse for public debate on matters of policy. As Confucius said, "He who holds no rank in a state does not discuss its politics."[88] Even as China began the slow process of reform in the wake of the Opium War, movement toward a public politics outside the state was exceptionally slow. When Lin Zexu, in disgrace after the outbreak of the Opium War, revealed in a letter to a friend his support for the acquisition of ships and guns, he closed by urging, "I only beg that you keep [these ideas] confidential. By all means, please do not tell other persons."[89] Even the famous reform essays of Feng Guifen, written around 1860, were not published until they were brought to the attention of the emperor in 1898.[90] But after the Sino-Japanese War of 1894–1895, and especially in the course of the twentieth century, Chinese politics changed fundamentally, and central to that change was the emergence of a new space for, and new kinds of, political theater.

Political Theater in Twentieth-Century China

In the final years of the Qing dynasty, the New Policies introduced a series of reforms that ushered in a new era of Chinese politics. First, there were the new schools, which brought together a politically engaged student class in urban centers across China. Soon these students were organizing protests against foreign-financed railways, boycotts of U.S. goods because of U.S. restrictions on Chinese immigration, and broad movements for political reform. They wrote big-character posters, spoke from street corners, and staged mass demonstrations (sometimes including costumed characters) to dramatize their concerns.[91] Some of these demonstrations built upon classic ritual forms—as in a 1906 funeral procession by Changsha students to bury the ashes of two revolutionaries who had committed suicide.[92] As Mary Rankin and William Rowe have shown, an increasingly assertive civil society grew out of earlier networks of gentry activists, local managers, merchant guilds, and charitable organizations. Chambers of commerce and educational associations aggressively sought to set agendas for local political

affairs. As constitutional reforms began in 1909–1910, China had its first experience with electoral politics. Provincial assemblies elected in 1909 immediately provided the basis for political parties, as like-minded individuals
grouped together in a variety of reformist associations. But reformers also
relied upon analogies to establish political forms to press their views—most
notably the series of petitions presented to the court in favor of a rapid transition to full constitutional government. The new local, provincial, and national assemblies became forums for speech-making. Political rhetoric began
to be an important part of the political process. Radical Chinese students in
Japan founded the Society for the Practice of Oratory (Yanshuo Lianxi Hui),
and some dissidents (like Wang Jingwei) established their political reputa-
tions as eloquent public speakers.[93]

Chambers of commerce and the provincial assemblies were two of the
most prominent institutions of this new civil society. It is significant that all
of the provincial assemblies and many of the chambers of commerce were
located in new, specially constructed buildings. The architecture of these
structures symbolized the break with the past. Chinese styles of walled com-
pounds and enclosed courtyards were generally eschewed. Instead, the
chambers and assemblies were located in large, Western-style buildings of
brick or stone, opening directly onto the streets and including spacious auditoriums (*huitang*) for a modern politics of meetings. The new schools also
built auditoriums, especially in the Republican period, and the function of
the new architecture was explicitly acknowledged. One commentator on the
auditorium at Qinghua University in Beijing noted that because the art of
public speaking was so undeveloped in China, the school's new auditorium
"may well be regarded as the Forum Romanum where budding Ciceros will
deliver their orations."[94] Sports stadiums attached to missionary schools,
another imported form of architecture, also provided venues for the new
politics.[95]

This politics of public meetings, speeches, and demonstrations was so new
in China that its forms and models had to be borrowed from other types of
performances. Foreign models were one natural source of inspiration for
these public activities, especially as so many speakers and protesters had
either studied abroad or been trained in missionary schools in China (where
preachers' sermons provided regular reminders of the power of oratory). A
North China Herald account of a 1903 protest meeting held to condemn Russian imperialism notes that at the beginning of the meeting "a set of rules,
translated from the English [*Robert's Rules of Order?*], for the governance of
public speakers and meetings were . . . read, printed copies of which were
also distributed to the audience."[96] Two years later, in an article on the anti-
U.S. boycott of 1905, the same Shanghai newspaper noted that the United
States should at least be heartened that the movement was being carried out
in a "characteristically American manner," complete with public assemblies
and the election of delegates to representative bodies.[97] Many of the most ardent protesters in 1905 had been trained by U.S. missionaries, and these missionaries' conferences and assemblies may well have served as influential
"object lessons" in governance for radical Chinese youths. It is no mere coin-

cidence that one of the most effective public speakers at boycott meetings in Shanghai was Ma Xiangpo, an educator and former priest who had studied under those most skillful of Western rhetoricians: the Jesuits.[98]

Besides foreign models for oratory and rallies, activists in the new politics also borrowed metaphors and techniques from Chinese theater. When the first public organizing went on in the late nineteenth and early twentieth centuries, before the new architecture was in place, the most common meeting places were guild halls (*huiguan*) and temples, which were equipped with stages for operatic performances. There politicians mounted platforms (*tai*) to address the audience. Meetings began with a *kaimushi*, a curtain-raising. Speechmaking was a kind of performance (*yanjiang* or *yanshuo*).

Given the influence of imported political models and theatrical venues and metaphors, it should come as no surprise that both operas and *xinju* (new theater) plays—dramatic performances that mixed elements of Chinese and Western dramatic genres—became "important vehicles of propaganda" for revolutionaries.[99] Shanghai's Chunliu She (Spring Willow Society) performed *xinju* works with names such as "Blood of Patriotism" that "advocated revolution and satirized and laid bare the corruption of the ruling government."[100] The founder of this troupe, Wang Zhongsheng, was executed for his activities in 1911—a sign that the Manchus were well aware of the potential persuasive power of theatrics—earning him a reputation as a revolutionary martyr to the Republican cause.[101]

The new republic inaugurated in 1912 brought forth a political theater appropriate to China's new democratic forms. We see this in magazines and photo albums about this period.[102] Politicians array themselves at railway stations or in front of meeting halls for ceremonial portraits. Naturally, they mount stages to deliver speeches. They parade into cities in open limousines, with flag-waving crowds lining the streets. Now, for the first time, political leaders are brought face to face with the people: Gone is the bowing and the taboo on visual contact. The people see, hear, evaluate, and react to the politicians of the early republic. The purpose, of course, is to make the new politics public and *open*. Indeed this new politics is symbolized in the term for holding a meeting: *kaihui*, or to open an assembly.

The Kuomintang's experiments with patriotic mass mobilization were the most conscious efforts to use political theater to foster political commitment and legitimacy for the new regime. Their most dramatic efforts would begin with an incident that threatened China's national sovereignty. KMT leaders at the national and local levels would sponsor mass rallies against the aggressor, usually Japan. Yellow trade unions, pro-KMT youth groups, and other loyalist organizations would mobilize people to attend these rallies, at which official speakers would praise the Kuomintang as the nation's leading patriotic and revolutionary force, and the crowd would be encouraged to mix cries of "Long live the republic" and "Long live the Nationalist party" with slogans criticizing the foreign foe. Later, local party branches or government bureaus might arrange for petitioners or carefully screened representatives of "legitimate" groups to travel to Nanjing to present their views to top KMT figures, or urge civic groups to launch patriotic fundraising drives.[103]

Whatever the specific techniques the KMT used, the intent was the same: to mobilize popular outrage to reinforce rather than subvert the status quo. Sometimes, as during the New Life Movement, this mobilization merged with attempts to foster Chiang Kaishek's personality cult. Even when not directly associated with cultic practices, however, KMT mass mobilization drives always relied heavily on ritual forms—bows to party and national flags, recitations of Sun Yatsen's last will at the start of meetings, orchestrated visits to the National Father's tomb by petitioners who visited the capital.

Most of these drives left a great deal of room for spontaneous political theater. As such, they might have served as the basis for a new form of politics, in which mass expressions of popular opinion, albeit carefully stage-managed, would play a role in determining and legitimizing public policy. But these new forms of public performance never seemed to catch on in China. The foreign rhetorical models were alien, and the analogy to theater linked politics to an occupation viewed as morally suspect in China.[104]

Political theater encountered two concrete problems. First, China's rulers never developed a mechanism to connect this new open politics of speeches and meetings to the "real" politics of governing. As studies by Andrew Nathan and Lloyd Eastman have shown, the governance of China remained a matter of factional alliances and patronage networks, of personal connections and secret deals.[105] Electoral politics, the most common Western form for connecting political theater to the business of governing, never appealed to the Chinese. Liang Qichao observed it in the United States and found it fraught with fraud, ignorance, and corruption.[106] When Yuan Shikai disbanded the elective assemblies in 1914, there was minimal protest from the disenfranchised citizenry.[107] In the years after 1927, the Kuomintang sporadically tried to reimplement electoral politics. But campaigns at the local level were so corrupt that they convinced neither foreign observers nor the Chinese electorate that the casting of votes had any real impact on governance. If these campaigns and elections qualified as theater at all, they represented burlesque or farce rather than serious political drama.[108]

Second, experiments at mass mobilization were consistently undermined by the tendency of patriotic popular movements to get out of hand and end up as attacks on those in power. Thus the Nationalist era witnessed periodic swings between official encouragement of and violent repression of popular mobilization, the complex dynamics of which are explicated in recent works by Christian Henriot and Wang Ke-wen.[109] The first major swing took place in spring 1928, when party leaders first supported then suppressed popular expressions of outrage over the Jinan incident in which the forces of Chiang Kaishek had been temporarily blocked by Japanese troops; one of the last important swings came in spring 1946, when party leaders encouraged urbanites to attend rallies against "Soviet imperialism" in February, then, as the United States replaced the USSR as the target of popular patriotic indignation, quickly began to argue that all mass gatherings were subversive acts.[110]

When officials failed to shape the mass movements into controlled performances, they turned to a set of repressive tactics that observers of last year will find all too familiar. The regime would declare all collective gatherings illegal, close newspapers (except for foreign ones protected by extraterritoriality) that printed favorable accounts of popular protests, arrest activists, and, if necessary, use violence against those who continued to take to the streets. This kind of repression reflected a continuation of the traditional dichotomy of *li* (ritual) and *fa* (law or coercive control) alluded to above. Though imperial emperors and officials called forms of collective action that threatened the hegemony of their rule "heterodox" whereas the KMT branded such behavior "counterrevolutionary," both regimes saw force as the only response left when they lost control of ritual or "ritualized" political theater.

The Kuomintang's failure to make either elections or mass mobilization an integral part of governance meant that the open politics of political theater became increasingly associated with protest. The traditional forms for mass petitions provided protest movements with a well-established Chinese repertoire that was lacking for hegemonic political theater. The events of May 4, 1919, established the Republican model for petition-based mass action: Students from the leading universities marched to the central square, Tiananmen, and attempted to present their petitions. Further demonstrations followed in Beijing in the early 1920s, but the May Thirtieth Movement was the next episode of truly national significance. These were, in the words of Mao Zedong, the years in which "the Chinese proletariat and the Chinese Communist Party mounted the political stage."[111] A new wave of activism followed the Japanese invasion of Manchuria, culminating in the December Ninth Movement of 1935.

These dates—May 4, May 30, and December 9—were all watersheds in the history of Republican China. They form the markers for conventional periodization, the topics of classroom lectures. They also became anniversaries calling forth celebratory rituals modeled on the original events. Most importantly, they defined the repertoires for a new political street theater. Students always played a leading role, marching from their campuses behind banners proclaiming their school affiliations, They shouted slogans, waved flags, cheered onlookers, petitioned the authorities, and clashed with police. On their campuses they wrote big-character posters; outside they set up platforms to speak to the citizenry. Although the authorities criticized them for neglecting their studies, suppressed their illegal marches, and condemned their disruption of law and order, the press broadcast news of their activities throughout the country and the power of theater was undeniable. From the December Ninth Movement of 1935, and increasingly in the late 1940s, the Communists recognized the power of this theater and its capacity to delegitimize KMT rule, and they worked quietly behind the scenes to encourage further demonstrations.

After 1949 the Communist Party sought to ritualize this theater: to incorporate and domesticate its repertoires into campaigns. The Party was well aware of the danger of uncontrolled political theater: Many of its key leaders had risen to prominence through their roles in student and worker demonstrations. They understood the power of independent student unions, which were called, under the Kuomintang as in 1989, *xuesheng zizhihui* (student self-government societies).[112] Accordingly, the Communists banned all autonomous associations. But they did not wish to abandon the theater—only to monopolize the capacity to organize it, to succeed here (as elsewhere) where the KMT had failed. Thus it became one of the important functions of work units and the party-sponsored mass organizations (of youth, women, workers, peasants, etc.) to mobilize constituencies for mass demonstrations.

The result was the "campaign style" of Maoist politics—a style that prevailed until the late 1970s.[113] In the ritualized demonstrations that accompanied every major campaign, or that marked important dates on the revolutionary calendar, people would march forth behind their unit's or mass organization's banners, with lots of red flags, drums, and cymbals, and head for the central square. In the nation's capital, national minorities would join in native costume while the party leaders looked down from the elevated platform of Tiananmen itself. The same ritual would be repeated in cities across the country, with local leaders in their own elevated reviewing stands.

During the Cultural Revolution, Mao loosened the controls on these political rituals, and the students quickly devised their own innovative repertoires of street theater. "Ghosts and monsters" were paraded through the streets in dunce caps; offending teachers and cadres were put on stage with arms bound behind their backs in the airplane position; books were burned, art destroyed. But Cultural Revolution street theater quickly degenerated into something too disorderly even for Mao, as rival Red Guard gangs fought physical battles in schools, factories, and streets.

By the late 1960s, this revived theater had to be suppressed, and by 1980 the party revised the constitution to prohibit all big-character posters, leaflets, and demonstrations. In fact, under Deng Xiaoping, the party tried to abandon both the campaign ritual of the pre-Cultural Revolution period and the political theater of the "ten years of chaos" and rule purely by administrative routine. But the Tiananmen demonstrations in honor of Zhou Enlai and against the Gang of Four in 1976, the Democracy Wall Movement of 1978–1979, the Hunan protests of 1980, the student demonstrations in Beijing in 1985 and in Shanghai and other cities in 1986 and 1987, and finally China's spring of 1989 demonstrated that political theater cannot be totally suppressed. Some public rituals are always necessary, and in those events, there is always the danger that students or other actors will usurp the stage and turn the official ritual into their own political theater.[114]

Interpreting the Political Theater

As performance, the truth-value of the words and actions in this political theater is not terribly important. But that does not imply that this theater is meaningless—only that we have to pay more attention to its symbolism than to the literal meaning of its utterances. Let us consider the symbolism of 1989. The first function of political theater is quite simply to be heard. The point of the street demonstration is to gain attention. Initially, the audience is a dual one: the general population (both urban residents who witness the demonstration directly and those who can be reached through the medium of television) and the authorities. But it is the authorities who are the real audience; the value of the people is largely instrumental. The more support the demonstrators can gain from the citizenry—the larger the applauding crowds lining the demonstration route, the more concrete contributions of food and drink, the more symbolic aid in the form of banners or citizens' support groups, the greater the monetary contributions from citizens and small business—the more leverage the demonstrators will gain with the authorities.

That the authorities are the real audience is demonstrated by the petition format. But this petition is also important in that it acknowledges the fundamental legitimacy of the government to which one appeals for redress. Later, the petition is replaced by the appeal for a dialogue. Again, this is fundamentally a demand to be heard. But underlying this demand—even more clearly in dialogue than in petition—is a claim to entrance into the polity.[115] Groups previously excluded from the political process seek through demonstration, petition, and dialogue to be taken seriously by the authorities as participants in the political decision-making process. Even some of the violence of the demonstrations, the rock throwing and arson, can be interpreted as efforts to gain attention, to be heard—efforts by those less skillful with and less trusting of words than intellectuals and university students.

The *public* nature of political theater is its second most important characteristic. Street theater invites all citizens to join. Once Tiananmen Square was occupied, the students often debated strategy and made decisions in public, there for all to see. They demanded a live broadcast of their dialogue with the government leaders. Symbolically, such theater stands in direct contrast to the secrecy of the Party-state. Significantly, the model for all such demonstrations in China, the May Fourth demonstration of 1919, protested against the secret diplomacy that had preceded the Versailles conference. Street theater invariably symbolizes a call to open up the political process, and the very secrecy (and lack of accountability) of the Party-state in China naturally calls forth this sort of dialectical opposite.

Finally, student strikes and, even more dramatically, the hunger strike, present images of selflessness—a key value in contemporary China, with models from Norman Bethune to Lei Feng. These acts were extraordinarily effective. The most common praise of the student movement was that their motives were entirely patriotic, for love of country (*aiguo*). They sought nothing for themselves—unlike, some said, workers who might strike for higher pay. These students asked nothing, accepted not even food, and wished no more than the good of the nation. Their acts of self-denial stood in obvious contrast to the self-serving and corrupt leadership they attacked. No privilege of the Party leadership was more visible than the enormous banquets they consumed at public expense. Now here were students refusing to eat anything at all.[116]

Finally, the last testaments that the students wrote out, plus the hunger strike and related gestures, located the students within a rich tradition of political martyrs. These activities, as Dru Gladney and others have noted, linked the students to Qu Yuan, the loyal minister of the third century B.C.

who showed his willingness to "die for the affairs of the nation" by committing suicide after his ruler refused to heed his advice.[117] Such actions also
recalled earlier generations of student martyrs, from Chen Dong (a Song dynasty protester who was executed for his criticisms of government corruption and who served as a model for some May Fourth activists) to Yao
Hongye and Chen Tianhua (two frustrated Hunanese activists who committed suicide in 1906), and the hundreds of youthful demonstrators killed by
foreign and native authorities during the Republican era. When students at
Tiananmen Square swore collective oaths to sacrifice their lives—the last and
most prophetic of which was taken on June 3—they were enacting a scene
from the May Fourth Movement. Similarly, when Chai Ling bit her finger and
wrote out a protest slogan with her own blood, she stepped into a role that
student protesters of 1915 and 1919 had played.[118] With all this theater, the
students appealed to a tradition of principled dissent and revolutionary action that the Party itself had legitimized and mythologized in the attempt to
claim such theater as its own.

If we are to understand the enormous appeal of the student demonstrations in Beijing and across China, we must begin by appreciating these symbolic meanings of their protest. The slogans—attacking the corruption of official profiteers (*guandao*), calling for a freer press, mocking China's highest
leaders, advocating a never-defined "freedom" and "democracy"—were certainly important. But they gained their power because the very repertoire of
the movement symbolized a demand for a voice in government, for a more
open political process, and for an end to leadership by a self-serving elite.

A Comparative Perspective

As Chirot argues in more detail in Chapter 11, the 1989 demonstrations in
China were clearly part of a larger, worldwide crisis of state socialist systems.
In Eastern Europe the Communist Party has been toppled from power in one
country after another. In the Soviet Union the Party is in the process of
renouncing its monopoly on power, and various ethnic groups—led by
Lithuania, but including all the Baltic states and the peoples of the Caucasus
region—have been moving steadily toward some form of greater autonomy
from Moscow. Increasingly, China (along with North Korea, Vietnam, and
Cuba) is looking like the last refuge of socialism. As a current Chinese joke
has it—playing on the official cant that "Only socialism can save China"—
now "Only China can save socialism."

In each of the European transitions, street demonstrations have played a
critical role. This was, of course, most obvious in the dramatic events of East
Germany and Czechoslovakia. There, an utterly peaceful political transformation—a "velvet revolution," to use the Czech phrase—was brought about
by unarmed civilians protesting in the streets. Because exactly the same sort
of political theater brought forth troops and tanks and unprecedented bloodshed in China, it is necessary to try to explain the contrasting result.

Part of the answer clearly lies in factors quite beyond the scope of this es-

Contrast

say. The Communist Party of China (and the parties of Vietnam, Cuba, and, to a lesser degree, Korea) made its own revolution. Each of these countries thus differs from the state socialist regimes of Eastern Europe, which were to one degree or another brought into being and propped up by the Soviet Red Army. Consequently, when Gorbachev made it clear that the Brezhnev Doctrine was dead and the Soviet Union would no longer come to the rescue of unpopular East European regimes, those regimes fell very quickly.

In addition, China and the remaining state socialist regimes are all poor Third World countries. They have large, impoverished, and still poorly educated rural populations. At least in China, there is unquestionably substantial peasant discontent over a variety of issues—the payment for grain requisitions in IOUs instead of money, the government's failure to deliver promised supplies of chemical fertilizer. But in general peasants displayed little sympathy for the demands of the student demonstrators. Only the attack on corruption struck a responsive chord. And when the crackdown came, rural residents tended to believe the government contention that the peasant soldiers of the People's Liberation Army would not fire on unarmed civilians unless there was a genuine threat to law and order. In short, China's large peasant population remained largely preoccupied with its own immediate material interests, and it viewed these interests as dependent on continued political stability. Consequently, China's peasantry provided a reservoir of support for the hard-liners in Beijing that was missing in any East European regime.[119]

More germane to our discussion, however, is the role played by the institutions of civil society in Eastern Europe—a role that Chirot alludes to as well in his chapter. These long-neglected institutions proved to have sufficient life to structure the opposition movement and sustain it until victory. The most obvious example is the Catholic church in Poland. As a gathering place and refuge for dissidents in the Solidarity movement, the Catholic opposition was fundamental to the breakthrough in Poland—which was, after all, the first domino to fall. It clearly did not hurt to have a Polish pope during Solidarity's long years of travail. Hungary was the next country to make serious moves in the direction of pluralism, and here the old democratic parties played a crucial role. In Czechoslovakia, the dissident groups among the intellectuals were clearly better organized than anyone previously believed. In East Germany, the Evangelical (Lutheran) church helped to shelter dissident intellectuals and a small independent peace movement. Bulgaria witnessed a nascent environmental movement, which played a critical role. In Lithuania, there was again the Catholic church, plus the role of national movements and linguistic solidarity.[120]

Virtually all of the institutions of civil society in Europe are imbued, to one degree or another, with aspects of democratic culture. We sometimes forget, as we focus on the hierarchic structures and stately rituals of the Catholic church, that the pope is elected and councils of bishops and other more local institutions have often operated on democratic principles. On a more mundane level, artisan guilds would, on their feast days, constitute themselves as a "republic" to manage their affairs and discipline their members.[121] When, therefore, civil society has been allowed to prosper, it has brought with it, in the West, a discourse and a culture already shaped by electoral forms and at least a minimal tolerance of dissent.

In Eastern Europe, such institutions of civil society played the absolutely critical role of translating the symbolic meaning of street theater into systematic programs for political change. When the Party-states of Eastern Europe were forced to sit down to negotiate with the street protesters, there were people with organizational experience and programmatic ideas who could negotiate the delicate transition to democracy. The glamour-seeking media has hardly focused on this process, sometimes leaving the impression that dramatic demonstrations led to government collapse and then a natural evolution to electoral forms. But that is hardly a plausible scenario, and when the full story is told we will surely find a critical role of civil society in presiding over that perilous political process.

It is not enough, however, to focus on institutions alone. The small and vulnerable groups of dissident intellectuals and workers in Eastern Europe could certainly not match the organizational might of the Party-state in these countries. But if there is one lesson that the rapid collapse of Communist parties in Eastern Europe and Russia has taught us, it is that social scientists have misled us into accepting an excessively reified notion of what "institutions" are. We have been led to think of the Party-state almost as a physical structure, of unshakable size and weight and power. Now we are in a position to recall that such "structures" are, in fact, made up of *people* who are bound together by certain rules and habits, interests and aspirations, rituals and shared identities, a theme that Calhoun and Saich return to hereinafter in Chapter 4 and Chapter 12, respectively. The people who make up these institutions are not mindless parts of a party "machine," acting always and unfailingly in the interest of that machine. (Gorbachev and his supporters in the Soviet Union obviously cannot be understood if we identify them only as leaders and servants of the Communist Party machine.)

Once we escape an excessively institutional approach to politics in state socialist systems, we are in a better position to appreciate the impact of the culture of civil society, or (to use Pierre Bourdieu's useful term) the habitus that reemerged from the collective memory to give life to the East European movements of dissent. One participant/observer of the Polish experience has noted "the explosion of national memory . . . the massive turnout for anniversary celebrations" that followed the first Solidarity struggles of 1980–1981.[122] In small rituals and mass celebrations, the habitus of democratic governance was revived from a culture rich in civic rituals and the theater of popular rule.

As we noted above, China's imperial state allowed minimal development of civil society. The late Qing and the Republican era witnessed a brief flowering of civil society, but its roots were not deep. In addition, as David Strand has shown, this new civil society found it difficult to escape the old politics of personal networks, and the leaders of the new civic institutions tended to look for patrons within the state.[123] The habitus of autonomous associations was still weakly developed. In addition, civil society in China never pro-

[handwritten marginalia: "opposition parties"]

vided an adequate foundation for pluralist politics. To a large degree, it revealed this weakness in its rhetoric. Mary Rankin has observed that the Chinese press (both a component and a mouthpiece of China's nascent civil society) tended to speak of the "people" as an undifferentiated whole— usually standing against an opposing symbolic category, "officials," that is, the state.[124] Thus when Chinese began to speak of "rule by the people" *(minzhu)*, the "people" were an undifferentiated whole. The separate "republics" of civil society were not sufficiently legitimized to bring, with the idea of democracy, the pluralism bred in the corporate roots of European civil society.

Under the PRC, the budding sprouts of republican civil society were cut off altogether. The rhetoric of the undifferentiated people was usurped by the state to establish a "people's democratic dictatorship." Dissidents were safely excluded as "enemies of the people." Pluralism existed neither in the organization of society nor in the rhetoric of politics. Both the Party-state and its opponents appealed to the virtue of "unity." But only the party existed as a functioning political organization. The tragic result of this combination of circumstances is that the Chinese Communist Party can justly claim that there is no political force outside the Party capable of ruling China. Many of the hunger-strikers conceded this point in May 1989, and they were probably reflecting the consensus of most of the protesters. In the wake of the June Fourth Massacre, the party's claim to legitimacy rests on little more than this fact: There is no alternative to the CCP. The *reason* there is no alternative is simple enough: The Party will not permit one to exist. To preserve their fragile legitimacy, the Party leaders must rigorously suppress any hint of pluralism: no autonomous student or workers' unions, no publications that might provide an alternative voice, no civil society. Then they can present the Chinese people with a bleak choice: either continued Communist rule or chaos.

Without a civil society, only street theater remains as a mode of political expression. No Chinese regime has ever been able to suppress it altogether. The smooth functioning of Chinese politics requires public rituals to celebrate the ideals of the revolution and the Party-state that emerged from it. In time, students will again find an opportunity to usurp those rituals to perform their own political theater. Then the question will again arise: Can they (and the state) find a mechanism to connect this theater to the complex task of governing more than a billion Chinese?

Postscript

During the months since this essay first appeared in the November 1990 issue of the *Journal of Asian Studies* (JAS), we have received a number of instructive comments from fellow historians and specialists in disciplines (anthropology, philosophy, literature) other than our own. In addition to the criticisms and queries in these informal communications, scholarly contributions—such as the essay by Ann Anagnost that appeared in the first edition of this book—have extended or challenged certain points we made. All of this has led us to look back at some parts of our original essay with a critical eye, though, upon reflection, we remain committed to our central argument. As a result we have decided to make only minor changes in preparing this essay for this volume. Nonetheless, it seemed worthwhile to address briefly three of the most important issues that our colleagues have raised.

1. Definitions of *li* and *ritual*. Both before and after the piece appeared in JAS, a number of people (including Henry Rosemont, Jr., and Frank Pieke) raised objections to our definitions of these concepts, arguing that we left too little room for the kind of innovation that often takes place during the performance of ritual acts and the way in which codes of *li* change over time as a result of such creative departures from received scripts. These critics have a valid point. However, we continue to see an important (though admittedly slippery) distinction between political theater and cultural performances that put a much higher premium upon faithful replication of a series of actions in a traditional fashion. To avoid confusion, we would be happy to find words other than *ritual* and *theater* to distinguish these two types of performance, but we have yet to discover more suitable terminology.

2. The unimportance of public speaking and public ritual in imperial China. Several colleagues have suggested that we may have overstated the seclusionary and nonoratorical nature of pre–twentieth-century politics. Most particularly, some (including Mary Rankin and Ann Anagnost) have raised questions about our claims regarding the lack of public speaking traditions. We have little doubt that, at least compared to the European case, political oratory was relatively unimportant in China prior to the twentieth century and that, above the most local level, public speaking played a decidedly minor part in formal politics. Nonetheless, some scholars have observed that the political content of storytelling performances suggests that the contrasts may not be as stark as we have drawn them. Others have noted that public speaking skills were often seen as a prerequisite for village leadership, though we would observe that the "ability to talk" (*huishuo*) is as likely to refer to interpersonal mediating and brokering skills as to a capacity for oratory. It is clear that China specialists need to study public speaking more closely. We also need a much better sense of how state rituals at the imperial, provincial, and local levels operated in practice. Were they always as "private" as they were supposed to be in theory? Work in progress by James Hevia, Angela Zito, and others promises to speak to this issue.

3. Civil society, East and West. Finally, comments on our JAS article and recent work on related topics (including various contributions to this volume) suggest that the reemergence or stifling of civil society traditions in differing political environments will continue to be a topic of considerable interest within the China field (and Eastern European studies) for some time to come. Most of what we have heard on this issue has reaffirmed our conviction in our original arguments. Nonetheless, there are certainly avenues that deserve more detailed exploration. Michael Duke, for example, has (in personal correspondence) brought up the question of the different degrees of ruthlessness shown by Eastern European Communist parties and the CCP when dealing with political dissidents. He notes that people like Vaclav

Havel and Lech Walesa were able to emerge from prison alive and sane and were apparently treated quite differently from Chinese dissidents like Wei Jingsheng. Duke suggests a distinctive Eastern European habitus in such matters that does not exist in contemporary China. To begin to address such issues, we need first to get a much more nuanced picture of both Chinese and Eastern European civil society traditions. Fortunately, important steps in this direction are already being made by people like Daniel Chirot (whose contribution to this volume addresses the Eastern European case) and David Strand (whose valuable discussion of Beijing's "public sphere" appeared as we were preparing our JAS piece to go to press).[125]

Notes

1. Jonathan Mirsky's "The Empire Strikes Back," *New York Review of Books*, February 1, 1990, discusses early English-language works by journalists and sinologists; Tony Saich and Nancy Hearst, "Bibliographic Note," in Tony Saich, ed., *Perspectives on the Chinese People's Movement* (Armonk, N.Y.: M. E. Sharpe, 1990), pp. 190–196, provides an extremely useful overview of these and somewhat later English-language works, as well as of books in other Western languages and Chinese. Of extant English-language works, Human Rights in China, ed., *Children of the Dragon* (New York: Macmillan, 1990) provides perhaps the best single-volume introduction to the movement, combining as it does accounts by foreign eyewitnesses (including Orville Schell and Perry Link), background essays by leading sinologists (such as Jonathan Spence), an impressive collection of photographs, and translations of some key Chinese-language speeches, interviews, and documents.

2. Keith Forster, "Impressions of the Popular Protest in Hangzhou, April/June 1989," and Josephine Fox, "The Movement for Democracy and Its Consequences in Tianjin," *Australian Journal of Chinese Affairs*, 23 (1990), pp. 97–120 and 133–144; Frank Niming [pseud.], "Learning How to Protest," in Saich, *Chinese People's Movement*, pp. 82–104.

3. Although official references to the Red Guard legacy had some effect in alienating support for the students in 1986, such Cultural Revolution imagery was much less effective in 1989, in part because the students confronted the argument head on. They demanded that the leadership apologize for labeling the movement a form of *dongluan* (turmoil)—a term that has become a code word for the Cultural Revolution.

4. For example, a report in the *San Franciso Chronicle*, May 19, 1989, p. A24, quotes a worker from Hubei saying: "At least Mao was honest. ... He even sent his son to the Korean War. Nowadays, the leaders send their sons to America."

5. For an interesting comparison of the uses Red Guards and the protesters of 1989 made of Mao portraits, see *Washington Post*, May 24, 1989, p. 1. For additional discussion of the similarities and differences between the Red Guards and the protesters of 1989, see Jeffrey N. Wasserstrom, *Student Protests in Twentieth-Century China: The View from Shanghai* (Stanford: Stanford University Press, 1991), epilogue, and the chapters by Schwarcz and Young in this volume.

6. See, for example, Lowell Dittrner, "China in 1989: The Crisis of Incomplete Reform," *Asian Survey*, 30, 1 (1990), pp. 25–41; and Gerrit W. Gong, "Tiananmen: Causes and Consequences," *Washington Quarterly*, 13, 1 (1990), pp. 79–95.

7. *Renmin ribao* (People's daily), May 19, 1990, p. 1; Zhaoqing, Gejing, and Suyuan, *Xueran de fancai* (Bloody scenes) (Hong Kong: Haiyan, 1989), p. 204. Interestingly, the U.S.-government–operated Foreign Broadcast Information Service: China (hereafter,

FBIS-CHI) reversed the meaning of this passage in its translation. See FBIS-CHI-89-096 (May 19, 1989), p. 15. Perhaps FBIS was uncomfortable with this explicit rejection of majority rule.

8. *Sun Zhongshan xiansheng huace* (Dr. Sun Yatsen: A photo album) (Beijing and Hong Kong, 1986), plate 199.

9. *Enlightenment*, no. 2, cited in Andrew Nathan, *Chinese Democracy*, (Berkeley: University of California Press, 1985), p. 6.

10. Although *Chinese Democracy* is replete with useful examples of this sort, Nathan seems blind to this issue and concludes with a quite unsupported discussion of "the West's—and the Chinese democrats'—identification of democracy with pluralism" (p. 227).

11. Here we follow the argument Richard C. Kraus presents in "The Lament of Astrophysicist Fang Lizhi," in Arif Dirlik and Maurice Meisner, eds., *Marxism and the Chinese Experience* (Armonk, N.Y.: M. E. Sharpe, 1989). For an alternative view of Fang's version of democracy, see Chapter 9 of this volume.

12. Mary S. Erbaugh and Richard C. Kraus, "The 1989 Democracy Movement in Fujian and Its Consequences," *Australian Journal of Chinese Affairs*, 23 (1990), pp. 145–160, esp. p. 153.

13. See, for example, Forster, "Hangzhou," p. 98; Niming, "Learning"; Henry Rosemont, Jr., "China: The Mourning After," *Z Magazine* (March 1990), pp. 85–96; Anita Chan and Jonathan Unger, "China After Tiananmen: It's a Whole New Class Struggle," *Nation*, January 22, 1990, pp. 79–81.

14. Note this May 1989 exchange between a youth, barred from boarding a bus where Wuer Kaixi was resting, and a student security guard. "'What kind of democracy is this?' [the youth] fumed. 'What kind of freedom? You are just like the country's leaders.' Responded the guard: 'You are right. But you are harming our unity. Don't say such things.'" *Newsweek*, May 29, 1989, p. 21. One of the earliest (and still one of the best) discussions of this sort of behavior at Tiananmen Square is Sarah Lubman, "The Myth of Tiananmen Square: The Students Talked Democracy But They Didn't Practice It," *Washington Post*, July 30, 1989. Criticisms of the new exile leagues appear in Yuen Ying Chan and Peter Kwong, "Trashing the Hopes of Tiananmen," *Nation*, April 23, 1990, pp. 545, 560–564; and Chan and Unger, "China After Tiananmen," pp. 79–81.

15. Comments at a roundtable at the 1989 national meetings of the American Historical Association.

16. Thompson, "Patrician Society, Plebeian Culture," *Journal of Social History*, 7, 4 (1978), pp. 382–405, and "Eighteenth-Century English Society: Class Struggle Without Class?" *Social History*, 3, 2 (1978), pp. 71–133; Clifford Geertz, *Negara: The Theatre-State in Nineteenth-Century Bali* (Princeton: Princeton University Press, 1980).

17. Frank Pieke, "Observations During the People's Movement in Beijing, Spring 1989" (paper presented at the International Institute of Social History, Amsterdam, July 7, 1989), and "A Ritualized Rebellion: Beijing, Spring 1989" (unpublished conference paper, 1990); Dru Gladney, "Bodily Positions and Social Dispositions: Sexuality, Nationality and Tiananmen" (paper presented at the Institute for Advanced Study, Princeton, April 26, 1990); Lucian Pye, "Tiananmen and Chinese Political Culture: The Escalation of Confrontation from Moralizing to Revenge," *Asian Survey*, 30, 4 (1990), pp. 331–347; and David Strand, "Protest in Beijing: Civil Society and Public Sphere in China," *Problems of Communism*, 34, 3 (1990), pp. 1–19. All unpublished papers cited with authors' permission; Link's comments on Beijing opera are cited in Strand, "Protest in Beijing."

18. Charles Tilly, *From Mobilization to Revolution* (Reading, Mass.: Addison-Wesley, 1978).

19. Strand, "Protest in Beijing"; Jeffrey Wasserstrom, "Student Protest in the Chinese Tradition," in Saich, *Chinese People's Movement*.

20. This phenomenon of protesters transforming an authorized procedure into radical street theater is by no means unique to China, as Charles Tilly's discussion of rural unrest in *The Contentious French* (Cambridge: Harvard University Press, 1986), esp. pp. 116–117, illustrates.

21. Pye, "Tiananmen and Chinese Political Culture."

22. *North China Herald*, November 19, 1902, pp. 1076–1077; November 24, 1917, pp.467–468.

23. For a more detailed discussion of the importance of funerals in Chinese political, social, and cultural life, and references to relevant works on the topic, see James Watson's contribution to the first edition of this volume.

24. Turner, *The Ritual Process: Structure and Anti-Structure* (Ithaca: Cornell University Press, 1969), esp. ch. 3: "Liminality and Communitas."

25. Yan Jiaqi and Gao Gao, *"Wenhua dageming" Shinianshi* (A ten-year history of the "Cultural Revolution") (Tianjin: Tianjin renmin chubanshe, 1986), pp. 586–640.

26. This pattern is hardly unique to China. Compare this account of a key demonstration by tens of thousands of youths on November 17, 1989, in Prague. It was one of the major events leading to the fall of the Communist government in Czechoslovakia. "The memorial for Jan Opletal, the student killed by the Nazis, was sponsored by the official student organization but was transformed into a demonstration for freedom, political change and the dismissal of the Communist Party leader, Milos Jakes." (*New York Times* [national ed.], November 18, 1989.) Needless to say, Czechoslovakia—where the theaters were transformed into the headquarters of the democratic opposition, and a playwright, Vaclav Havel, was elected president—is an excellent place to look for examples of political theater.

27. For student comments on hunger strikes in other parts of the world, see Yi Mu and Mark V. Thompson, *Crisis at Tiananmen* (San Francisco: China Books, 1989), p. 172; and *Newsweek*, May 29, 1989, p. 21. For more comprehensive treatments of the hunger strikes of 1989, see James L. Watson, "The Renegotiation of Chinese Cultural Identity in the Post-Mao Era: An Anthropological Perspective," in Kenneth Lieberthal et al., eds., *Perspectives on Modern China: Four Anniversaries* (Armonk, N.Y.: M. E. Sharpe, 1991), pp. 364–386; and Frank Pieke, "The Ordinary and the Extraordinary: An Anthropological Analysis of Chinese Life and Protest in the Reform Era" (doctoral dissertation, University of California, Berkeley, 1991).

28. For general discussions of the goddess of democracy statue's construction and symbolism and photographs of the statue, see Han Minzhu, ed., *Cries for Democracy* (Princeton: Princeton University Press, 1990), pp. 342–348; Human Rights in China, *Children*, pp. 116–122; Yi and Thompson, *Crisis*, p. 372; and Chapter 8 in this volume. Dru Gladney notes the parallels between the goddess and Cultural Revolution Mao icons in his "Bodily Positions and Social Dispositions"; for photographs of such statues being carried through Tiananmen Square, see *Beijing Review*, October 3, 1969, p. 7, and *China Reconstructs* (December 1986), p. 3; and for a photograph of Shanghai students carrying a replica of the Statue of Liberty, see the *New York Times Magazine*, June 4, 1989, p. 28.

29. Insightful firsthand accounts of audience reaction to and participation in Beijing events are provided in Pieke, "Observations," and Niming, "Learning."

30. Suggestions from Barry Naughton were very helpful in inspiring and formulating these ideas.

31. Among the students, there was significant criticism of the servile posture of the kneeling petitioners. But it appears that by adopting this traditional ritual, the petitioners gained substantial sympathy and support among the general populace. See Lianhebao editorial department, ed., *Tiananmen yijiubajiu* (Tiananmen 1989) (Taipei: Lianjing chuban shiye gongsi, 1989), pp. 60–61; Han, *Cries*, pp. 63–64.

32. *North China Herald*, June 8, 1918, pp. 571–572; *Minguo ribao*, June 1 and 2, 1918;

John Israel, *Student Nationalism in China, 1927–1937* (Stanford: Stanford University Press, 1966), pp. 60–61 and passim.

33. "Dueling Demonstrations in Beijing," *San Francisco Chronicle*, June 1, 1989, pp. A21–A25.

34. We are grateful to Henry Rosemont, Jr., who witnessed this performance, for describing it to us.

35. Wu Mouren et al., *Bajiu Zhongguo minyun jishi* (Annals of the 1989 Chinese democracy movement) (New York: privately published, 1989), pp. 262 and 267.

36. Michel Oksenberg provoked our thinking on this point. It became clear during Nixon's visit to China in November 1989 that Chinese and Western connotations of the term *tragedy* are quite different. Western notions derived from Greek drama link tragedy to unalterable fate or to some "tragic flaw" of the person who suffers the tragic fate. Thus, from a Western perspective, calling the events of June 3–4 a "tragedy" tends to objectify them and even to remove responsibility for the bloodshed from the hands of the Chinese leadership. In this sense, use of the term *tragedy* was an attempt to soften the implications of the term *massacre*; it is perhaps significant that years earlier, Nixon had no difficulty terming the student deaths at Kent State a "tragedy." But the Chinese word is closer to our sense for *melodrama* and implies a clear villain—which the Chinese leadership correctly understood to be themselves. For an example of an official denial that June 4 was a tragedy, see *New York Times*, September 27, 1989, p. 8; for Nixon's comment on Kent State ("when dissent turns to violence it invites tragedy"), see Kirkpatrick Sale, *SDS* (New York: Random House, 1973), p. 638; and for further discussion of the differences between English and Chinese understandings of *tragedy*, see the Afterword to this volume.

37. Here and in later sections, we draw heavily upon the discussion in Richard Schechner, "From Ritual to Theater and Back," in Richard Schechner and Mady Schuman, eds., *Ritual, Play, and Performance* (New York: Seabury Press, 1976), pp. 196–222.

38. Steven Lukes, "Political Ritual and Social Integration," *Sociology*, 9, 2 (1975), pp. 289–305, criticizes overly broad definitions of the term, but Lukes's own more limited definition still encompasses most forms of popular protests as well as ceremonials that serve to uphold the status quo. In an earlier work, one of us has followed Lukes's lead and analyzed Chinese student demonstrations as "political rituals"; see Jeffrey Wasserstrom, "Taking It to the Streets: Shanghai Students and Political Protest, 1919–1949" (Ph.D. dissertation, University of California, Berkeley, 1989).

39. See in particular, Clifford Geertz, "Religion as a Cultural System," in his *Interpretation of Cultures* (New York: Basic Books, 1973), pp. 87–125.

40. See Emile Durkheim, *The Elementary Forms of the Religious Life*, trans. J. W. Swain (London: Allen and Unwin, 1915); for citations to and a highly critical review of other Durkheimian studies of ritual, see Lukes, "Political Ritual."

41. Robin Horton, cited in Victor Turner, *From Ritual to Theater* (New York: Performing Arts Journal Press, 1982), p. 82.

42. For Geertz's approach, see the various essays in *The Interpretation of Cultures* and his "Blurred Genres: The Refiguration of Social Thought," *American Scholar* (Spring 1980), pp. 172–176.

43. Turner's classic statement on the topic was *The Ritual Process: Structure and Anti-Structure* (Ithaca: Cornell University Press, 1969); see also his "Social Dramas and Ritual Metaphors," in Schechner and Schuman, *Ritual, Play, and Performance*, 97–122.

44. If, for example, a priest were just to pour wine into a chalice, dump wafers into a bowl, and pass them around without the proper words and gestures, transsubstantiation would not occur and the communicants would not partake in the body and blood of Christ. Schechner uses the believed efficaciousness of rituals as the main criterion for

differentiating them from theatrical performances in his essay "From Ritual to Theater and Back."

45. Jean-Christophe Agnew, *Worlds Apart: The Market and the Theater in Anglo-American Thought* (Cambridge: Cambridge University Press, 1986), pp. 103–112. The concept of "orthopraxy" is discussed in Watson, "The Renegotiation of Chinese Cultural Identity."

46. Turner, *From Ritual to Theater*, esp. pp. 52–55. Geertz is less helpful in this regard. Although he writes at length about the "theater state" of Bali, his language (e.g., in *Negara*, p. 102, he writes of "the ritual extravagances of the theater state") both fails to distinguish between ritual and theater and tends to treat theater as a mass ritual to which all responded with a uniform belief.

47. *Li Ji* (Classic of ritual), ch. 1, verses 27, 63, in Fung You-lan, *A History of Chinese Philosophy*, vol. 1, trans. Derk Bodde (Princeton: Princeton University Press, 1952), p. 339.

48. Ibid., Chapter 1, 28, 97–99, p. 343.

49. Schechner, "From Ritual to Theater and Back," p. 211.

50. In both "Patrician Society, Plebeian Culture," and "Eighteenth-Century English Society," Thompson analyzes "countertheater" of "threat and sedition" through which England's common people challenged the gentry's "theater of hegemony." Although these insightful articles forcefully illustrate the subversive potential of theater, we have avoided Thompson's "theater/countertheater" terminology because "theater of hegemony" blurs the important distinction between regularly repeated "rituals" (such as coronations) and other kinds of improvised, theatrical shows of force or majesty that support the status quo.

51. Nicholas Rogers, "Popular Protest in Early Hanoverian England," *Past and Present*, 79 (1978), pp. 70–100; Susan G. Davis, *Parades and Power: Street Theatre in Nineteenth Century Philadelphia* (Philadelphia: Temple University Press, 1975); Konrad Jarausch, *Students, Society, and Politics in Imperial Germany* (Princeton: Princeton University Press, 1982), pp. 3–6.

52. J. L. Austin, "Performative Utterances," in Austin, *Philosophical Papers* (London: Oxford University Press, 1962), pp. 220–239.

53. The proper forms of these rituals were precisely delineated in the ancient text, the "Ceremonies and Rituals." For a translation, see John Steele, *The I-li* (London, 1917).

54. In divination rituals that mimic these social transactions, an undesirable result may come from choosing the wrong polite words. Therefore, according to one informant, "You keep throwing the blocks until a yes comes up, each time slightly changing what you say. That is because you might have made a mistake in giving your address, or you might not have been polite . . . enough in speaking to the god." Emily M. Ahern, *Chinese Ritual and Politics* (Cambridge: Cambridge University Press, 1981), p. 32.

55. Lianhebao, *Tiananmen yijiubajiu*, pp. 69–71; Han, *Cries*, pp. 126–127; Pye, "Tiananmen and Chinese Political Culture," p. 341.

56. Jacques Burdick, *Theater* (New York: Newsweek Books, 1974): pp. 7–41; E. T. Kirby, "The Shamanistic Origins of Popular Entertainments," in Schechner and Schuman, *Ritual, Play, and Performance*, pp. 139–149.

57. Colin MacKerras, *The Chinese Theatre in Modern Times* (Amherst: University of Massachusetts Press, 1975), p. 13.

58. For relevant citations concerning funeral rites, see Watson's chapter; for other kinds of dramas performed for the gods, see Joseph Esherick, *The Origins of the Boxer Uprising* (Berkeley: University of California Press, 1987), pp. 63–64 and passim.

59. Natalie Davis, "The Rites of Violence," in *Society and Culture in Early Modern France* (Stanford: Stanford University Press, 1975), pp. 152–188. Other chapters in this

book, such as "The Reasons of Misrule," also provide insights into the relationship between rituals and political theater.

60. For relevant citations, see Wasserstrom, *Student Protests*, ch. 10; see also Lukes, "Political Ritual," pp. 294 and 299.

61. "Social Dramas and Ritual Metaphors," in Schechner and Schuman, *Ritual, Play, and Performance*, pp. 97–122.

62. Some sample rituals that reenact violent struggles can be found in Schechner, "From Ritual to Theater and Back," pp. 196–202. The final moments of U.S. electoral campaigns, after the voting ends, often take on a ritual character: First groups converge at the headquarters of rival candidates, where they revel and make their final symbolic attacks upon the character of the opponent; then, to conclude the ritual, the losing candidate calls the winner to politely concede to and congratulate his or her former adversary.

63. Lynn Hunt, *Politics, Culture and Class in the French Revolution* (Berkeley: University of California Press, 1984), p. 99; see also Mona Ozouf, *Festivals and the French Revolution* (Cambridge: Harvard University Press, 1988).

64. Hunt, *Politics, Culture, and Class*, p. 60.

65. Schechner, "From Ritual to Theater and Back," p. 211.

66. For a provocative discussion of these uses of May 4, see Vera Schwarcz, *The Chinese Enlightenment* (Berkeley: University of California Press, 1986), pp. 240–282; this topic is dealt with at length in Jeffrey N. Wasserstrom, "Revolutionary Anniversaries in Guomindang and Communist China" (paper presented at the Pacific Coast regional Association for Asian Studies meetings, Stanford, June 1990).

67. Confucius, *Lunyu*, 12:1, in Arthur Waley, trans., *The Analects of Confucius* (New York: Vintage, no date), p. 162.

68. Susan Naquin and Evelyn Rawski, *Chinese Society in the Eighteenth Century* (New Haven: Yale University Press, 1987), p. 88 and passim; Charles Hucker, *The Traditional Chinese State in Ming Times* (Tucson: University of Arizona Press, 1961), pp. 67–68; various contributions to Kwang-Ching Liu, ed., *Orthodoxy in Late Imperial China* (Berkeley: University of California Press, 1990); and Angelo Zito, "Grand Sacrifice as Text-Performance: Writing and Ritual in Eighteenth-Century China" (Ph.D. dissertation, University of Chicago, 1989).

69. Herbert Fingarette, *Confucius: The Secular as Sacred* (New York: Harper and Row, 1972).

70. For more details on imperial rituals, see Zito, "Grand Sacrifice as Text-Performance"; Naquin and Rawski, *Chinese Society;* and Gugong bowuguan yuan (Palace Museum), eds., *Zijincheng dihou shenghuo* (Lives of the emperors and empresses in the Forbidden City) (Beijing: China Travel and Tourism Press, 1983), pp. 108–111.

71. The quote is from Jean Baptiste Du Halde, *The General History of China,* trans. Richard Brooks (London: J. Watts, 1736), p. 349; for a general treatment of the tours and comments on the official record, see Jonathan D. Spence, *Ts'ao Yin and the K'anghsi Emperor, Bondservant and Master* (New Haven: Yale University Press, 1966), pp. 125–136.

72. Alexander Woodside, "Emperors and the Chinese Political System," in Lieberthal et al., eds., *Perspectives on Modern China*, pp. 5–30.

73. Kung-chuan Hsiao, *Rural China: Imperial Control in the Nineteenth Century* (Seattle: University of Washington Press, 1967), pp. 449–450.

74. Especially when compared to Chinese theater audiences, the silence of ritual "audiences" is notable. In this regard, the "profound silence" that Jesuit observers recorded in the vast crowds greeting the Kangxi emperor suggests that imperial tours were closer to rituals than theatrical performances; Spence, *Ts'ao Yin*, p. 136.

75. Roy Strong, *Art and Power: Renaissance Festivals, 1450–1650* (Berkeley: University of California Press, 1984), pp. 7–11.

76. Thomas A. Brady, Jr., "Rites of Autonomy, Rites of Dependence: South German Civic Culture in the Age of Renaissance and Reformation," in Steven Ozment, ed., *Religion and Culture in the Renaissance and Reformation* (Kirksville, Mo.: Sixteenth-Century Journal Publishers, 1989).

77. Lawrence M. Bryant, *The King and the City in the Parisian Royal Entry Ceremony* (Geneva: Librairie Droz, 1986), p. 22.

78. David M. Bergeron, *English Civic Pageantry, 1558–1642* (Columbia: University of South Carolina Press, 1971); Edward Muir, *Civic Ritual in Renaissance Venice* (Princeton: Princeton University Press, 1981).

79. Hsiao, *Rural China*, pp. 194–201; Victor Mair "Language and Ideology in the Written Popularizations of the *Sacred Edicts*," in David Johnson, Andrew Nathan, and Evelyn Rawski, *Popular Culture in Late Imperial China* (Berkeley: University of California Press, 1985), pp. 325–359.

80. In Waley, *Analects*, 1:3; Wing-Tsit Chan, *A Sourcebook of Chinese Philosophy* (Princeton: Princeton University Press, 1963), p. 20.

81. For an important recent discussion of the contrasting meanings of *li* and *fa*, which inter alia shows the extent to which these two terms dominate classical Chinese conceptions of politics, see Benjamin Schwartz. *The World of Thought in Ancient China* (Cambridge: Harvard University Press, 1985), pp. 102–104, 321–349, and passim. As Schwartz notes (pp. 102–104), even idealistic Confucians such as Confucius himself accepted that their vision of rule by *li* alone was utopian, and that in reality punishments and force would have to play some role.

82. An interesting discussion of this topic by a nonsinologist that draws attention to contrasts between the Chinese and Greek traditions is J.G.A. Pocock, "Ritual, Language, Power," in *Politics, Language and Time: Essays on Political Thought and History* (Chicago: University of Chicago Press, 1989), pp. 42–79. We are grateful to Daniel Gargola for drawing our attention to this piece.

83. John Meskill, "Academies and Politics in the Ming Dynasty," in Charles Hucker, ed., *Chinese Government in Ming Times* (New York: Columbia University Press, 1969), pp. 149–174.

84. Derk Bodde and Clarence Morris, *Law in Imperial China* (Philadelphia: University of Pennsylvania Press, 1973), pp. 464–466.

85. For some relevant examples, see Elizabeth J. Perry, "Tax Revolt in Late Qing China," *Late Imperial China*, 6, 1 (1985), pp. 83–112; Tsing Yuan, "Urban Riots and Disturbances," in Jonathan Spence and John Wills, eds., *From Ming to Ch'ing* (New Haven: Yale University Press, 1979); and Lin Yu-tang, *A History of the Press and Public Opinion in China* (1936; reprint, New York: Greenwood, 1968).

86. William Martin, *A Cycle of Cathay* (New York: F. H. Revell, 1900), pp. 91–92, cited in Hsiao, *Rural China*, p. 434.

87. Ahern, *Chinese Ritual and Politics*, p. 92.

88. *Lunyu*, 8:14, in Waley, *Analects*, p. 135.

89. Cited in Ssu-Yu Teng and John K. Fairbank, eds., *China's Response to the West: A Documentary Survey, 1839–1923* (Cambridge: Harvard University Press, 1979), p. 28.

90. Ibid., p. 50.

91. Edward J. M. Rhoads, *China's Republican Revolution: The Case of Kwang-tung, 1895–1913* (Cambridge: Harvard University Press, 1975), pp. 86 and 95–96.

92. Joseph W. Esherick, *Reforms and Revolution in China: The 1911 Revolution in Hunan and Hubei* (Berkeley: University of California Press, 1977), p. 56; see also Rhoads, *China's Republican Revolution*, p. 88.

93. Mary Rankin, *Elite Activism and Political Transformation in China: Zhejiang Province, 1865–1911* (Stanford: Stanford University Press, 1986); William Rowe, *Hankow: Commu-*

nity and Conflict (Stanford: Stanford University Press, 1989). Rankin mentions the oratory society in "The Emergence of Women at the End of the Ch'ing: The Case of Chiu Jin," in Margery Wolf and Roxann Witke, eds., *Women in Chinese Society* (Stanford: Stanford University Press, 1975), p. 51.

94. Chao Hsueh-hai, "Tsing Hua New Buildings," *Tsing Hua Journal*, 3, 7 (June 1918), p. 38. We are grateful to Jeffrey Cody for bringing this quote to our attention.

95. "The First Stadium in Shanghai," in Zhou Yuehua, ed., *Anecdotes of Old Shanghai* (Shanghai: Shanghai Cultural Publishing House, 1985), pp. 154–156, describes various political gatherings held at the St. John's sports field. Complaints about the lack of appropriate public gathering places can be found in various early twentieth-century newspaper reports; see, for example, Cai Yuanpei's comments in *North China Herald*, May 7, 1903, p. 885.

96. *North China Herald*, May 7, 1903, p. 885.

97. Ibid., August 11, 1905, p. 322.

98. Ruth Hayhoe, "Towards the Forging of a Chinese University Ethos: Zhendan and Fudan, 1903–1919," *China Quarterly*, no. 94 (June 1983), pp. 323–341; and British Foreign Office records 228/2155.

99. MacKerras, *Chinese Theatre*, p. 48.

100. Zhou, *Anecdotes*, p. 32.

101. MacKerras, *Chinese Theatre*, p. 49.

102. See, for example, *Sun Zhongshan xiansheng huace*; and *Guomin geming huace* (An illustrated history of the national revolution) (Taipei, 1965).

103. For more details on KMT-sponsored mass movements (and citations to the relevant literature on the topic, some of which is discussed below as well), see Wasserstrom, *Student Protests*, ch. 6, 7, and 9.

104. MacKerras, *Chinese Theatre*, pp. 78–79 and 95–96.

105. Andrew Nathan, *Peking Politics, 1918–1923: Factionalism and the Failure of Constitutionalism* (Berkeley: University of California Press, 1976); Lloyd Eastman, *The Abortive Revolution: China Under Nationalist Rule, 1927–1937* (Cambridge: Harvard University Press, 1974).

106. Chang Hao, *Liang Ch'i-ch'ao and Intellectual Transition in China* (Cambridge: Harvard University Press, 1971), p. 239.

107. Ernest P. Young, *Liberalism and Dictatorship in Early Republican China: The Politics of the Yuan Shih-K'ai Presidency* (Ann Arbor: University of Michigan Press, 1976), pp. 148–155.

108. Various pieces in the March and April 1946 issues of *China Weekly Review*, which describe Shanghai's first "free" elections and include admissions by KMT officials concerning some improprieties, illustrate this point. See particularly "Democratic Elections," March 16, pp. 48–49; "Scandal in Yunnan: Bribery (Quite Common in 'Elections' Paper Declares," April 27, pp. 184–185; and "Officials Held on Ballot Box Stuffing Charge," May 11, p. 235.

109. Christian Henriot, "Le Gouvernement Municipal de Shanghai, 1927–1937," (doctoral dissertation, Sorbonne, 1983); Wang Ke-wen, "The Kuomintang in Transition" (Ph.D. dissertation, Stanford University, 1985). See also John Israel, *Student Nationalism in China, 1927–1937* (Stanford: Stanford University Press, 1966); and Patrick Cavendish, "The 'New China' of the Kuomintang," in Jack Gray, ed., *Modern China's Search for a Political Form* (London: Oxford University Press, 1969).

110. For details, see Wasserstrom, *Student Protests*, ch. 9.

111. Mao Zedong, "Xin minzhu zhuyi lun" (On new democracy), in *Mao Zedong xuanji* (Collected works of Mao Zedong), vol. 2 (Beijing: People's Publishing House, 1952), p. 690.

112. Israel, *Student Nationalism*, p. 24.

113. Charles P. Cell, *Revolution at Work: Mobilization Campaigns in China* (New York: Academic Press, 1977).

114. Along with examples given earlier, the student protests of 1985 and those of 1986–1987 began on anniversary dates—September 18 and December 9—set aside for official commemorations.

115. This point owes much to Charles Tilly's studies of collective action, see esp. *From Mobilization to Revolution.*

116. The symbolic appeal of this selflessness helps to explain why, especially since June 4, criticisms of student movement leaders within the dissident community have focused on acts of extravagance and indulgence as well as undemocratic procedures. As Chan and Kwong note ("Trashing the Hopes of Tiananmen," p. 562), attacks on Wuer Kaixi and others have tended to stress allegations that they have squandered funds on "luxury hotel accommodations, banquets and other questionable expenses."

117. Gladney, "Bodily Positions and Social Dispositions."

118. For further information on and relevant citations for the various continuities between student protests, past and present, alluded to in this paragraph, see Wasserstrom, *Student Protests*, chs. 2, 3, and epilogue.

119. David Zweig, "Peasants and Politics," *World Policy Journal* (Fall 1989), pp. 633–645. Esherick's impressions from fieldwork in North Shaanxi in June and July 1989 generally support Zweig's analysis.

120. See Vladamir Tsimaneau, "Eastern Europe: The Story the Media Missed," *Bulletin of Atomic Scientists*, 46, 2 (1990), pp. 17–21; Pawel Machcewicz, "The Solidarity Revolution," *Polish Perspectives*, 32, 3 (1989), pp. 14–25; and, for further discussion and additional citations, Chapter 11 below.

121. Robert Darnton, *The Great Cat Massacre and Other Episodes in French Cultural History* (New York: Vintage, 1985), pp. 85–89.

122. Machcewicz, "The Solidarity Revolution," p. 19; Bourdieu defines his concept of habitus in *Outline of a Theory of Practice*, trans. Richard Nice (Cambridge: Cambridge University Press, 1977), pp. 72–87.

123. David Strand, *Rickshaw Beijing* (Berkeley: University of California Press, 1989), and "Protest in Beijing."

124. Rankin, *Elite Activism*, p. 166.

125. Strand, "Protest in Beijing."

Part Two

CLASS, GENDER, AND IDENTITY: 1989 AS A SOCIAL MOVEMENT

Although each of the contributors to this section represents a different discipline—Perry is a political scientist, Feigon a historian, and Calhoun a sociologist—they share a common concern with the social and cultural dimensions of the collective actions that took place on the streets of China's cities in 1989. As diverse as their specific interests and approaches are, there are at least two important common threads running through these three essays. First, like the contributors to Part 1, all three of these authors are interested in the ways in which symbols and structures inherited from the past can constrain or give special meaning to contemporary struggles for change. Second, all three find the kinds of theatrical metaphors discussed in Esherick and Wasserstrom's chapter useful for describing and making sense of social movements. This is most obvious in the case of Perry's chapter, which draws attention to the contrasting types of roles that members of different social classes chose or were allowed to play in the street theater of 1989. Feigon uses dramatic imagery in a similar fashion to highlight the tendency of male students to monopolize most of the starring roles in the occupation of Tiananmen Square. Calhoun, finally, refers to scripts and performances in his analysis of the effects that participation in symbolically charged public dramas can have on the self-images of the actors involved. The supplementary materials list for this section includes everything from essays that look at the protest activities of Chinese political actors who belong to social classes other than those of primary concern here, to studies of social movements that have occurred in times and places far removed from 1989's Tiananmen Square, to theoretical works on the formation of collective identities.

Recommended Supplementary Materials for Classroom Use

Scholarship on China: Contemporary Politics

Gladney, Dru. "The People of the People's Republic: Finally in the Vanguard?" *Fletcher Forum of World Affairs*, vol. 12, no. 1 (Winter 1990), pp. 62–76. Gladney looks at the important roles that members of national minority groups played in the protests of 1989.

Goldstein, Carl, and Lincoln Kaye. "Get Off Our Backs." *Far Eastern Economic Review*, vol. 156, no. 28 (July 15, 1993), pp. 68–71. A study of the causes and forms of rural unrest in post-1989 China.

Perry, Elizabeth J. "Rural Violence in Socialist China." *China Quarterly*, 103 (September 1985), pp. 414–440. Perry surveys various types of village protest during the first thirty-five years of CCP rule and pays particular attention to the early 1980s.

Walder, Andrew G., and Gong Xiaoxia. "Workers in the Tiananmen Protests: The Politics of the Beijing Workers' Autonomous Federation." *Australian Journal of Chinese Affairs*, 29 (January 1993), pp. 1–30. A study of the activities of one of the most important nonstudent organizations involved in the struggles of 1989.

Watson, James L. "The Renegotiation of Chinese Cultural Identity in the Post-Mao Era: An Anthropological Perspective." In Kenneth Lieberthal et al., eds., *Perspectives on Modern China: Four Anniversaries*. Armonk, N.Y.: M. E. Sharpe, 1991, pp. 364–386. Watson traces the changing forms through which a sense of national identity is cultivated, expressed, and contested in the PRC; his work also appeared in the first edition of this book.

Scholarship on China: Historical Perspectives

Chan, Anita. *Children of Mao: Personality Development and Political Activism in the Red Guard Generation*. Seattle: University of Washington Press, 1985. Chan analyzes the socialization and political activities of those who came of age during the early years of the Cultural Revolution.

Chesneaux, Jean, ed. *Popular Movements and Secret Societies in China, 1840–1950*. Stanford: Stanford University Press, 1972. A collection of essays by leading specialists from several countries; includes discussion of a wide range of different types of urban and rural protests.

Kazuko, Ono. *Chinese Women in a Century of Revolution, 1850–1950*. Stanford: Stanford University Press, 1989. A survey that includes chapters detailing female involvement in social movements ranging from the Taiping Uprising of the mid-nineteenth century to the land reform campaigns of the 1940s.

Rawski, Evelyn. "The Social Agenda of May Fourth." In Kenneth Lieberthal et al., eds., *Perspectives on Modern China: Four Anniversaries*. Armonk, N.Y.: M. E. Sharpe, 1991, pp. 139–157. An analysis of New Culture Movement activists' attempts to create a "new citizen" through efforts aimed at promoting mass literacy, doing away with inequalities related to class and gender, and changing China's family system; ends with a comparison of those aspects of the agenda that have and have not been realized in the PRC and the Republic of China on Taiwan.

Strand, David. *Rickshaw Beijing: City People and Politics in the 1920s*. Berkeley: University of California Press, 1989. A study of urban life and social protest in China's capital, which pays particular attention to alliances and tensions between different social groups.

Comparative Works and Case Studies of Other Countries

Bourdieu, Pierre. "What Makes a Social Class? On the Theoretical and Practical Existence of Groups." *Berkeley Journal of Sociology,* vol. 32 (1987), pp. 1–17. An essay on the contested nature of group identities; adapted from a public lecture given in the United States by one of France's leading cultural theorists.

Kruks, Sonia, et al., eds. *Promissory Notes: Women in the Transition to Socialism.* New York: Monthly Review Press, 1989. A collection of essays on the roles women have played in twentieth-century revolutions occurring in various parts of the world, and the way state socialist regimes have come to terms with the "woman question" after gaining power; the book includes pieces on China by Christina Gilmartin, Marilyn B. Young, and Delia Davin.

Lipset, Seymour, and Philip Altbach, eds. *Students in Revolt.* Boston: Houghton Mifflin, 1969. A collection of essays on campus activism in the United States and a variety of other countries; includes an essay on China by historian John Israel.

Tilly, Charles. *From Mobilization to Revolution.* Reading, Mass.: Addison and Wesley, 1978. Tilly's general introduction to various approaches to the study of social movements; the book includes a chapter outlining his influential conceptualization of "repertoires" of collective action.

Tilly, Louise. "Gender, Women's History, and Social History." *Social Science History,* 13:4 (Winter 1989), pp. 439–462. Tilly looks at strategies for engendering the study of revolutions, including particular focus on the roles women play in social protests, and also refers to the gendered dimensions of revolutionary rhetoric and symbolism.

Primary Sources

Honig, Emily, and Gail Hershatter. *Personal Voices: Chinese Women in the 1980s.* Stanford: Stanford University Press, 1988. This work contains translations from contemporary newspaper and magazine articles that deal with the gendered dimensions of subjects ranging from courtship to domestic violence and includes analytical introductions by two leading specialists in Chinese women's history.

Long Bow Film Group. "Small Happiness." This documentary film uses interviews with the inhabitants of a Chinese village to explore the changing status of women since 1949, the impact of the economic reforms of the early 1980s, and the shifting senses of individual and group identity in the countryside.

Perry, Elizabeth J., and Jeffrey N. Wasserstrom, eds., *Shanghai Social Movements, 1919–1949,* a special double-issue of *Chinese Studies in History* (Fall-Winter 1993–94). This work contains translations of memoirs, scholarly articles, and speeches by Chinese authors who participated in and/or are students of the campus unrest and labor strikes of the Republican era.

3

CASTING A CHINESE "DEMOCRACY" MOVEMENT: THE ROLES OF STUDENTS, WORKERS, AND ENTREPRENEURS

Elizabeth J. Perry

Of all the momentous political upheavals in 1989, few captured wider attention and sympathy than the Chinese protests that spring. Taking full advantage of the international media (then focused on Beijing to cover first the Asian Development Bank meetings and then the Gorbachev summit), the demonstrators engaged in a style of political showmanship that seemed tailor-made for their new global television audience: festive marches complete with colorful banners and contemporary music, somber hunger strikes punctuated by the wail of ambulance sirens, even a twenty-seven-foot "goddess of democracy" guaranteed to strike a resonant chord in foreign viewers.

Undoubtedly this adept handling of symbolic politics contributed to the widespread publicity and enthusiasm that the events in China elicited around the world. The revolutions in Eastern Europe later in the year were surely stimulated in part by the Chinese example. And yet whereas the Berlin Wall came tumbling down, the walls surrounding Tiananmen Square stand more heavily fortified than ever. International opinion was obviously not sufficient to break a Chinese regime whose leadership operated according to

An earlier version of this essay appeared in Daniel Chirot, ed., *The Crisis of Leninism and the Decline of the Left: The Revolutions of 1989* (Seattle: University of Washington Press, 1991). This revised version is printed with the permission of the University of Washington Press. The author would like to thank participants in the "Revolutions of 1989" conference (Seattle, October 1990) for their helpful comments.

its own political logic. Moreover, despite the apparent sophistication of the young Chinese protesters in dealing with the international media, their movement also remained for the most part within a distinctly Chinese political pattern. The shared assumptions of rulers and rebels served to reinforce preexisting authority relations, helping to ensure that China's protest movement did not become its revolution of 1989.

Why No Revolution in 1989? The Standard Explanations

When compared to the head-spinning transformations in Eastern Europe, the Chinese outcome has been tragically anticlimactic. To account for this difference, two sorts of explanations are commonly given. The first, ironically enough, points to China's *revolutionary heritage*. In contrast to the communism in most of Eastern Europe, Chinese communism was the outcome of a hard-fought civil war. Having been won from within rather than imposed by alien tanks, the Chinese system was said to enjoy a considerably higher level of popular legitimacy than its East European counterparts.

In the early 1960s, Chalmers Johnson highlighted China's (and Yugoslavia's) indigenous revolutionary experience—which he termed "peasant nationalism"—as an explanation for the emergence of the Sino-Soviet rift.[1] At that time it seemed that nationalist revolutions had engendered independent and dynamic variants of socialism: Maoism in China, Titoism in Yugoslavia. Today, however, that same revolutionary heritage (lingering on in Cuba, Vietnam, and to some extent North Korea as well) reputedly acts as a brake on further political transformation.

If legitimacy was once the product of a revolutionary past, however, it is surely being eroded by a repressive present. Presumably, then, this explanation for contemporary political stagnation is a short-lived one; as the reservoir of popular support is drained by the heavy-handed tactics of obsolescent polities, the aging rulers' claim to revolutionary legitimacy is rendered less and less convincing.[2]

A second type of explanation would seem to have more staying power. This is the view that stresses the *peasant nature* of China. Mired in poverty and ignorance, the 800 million rural dwellers are held responsible for China's political impasse. The tendency to lay the blame for tyranny at the feet of the peasantry is a familiar theme in social science analysis on both the left and the right. Marx claimed that Louis Napoleon's rise could be attributed to those French "potatoes in a sack," a notion that parallels the explanation many a modernization theorist has proffered for Third World dictatorships. Among Chinese intellectuals, this line of reasoning has been especially pronounced. Mao's cult of personality—and the resultant tragedies of the Cultural Revolution and its aftermath—are said to have sprung from the benighted peasantry's undemocratic messianic yearnings. It was these peasants, we are told, who were so attached to the anthem of the Cultural Revolution: "The East is red; the sun is rising. China has given birth to a Mao Zedong. He works for the people's happiness; he is our great savior." The same adulation that had propped up imperial despots for thousands of years was now being transferred to Communist tyrants—first Mao and then Deng Xiaoping. Little wonder that democracy advocates like Fang Lizhi allude to the need to limit peasant political participation; democracy demands an enlightened citizenry—something that in China only the intellectuals claim to be.[3]

The use of peasants as convenient scapegoats is an old practice among Chinese thinkers. Whenever political change failed to occur in the desired manner, the fault could always be said to lie with the backward inhabitants of the countryside. In fact, however, most of China's twentieth-century political follies have been centered in the cities, where intellectuals themselves have played a central role. Certainly this was true for the Cultural Revolution; not ignorant peasants but educated students proved the most zealous disciples of Chairman Mao. In the post-Mao period as well, intellectuals were a bastion of support for Deng Xiaoping through much of the 1980s. History might well have taught them better. In 1957 Deng had taken charge of implementing the notorious antirightist campaign that ruined the careers of hundreds of thousands of the nation's finest intellectuals.[4] In 1979–1980 Deng's harsh crackdown on the Democracy Wall Movement again indicated his intolerance for intellectual criticism. Yet despite this record of repression, Chinese intellectuals continued to express enthusiasm for Deng Xiaoping. To a greater degree than the peasants (most of whom have, after all, benefited materially from Deng's agrarian reforms), it is the intellectuals whose complicity in despotism seems based less on realistic interests than on traditional patterns of authority.

Intellectual Traditionalism

To explain the weaknesses of China's 1989 protests, one must not stop with the country's revolutionary heritage or peasant population. Rather, the very people who launched the Tiananmen protest—urban intellectuals—were perhaps a greater fetter on its further development. The seemingly cosmopolitan and contemporary style of the demonstrations masked a deeper continuity with longstanding patterns of state-society relations in China.

Educated Chinese have tended to identify closely with the regime in power, as Cheek argues (Chapter 9). For much of imperial history, this identification was of course institutionalized in the examination system; the highest honor for a Confucian scholar was to win official position by an outstanding examination performance. Although a vigorous tradition of remonstrance did develop among Chinese intellectuals, it remained for the most part within officially prescribed channels. In contrast to early modern Europe, an alienated academy did not emerge in China until the twentieth century under foreign tutelage. The May Fourth Movement of 1919 revealed the explosive potential of this new critical stance, but it was a short-lived enlightenment indeed. The tendency for subsequent generations of Chinese intellectuals to invoke the May Fourth model—most recently on the seventieth anni-

versary of that historic occasion—reflects nostalgia for a truncated event
rather than the completion of its critical mission.[5] Contemporary intellectuals
have fallen into the trap of trying to "replay the old tune of May Fourth" that
the literary critic Lo Changpei so presciently warned against on the eve of
liberation in 1949 and that Schwarcz describes in Chapter 8. In endeavoring
to imitate the May Fourth exemplar, recent generations of intellectuals have
been guilty of the same "emperor-worship mentality"—characterized by
submission to a familiar pattern of ceremonial politics—against which the
May Fourth Movement was directed.

A dramatic example of this recycling of tradition was seen on April 22,
1989, a day of government-scheduled memorial services for former Party
General-Secretary Hu Yaobang. As they had on many previous occasions
(e.g., the Qingming remembrance for the late Premier Zhou Enlai thirteen
years earlier, which sparked the momentous Tiananmen incident of April 5,
1976), students managed to convert an official ceremony into a counterhegemonic performance.[6] The inversion of state rituals has been used to considerable effect by protesters in other parts of the world as well, of course.[7] In taking charge of the occasion (in the Chinese case by claiming control of the
official site for such events: Tiananmen Square), the demonstrators are able to
challenge the legitimacy of the regime and gain a forum for conveying their
own political messages. Yet a striking feature of the April 22 countercere-
mony was its adherence to traditionally sanctioned modes of behavior. Three
student representatives attempted—in the age-old manner of Chinese scholarly remonstrance—to present a petition demanding an explanation for the
ouster of Hu Yaobang and a meeting with the current premier, Li Peng. Denied entrance to the Great Hall of the People, the young emissaries suddenly
fell to their knees and began to kowtow. Embarrassed officials eventually
opened the doors, allowing the students to present their petition to a low-
ranking functionary who summarily rejected the demands.[8] The obsequious
demeanor of the petitioners was a stark reminder of the degree to which contemporary intellectuals continue to practice traditional styles of protest.

Perry Link, a specialist in Chinese literature who was an eyewitness to the
memorial demonstration, offers an insightful account:

> The students knelt on the steps of the People's Hall and asked the Premier, "Will
> you just come out and see us, just give us your acknowledgement of our trying to
> be patriotic and trying to help?" From our point of view the demand for dialogue
> with somebody might not really have punch. But for them it was really important,
> and in fact I can view that whole square through those thrilling days of April and
> May as a Beijing Opera Stage . . . in that morally charged Beijing Opera sense . . .
> when one after another unit would come out, and say, "Here we are with our ban-
> ner." This to me meant two things. It meant literally, "We have shown up," but it
> also meant, "We have presented ourselves in this drama."[9]

The presentation of banners representing one's unit was both a theatrical
convention and part of the standard protest repertoire.[10] It was, moreover, a
tradition not confined to Beijing. When a delegation of graduate students
from the Shanghai Academy of Social Sciences attempted on May 25 to

present their banner to the Shanghai Garrison Command,[11] the scene was reminiscent of the Shanghai workers' militia presentation of their banner to Chiang Kaishek following a major labor uprising in spring 1927.[12] In all these instances, the protesters were in effect seeking recognition from the ruling authorities of their unit's place on the political stage.

The Limits of Tradition

To be sure, the protesting units had changed somewhat since the Republican period. Though schools remained central, gone now were the native-place associations, guilds, and professional societies that had served as the building blocks of urban unrest during the first half of the twentieth century. Thanks to the reordering that took place under communism, in 1989 many of the participating groups were the *danwei* (or units) created by the state itself. In fact, at one point members of more than ten organs directly under the Central Committee of the Chinese Communist Party—including the propaganda department—could be counted among the marchers.[13]

The incestuous relationship between state and society that had developed as a consequence of communism rendered familiar forms of protest ineffective. Although danwei could serve as a vehicle to mobilize millions of people for a Tiananmen demonstration, because these units (whether schools, factories, or Party organs) were ultimately dependent on the state for their very survival, they could easily be *demobilized* once the state leadership was united in its determination to take action. The frailty of "civil society" in contemporary Chinese cities, even when compared to the late imperial and Republican scene,[14] has made much of the old protest repertoire anachronistic. Lacking autonomy from state domination, urbanites restage the pageant of May Fourth without the *social* power that invigorated the initial performance.

The actors in the most recent rendition of this continuing drama were certainly capable of putting on an exciting show. In their contribution to this volume, Esherick and Wasserstrom characterize the 1989 protest as "street theater: untitled, improvisational," but following "a historically established 'repertoire' of collective action." They rate Wuer Kaixi's performance in the May 18 dialogue with Li Peng as "one of the best acts" in this "instance of political theater"; costuming, timing, and props were all exquisitely handled.

But if the theatrics were first-rate, the politics were less impressive. A particularly disappointing feature of this self-styled "democracy" movement was its fickle search for patrons. Hu Yaobang, posthumous hero to the students of 1989, had been vilified in the huge demonstrations that broke out during his tenure as general-secretary just a few years earlier. In winter 1986–1987, a popular protest slogan had called for the overthrow of Hu Yaobang, comparing him unfavorably to the Gang of Four of Cultural Revolution notoriety.[15] Yet once Hu was ousted in January 1987, and particularly after his death from a heart attack on April 15, 1989, he became a martyr to the movement. Hu's successor as general-secretary, Zhao Ziyang, now suffered the wrath of the students. Whereas Hu had been criticized for his buffoonery, Zhao was attacked for the corruption of his children.[16] Even so, when Zhao Ziyang deigned to visit the hunger strikers in Tiananmen Square on May 19, he became an instant hero, with students clamoring for his autograph. And just as soon as Zhao was deposed, he too attained martyrdom.

Although it would be grossly unfair to accuse the 1989 activists of anything close to the degree of adulation that surrounded Mao's cult of personality during the Cultural Revolution, nevertheless the longing for heroes remained disturbingly evident. Among many young intellectuals, this tendency found expression in support for the doctrine of "New Authoritarianism" (xin quanweizhuyi), which looked to a political strongman—in the tradition of Chiang Kaishek in Taiwan or Park Chung-Hee in South Korea—to push forward with economic reform. There were important differences among advocates of this doctrine,[17] but a number of its adherents played a leading role in the early stages of the 1989 demonstrations.[18] To them, state strengthening was the sine qua non of democracy—an argument that, as Andrew Nathan has shown, has been common among Chinese "democrats" since the late nineteenth century.[19] But whereas earlier generations lived under imperial and Republican regimes that were indeed too weak to effect the economic and political transformation of which young activists dreamed, the current dilemma is of an entirely different sort. Genuine change will almost certainly require breaking, not buttressing, the state's control.

The students' deference to state authority was seen in their demand for dialogue—for a place on the political stage, as it were. Xinhua News Agency reported on April 30, "Dialogue has become a household word here as millions of Beijing residents watched last night and tonight the television program of the dialogue between Yuan Mu, the spokesman for the State Council, and the college students."[20] Dramatic as it was, the demand for dialogue was also an admission of the hold that the state continued to exert; protesters wanted a role in the official political pageant, which for them remained the only real show in town. As Geremie Barmé observes, "students and intellectuals alike have craved above all for some form of official recognition, their own place at the helm of the ship of state."[21] In sharp contrast to their counterparts in Eastern Europe, Chinese urbanites certainly had not "simply . . . [begun] to turn away from the state, by refusing to take it seriously," as Chirot notes in Chapter 11.

Perhaps the most distressing aspect of the demand for dialogue was the limited cast of characters included in the request. Perpetuating a Confucian mentality that assigned to intellectuals the role of spokespeople for the masses, students assumed that they were the only segment of society whose voice deserved to be heard. The disregard for peasants and workers was a prejudice that intellectuals shared with state leaders. As Young argues in Chapter 1, Deng Xiaoping—like Chiang Kaishek and Yuan Shikai before him—was a reformer who viewed the Chinese peasantry as an obstacle to the fulfillment of national objectives. When each of these reformers turned repressor, he pointed to the "backward" peasants as the reason why China's march toward representative government would have to be postponed.

Similarly, in 1989's "democracy" movement, students were reportedly "horrified at the suggestion that truly popular elections would have to include peasants, who would certainly outvote educated people like themselves."[22] As a young intellectual in Wuhan explained, "While the people support our aims of stamping out corruption, they just don't understand the ideas of freedom and democracy."[23]

Confucian Moralism

From the perspective of the students, peasants and workers appear motivated by crass materialism, whereas their own politics are selflessly pure. The link to Confucian morality is evident here. When hunger strikers wrote out their last testaments—vowing to sacrifice their very lives for their beliefs—they joined an ancient tradition of scholar-martyrs dating back to the third century B.C. (on this point, see Chapters 2 and 4).

The intense moralism of the Tiananmen protesters has been noted by many analysts. Lee Feigon writes of the hunger strikers: "By fasting they hoped to contrast the *moral righteousness* of their behavior with that of the corrupt and despotic government against which they protested."[24] Dorothy Solinger highlights the "proclivity to *moralize* and demand high behavioral standards from rulers."[25] And Esherick and Wasserstrom (see Chapter 2) point out that the statements of the protesters were filled with "*moral* statements of resolve" (emphasis added).

In this respect, the Chinese case would seem to fit comfortably into Daniel Chirot's interpretation of the revolutions of 1989; the cause was essentially moral. Chirot's chapter in this volume links "the endless corruption, the lies, the collapse of elementary social trust, the petty tyranny at every level" to a moral backlash. Similarly, at the height of the Chinese protests, Fang Lizhi offered the following analysis: "The corruption is so obvious now. People see it every day in their factories and offices. Everybody understands what is going on. The blatant profiteering of state officials is now the focal point of the movement because it is this profiteering that has directly led to the failure of the economic reform."[26] An attitude survey conducted in Beijing at about the same time provided support for Fang's assertions; the overwhelming majority of respondents saw anticorruption as the most important goal of the movement and predicted that corruption was the most likely precipitant of future unrest in China.[27] A startling indication of this moralism was the nostalgia for Chairman Mao that surfaced during the spring protests.[28] One popular ditty expressed the general sentiment: "Mao Zedong's son went to the front lines [and was killed as a soldier in the Korean War]; Zhao Ziyang's son smuggles color television sets."

The 1989 demonstration was, in David Strand's words, "a morality play done in Beijing opera style."[29] As a morality play, it shared many features of the East European scenario. But its Beijing opera style limited the stars of the show to the Confucian elite: scholars and officials. Indeed, the criticisms that Mao's wife Jiang Qing had leveled against the Beijing opera during the

Cultural Revolution could be applied with equal force to 1989's Tiananmen drama: The plot followed a standard format that denied heroic roles to workers and peasants.

Rank-and-File Participation

That the ordinary populace is in fact fully capable of dramatic action is revealed not only by its revolutionary history but by its recent behavior as well. In the post-Mao era, despite major gains for agriculture under the reforms, unrest in the Chinese countryside has been remarkably prevalent.[30] Significantly, this rural protest is accompanied by a strong resurgence of folk religion; many of the incidents have involved shamans, ancestral temples, "jade emperors descended to earth," and the like. Undoubtedly the popular religion of the contemporary countryside differs significantly from its pre-1949 forerunners; the socialist experience has left a visible imprint on the mentality of today's peasantry.[31] But regardless of how old or new these practices may be, they suggest the fuzzy outlines of a "civil society" in the sense of a domain of public interaction not fully controlled by the state. The drive to institutionalize this domain (as seen in the privately financed rebuilding of local earth-god temples or rewriting of lineage genealogies, for example) further attests to the efforts of the rural populace to carve out a niche of independence from state authority. We are not, of course, seeing here a Chinese Solidarity or Neues Forum. Yet we are witnessing the consolidation of organizational forms that have for centuries provided a foundation for popular protest.[32] When they join state officials in dismissing these practices as "feudal superstition" (*fengjian mixin*), contemporary intellectuals mirror the prejudice of their Confucian forefathers as well as of the ruling regime. In failing to take seriously the peasantry's capacity for collective action, would-be democrats deny themselves a powerful and essential ally.

Equally damaging to the democratic project has been the exclusion of other key social groups: entrepreneurs and workers in particular. With the liberalization of marketing under the post-Mao reforms, an explosion in entrepreneurship occurred. Enticed by the profits to be made in commercial activity, hundreds of thousands of peasants and town dwellers rushed to join the burgeoning ranks of the *getihu*, or independent entrepreneurs. Their transactions gave new life to the realm of nongovernment economic activities that G.W.F. Hegel, Karl Marx, and Antonio Gramsci all viewed as central to the emergence of civil society. The importance of the growth of this commercial class for the advent of democratic politics has often been posited. In Barrington Moore's memorable formulation, "No bourgeoisie, no democracy." The defense of property and profits encourages ordinary citizens to fight for the freedoms associated with liberal democracy.[33]

The support provided by Chinese entrepreneurs for the student protests in 1989 was in fact substantial. In Shanghai on May 21, "hundreds of people with 'entrepreneur' banners staged a sit-in" in sympathy with the students.[34] Unlike most Chinese, the independent *getihu* could engage in political action without fear of sanctions from their work units. Many of them were, more-over, financially well off. Their largess proved crucial in sustaining the stu-dent movement. As one private entrepreneur recalled, "Whenever the *getihus* passed by one of the students' donation checkpoints, they would stop to give money—from ten, several tens to a thousand or even tens of thousands of dollars, to show that the *getihus* were sincere from the bottom of our hearts."[35] Such monetary contributions made possible the purchase of bat-tery-operated megaphones for the student leaders.[36] One of the largest of the new private enterprises, the Stone Corporation, is estimated to have donated tens of thousands of dollars' worth of sophisticated equipment—including facsimile machines—to the protesters.[37] As military intervention grew imminent, the Flying Tiger Brigade of *getihu* on motorbikes delivered news of troop movements to the students. After the crackdown, the pedicabs of the *getihu* carried off the casualties.

Despite this crucial help, the entrepreneurs received from the students the same disparaging appellation that the regime used to discredit them. Intel-lectuals and officials alike referred publicly to the getihu as *xiansan ren*—idle drifters.[38] In Communist China as in Confucian China, commercial elements are scorned as rootless, amoral figures who cannot be trusted.[39] (Significantly, the Chinese societies where merchants *have* flourished—Taiwan, Singapore, and Hong Kong—are also societies where the link between state and scholar was broken by colonialism.)[40] The recent experience of Taiwan in particular establishes the catalytic role that the commercial middle class can play in the democratization process. Chirot (see Chapter 11) similarly points to the cen-trality of the East European middle class in the upheavals of 1989. In den-igrating this key social element, Chinese students undervalued the contribu-tions of one of the most enthusiastic supporters of their cause.

Another group in the Tiananmen drama relegated to a role well beneath its actual performance ability was the urban working class. A review of Chinese popular movements of the past century reveals the extraordinary power of a worker-student alliance. The May Fourth Movement of 1919, which began as a demonstration by 3,000 students in Beijing, became a historical watershed only after it had been joined by tens of thousands of Shanghai workers in a general strike the following month. It was this participation by labor that persuaded the government to disavow the terms of the Versailles treaty that threatened to turn China's Shandong Province into a virtual colony of Japan. And it was this same worker activism that in 1921 persuaded young student organizers to establish a Communist Party dedicated to the proletarian cause. Four years later the influence of this new party was seen in the mo-mentous May Thirtieth Movement of 1925—again precipitated by a worker-student protest against imperialism—which marked a high point of Commu-nist strength in the cities. Although subdued by Chiang Kaishek's "white terror" of repression against the Left in spring 1927, the urban coalition re-gained force after the Japanese invasion of 1937. Fueled first by anti-Japanese sentiment and then, after 1945, by anti-Americanism, worker-student nation-alism was a key ingredient in the Communist victory of 1949.[41]

The founding of the People's Republic, although ushering in a self-proclaimed "dictatorship of the proletariat," certainly did not spell the end of labor unrest. In fact, every decade has brought a new round of widespread strikes. In 1956–1957, the Hundred Flowers Movement saw a major outburst to protest the inequities of the First Five-Year Plan.[42] In 1966–1967 the Cultural Revolution prompted another explosion of labor protest.[43] In 1974–1976 resentment against the austere policies of the Gang of Four resulted in a further display of working-class dissatisfaction.[44] And in 1986–1988, strikes erupted at factories across the country to protest the inflationary consequences of the post-Mao reforms.[45] In contrast to the pre-1949 situation, however, the contemporary upheavals elicited little enthusiasm from students. To be sure, much of the explanation for the separation of worker and student politics in the socialist era can be attributed to the effectiveness of state controls.[46] But a certain amount of the responsibility must also be assigned to the intellectuals' disdain for a working class whose aspirations are dismissed as crass "economism."

That workers are actually attracted to larger social causes than many intellectuals give them credit for is shown in their reaction to recent student demonstrations. When tens of thousands of students marched in Shanghai during winter 1986–1987 to demand freedom of expression and an end to police brutality, an even larger group of workers gathered in support. Although a tight police cordon was formed to prevent anyone without valid student identification from entering the center of the demonstration, sympathetic workers stood just outside the police lines yelling, "Younger brothers, your elder brothers support you!" and tossing in bread and cigarettes as a gesture of solidarity. The immediate precipitant of this massive demonstration was the police beating of a college student during a concert by a U.S. rock group in Shanghai. When fellow students erupted in fury, the mayor of Shanghai (now secretary general of the Communist Party), Jiang Zemin, went to the campus of the injured student to offer an explanation. The police, he assured his audience, had mistaken the young concert-goer for a worker; had they only realized he was an intellectual, such heavy-handed treatment would never have been applied. Most members of the campus community reportedly found nothing improper in the mayor's line of reasoning.[47]

Many workers, increasingly disadvantaged by the post-Mao industrial reforms, had ample cause for concern about government policy. For one thing, double-digit inflation was threatening their standard of living. For another, the reforms promised to put more money into industrial reinvestment at the expense of workers' housing and bonuses. "Economistic" as such issues may be, they could form the backbone of a lively protest. Moreover, workers were no less aware or intolerant of corruption and petty tyranny than other Chinese. In short, the basis for a potent worker-student alliance seemed to exist. As in the pre-1949 era, such an urban coalition might have been constructed on the foundations of both *consumer* identity and *citizen* identity. As consumers, urbanites could unite against the debilitating effects of runaway inflation (also a central issue during the general strikes of May Fourth and the Civil War years). As citizens, they could condemn government corruption (again an issue, along with imperialism, in all the major pre-1949 urban movements). Orthodox historiography notwithstanding, it was not *class* identity (or protest against on-the-job exploitation) that had fueled the massive worker strikes of early twentieth-century China. Labor was accustomed to performing on a larger stage than the narrow confines of the workplace.[48]

In spring 1989, workers again sought to play a major role in the drama unfolding in Tiananmen Square. On April 20, laborers from a number of Beijing factories made speeches at the square, proclaiming that "workers and students should work together for the introduction of a more democratic and less corrupt system."[49] Fearing the dangers of growing working-class participation, especially as the May Fourth anniversary drew near, the Beijing city government issued an order forbidding any worker to take leave of absence between April 25 and May 5.[50] At this same time, Deng Xiaoping—explaining that "the movement might soon spread to workers and peasants, as in Poland, Yugoslavia, Hungary, and the Soviet Union"[51]—arranged for two divisions of the Thirty-eighth Army to be called into the city. But the leadership's fears of a worker-student coalition were in fact ungrounded. As Anita Chan and Jonathan Unger have observed, until the very end of the movement, "the students had disdainfully tried to keep the workers at arm's length."[52] This was literally the case, with students linking arms to prevent workers from joining directly in their ranks.[53] As the member of one working-class family observed, "The workers could see that participation was being strictly restricted by the students themselves, as if the workers were not qualified to participate. . . . The issues that the students raised had nothing to do with the workers. For example, Wuer Kaixi in his speeches only talked about the students. If he had mentioned the workers as well, appealed to the workers, appealed to them in a sincere manner, the workers might really have come out in a major way."[54] Only during the last week of May, beleaguered by the growing threat of military suppression, were student delegations sent to the major factories to seek support.[55]

Considering the lack of student initiative, the extent of worker participation was really rather remarkable. In late April an unofficial workers' group calling itself the Beijing Workers' Autonomous Association issued a statement condemning inflation and the gap between wealthy government leaders and the ordinary people. The group called for wage raises, price stabilization, and publication of the incomes and material possessions of Party and government officials and their families.[56] A month later, claiming a membership of more than 6,000 workers, the association's goal was "to set up a nationwide non-Communist union along the lines of Poland's Solidarity trade union."[57] At this time it issued a stinging attack, in cynical Marxist language, on official corruption and its deleterious consequences for the Chinese working class:

> We have carefully considered the exploitation of the workers. Marx's *Capital* provided us with a method for understanding the character of our oppression. We deducted from the total value of output the workers' wages, welfare, medical welfare, the necessary social fund, equipment depreciation and reinvestment expenses. Surprisingly, we discovered that "civil servants" swallow all the remaining value produced by the people's blood and sweat! The total taken by them is really

vast! How cruel! How typically Chinese! These bureaucrats use the people's hard earned money to build luxury villas all over the country (guarded by soldiers in so-called military areas), to buy luxury cars, to travel to foreign countries on so-called study tours (with their families, and even baby sitters)! Their immoral and shameful deeds and crimes are too numerous to mention here.[58]

To fight such "typically Chinese" bureaucratic corruption, the autonomous union pledged to support the student hunger strikers and to "promote democratization in alliance with students and citizens from all walks of life."[59]

Pressured by this competition from an unofficial labor association, the official All-China Federation of Trade Unions (ACFTU) began to assume a more active role in responding to working-class concerns. On May 1 (International Workers' Day), the president of the ACFTU conceded that government-sponsored unions "should fully support workers in their fight against corruption."[60] Thanks to this encouragement, workers became more involved in the demonstrations. On May 17, as the hunger strike entered its fifth day,

Millions of workers, peasants, and clerks from government organs, personnel from cultural and publishing circles and from the press took to the streets to show they supported and cared for the students. . . . Particularly noticeable were the massive marching columns of workers. They came from scores of enterprises such as the Capital Steel Corporation, the main factory of the Beijing Internal Combustion Engines, Beijing Lifting Machinery Factory and the state-run Number 798 Factory. The demonstrating workers were holding banners and placards carrying slogans stating: "Students and workers are bound by a common cause" and "Workers are grieved seeing students on hunger strike."[61]

The next day the ACFTU took the bold step of donating 100,000 yuan (about $27,000) for medical aid to students in the sixth day of their hunger strike. Explained a spokesperson for the federation, "We workers are deeply concerned about the health and lives of the students."[62] The same day, the Shanghai Federation of Trade Unions added its voice in support of the movement: "Workers in the city have expressed universal concern and sympathy for the patriotism of students who are demanding democracy, rule of law, an end to corruption, checking inflation, and promoting reform. The municipal council of trade unions fully affirms this."[63]

There were limits beyond which the official unions could not go, however. On May 20, a crowd of workers gathered in front of the ACFTU offices to demand that the unions order a national strike.[64] Three days later, after the declaration of martial law, Beijing television announced: "In the last few days, there have been rumors in some localities saying that the All-China Federation of Trade Unions has called for a nationwide general strike. A spokesman for the Federation said that this is merely a rumor with ulterior motives. The spokesman emphatically pointed out that the ACFTU has recently stressed that the vast number of staff members and workers should firmly stay at their posts and properly carry out production work."[65] By the end of the month, Ruan Chongwu, a former minister of public security, had been appointed to the post of labor minister. His brief was "to ensure that workers remain loyal to the party and government—and that they not take part in activities that challenge the regime."[66] Reported the Hong Kong press, "A top priority with Mr. Ruan and the restructured leadership of the trade unions federation will be to prevent nonofficial unions from being organized."[67]

In the drive to recapture control of labor, three leaders of the Beijing Workers' Autonomous Association were detained by the police on May 30. Also rounded up were eleven members of the Flying Tiger Brigade—the contingent of 300 motorbikers, at least 200 of whom were independent entrepreneurs—which was providing information on troop deployment to the students.[68] Once again workers and other nonstudents were being made to pay the price for a movement in which they had played only supporting roles.[69] Even so, many continued to defy the authorities. On June 9 at a huge demonstration and memorial service in Shanghai for victims of the June 4 massacre, among the marchers were about 1,000 workers holding high a banner that read "Shanghai Autonomous Federation of Labor Unions."[70]

Conclusion

The tragic ending to China's uprising of 1989 is explained neither by the salience of its revolutionary ideology nor by the silence of its rural inhabitants. If the persistence of "tradition" served as a brake on political transformation, the relevant tradition was not that of the committed revolutionary or the conservative peasantry. Ironically, it was the very instigators of the Tiananmen protest—the urban intellectuals—who appeared most wedded to a limiting legacy. In their *style of remonstrance* (presenting petitions and banners and demanding dialogue with the authorities), their *search for political patrons* (emphasizing the need for state strengthening and switching quickly from one "hero" to the next), and above all their *stress on moralism* (contrasting their own selfless martyrdom to the crass materialism of the masses), the students evinced a brand of political behavior and belief replete with the stigmata of the past.

The traditionalism of student protesters was not due to some immutable Confucian culture, forever lurking like a sea monster beneath the surface of China's political waters—waiting to seize and sink any unsuspecting would-be democrat who happened to swim by.[71] Rather, the intellectuals' political proclivities were shaped by the close links between state and scholar that persist in contemporary China.[72]

Though the Confucian examination system was abolished in 1905, the Communists instituted a *fenpei* (allocation) system whereby the state assigns college graduates to jobs commensurate with their scholastic records, political loyalties, and of course personal connections. Even more than under the imperial regime, the socialist state exercises a virtual monopoly over meaningful job opportunities for intellectuals. Little wonder, then, that these intellectuals—even in the act of protest—should evidence such state-centric tendencies. It was only during the Republican interregnum, when the state's hold over the scholar was effectively eased, that a different sort of student protest emerged. That "May Fourth Tradition," which held sway from 1919 until the founding of the PRC in 1949, was a brilliant but brief chapter in the history of Chinese popular protest. Occurring during an unusual period of state retrenchment (at least with respect to control over intellectuals), the protests of that generation demonstrated an unprecedented independence and enthusiasm for active alliance with workers, peasants, and merchants. It was these qualities of autonomy and mass involvement which imbued the collective action of the Republican era with such social fire. By contrast, contemporary intellectuals who attempt to resuscitate the spirit of May Fourth are hampered by the inability to liberate themselves from the hegemonic claims of the state and thereby embrace the interests of other social elements. As a consequence, their rendition of the May Fourth drama is much less powerful—politically, if not necessarily theatrically—than pre-1949 performances.

The omnipresence of the Chinese Communist state, even more than its Confucian forerunner or its East European counterparts, has inhibited the florescence of "civil society" and rendered the formation of cross-class coalitions correspondingly difficult and dangerous. Accordingly, Andrew Walder cautions against interpreting the Tiananmen upheaval "as a direct expression of the growth of an independent society. Such independence was greatly restricted in China relative to Poland, Hungary, and the Soviet Union."[73] But if the answer lies not in a developed "civil society," how *do* we explain China's recent turmoil? For Walder, "the key to the 1989 upheaval appears to be the splintering of the central leadership and the Party-state apparatus after the initial student protests of April."[74] There is considerable merit in Walder's emphasis on elites and political institutions. As we have seen in the case of the All-China Federation of Trade Unions, elements of the state did indeed play a significant role in facilitating the protest movement of 1989. At the same time, however, we must not underestimate the potential for self-generated political action by nonstate entities. The traditions of Chinese civil society are admittedly weaker and different from those of Eastern Europe. Absent in China are the Catholic church of Poland, the old democratic parties of Hungary, or the dissident intellectual circles of the Soviet Union and Czechoslovakia. Yet there is evidence that recent reforms have encouraged the resurgence of meaningful traditions of extrastate economic and associational behavior in China, just as in Eastern Europe. Today's independent entrepreneurs, practitioners of folk religion, and members of autonomous labor unions are all building on patterns of collective identity and action with proven records of resisting state domination in the Chinese context. These practices may well lack the democratic character of the institutions of civil society in Eastern Europe.[75] But as Strand has noted, "When Chinese seek to revive a democratic tradition, it is a tradition of movements, not institutions, they are drawing upon."[76] And China's merchants, peasants, and workers—as well as students—can rightfully lay claim to a vital part of that inheritance.[77]

In accounting for the timing of the 1989 protest movement, it is clear that the efforts of the Chinese state to undertake reform have played a major hand in encouraging dissent on the part of both political elites and ordinary citizens. Although the relationship between reform and revolution is poorly understood, it is obviously significant. As the history of modern China shows, reform is often the harbinger of revolution. The 1911 Revolution that toppled the imperial system followed upon the Hundred Days' reform and New Policies of the ailing Qing dynasty. The reformist New Life Movement of Chiang Kaishek's Kuomintang heralded the imminent demise of the Nationalist regime. Serious reforms exact substantial costs on at least some sectors of both state and society. Furthermore, they raise expectations to levels that can seldom be attained. Most important, reforms are admissions by the regime of its own inadequacies. As a result, they encourage widespread disbelief. This is especially unsettling in Communist systems, where claims to ideological truth have been so central. When the leadership publicly repudiates many of its past practices, it invites ordinary citizens to engage in open criticism as well.

The uprising of 1989 was a dramatic expression of the Chinese people's appetite and aptitude for political criticism. Influenced by forty years of socialism as well as by international cultural currents, the demonstrators staged an innovative performance. Dunce caps from the Cultural Revolution, rock music from Taiwan, headbands from South Korea, and a hunger strike from Gandhi's India all contributed a seemingly contemporary and cosmopolitan flavor. Yet in its core values the student movement was in fact remarkably Confucian. Thanks to the special bond between state and scholar that had persisted for so long under the imperial system and was reconstituted (on different terms, to be sure) under the socialist system, Chinese students engaged in an exclusionist style of protest that served to reinforce preexisting authority relations. At the same time, however, other social groups showed themselves ready to reclaim the true spirit of the May Fourth Movement—in which a fledgling civil society had challenged a troubled Chinese state on both moral and material grounds.

Notes

1. Chalmers Johnson, *Peasant Nationalism and Communist Power: The Emergence of Revolutionary China, 1937–1945* (Stanford: Stanford University Press, 1962).

2. Of course, powerholders in Beijing see the situation differently. Jiang Zemin, general secretary of the Chinese Communist Party, offered five reasons why his country would not go the way of eastern Europe: (1) The CCP is armed with Marxism-Leninism-Mao Zedong Thought and has grown strong through armed struggle; (2) the Chinese military is armed with Maoism and led by the CCP; (3) Chinese socialism was created by the Chinese people themselves and not forced upon them by the Soviet Red Army; (4) China is not surrounded by capitalist countries; and (5) Marxism has been sinicized by Mao Zedong and Deng Xiaoping and is thus not subject to a Soviet type of reform movement. Quoted in *World Policy Journal*, December 22, 1989, p. 20.

3. Richard C. Kraus, "The Lament of Astrophysicist Fang Lizhi: China's Intellectuals in a Global Context," in Arif Dirlik and Maurice Meisner, eds., *Marxism and the Chinese Experience* (Armonk, N.Y.: M. E. Sharpe, 1989), pp. 294–315.

4. On Deng's role in the antirightist campaign, see David Bachman, *To Leap Forward: Bureaucracy, Economy and Leadership in China, 1956–57* (New York: Cambridge University Press, 1991), ch. 8.

5. Vera Schwarcz, *The Chinese Enlightenment: Intellectuals and the Legacy of the May Fourth Movement of 1919* (Berkeley: University of California Press, 1986), pp. 283–291. Schwarcz argues convincingly that the incompleteness of the May Fourth enlightenment is linked to the tension in twentieth-century China between commitment to cultural criticism and commitment to national salvation. Those who raised the most serious criticisms have been open to the charge of being unpatriotic.

6. Examples of this technique during the Republican period can be found in Jeffrey N. Wasserstrom, *Student Protests in Twentieth-Century China: The View from Shanghai* (Stanford: Stanford University Press, 1991).

7. See Charles Tilly, *The Contentious French* (Cambridge: Harvard University Press, 1986), for a discussion of comparable protest behavior in France.

8. Lee Feigon, *China Rising: The Meaning of Tiananmen* (Chicago: Ivan R. Dee, 1990), p. 146; Foreign Broadcast Information Service (FBIS) (April 27, 1989), pp. 11–12.

9. Perry Link, *Chinese Writers Under Fire*, pp. 21–22; quoted in David Strand, "Civil Society and Public Sphere in Modern China: A Perspective on Popular Movements in Beijing, 1919–1989," *Working Papers in Asian/Pacific Studies* (Durham, N.C.: Duke University Press, 1990), pp. 30–31.

10. On the continuity with earlier student movements, see Jeffrey Wasserstrom, "Student Protests in the Chinese Tradition, 1919–1989," in Tony Saich, ed., *Perspectives on the Chinese People's Movement: Spring 1989* (Armonk, N.Y.: M. E. Sharpe, 1990). At least since the May Fourth Movement, groups of students had paraded with banners naming their alma mater as they marched from school to school, calling on those at other institutions to join in the task of saving the nation.

11. Wu Mouren et al., *Bajiu Zhongguo minyun jishi* (Annals of the 1989 Chinese democracy movement) (New York: privately published, 1989), p. 446.

12. Jean Chesneaux, *The Chinese Labor Movement, 1919–1927* (Stanford: Stanford University Press, 1968).

13. FBIS (May 18, 1989), pp. 49–50.

14. On the earlier situation, see William Rowe, *Hankow: Conflict and Community in a Chinese City, 1796–1895* (Stanford: Stanford University Press, 1989); Susan Mann, *Local Merchants and the Chinese Bureaucracy, 1750–1950* (Stanford: Stanford University Press, 1987); and Mary Rankin, *Elite Activism and Political Transformation in China* (Stanford: Stanford University Press, 1986).

15. Personal observation, Shanghai, December 1986. The slogan was: "Dadao Hu Yaobang; Ningyuan Sirenbang!" (Down with Hu Yaobang; better the Gang of Four!).

16. A son who had allegedly used his family connections to make huge profits from an illicit trading company in Hainan was the cause of much of the public hostility.

17. The Beijing variant, formulated by Rong Jian and others close to Zhao Ziyang, argued for a coercive government to carry out radical liberalization of the economy. The southern variant, as formulated by Xiao Gongqin at Shanghai Normal University, favored a more gradual reform program. See Xiao Gongqin, "Lun guodu quanweizhuyi" (On transitional authoritarianism), *Qingnian xuezhe*, 2 (1989).

18. Feigon, *China Rising*, ch. 6.

19. Andrew J. Nathan, *Chinese Democracy* (Berkeley: University of California Press, 1985).

20. FBIS (May 1, 1989), p. 50.

21. Geremie Barmé, "Blood Offering," *Far Eastern Economic Review*, June 22, 1989, p. 39. As Barmé explains this phenomenon: "The traditional role of the scholar-bureaucrat dovetailed neatly with the Stalinist talk of engineers of the human soul."

22. Mary S. Erbaugh and Richard C. Kraus, "The 1989 Democracy Movement in Fujian and Its Consequences," *Australian Journal of Chinese Affairs*, 23 (1990), p. 153.

23. Eddie Yuen, "Wuhan Takes to the Streets" (unpublished paper, 1990), p. 11. However, as Yuen notes (pp. 10, 12), hundreds of workers did in fact participate in the Wuhan protests by attending demonstrations and driving out in factory trucks after their work shifts were over.

24. Feigon, *China Rising*, p. 196 (emphasis added).

25. Dorothy Solinger, "Democracy with Chinese Characteristics," *World Policy Journal* (Fall 1989), p. 625 (emphasis added).

26. *South China Morning Post*, May 22, 1989, p. 23.

27. *China Information*, 4, 1 (1989), p. 4.

28. Feigon, *China Rising*, p. 206. The carrying of Mao posters was one expression of this phenomenon.

29. Strand, "Civil Society and Public Sphere," p. 16.

30. Elizabeth J. Perry, "Rural Collective Violence: The Fruits of Recent Reform," in Elizabeth J. Perry and Christine Wong, eds., *The Political Economy of Reform in Post-Mao China* (Cambridge: Harvard University Press, 1985).

31. For this argument, see Helen Siu, *Agents and Victims* (New Haven: Yale University Press, 1989). See also Elizabeth J. Perry, "Rural Violence in Socialist China," *China Quarterly*, no. 103 (September 1985), pp. 414–440.

32. On rural religion as a basis for antistate rebellion, see Susan Naquin, *Millenarian Rebellion in China: The Eight Trigrams Uprising of 1813* (New Haven: Yale University Press, 1976). On kinship and village as organizational bases of rural protest, see Elizabeth J. Perry, *Rebels and Revolutionaries in North China, 1845–1945* (Stanford: Stanford University Press, 1980).

33. Barrington Moore, Jr., *Social Origins of Dictatorship and Democracy* (Boston: Beacon Press, 1966), ch. 6. For a dissenting view, see Nina P. Halpern, "Economic Reform and Democratization in Communist Systems: The Case of China," *Studies in Comparative Communism*, 22, 2/3 (1989).

34. Wu, *Bajiu Zhongguo minyun jishi*, p. 355.

35. *Jiushi niandai* (The nineties) (December 1989), pp. 15–16, quoted in Anita Chan and Jonathan Unger, "Voices from the Protest Movement, Chongqing, Sichuan," *Australian Journal of Chinese Affairs*, 24 (July 1990), p. 264.

36. Feigon, *China Rising*, p. 183.

37. Ibid., p. 184.

38. Interviews with participants, Seattle, April–May 1990. An exception was the dissident writer Wang Ruoshui, who argued for an affinity of interests between intellectuals and entrepreneurs. See the interview with Wang in *Jiushi niandai* (The nineties) (April 1989), p. 37.

39. On public disdain for the *getihu*, see Thomas B. Gold, "Guerrilla Interviewing Among the *Getihu*," in Perry Link, Richard Madsen, and Paul Pickowicz, eds., *Unofficial China: Popular Culture and Thought in the People's Republic* (Boulder: Westview, 1989), pp. 175–192.

40. In Taiwan, the role of intellectuals was further weakened after the KMT takeover via a land reform that undermined their traditional economic base and (by compensating dispossessed landlords with stock in nascent industries) converted the intellectuals themselves into members of the bourgeoisie.

41. Suzanne Pepper, *Civil War in China* (Berkeley: University of California Press, 1980).

42. François Gipouloux, *Les cents fleurs dans les usines* (Paris: L'Ecole des Hautes Etudes en Sciences Sociales, 1986).

43. Hong Yung Lee, *The Politics of the Chinese Cultural Revolution* (Berkeley: University of California Press, 1978).

44. Lowell Dittmer, *China's Continuous Revolution* (Berkeley: University of California Press, 1988).

45. Interviews at the Shanghai Federation of Trade Unions, Shanghai, May 1987 and September 1988.

46. See Andrew Walder, *Communist Neo-Traditionalism: Work and Authority in Chinese Industry* (Berkeley: University of California Press, 1986). Walder provides an insightful discussion of the operation of state controls in state-owned factories. In my view, however, he underestimates the possibility of autonomous worker protests.

47. Personal observations and interviews, Shanghai, December 1987–January 1988.

48. Elizabeth J. Perry, *Shanghai on Strike: The Politics of Chinese Labor* (Stanford: Stanford University Press, 1993).

49. FBIS (April 20, 1989), p. 18.

50. FBIS (April 26, 1989), p. 17.

51. Feigon, *China Rising*, p. 153.

52. Anita Chan and Jonathan Unger, "China After Tiananmen," *Nation*, January 22, 1990, pp. 79–81. See also Henry Rosemont, Jr., "China: The Mourning After," *Z Magazine* (March 1990), p. 87. Rosemont notes that for the first four of the six weeks of demonstrations, students kept their distance from workers. Workers were primarily concerned with inflation and job security, issues that did not gain student attention.

53. Feigon, *China Rising*, p. 203.

54. Chan and Unger, "Voices," p. 273. Similar sentiments were expressed in an open letter to the students from a Beijing worker. See Mok Chiu Yu and J. Frank Harrison, eds., *Voices from Tiananmen Square* (Montreal: Black Rose Books, 1990), pp. 111–112.

55. FBIS (May 26, 1989), p. 52.

56. The founding manifesto of the union can be found in Yu and Harrison, *Voices*, p. 107. See also FBIS (April 28, 1989), p. 11.

57. FBIS (May 30, 1989), p. 9; FBIS (May 31, 1989), p. 44.

58. Yu and Harrison, *Voices*, p. 109.

59. Ibid., p. 114.

60. *China Daily*, May 1, 1989, p. 1.

61. FBIS (May 18, 1989), p. 49.

62. Ibid., p. 76.

63. FBIS (May 22, 1989), p. 91.

64. Ibid., p. 45. See also Yu and Harrison, *Voices*, p. 114.

65. FBIS (May 23, 1989), p. 58. Whatever the ACFTU leadership may really have felt about a general strike, theirs was one of the last government/Party units to express support for martial law. See FBIS (May 30, 1989), p. 9.

66. FBIS (May 30, 1989), p. 9.

67. Ibid.

68. FBIS (May 31, 1989), p. 44.

69. On the detention of additional workers and entrepreneurs in early June, see FBIS (June 2, 1989), p. 11. Wuhan also saw more severe treatment for workers than for students. See Yuen, "Wuhan," p. 13. Rosemont states that at least forty-two workers were executed after the June 4 crackdown, whereas no student executions had been reported. Rosemont, "China," p. 87.

70. Wu, *Bajiu Zhongguo minyun jishi*, p. 787. Members of the Workers' Autonomous Union and a handful of small radical workers' groups had assisted Shanghai students in erecting barricades on the morning of June 4. Official workers' militia (composed largely of Party members and cadres) dismantled these barriers on June 8, however. See Shelley

Warner, "Shanghai's Response to the Deluge," *Australian Journal of Chinese Affairs*, 24 (July 1990), pp. 303, 312.

71. The "unchanging China" argument can be found in Lucian Pye, *The Spirit of Chinese Politics* (Cambridge: MIT Press, 1968); Richard Solomon, *Mao's Revolution and Chinese Political Culture* (Berkeley: University of California Press, 1971); and Lucian Pye, "Tiananmen and Chinese Political Culture: The Escalation of Confrontation from Morality to Revenge," *Asian Survey*, 30, 4 (April 1990), pp. 331–347. Pye and Solomon argue for a unitary Chinese culture (across time and social class) instilled during childhood socialization experiences.

72. In Taiwan, where the bonds between state and scholar were weakened first by Japanese colonialism and then by the KMT takeover, intellectuals have found it easier to make common cause with other social elements, especially entrepreneurs. This has been apparent in the development of the Democratic Progressive Party, the main Opposition party to the ruling KMT. It is also seen in the active participation of intellectuals (along with virtually all other social groups) in Taiwan's recent stockmarket boom.

73. Andrew G. Walder, "Political Upheavals in the Communist Party-States," *States and Social Structures Newsletter*, 12 (Winter 1990), p. 8. See also Walder, "The Political Sociology of the Beijing Upheaval of 1989," *Problems of Communism* (September–October 1989), pp. 39–40.

74. Ibid.

75. For this interpretation, see Chapter 2 by Esherick and Wasserstrom.

76. Strand, "Civil Society and Public Sphere," p. 3.

77. This is not to say that protests by peasants, workers, and entrepreneurs were invariably less exclusionist than student protests. We can, of course, point to numerous examples of labor unrest or rural uprisings that eschewed alliance with outside forces. But in contrast to the student movement, these were not self-proclaimed "democracy" protests. The argument here is simply that a successful effort at democratization must incorporate the interests of a diverse array of social elements. Another important source of potential allies left untouched by the students in 1989 were the national minorities. Disaffection in Tibet, Xinjiang, and elsewhere might well have been creatively addressed by student leaders—several of whom (including, most notably, Wuer Kaixi) were themselves of minority descent. However, any overt expression of sympathy with minority aspirations for freedom would have immediately elicited charges of lack of patriotism (not only from the government, but most likely from many ordinary Han Chinese as well).

4

SCIENCE, DEMOCRACY, AND THE POLITICS OF IDENTITY

Craig C. Calhoun

In China's 1989 protest movement, students self-consciously identified themselves with the May Fourth Movement of 1919. They repeated the old slogan, "science and democracy," echoing not just the May Fourth but the "New Culture" Movement of the late 1910s and 1920s generally. On May 4, 1989, for example, Wuer Kaixi read to the handful of the massive Tiananmen Square crowd who could hear him a "New May 4th Manifesto":

> Fellow students, fellow countrymen, the future and fate of the Chinese nation are intimately linked to each of our hearts. This student movement has but one goal, that is, to facilitate the process of modernization by raising high the banners of democracy and science, by liberating people from the constraints of feudal ideology, and by promoting freedom, human rights, and rule by law."[1]

History repeated itself, Wuer and other students seemed to be saying. Sometimes there was a hint of farce: "Science and Democracy" T-shirts were sold in Tiananmen Square. However, as other contributors to this volume—such as Schwarcz (Chapter 8) and Wasserstrom (Chapter 13)—emphasize, the 1989 events were not a repetition of 1919, nor was there a simple continuity between the two protest movements. But this does not mean that the link is spurious. The link is an identity claim, a call by the 1989 student protesters for recognition alongside those of 1919, for recognition at once as modernizers and patriots, serious intellectuals, and democrats.

Social movements, including that of 1989, are commonly analyzed in terms of underlying conditions, motives, strategies, political opportunity, and the mobilization of resources. All these are important.[2] But even taken together, all these aspects of the production of social movements miss certain crucial aspects of their meaning. They tend to reduce social movements to some combination of the calculating pursuit of relatively clear ends (as, for example, labor movements seek better wages) or to the product of structural conditions, such as strong social networks or weaknesses in otherwise repressive governments. These approaches underestimate culture. They also take the identities of participants as more or less fixed and as easily translatable into a specific set of interests.

That this understanding of social movements misses something important has been articulated by many movement protagonists as well as analysts since the 1960s. Addressing or producing what they called "new social movements," these thinkers and actors have stressed the extent to which cultural meaning and both personal and collective identity are objects of struggle in such social movements as feminism, some ethnic movements, the gay rights movement, and the green movement. I have argued elsewhere that this is a problematic way to state a powerful insight.[3] The new social movements literature implies that a linear historical change in the nature of social movements is at issue, accepting the notion that earlier movements like socialism and the labor movement were fundamentally different. It would be better, I think, to see the importance of struggles over culture and identity as of widespread importance in social movements at many points in history and in many sociocultural settings. I think this was clearly true of the New Culture Movement, and in this chapter, I will suggest some of the ways in which these themes are central to understanding the 1989 protests.

Cultural Crisis

It has recently become commonplace to observe that communism stifled the development of civil society. This is one of the most meaningful senses in which Communist rule was "totalitarian," for "civil society" denotes the capacity for social self-organization outside state control. In China especially, the state not only dominated the public realm and prohibited nonstate organizations but also penetrated the putatively private realm of the family—indeed, undermining the very distinction of public from private.[4] But democrats and modernizers faced the problem of the absence of civil society well before Mao and his fellow Communists rose to power. As the opening article of the *New Tide* monthly put it in 1919, "Our society is very strange. Western people used to say that China has 'masses' but no 'society.'"[5]

In 1989, one of the first and most important things student protesters were saying was that they were unwilling to be part of the government's masses but insisted on differentiated identities, as students, as intellectuals, and as individuals. Even popular music was an important medium for transmission of this sort of political dissent, linking national to personal concerns. Cui Jian, for example, expressed many senses of bankruptcy when he sang the following lyrics, as much to China as to a girlfriend:

I want to give you my hope
I want to help make you free
But all you ever do is laugh at me, 'cause
I've got nothing to my name.[6]

The song was perhaps the most popular of the late 1980s among Beijing students. Cui Jian's songs gave encapsulated, often repeated, expression to powerful grievances and desires; the very style of much of his music—as close as Chinese performers came to "hard rock"—combined Westernization with countercultural critique.

The sense of being left without opportunities, resources, possessions—and therefore without the chance to live an autonomous individual life—was palpable among Chinese students in the late 1980s. In Cui Jian's song and in everyday life, thise sense extended into the most intimate and emotionally powerful relations. Cui Jian sings of his expectation that the girl of his dreams will forsake him because he has nothing to offer her (as well as implicitly of the system that left him in that situation). And so, too, Chinese students smarted under postponed marriages, spouses who had to be left at home because it was too expensive to house them near school, and girlfriends more interested in *getihu*—young businessmen with the money to show them a nice time. Yet the aspiration to be masters, at least of their own lives, was powerful. Another popular singer's simple lyric, Su Rui's "follow your own feelings," summed up one of the powerful urges, even moral mandates, for Chinese students. Hou Dejian's "Children of the Dragon" called for them to live up to the obligations of Chinese national identity, complexly evoking both the problematic past and aspirations for the future.[7] Basically, the song posed the central dilemma of modern China—how could a country with such a rich history be so poor and weak? Hou summarizes "Children of the Dragon" in the following way:

> The song just talks about the Chinese. We are a very ancient and very historic people, but our quality of life is still very poor. Can anyone tell us why? Have we ever thought about these questions—deep in our heart? The major power to destroy the family, or the people, or the nation, is not from foreigners. It comes from ourselves. With that song, I wanted to make it clear that everybody should be thinking from the inside; that we should take a good long look at ourselves.[8]

At the heart of students' concerns lay basic questions about China's fate and what it might mean to be Chinese at the end of the twentieth century.[9] This multifaceted concern was a product, above all, of a shared sense of China's weakness and backwardness. When China opened to the West in the reform era, travel and television footage showed capitalist societies to be full of gleaming highrises and such wealth that ordinary people drove cars and occupied huge houses. Such images jarred with the previous Maoist message that capitalism was on the skids. But while many Chinese drew rather simple economic conclusions—rooted in desire and envy—students and intellectuals also asked deeper questions about what the comparison said about Chinese culture. Had China not really advanced in relation to the rest of the world for a hundred years? Had it actually fallen farther behind?

Many intellectuals and even more young students responded by a simple out-and-out embrace of the West, at least as they understood it. As physicist Fang Lizhi put it, for example, "I sincerely believe that if we want things to change, 'complete Westernization' is the most viable approach."[10] More dramatic and troubling were the Chinese youths who simply could not see any fault with the West and simultaneously lost the capacity to find virtue and resources in Chinese culture. Their difficulties of self-image were manifested in everything from clothing styles to a fad for "de-sinicizing" cosmetic surgery to an eagerness to embrace Western social science theories as the solutions to China's ills.[11]

Su Xiaokang, a journalist and television writer, referred to what he saw as the recurrence of a fin de siècle mentality among intellectuals during the reform era—particularly in the two dragon years of 1976 and 1988.[12] From popular music to learned debates, poetry to television, social science research to the fad for *qigong* breathing exercises, thoughtful citizens of the People's Republic were caught up in a "culture fever"; in the later 1980s, they took up a passionate reexamination of the virtues, failings, and possibilities of Chinese culture. The government, by contrast, sought to keep the lid on cultural concerns, to pursue modernization while resisting "bourgeois liberalization" and "wholesale Westernization." This echoed a late-Qing codification of official Confucian views: "Chinese learning for [spiritual] essence, Western learning for utilitarian ends" (*Zhongxue wei ti, Xixue wei yong*, or simply *ti-yong* in slogan form).[13] The familiarity of the distinction encouraged those party leaders who wanted economic reform without political change or threats to their power to pursue the virtually impossible line of trying to import Western technology, economic thought, and bits of business practice without accepting any political or cultural baggage. But in both the 1920s and the 1980s, there were enough people prepared to embrace a more robust notion of learning from the West to give ulcers to the Chinese government and even the moderate reformers attached to it.

Yet Western culture excited great anxiety at the same time that it exerted a powerful attraction. Likewise, Chinese culture was the object of both nationalist ardor and great disappointment. Many intellectuals were unable to reconcile their opposing feelings and vacillated from one side to the other. For many, problems of culture predominated over practical possibilities of institutional reform. Among the most important of these cultural thinkers was Li Zehou, a philosopher at the Chinese Academy of Social Sciences, and an author, for example, of important work on traditional Chinese aesthetics—but best known for his influential historical study of "the six generations" of modern Chinese intellectuals. In 1989, he suggested that Chinese intellectuals ought to reverse the old *ti-yong* formula and work out practical Chinese ways to apply the "essence" of certain aspects of Western culture.[14]

National Salvation and Enlightenment

Facing a similar combination of cultural crisis and corrupt, authoritarian politics in 1915, Chen Duxiu, a classically trained scholar turned vernacular writer, editor, and radical activist, advised intellectuals to turn away from politics to pursue culture. Yet he did not really do this himself. Instead, he sought with some success to forge a cultural politics. To this end, he devel-

oped personifications of science and democracy as vehicles for spreading enlightenment among the less educated in China (and thereby strengthening
the nation both domestically and internationally). Writing in *New Youth*, the
most important of all the many journals created to encourage the "new culture" of the era, Chen responded to critics' charges against the magazine in
the following manner:

> They accused this magazine on the grounds that it intended to destroy Confucian-
> ism, the code of rituals, the "national quintessence," chastity of women, traditional
> ethics (loyalty, filial piety, and chastity), traditional arts (the Chinese opera), tradi-
> tional religion (ghosts and gods), and ancient literature, as well as old-fashioned
> politics (privileges and government by men alone).
>   All of these charges are conceded. But we plead not guilty. We have committed
> the alleged crimes only because we supported the two gentlemen, Mr. Democracy
> and Mr. Science. In order to advocate Mr. Democracy, we are obliged to oppose
> Confucianism, the codes of rituals, chastity of women, traditional ethics, and old-
> fashioned politics; in order to advocate Mr. Science, we have to oppose traditional
> arts and traditional religion; and in order to advocate both Mr. Democracy and Mr.
> Science, we are compelled to oppose the cult of the "national quintessence" and
> ancient literature.[15]

"Mr. Science" and "Mr. Democracy" (often presented not through the full
Chinese terms but as the equivalent of "Mr. Sci" and "Mr. De") were widely
touted as solutions to China's problems. These problems were many and varied, but were perceived centrally in terms of modernization and relations
with the West.

Political weakness was seen simultaneously in traditional terms of a corrupt, declining dynasty and in the newer terms of failed modernization and
lack of national strength. The May Fourth Movement was clearly nationalist,
yet "many of the important student leaders concerned in the incident felt
from the beginning that the real spirit of their movement was not one of simple patriotism but was bound up with concepts of the supremacy of public
opinion, people's rights, and an intellectual renaissance."[16] Similarly, China's
poverty had become an increasing concern, and the importance both of "Mr.
Science" and of political reform lay substantially in paving the way for economic modernization and improvement in material standards of living. Last
but not least, as the Enlightenment imagery suggests, May Fourth intellectuals worried about the cultural state of the nation. Illiteracy, primitive technology, and in general a low level of cultural attainment among the mass of
the population formed part of the story. Beyond it, though, there was a critique of traditional Chinese culture—from the binding of women's feet
through the patriarchal family to feudal relations in the countryside and the
emphasis on stultifying rote learning and the archaic formal essays in the imperial examination system. China, it seemed, needed not only more but different culture. The old was not merely an obstacle to progress but an embar-
rassment.[17]

In this context, the idea of distinguishing sharply between Chinese culture
for essence and Western culture for utilitarian ends was not satisfactory.

China needed change in institutions—not just new technology. In the late nineteenth and early twentieth century, some thinkers like Yan Fu urged the view that what mattered was not whether a particular practice or idea was Western or Chinese but whether it worked. As Yan Fu put it:

> What are China's principal troubles? Are they not ignorance, poverty, and weakness? In a nutshell, any method which can overcome this ignorance, cure this poverty, lift us out of this weakness, is desirable. The most urgent of all is the overcoming of ignorance, for our failure to cure poverty and weakness stems from our ignorance. In overcoming ignorance we must exert our utmost efforts to seek out knowledge. We have no time to ask whether this knowledge is Chinese or Western, whether it is new or old.[18]

Indeed, one of the intellectual problems Chinese thinkers faced was that they had constructed a view of Chinese and Western culture in which each was understood too much as a homogeneous whole; they had a hard time dealing with the argument that certain ideas did not fit neatly and exclusively into one category or the other. But consciously or not, they had embarked on a program of theoretical questioning and practical reform that among other far-reaching consequences rendered them caught between the two poles of pursuing national salvation or enlightenment.

The politics of national salvation (*jiugao*) seemed to involve a subordination of all other goals to political and technical strength. After the Republican revolution of 1911, the Chinese government was stripped of much of its Confucian rhetoric and appeared even more clearly as devoted to material power. Schwarcz sums up the progression in this way:

> Precursors of the May Fourth enlightenment, in spite of the political differences among them, had all been motivated by a single-minded commitment to *jiuguo*, national salvation. Their intellectual and emotional energies had been focused on making China strong and enabling it to survive foreign aggression. The iconoclasts [i.e., the adherents of enlightenment and New Thought], less concerned with China's political weakness, went on to probe the indigenous sources of their nation's spiritual and intellectual backwardness.[19]

Patriotism implied the need for unity, an anxiety about foreign threats, and the importance of seeking national salvation; enlightenment implied rationalism and an "opening to science and democracy" and to the rest of the world.[20] Few students feared foreign military aggression in 1989, but the economic and cultural incursions of both the Japanese and Westerners raised the students' anxieties about China's future.

The themes of national salvation and enlightenment were not strictly in conflict with each other; students wanted both. Intellectuals had long seen strengthening of the nation as one of the benefits of enlightenment. But thought about national salvation had roots in more technocratic conceptions of the role of intellectuals, while enlightenment suggested more their role as producers and disseminators of culture.[21] In 1989, students and intellectuals thought about national salvation in ways that stressed the unity of the entire nation but also thought about enlightenment in ways that reflected their desire for more freedom.

The sense of crisis in Chinese culture not only produced arguments among literary critics, it exerted a profound influence on students' identities and ideas, including their understanding of democracy. The discourse of national salvation, for example, carried gender biases, which went hand-in-hand with the male monopolization of leadership roles within the movement that Feigon describes in the following chapter. Posters encouraging a reinvigoration of the "national essence" often criticized Chinese men as effeminate.[22] Deng Xiaoping was doubly mocked (as both feudal and female) when he was caricatured as the Empress Cixi. The national essence was presented as basically male.

While the discourse of national salvation flourished in innumerable poems, essays, books, magazine articles, and debates over the dinner table, one cultural product was perhaps the most influential. This was the television series *He shang* (River Elegy), shown in the fall of 1988. As the following portion of script of the show indicates, the issue of the relationship between Chinese and foreign cultures was once again central:

> For thousands of years, the Yellow River civilization was under constant attack from the outside but never fell. We have always appreciated its great power to assimilate other cultures. But today at the end of the twentieth century, even though external attacks are no longer accompanied by cannons and iron hooves, our ancient civilization can no longer resist. It has grown old and feeble. It needs a transfusion of new blood for its civilization.[23]

Intellectuals faced with the challenge of the West were torn between xenophobic national salvation and enlightenment modernization:

> To save our nation from danger and destruction, we should try to keep the foreign pirates at bay beyond our country's gates; and yet to save our civilization from decline, we should also throw open our country's gates, open up to the outside, and receive the new light of science and democracy. These extremely contradictory antiphonal themes of national salvation and modernization have taken turns over the past century in writing China's abnormally shaped history; as complexly intertwined as myriad strands of hair, they can neither be trimmed by the scissors nor untangled by the comb, a situation which has caused the Chinese people to pay an immeasurably heavy price! (133–134)[24]

Much of the rhetorical power of *River Elegy* came from various ways of posing the question of how China, a nation with such a great past, could have such a problematic present.

> Why was it that the light of Chinese civilization, which had led the way for more than a thousand years, dimmed after the seventeenth century? Why has such a smart people become so slow-witted and decrepit? What was it, after all, that we possessed yesterday yet whose loss we have only discovered today? (140)

The Communist era is just a continuation of the old patterns, *River Elegy* suggested. Like previous dynasties, the Communists hoped to make the Yellow River run clear, but failed. Glamorous shots of skyscrapers represented the attractions of the West, and shots of Hong Kong stressed that such glories were within the reach of the Chinese people, if only they would accept change.

> New China for a while was indeed able to make Chinese all over the world swell with pride; but who would have thought that after a mere thirty-some years, when we had awakened from a civil turmoil in which we had tried to strangle ourselves, that we would discover ourselves in the company of poor nations such as Tanzania and Zambia; that even South Korea, Singapore, and Taiwan would have outpaced us, and that the Japanese would have come back laughing, bearing their Toshibas, Hitachis, Toyotas, Yamahas, and Casios? (276)

Faced with similar failures of modernization, China's intellectuals have often retreated into Confucianism:

> Even in the 1980s, in the midst of our great debate stirred up by the "passion for studying Chinese culture," people still continue the century-old inconclusive argument over the strong and weak points of Chinese versus Western culture. No matter whether it is the fantasy of "wholesale Westernization" or the fervent wish for a "third flowering of Confucian civilization," it all seems to be going over the same ground as before. No wonder some young scholars say with a sigh that their tremendous cultural wealth has become a tremendous burden, that their feeling of tremendous cultural superiority has become a feeling of tremendous cultural inferiority; and this we cannot but admit is a tremendous psychological obstacle standing in the course of China's modernization. (210–211)

"China is pondering," the television series told its viewers. "Young people are questioning history" (153). History gave innumerable lessons in how difficult it was to escape the dynastic cycle, to achieve meaningful modernization. History had also created a situation in which China's intelligentsia was both the group that had the best chance of saving the nation and a social class whose members could only accomplish this goal if they developed new strategies to overcome structural and cultural problems inherited from earlier eras. The narrator of the series summed up the dilemmas relating to China's intellectuals as follows:

> It is very difficult for them to have economic interests in common or an independent political stance; for thousands of years they have been hangers-on. Nor can they become a solid social entity that employs a steel-hard economic strength to carry out an armed critique of the old society. Their talents can be manipulated by others, their wills can be twisted, their souls emasculated, their backbones bent, and their flesh destroyed. And yet, they hold in their hands the weapon to destroy ignorance and superstition: It is they who can conduct a direct dialogue with "seafaring" civilization. It is they who can channel the "blue" sweetwater spring of science and democracy onto our yellow earth! (219)

According to *River Elegy*, intellectuals faced two major obstacles in carrying out this historical mission. The first was simply their weakness. Intellectuals were able to discover the faults of tradition but lacked the ability to change it. It was crucial that they form common cause with the entrepreneurs who were bringing new social energy and greater practical strength to China. The second obstacle came from within the intellectuals themselves—their identity crisis: "The greatest difficulty of reform lies perhaps in that we are always worrying: "Are the Chinese people still Chinese?" (212) These ideas and this sense of cultural or identity crisis was nearly ubiquitous among elite Beijing students in 1989.

At the same time, intellectuals were disillusioned in both 1919 and 1989 with political involvements that seemed always disappointing at best because once-idealistic regimes turned corrupt. This is a key reason why students took the lead in the 1919 protests. As Schwarcz puts it, students "were free of the weight of disappointment that still burdened their older contemporaries in the spring of 1919." And virtually the same could be written about 1989. The same debate about national salvation versus enlightenment still raged. Li Zehou had written a provocative and widely read essay on the subject, suggesting that the turn away from enlightenment and toward blind passion for national salvation that Chen Duxiu had spotted seventy years earlier was a recurrent problem.[25] The theme was taken up by protesting students in this late-May poster:

> Li Zehou has said that well: after May 4th, in the democratic movement, the struggle for national salvation replaced the introduction of Enlightenment, the fundamental democratic mechanisms were not effectively understood, and each time the democratic movement had to start again at zero. Drawing the lessons of history, we must place the mission of introducing Enlightenment and the promotion of fundamental democratic mechanisms at the center of our preoccupations.[26]

In 1988, Xu Jilin had written an essay, "On the Independent Personality of Intellectuals"—a title echoing Chen Duxiu's concern with autonomy. It was, indeed, published in the "New Enlightenment Series," a further reminder of the link to the New Culture Movement of the Republican era—as well as to the Western Enlightenment. Xu argued that intellectuals were called upon to play two roles, enlightener and public conscience. The latter modified the national salvation ideal by emphasizing a more critical as well as holistic perspective.[27]

Individualism and Authenticity as Causes

Chinese radicals and reformers had long seen literary efforts as central to the basic changes they wanted to produce. As Liang Qichao wrote in 1902:

> To renovate the people of a nation, the fictional literature of that nation must first be renovated . . . to renovate morality, we must renovate fiction, to renovate manners we must first renovate fiction . . . to renew the people's hearts and minds and remold their character, we must first renovate fiction.[28]

In the Chinese case, reform of the very language itself was crucial, so much was the classical language tied up with Confucianism and imperial rule. Yu Pingbo, a veteran of the May Fourth protest, wrote in a commemorative poem on the sixtieth anniversary in 1979, "We did not worry if our words were sweet or bitter / We just wrote in the newly born vernacular."[29] China's Communists made an attempt to harness literature to class struggle and the task of building socialism. But immediately after Mao's death, unauthorized literature surfaced in ways more critical of the Party. During the Democracy Wall Movement in 1978, a ninety-four page wall poster, the "God of Fire Symphonic Poems," spoke of a monstrous idol that suffocated the Chinese people and subjected them to a "war of spiritual enslavement":

> The war goes on in everyone's facial expression.
> The war is waged by numerous high-pitched loudspeakers.
> The war is waged in every pair of fearful, shifting eyes.[30]

Poetry and fiction remained controversial throughout reform-era China. Authors had experimented with new styles, from a sort of vague, evocative poetry that came to be known as "misty" or "obscure" to stream of consciousness novels.[31] The most important common thread was a new preoccupation with individual experience and especially its distinctiveness—a theme previously forbidden in Communist China. A debt to Western modernism was also apparent. When poets like Bei Dao, Shu Ting, and Jiang He began to write the new sort of poetry, particularly in the journal *Today*, founded during the 1978–79 democracy movement, it was widely understood to carry simultaneous political, cultural, and personal messages. But the messages were seldom blunt. In Shu Ting's famous 1982 poem, "The Wall," for example, her opening and closing verses read:

> I have no means to resist the wall,
> Only the will.
>
> Finally I know
> What I have to resist first:
> My compromise with walls, my
> Insecurity with this world.[32]

A factory worker as well as a poet, Shu was initially celebrated in part for the particular female strength she brought to her writing. In the late 1980s, she was criticized for making accommodations with the literary and Party establishment. This complaint itself suggests the demand for radical authenticity. The pursuit of authenticity was linked to both reflection on individual experience and an unwillingness to subordinate art to political ends. This did not mean, as some critics charged, that there was no socially decipherable point to the art. "The irony remains, however, that, accustomed to message-hunting, critics do not realize that having no message is itself a kind of message."[33] A focus on "mere" sensory perceptions could, in the context of China at that time, carry implicit statements about the importance of the perceiving self and of the art that records the perception—both distinct from the socially recognized projects that evaluate poetry by instrumental criteria.

Older poets like Ai Qing attacked the new poetry, likening it to an intellectual version of the Red Guards, even calling it the "Beat and Smash Poetic School." Indeed, it did have roots in the Cultural Revolution, in both the intensity of the commitment and the later disillusionment of young participants and the wounds with which so many Chinese people were left. It was also this poetry, more than any directly political texts, that established the crucial link between the protesting Chinese students of 1989 and their forebears of 1978–79.[34] Protesting students in 1989 frequently quoted Jiang He's "Motherland, O My Motherland" and Bei Dao's "The Answer," particularly the latter's stanzas reading:

> Baseness is the password of the base,
> Honour is the epitaph of the honourable.
> Look how the gilded sky is covered
> With the drifting, crooked shadows of the dead.
>
> I come into this world
> Bringing only paper, rope, a shadow,
> To proclaim before the judgment
> The voices of the judged:
>
> Let me tell you, world,
> I—do—not—believe!
> If a thousand challengers lie beneath your feet,
> Count me as number one thousand and one.
>
> I don't believe the sky is blue;
> I don't believe in the sound of thunder;
> I don't believe that dreams are false;
> I don't believe that death has no revenge.[35]

On May 4, 1989, I saw a marcher heading from the universities in the Haidian district toward Tiananmen, carrying aloft a sign with no words, simply a piece of paper, a bit of rope, and a cut-out shadow.

Novelists and short-story writers of the same era as the misty poets were perhaps less radical and struck less often to the very heart of their Chinese readers, but they were also influential. "Exploring" writers such as Jiang Zilong, Chen Rong, and Liu Xinwu (editor of *People's Literature*) also took up the implicit critique of the Cultural Revolution and remaining "leftist" tendencies and also tried to rehabilitate a certain individualism. In his famous "Black Walls," Liu has his protagonist paint the apartment entirely black, only to confront the puzzlement and ultimately the hostility of his neighbors. The point is made apparent even by an orthodox literary critic who claims he cannot find it:

> A certain fellow by the name of Zhou—a man recognized as being a little 'odd'— paints the walls and ceiling of his apartment black without providing the slightest explanation. An egotistical 'indulgence' of this nature can hardly be seen as

normal or acceptable . . . the problem, however, is that the author . . . regards the
'abnormal' as 'normal,' and is critical of the attempted suppression of Zhou's desire to express his quirky individuality. . . ."[36]

The stifling of individuality was linked to the stifling of artistic and literary
creativity. As Wang Ruowang put it, turning a government condemnation on
its head, "we should say that those people who opposed the freedom of
creativity are themselves the greatest source of contamination in spiritual
pollution."[37]

Liu Xiaobo, a young literary critic whose recent essay on the term "Revolution" is included as Chapter 14 of this volume, brought much of this sensibility to the 1989 protests. He was a popular teacher to many of the protesting
students and a bridge to the generation of the misty poets. He was an enthusiastic Westernizer, an antitraditionalist radical, and even something of a self-
conscious "enfant terrible."[38] In this context, "traditional" meant seeking a
good balance of emotion and rationality and a stress on the collectivity and
the social responsibility of the artist. "Radical," by contrast, meant a focus on
the expression of personal feeling, individuality, auratic art (to borrow Benjamin Schwartz's term), and the autonomy of artistic production and its potential independence of national particularity in the modern metropolitan
culture. "It is this stance as the 'angry young man,' a bohemian and his antisocial truculence that made him so popular with audiences of Chinese
university students since 1986."[39] Similarly, it is no accident that Liu
Xiaobo's participation in the 1989 protests (as one of the last four hunger
strikers) should seem so akin to nineteenth-century European romantics and
yet strike a chord among many Chinese. As Barmé puts it, "Liu Xiaobo expressed the desire for people to participate in protest as part of a civil action
of redemption."[40]

Literature rooted in authentic self-expression was indeed "renovating"
Chinese culture, but not always with Liang Qichao's focus on practical social
ends. This left a tension that was played out in differences between "creative
writers" and "reportage writers." The latter were journalists of a sort, posi-
tioned between social scientists and more literary writers. The Communist
Party, long holding that social reportage (and sometimes only social reportage emphasizing the moral-building good side of socialist society) was the
main responsibility of writers, saw reporters as central to literature. Many
young poets and fiction writers disagreed, wishing to claim the turf of literature entirely for art and not social commentary. Indeed, the call of "art for
art's sake" was paradoxically not apolitical at all. In "The Life of an Artist,"
for example, Bei Dao describes "the betrayal of the artist to the cultural orthodoxy,"[41] presenting himself at the end as "a doctor, a large syringe in
hand," pacing "up and down the hallway to while the nights away." The
point, Michelle Yeh suggests, is that "in a society that operates on absolute
authority (assigning jobs with little regard for personal ability or proclivity)
and rigid conformity, the artist—the artist who insists on creative freedom
and pursues personal ideals—has no place."[42] The misty poets portrayed
alienation—and portrayed it as produced by the socialist People's Republic

of China—even though the official position of the PRC was that alienation was "the product of the decayed capitalist system only."[43]

This linked the misty poets to the more prosaic efforts of theorist Su Shaozhi, who at the same time was attracting attention with his explorations of the writings of the young Marx and also raising the forbidden question of whether there might be alienation in socialist China.[44] Though there was, at least sometimes, a politics to the individualism and aestheticism of the misty poets—as, for example, there had been a politics to European existentialism—it clashed with the more immediately practical political imaginary not only of the government but of many of the government's most famous critics, such as Su Shaozhi and the famous dissident journalist Liu Binyan, who publicly clashed with the poet Bei Dao at a conference held in California in April 1989. When Liu (who was already living in the United States) accused the literary avant garde of producing impenetrable works that were "read only by a few" and had little real political impact, Bei responded by arguing that: "True art does not ask about its own 'social effects.'" This is because artists are primarily concerned "with life itself, not social engineering."[45] Though both Liu Binyan and Bei Dao helped pave the way for the 1989 protests, the sensibility of the Beijing students was closer to Bei Dao's call for artistic autonomy.

as opposed to antagonist (against)

The Affirmation of Ordinary Life

Salient identities and perspectives are not fully formed in advance of participation in the public sphere. On the contrary, when political debate and broader cultural discourse are really effective, they have the potential to shape both the identities and the perspectives of their protagonists.[46] Thus for the Chinese students in 1989, participation in the public discourse of the social movement was not just an occasion for articulating preestablished interests or expressing the identities with which they began. It was an occasion for trying on new identities and, accordingly, shifting their interests and the bases of their discourse. For example, the identity "Chinese patriot" became increasingly salient and more strongly linked to the specific identity of "student/intellectual" the longer students participated in the movement; the students' discourse shifted away from "special-interest" demands and toward broader "populist" and patriotic claims. As a People's University poster put it:

> . . . as intellectuals, we made significant concessions in our banners and slogans. The original slogans that were suggested—"improve the treatment of teachers" and so on—were only shouted by some marchers from the teachers' colleges. The march's main purpose was changed to "petition for the people" and "appeal for redress of wrongs suffered by the students. . . ."[47]

This shifting discourse is one of the reasons it is sometimes hard to pin down precisely what students wanted when they called for democracy. Indeed, reference to democracy by itself was more common in posters aimed at foreigners; the discourse of the movement itself generally linked patriotism and democracy. The strong sense of nationalism was one reason why students took such offense at the suggestion of the April 26 *People's Daily* editorial that they were an unpatriotic source of chaos.

At the same time, students' concerns (and those of many others in China) were rooted in personal existence as well as politics at large; in an "affirmation of ordinary life"—an assertion of the value of everyday personal and family life, of simply being happy. This was celebrated in pop songs, poetry, short stories, and novels. After decades of deferring gratification to the higher ends of the Communist Party and the building of socialism, many Chinese—especially in younger generations—simply wanted more food, more fun, and more freedom. They were prepared, moreover, to defend these as real values—not merely personal desires.

Charles Taylor coined the phrase, "the affirmation of ordinary life," as part of an account of how early modern Christians came to shift their moral sensibilities away from a sharp separation of "higher moral goods" and "base human existence" and toward a directly positive evaluation of "those aspects of human life concerned with production and reproduction, that is, labour, the making of the things needed for life, and our life as sexual beings, including marriage and the family."[48] I borrow the phrase here to call attention to a partially parallel development in reform-era China. The Communist leaders of China's first thirty years had not taken second place to any Protestants in their praise of productive labor. They were not, like medieval Catholics or ancient Greeks, oriented to a spiritual or an ideal realm rather than to a material one. All in all, they were rather more like Puritans. While affirming the importance of ordinary life in general, the Puritans—like the citizens of the . People's Republic in its first thirty years—were called upon to renounce selfish pleasures: purely personal enjoyments that would turn attention away from dedication to the general good and duty before God. They were still called to subordinate or harness their affirmation of ordinary life to transcendental goals.

In Maoist China, socialist realist art glorified everyday life and material production with paintings of rosy-cheeked peasants cheerfully laboring in their fields and eager factory workers smiling as new tractors rolled off assembly lines. A wide range of concrete policies sought to make the everyday lives of ordinary people better—by housing them better, feeding them better, and providing better healthcare for them. This was a striking departure not only from the transparent greed of much of the early Republican and warlord years but from the ancient imperial system that drew resources from ordinary people and ordinary life that elites might enjoy extraordinary luxuries, refinements, and intellectual pursuits. But Maoist ideology did not see these gains as merely a sum of private benefits. They were public goods, to be achieved and enjoyed collectively. Personal desires were to be held in check not just so that there would be enough (and as good) for others but so that the people as a whole could flourish, build socialism, and make China strong. Communism developed like Puritan capitalism into a system of "worldly asceticism" (though without equally productive investment of the surplus retained). Maoist communism was also famously "puritanical" with regard to sexuality and other decadent pleasures. In one sense, it outdid its European religious counterpart—in regarding even the family as suspect and emphasizing higher loyalties against this crucial locus of ordinary life.

With the reform era, Deng ushered in a renunciation of much of Communist puritanism. "To get rich is glorious," he proclaimed, and while he may have meant mainly the accumulation of wealth, he and his colleagues in the leadership gradually legitimated greater and greater freedom in its consumption and eventually (especially after the Tiananmen massacre) its ostentatious display. But just as the affirmation of ordinary life in early modern Europe eventually outran Puritan and other strictures against hedonism, so a similar affirmation escaped the grasp of Deng and his fellow leaders.

The affirmation of ordinary life gained strength in the "literature of the wounded," in which victims of the Cultural Revolution recounted their torments and tried to rebuild their shattered lives. Children who had been forced to betray their parents, wives who had willingly or unwillingly condemned their husbands, parents whose disgrace had been visited on their children—all sought to rebuild family life. In doing so—especially in cities—they not only restored ancient Chinese values but reconstructed families as the objects of a new kind of attachment—not simply ubiquitous units of lineage. Similarly, as small clusters of cherished relationships among individuals and friendship was celebrated in some circles—including those of the students who protested in 1989—as a special and basic value. This was a sharp change from the Maoist era when "the Party and the state did not shine kindly on unauthorized personal relationships."[49] The ideology of romantic love spread widely through the population—nowhere more prominently than among students. The idea that marriage should bring personal fulfillment, including sexual satisfaction, not only challenged a variety of old norms but reinforced the idea that the basic happiness of ordinary people in their ordinary lives was a fundamental value.[50]

New consumption patterns also both responded to and encouraged a new emphasis on enjoyment in the here and now.[51] The government actively boosted some of this consumerism to create motivation for harder work and perhaps most importantly to draw money hidden under mattresses and buried on or near farms back into productive circulation. Increased personal consumption not only drove the economy, of course; it kept people's attention focused on economic ends rather than on politics or other more dangerous domains. Students who lived better than any of their predecessors had lived five or ten years before nonetheless chafed at lacking the material goods they could increasingly see around them.[52]

Students also chafed at lacking privacy; at being jammed four or more to a room. Students were no longer subject to such intense scrutiny of their personal lives as had been characteristic under Maoism and immediately thereafter; but because they no longer believed in the ideals that had justified the Maoist intrusions and because they were rapidly developing stronger senses of privacy and individual claims to autonomy, they found even modest levels of surveillance and involuntary publicness unpleasant. Most would agree with Sun Longji's argument about the pernicious effects of the Maoist refusal to recognize any realm of purely private life: "This intrusion into and control of private lives has no other function than to eradicate individual personality."[53]

Thus, in claiming rights to better material standards of living, students were not only demanding more material possessions but more respect and more individual autonomy. They were voicing the idea that it was alright to care about themselves, about lovers and friends, and about the day-to-day pleasures of ordinary life. This does not mean that they renounced the rhetoric of selflessness and sacrifice; on the contrary, they adopted it with the hunger strike. But even then, numerous speeches, placards, and interviews made the point that this was not simply routine selflessness, such as that demanded of all citizens by the Party based on the model of Lei Feng, a self-sacrificing soldier. The students made a point of reminding others that they had valuable ordinary lives and aspirations that they were prepared to sacrifice for the sake of the country. As Chai Ling put it in her late May interview, "I wanted to live a very peaceful life with children and small animals all around."[54]

The affirmation of ordinary life was dramatized publicly in the Square through the marriage of Li Lu and Zhao Ming.[55] This affirmation was not explicitly political, but it was an important ground for some of the students' more directly political ideas as well as for their action. It underpinned the claim to speak as citizens, or autonomous individuals joining together in a public discourse, rather than as an undifferentiated mass. The affirmation of everyday life and of the value of ordinary happiness offered straightforward criteria for assessing the performance of the government. Giving weight to ordinary life also implied giving weight to the experience and feelings of ordinary people. Though students were (perhaps unconsciously) ambivalent about this, torn between their affirmation of ordinary life and their own sense of superior access to knowledge, emphasizing such values nonetheless amounted to a very large step in the direction of democracy.

Intellectuals and Democracy

The more sophisticated students understood democracy as something with different levels, not as something simply present or absent. "People pursue higher and higher goals as they continuously improve their knowledge of democracy. Democracy is such that it usually moves to a higher and higher realm with every step ahead. 'Give me liberty or give me death' should be changed to 'struggle for freedom or wait for death.'"[56] Repeatedly, students reminded themselves—and their listeners—that this was just a step in a longer struggle, though this recognition was at odds with the enthusiasm of the moment. Sometimes the two were joined in the thought that the current dictators could be toppled immediately even though democracy would take a long time to build afterward: "We should, after dismissing the octogenarian party leaders, and still maintaining the party rule, embark on a large-scale movement of democratization and guide this process into sustained and gradual orbit, and eventually bring about genuine and modern democracy characterized by pluralist politics." This belief that the Party might be the agent of democratic reform was not uncommon. Even more widespread was the notion that "we"—that is, the "knowledgeable elements," students, and intellectuals—would need to guide the rest of the Chinese people through some period of tutelage before full democracy could take hold.

A stress on educating people in the ways of democracy was extremely widespread. "Putting emphasis on education is the precondition to the realization of democracy." Students did not seem to have conceived of the election process as itself a matter of political education (though their own movement ought to have shown them how political action can work this way). Rather, they envisaged education as something that has to be accomplished *first,* before elections will work. Moreover (and somewhat undemocratically), most regarded education as something that they—the intellectuals—should do *to* the people and not as a direct outgrowth of a participatory political process. This was a continuation of an older way of thinking. The May Fourth intellectuals, literary theorist Liu Zaifu argued, had seen themselves as the "subject," or those who did the enlightening, in regard to the "object," or the people they wished to enlighten.[57] The Communists had demanded the subject role, and now the intellectuals were demanding it back. Political philosopher Gan Yang, author of the May Twenty-fifth Declaration, has made a similar complaint. The problem with Chinese intellectuals lies in their obsessive determination "to speak for others and to speak the truth to others who have not seen the truth."[58]

Similarly, democracy seemed to be spoken of more as something that people might *have* than as something that people might *do.* That is, democracy meant having a government that took the interests of its people seriously, acted in their behalf rather than in behalf of its own cadres, listened to expressions of popular opinion, and was fair in its dealings with ordinary people.[59] The idea of democracy as a form of popular rule was much less well developed. The crucial forms of participation that the students sought to guarantee were extensions of the traditional idea of officials (and to a lesser extent ordinary people) remonstrating with the emperor, holding him to his responsibilities, and telling him what he needed to know in order to be a good ruler. Thus, a greater role for intellectuals was central to the students' vision of democracy. We in America sometimes emphasize the role of elections to the point of forgetting the importance of social movements and other less mechanical forms of democratic participation, particularly in determining which issues will be on the agenda of policymakers and behind the decisions made in elections. Chinese thinkers have often pointed to both the weaknesses of electoral democracy in the West and the problems of reliance on elections in a backward, undereducated country. Students implicitly postponed universal suffrage elections to a later stage, after popular consciousness had been raised. Thus, among other things, they put the role of intellectuals in the forefront and made their own actions the precondition of democracy.

For many, democracy turned not simply on who was in power but to whom those in power listened. A sound system of government called for top officials to consult and listen to the advice of intellectuals and experts. This could be as true for traditional imperial government as for democracy, of course; the difference being largely in the method of proffering advice. For leaders to consult with intellectuals and experts was good, regardless of the system. But more democratic intellectuals demanded not just private consultations or the right to send memorials to the emperor or to a Party secretary; they argued for the importance of a public sphere, an arena of public discussion and cultural production. This is a key reason why freedom of the press figured so prominently among student demands. Valuing this made them democrats and as democrats they knew they needed such a public arena.

As we have seen, the values of free expression and a free press were widespread leading up to the time of the protests. But just as corruption was clearly the first concern of ordinary people, intellectuals had a special sort of "elective affinity" for press freedom and the right of public discourse. After all, who wrote more articles and who conducted more discussions? For many students and intellectuals, one of the principal significations of democracy lay in the possibilities of speaking without fear, of gaining both due attention and respect, and of contributing to the progress of Chinese culture. In this hope for enfranchisement of the voice they thought proper to themselves, students did indeed express the elitist aspirations and self-image of intellectuals. But though elitist, this self-image was not simply self-interested.[60] It was an identity that could be expanded beyond narrow sectional interests— better jobs, more respect—to embody a sense of speaking for the Chinese nation as a whole. Students might or might not fairly represent the thoughts or aspirations of all Chinese people, but they certainly did (to paraphrase President Kennedy's famous paraphrasing of Rousseau) ask not solely what their country could do for them, but what they could do for it.

Bravery and the Politics of Identity

The sense of acting on behalf of the Chinese nation was a powerful motivator for protesting Chinese students. Part of the power of the rhetoric of nationalism comes from its capacity to join the living and the dead as members of the same nation.[61] The vocabulary of national identity also enabled students to affirm the higher purposes of democracy and freedom and to rise above their more narrowly self-interested claims and desires. "We defy death to win life for the nation," Chai Ling and her colleagues wrote in the Hunger Strikers' Declaration.[62] Indeed, on the night of June 3 and the morning of June 4, students in Tiananmen Square knowingly risked—arguably even courted— death at the hands of government troops.

Students took these risks knowing there was little, if any, near-term likelihood that their actions would succeed in improving their own or their fellow-students' circumstances or effect the political changes they sought in China. They did so despite the availability of apparent alternatives. Yet these students were not habitual risk-takers. Some of those who died that night had been too cautious even to identify themselves publicly with the boycott of classes that was held only a month before. Many of those who risked death that night went to great lengths to avoid attack or arrest in succeeding months. But at the crucial moment, they were willing to be brave to the point of apparent foolishness. Why?

The question is not idle. Were it not for this extraordinary bravery, the Chinese protest movement would not be remembered as it is. Were it not for similar cases of bravery elsewhere, revolutions would not have been made nor battles won nor rescues attempted. We cannot reduce heroic events to the mere exercise of interest and still make sense of history.[63] At the same time, we grasp heroism poorly if we treat it simply as a static attribute of certain persons rather than as a broader human potential that is activated often through situations and processes in which normally prudent people take on seemingly unreasonable risks. This bravery was stunning in Beijing and elsewhere in China in 1989 and was exemplified not just among students. At the heart of this bravery lies a question of representation or articulation, of how the students—or anyone—arrives at an understanding of who they are.

On April 27, in the early days of the "Beijing Spring," students marching on Tiananmen Square confronted soldiers. There had been no military violence yet, although many students were braced for some. The soldiers were young men from peasant families; the students came almost entirely from urban families and those from "academic" universities were the products of a selection system that allowed only about one and a half percent of their age-mates such an educational opportunity. "Go home to your fields," the students shouted to the soldiers, "you have no business here." Similarly, when Han Dongfang, the workers' leader, stood up to speak at the Monument to the People's Heroes on May 30, students shouted him down. "Who is this guy?" "We are the vanguard!" "Get down, leave!"[64]

Some of these same arrogant students, so self-important, were able to see something worth dying for in the fact that they, like the peasant soldiers and the rebel workers, were all Chinese. How are we to reconcile the risk-takers at the end with the students who began the protest movement of 1989 with such a strong sense of themselves as young or prospective intellectuals and such a strong sense of their own distinction from peasants, members of the working class, and officials? To be a student—an intellectual-in-the-making—was not a casually adopted role; it was a matter of basic personal identity. It had resonances with images of intellectuals going back thousands of years in Chinese history, and it was also manifest in the way people spoke, dressed, and comported themselves. Who they were as individuals was bound up with and indistinguishable from their participation in a whole variety of social relationships that were colored and shaped by reciprocal recognitions of class identity.

From the self-strengthening movement of the 1890s, through the 1919 protests, the ebbs and flows of Republicanism, and early stages of Chinese communism, intellectuals took on a stronger and stronger sense of their own crucial role in China's modernization. In the 1980s, Deng Xiaoping and other Communist leaders had courted intellectuals as important agents of reform.

union

This new respect and tolerance, however, encouraged intellectuals to resume their advocacy of "science and democracy" and, more generally, the combination of national salvation and enlightenment that had long been a collective agenda. On May 4, 1989, the unauthorized Federation made it clear in its declaration that it wanted to "Let Our Cries Awaken Our Young Republic!"

> Seventy years ago today, another group of students gathered here before Tiananmen. That was the beginning of a new, great chapter in the history of China. . . . Today we are gathered here not only to commemorate that great day, but also to carry on and develop the spirit of democracy and science upheld by the May 4th Movement. Standing before Tiananmen—the symbol of our ancient nation—we proudly declare to the people of the nation: We are worthy of the cause advanced by our predecessors seven decades ago. . . . For more than a century, the elitist elements of the Chinese people have been ceaselessly exploring the way to modernize their ancient and degenerating nation.[65]

Along with this relatively new cause, students and intellectuals also reclaimed the older idea of the intellectual's responsibility to remonstrate with an emperor (though that responsibility had never matured into a right to be free from punishment for doing so). A scholar, tradition held, should be responsible only to his ideals. This view was sometimes transmuted into a more modern notion of authenticity, of being true to oneself. In any case, when Chinese students in 1989 said that they were acting as "the conscience of the nation" and that this was not just a simple choice but a responsibility they had to live up to, they were speaking in line with a long tradition.

Students were different from other intellectuals not only by age-group, the lesser development of their ideas and skills, and their relative freedom from the burden of discouragement at past failures but in the fact that they did not have families to support or jobs to risk (at least in the immediate sense). They were therefore understood to be freer than their elders to act through public protest. Spatial concentration; subject, class, and cohort organization; and the web of communication among universities provided students with structural facilitation for mobilization. More senior intellectuals offered advice, tried to protect young activists, and pushed for change in quieter ways (though a special respect was paid to those elders who did put themselves on the line in public protest).

Of course, the student "fraction" of the intellectual class also had its own complaints. Students lived in crowded dormitories of poured concrete (often not even reinforced against earthquakes) with blank concrete walls and floors. Government stipends were inadequate. Good jobs were scarce after graduation. Students had little control over whether they would be assigned to remote teachers' colleges or major universities—except by toeing the line within the system and possibly working the corrupt game of *guanxi*, or connections. Furthermore, students shared in the broader frustrations of the intellectual class. The government seemed not to listen enough, public respect was not forthcoming enough, and pay was poor. As the common comparison put it, even the most senior university professors earned less than taxi drivers. Or more colorfully, "the doctor earns less than the old woman selling baked potatoes at the entrance of the hospital, and the barber who cuts a person's hair earns more than the surgeon who operates on the brain beneath it."[66]

To many Chinese observers, it seemed likely at first that the striking students were mainly interested in themselves. Demonstrating that students—as intellectuals—were prepared to place the interests of the Chinese people generally and the Chinese nation as a whole uppermost was in fact one of the major functions of the hunger strike. When, beginning May 19, the ordinary people of Beijing rallied to protect the student hunger strikers, this was not only because they saw students speaking for ideals they shared but because the act of refusing sustenance and courting government reprisals convinced onlookers that the students were not just seeking personal gains but sacrificing themselves for the Chinese people as a whole. As it so often had, 1989 directly echoed 1919. On May 26, 1919, in the first article to speak of the May Fourth protest as a 'movement,' Luo Jialun wrote:

> This movement shows the spirit of sacrifice of the students. Chinese students used to be eloquent in speech and extravagant in writing, but whenever they had to act, they would be overly cautious. . . . This time, and only this time, they struggled barehanded with the forces of reaction. . . . The students' defiant spirit overcame the lethargy of society. Their spirit of autonomy *(zijue)* can never be wiped out again. This is the spirit which will be needed for China to be reborn.[67]

Even when their concerns were for China and not simply for themselves, however, students and intellectuals understood China's needs in ways shaped by their participation in intellectual life. This was not merely something so simple as the idea that intellectuals were important and should be paid more, though this was certainly a commonly made point. It also involved contending visions of the nature of China's crisis and the role intellectuals were called to play in resolving that crisis.

We cannot, then, explain the student protest movement simply in terms of the elitist, self-interested consciousness of intellectuals. Certainly the students were elitist, and their positions in economic and prestige-related hierarchies exerted an influence on their participation in the movement. Certainly some part of the content of their "democratic" consciousness was focused on their identity as students and intellectuals and what that identity ought to mean in China. But the consciousness of the students changed in important ways during the course of the protest and the consciousness of Chinese intellectuals was changed by the protest and by its repression. These processes of change cannot be grasped through an understanding of consciousness that focuses on the recognition of interests alone.[68]

Students did see the movement for democracy through lenses colored by self-interest and elitism. Nevertheless, the basic self-identification of the protesting students in Tiananmen Square—and not just their intellectual self-categorization but their lived identity—was transformed and, at least for a time, radicalized by six weeks of activism. Their consciousness expanded beyond particularistic concerns to include national ones and—in important ways—universal ideals. In the midst of their struggle, the students identified emotionally with a general category—the Chinese people—that under more ordinary circumstances would not have been possible because of class divisions.

Heroes

As Chinese patriots, students who risked death on the night of June 3 and the morning of June 4 became heroes. But heroism is more complexly related to issues of identity than mere identification with the nation. The capacity for heroism was not just a natural attribute of this select group of Chinese students. It was forged in the protest movement itself, because the students cared deeply enough and threw themselves wholly enough into the action for constructions of their personal identities to be at stake. We cannot altogether make sense of the students' risk-taking without some sort of idea of the sense of honor that motivated these individuals and the sense of collective identification that made them more than *merely* individuals. Both of these aspects of identity were subject to remaking during the course of the movement. Not only is life always social but living is always a matter of action, not of statically possessing an identity or set of attitudes prior to action. What one does defines who one is, both for others and especially for oneself. Risky and unusual collective action places one's identity on the line in an especially powerful way.

Put another way, extremely risky actions, such as the protester who stood in front of a tank as it rolled down Chang'an Boulevard, depend on a sense of who one is as a person and what it means to go on living with oneself—such considerations are inextricably social as well as personal and are sufficiently powerful to outweigh what might ordinarily be paramount prudential concerns. When I stood in Tiananmen Square the evening of June 3, I felt a rush of adrenalin during the early stages of the fighting, a macho impulse to be where the action was, and deep anger at the government's decision to attack the protesters. I also contemplated all sorts of good reasons for my not being there—including personal safety—even though the army was not yet firing live ammunition. Prudential considerations won out, in large part because my sense of who I was had not been put on the line. I was not Chinese; it was not my government or my army that was beginning to attack. I was not even a journalist whose professional identity involved commitment to getting a story or a photograph; I was more committed to being an American husband and father and to finishing my book on critical theory. Furthermore, my family and my main circle of friends and colleagues were thousands of miles away. But none of these aspects of my identity was fixed and immutable. By early June I identified myself with the student protesters more than I had in mid-April, largely because I had been with them around the clock for six weeks. But I had not been on hunger strike, had not made speeches, and had not put my career in jeopardy. In other words, I had not been through nearly so transformative a sequence of events and actions as had many Chinese students. Perhaps in some basic sense, I was and am not as brave as they were.

But on June 3, some students were brave enough to risk death who only a month before had not been brave enough to be publicly identified with the boycott of classes.[69]

Yet another side of heroism is the goading of the crowd, as Lu Xun saw in the case of Qiu Jin.[70] Everyone in the crowd who demanded escalation, the next jolt of adrenalin, and the next shocking challenge to those in power must share in the responsibility for the deaths of 1989. At least one observer, Jane MacCartney, has described the students as caught up in a "cult of the hero," starting from their adulation for Fang Lizhi, extending through the near deification of Hu Yaobang, and resulting in an eagerness to achieve heroism for themselves. "The hero was important to the students because they needed someone to look up to but also because they each wanted a share of the limelight, the glory of action."[71] "The yearning for heroism extended to the ultimate sacrifice, an almost hysterical desire for blood."[72] MacCartney's comments are offered in a biting tone, but they certainly capture an aspect of what was going on. But she not only presents the whole of the student movement through a sketch of the hysterical few but also neglects the temporal dimension to the production of heroes and martyrs. Students were not simply sitting around for months or years before the movement, fully prepared for heroism by their admiration for Fang Lizhi (or their envy for his fame and courage). Many certainly tried on the mantle of heroism, making melodramatic declarations on the eve of the April 27 march or again with the start of the hunger strike. But that does not mean that as a group "the students were almost eager to attain the glory of death."[73] Superheated rhetoric can help prepare one for sacrifice but is not an altogether reliable indicator of readiness to face death. Just as the classic Chinese psychology of thought reform turns on getting individuals to begin to behave in "appropriate" ways even before they have altogether internalized its values (which are assumed to follow), so the students' recurrent writing of "last testaments" and discussions of possible "ultimate sacrifices" served as rehearsals for the real thing.

But though scripts and rehearsals for heroism were important, students (and workers) were not just reading pre-prepared lines. They were improvising; they were remaking their roles, in part, as they went along. They were also caught in a situation where martyrdom became plausible by the fact that they had thrown their identities so completely into the movement. Little of them was invested in other relationships, in everyday activities—or at least these other investments seemed to pale beside the magnitude of their cause and the radical commitment they made to it through weeks of fasting, shouting, living fear and excitement, and trying on the idea of being a hero.

As we improvise each action, we constantly construct and reconstruct our identities.[74] We do this always in a social engagement, not by ourselves in front of mirrors. Moreover, we do it in the midst of cultural currents offering us representations of historical memory. Qiu Jin and Tan Sitong, for example, contribute to contemporary Chinese protesters' scripts for action in the midst of radical struggle. The commonplace events of everyday action—shopping, flirting, asking questions in class, developing a style of dress—all have innumerable possible contemporary models. Even without innovation, the range of choice is wide and multiplied by print and electronic media that extend the proliferation of examples beyond one's direct observation. But the number of available models for how to challenge the legitimacy of the government or face the threat of military repression or suffer execution is fairly small. Moreover, those past protesters who backed down in the face of repression do not live on as heroic legends. Our daily lives are full of examples of caution, but our narratives of revolution and popular struggle contain mainly tales of bravery rather than prudent common sense. As the course of a movement takes its participants beyond the range of usual experience, they are thrown back more and more on such heroic images in their struggle to find acceptable guidelines for action.

An important part of these images is often the notion of honor. It stresses not only reputation and the opinions of others but a particular way of evaluating oneself. This involves a much greater stress on archetypal patterns of behavior.[75] The notion of honor does not break down into distinguishable justifications of specific acts so readily as do the notions of guilt and innocence or a calculus of interests. Honor places a strong emphasis on following commendable models that generally come as scripts linking together a whole series of actions and events.

There are other distinctive features of social identity reliant on the notion of honor. As Peter Berger remarked some years ago, "the obsolescence of the concept of honour is revealed very sharply in the inability of most contemporaries to understand insult, which in essence is an assault on honour."[76] One of the salient emotions driving the student protesters in Beijing was a shared, recurrent sense of insult. Government descriptions of the protests as "turmoil," accusations that the students were led or manipulated by a tiny band of foreign agitators, and charges that the students were hooligans engaged in antisocial (or antisocialist) behavior all offended the students' sense of honor deeply. On the night of May 19, I watched students dither in uncertainty about whether it was prudent to march yet again to Tiananmen Square, only to be galvanized into immediate action by Li Peng's speech declaring martial law. Amid their tears and shouts they repeated over and again their sense of anger and outrage at his insulting tone. "He lectures us like naughty children." "He speaks like a bad, old-fashioned teacher." "He is so arrogant." Earlier, students had felt a similar insult in the *People's Daily* editorial of April 26 that condemned their protests as unpatriotic. One of the central student demands became the call for an apology and an official recognition of student patriotism. To a Westerner, this demand seemed oddly abstract amid the more substantive calls for freedom of the press or of association and an end to corruption. But this may have been even more emotionally central to participants in the protest (though they were well aware that the other sorts of demands were more fundamental long-term goals).

The rhetoric of national salvation and redemption through blood sacrifice had been deployed at many times in the 1989 movement. Liu Xiaobo specifically called for participation in protest to be seen as a civic ritual of redemption. As Barmé puts it, "there was something about these young people who had pledged themselves to death for the sake of a cause that now had as much to do with honor and self-esteem as anything; it was reminiscent of that 'splendid death' *(rippana shi)* pursued by the Japanese *shimpu* pilots.[77]

A sense of honor is linked to a notion of the primacy of social hierarchy and is at odds with a conception of the world in which essentially equivalent individuals are primary.[78] Not only personal reputation but the evaluation of collective niches in the hierarchy are crucial sources of honor (or shame): one's group must defend its honor against presumption from below and slights from above. The notion of person that the students perceived as crucial was not that of purely equivalent, abstract individuals such as evoked most commonly in Western liberalism; certainly Chinese protesters were drawn to this liberalism and much of Western individualism, but they were also moved by a more social and more responsible notion of the individual person. Chen Ziming, for example, had taken the huge risk—one enormously fateful for his life—of reading *Xiaozibao* aloud for the crowd in 1976's Tiananmen Incident. He explained why he had done this with reference to a template of historical honor—*ting shen er chu*—a phrase from classical Chinese literature meaning "show resolve, strike the posture of the hero, stand up and be counted."[79] Chen's action helped lead him into a career of dissent and attempts at reform from just outside the system. It changed him from being one of the many members of the crowd to one who took risks; it rerouted his personal trajectory from more conventional academic life to activism. In addition, something of the same consciousness, I think, must have informed the thoughts of Chen's friend Wang Juntao when he wrote from prison to thank his lawyers for being brave enough to defend him at his show trial:

I feel sad when I see that so many leaders and sponsors of the movement, when facing the consequences, dare not shoulder their responsibility. They will certainly suffer less as a result. But what about the dead? . . . The dead are unable to defend themselves. Many of them intended to fight for China and her people, for truth and justice. I decided to take my chances to defend some of their points, even if I did not agree with all of them all the time. I know that my penalty was more serious because of all this action. But only by doing so can the dead rest in peace. . . . The trial has brought me a sort of relief and consolation. I once again have a clear conscience. . . . Yet what I am most concerned about is the loss of spirit and morality of our nation. . . . What I value is whether a human spirit has nobility—a noble and pure soul. . . . In China, even intellectuals lack it.[80]

During the spring of 1989, Chinese student protesters—and some adult intellectuals, such as Chen and Wang—went through a series of actions and experiences that shaped and reshaped the identities of many. They moved from small statements, such as marching, through boycotts of classes and signing of petitions, and to hunger strikes. They made speeches—to each other as well as on television—that affirmed the primacy or even irreducible priority of certain values. They linked these values—freedom, national pride, personal integrity, and honor—to their positional identity, seeing them as particularly the responsibility of intellectuals. But their actions were more than a reflection of positional interests. Students joined the protest movement largely in blocks of classmates, so their primary immediate social network supported the process of redefinition of identity. Indeed, it seems that those more centrally placed in everyday social networks—for example, class monitors and other leaders at school—were more active in the movement and felt more obligated to hold themselves to high standards of committed behavior.[81]

Of course, various other factors besides honorable defense of identity determined expressions of bravery among the protesters. Not least of all, I suspect, were detailed and largely arbitrary chains of events the night of June 3 that presented varying demands for heroism. Nonetheless, the student protesters of China's Beijing Spring certainly began their protest with a consciousness shaped by their class position and concrete material concerns (or interests). But the risks they took, the sacrifices they made, and the moral example they provided for the future of democratic struggles in China cannot be understood only in terms of that positional identity. This is not a matter of structural or holistic accounts being better than individualistic or microsocial ones. Rather, we have to see how—for some of the students—participation in the protest contributed, at least temporarily, to a transformation of personal identity. Not only did they identify with a larger whole—the Chinese people—or with democratic or other ideals. Crucially, these students understood who they themselves were on models of such high standards of courage and struggle that failing to accept the danger would have meant a collapse of personal identity or at least a bitter wound. That so many rose to the challenge of their own ideals was vital to giving the events of 1989 their enduring significance.

Notes

1. In Han Minzhu (pseudonym), ed., *Cries for Democracy: Writings and Speeches from the 1989 Chinese Democracy Movement* (Princeton: Princeton University Press, 1990), p. 136.

2. I have examined each of these aspects of the 1989 Chinese student protests in Calhoun, *Neither Gods Nor Emperors: Students and the Struggle for Democracy in China* (Berkeley: University of California Press, forthcoming).

3. Calhoun, "'New Social Movements' of the Early 19th Century," *Social Science History*, 17, 3 (1993), pp. 385–427. That article reviews the new social movement literature. Perhaps the most important contributions come from Alberto Melucci, e.g., *Nomads of the Present: Social Movements and Individual Needs in Contemporary Society* (Philadelphia: Temple University Press, 1989); Alain Touraine, e.g., *The Return of the Actor* (Minneapolis: University of Minnesota Press, 1988); as well as Jean Cohen and Andrew Arato, e.g., *The Political Theory of Civil Society* (Cambridge: MIT Press, 1992).

4. This sense of what "totalitarianism" means informs Hannah Arendt's classic usage in *The Origins of Totalitarianism* (New York: Meridian, 1951). For recent discussions of "civil society" in China, including the question of how well developed it was before communism, see Thomas B. Gold, "The Resurgence of Civil Society in China," *Journal of Democracy* 1, 1 (1990), pp. 18–31; Andrew Nathan, *China's Crisis* (New York: Columbia University Press, 1990); David Strand, "Protest in Beijing: Civil Society and Public

Sphere in China," *Problems of Communism*, 39 (1990), pp. 1–19; and Martin King Whyte, "Urban China: A Civil Society in the Making?" pp. 77–101. In A. L. Rosenbaum, ed., *State and Society in China: The Consequences of Reform* (Boulder: Westview Press, 1992), pp. 77–101. This discussion overlaps with concern for what sort of "public sphere" Chinese civil society supported; see the special issue of *Modern China*, 19, 2 (1993) and Calhoun, "Civil Society and Public Sphere," *Public Culture*, 5, 2 (1993), pp. 267–280.

5. Quoted in Chow Tse-tung, *The May 4th Movement: Intellectual Revolution in Modern China* (Cambridge: Harvard University Press, 1960), p. 59.

6. Translation in Geremie Barmé and John Minford, eds., *Seeds of Fire: Chinese Voices of Conscience* (New York: Hill & Wang, 1988), pp. 400–401.

7. "Children of the Dragon" was among the songs most familiar to the university students. Hou was born in Taiwan but moved to the People's Republic of China, though his relations with the Communist government were strained long before he became one of the four intellectuals who staged a hunger strike near the end of the occupation of Tiananmen Square.

8. Quoted in Scott Simmie and Bob Nixon, *Tiananmen Square: An Eyewitness Account of the Chinese People's Passionate Quest for Democracy* (Seattle: University of Washington Press, 1989), p. 165.

9. Leo Ou-fan Lee, "The Crisis of Culture," in A. J. Kane, ed., *China Briefing, 1990* (Boulder: Westview Press, 1990), pp. 83–105; James L. Watson, "The Renegotiation of Chinese Cultural Identity in the Post-Mao Era," in J. N. Wasserstrom and E. J. Perry, eds., *Popular Protest and Political Culture in Modern China*, 1st ed. (Boulder: Westview Press, 1992), pp. 67–84.

10. Fang Lizhi, "Intellectuals and the Chinese Society," *Issues and Studies*, vol. 23, 4 (1987), pp. 124–142 (esp. p. 127); Lizhi, *Bringing Down the Great Wall: Writings of Science, Culture, and Democracy in China* (New York: Knopf, 1991), p. 138. The phrase "complete Westernization" had been in use since Tan Sitong and the rebellion of the jinshi examination candidates in 1895.

11. Orville Schell nicely documents much of this in *Discos and Democracy: China in the Throes of Reform* (New York: Anchor Books, 1988). One student asked me in 1989 whether China could solve its problems by becoming "postmodern" immediately without first being modern.

12. Su Xiaokang, "The Distress of a Dragon Year—Notes on *Heshang*," (orig., 1989) transl. in Richard W. Bodman and Pin P. Wan, eds., *Deathsong of the River: A Reader's Guide to the Chinese TV Series, Heshang* (Ithaca: Cornell East Asia Series, 1991), pp. 271–299 (esp. p. 273).

13. This formula has numerous variations in translation, such as "Chinese learning as the goal, Western learning as the means." It was coined by Zhang Zhidong in 1898. The division of "essence"—fundamental structure of values and spirit—from "practical use"—mere utilitarian skill—reflected not only an opinion about Western knowledge in relation to Chinese but a classical division between the kind of intellectual scholarship and moral elevation deemed crucial to Confucian scholars and the merely practical skills not only of craftsmen but even of astronomers, builders of dams, and others whose achievements were more narrowly utilitarian, rooted in the accomplishment of some external result rather than the cultivation of personal qualities. Japanese thinkers had used somewhat similar formulas in their attempts to distinguish a Japanese cultural essence from the enormous range of Chinese imported knowledge: "Japanese spirit, Chinese skill" is attributed to Sugawara Michizane (845–903 A.D.). There are brief discussions in Chow, *The May 4th Movement*, pp. 13–14; and Vera Schwarcz, *The Chinese Enlightenment: Intellectuals and the Legacy of the May Fourth Movement of 1919* (Berkeley: University of California Press, 1986), pp. 5–6.

14. See Vera Schwarcz, "Memory and Commemoration: The Chinese Search for a Livable Past," in J. N. Wasserstrom and E. J. Perry, eds., *Popular Protest and Political Culture in Modern China*, 2d ed. (Boulder: Westview Press, 1992), chapter 8; Li Zehou and Vera Schwarcz, "Six Generations of Modern Chinese Intellectuals," *Chinese Studies in History*, vol. XVII, no. 2 (1983–4), pp. 42–57; and Li Zehou, *A Collection of Essays on Modern Chinese Intellectual History* (Beijing: East Publishing House, 1987), respectively.

15. Quoted in Chow, *The May 4th Movement*, p. 59.

16. Ibid., p. 5.

17. At the same time, it is worth noting that, in the 1919 protests, "science and democracy were widely accepted goals but conspicuously absent from the slogans of May Fourth, which voiced more immediate political demands"; see John Israel, "Reflections on 'Reflections on the Modern Chinese Student Movement,' " in J. N. Wasserstrom and E. J. Perry, eds., *Popular Protest and Political Culture*, 1st ed., pp. 85–108. By 1989, these words had both come to symbolize the May Fourth era protest and taken on a new significance as a way to liken the now devalued Communist regime to its own hated precursors. If the government of the People's Republic was "feudal" in 1989, as students charged, then it was likened not only to the imperial dynasties but to the warlords and Chiang Kaishek.

18. Quoted in Benjamin Schwartz, *In Search of Wealth and Power* (Cambridge: Harvard University Press, 1964), p. 49.

19. Schwarcz, *The Chinese Enlightenment*, p. 36.

20. Li Zehou, *A Collection of Essays . . .*; see also the similar remarks in Su Xiaokang, *The Memorandum of Freedom* (Beijing: Beijing Publishing House, 1989) and the discussion by Zhu Yongtao, "American Culture as Seen by Chinese Intellectuals Today," *Journal of American Culture*, 12, 4 (1989), pp. 35–42.

21. This was already true in the late-Qing and early Republican eras, as intellectuals might identify with the strengthening of the navy as much as with the production of "New Culture."

22. Anne Gunn, "Tell the World About Us: The Student Movement in Shenyang, 1989," *Australian Journal of Chinese Affairs*, 24 (1990), pp. 243–258.

23. This and all future quotations from the script are from the translation by Bodman and Wan, *Deathsong of the River*; I shall simply indicate page numbers in parentheses; this quotation is from p. 116.

24. Bodman and Wan note that the metaphor of hair that can neither be cut nor combed both comes from an ancient poem and can be read as a play of words suggesting the simultaneous futility and inescapability of both efforts to bring order *(li)* and turmoil *(luan)*.

25. Schwarcz, *The Chinese Enlightenment*, p. 38.

26. Translated in Jean-Philippe Beja, Michel Bonnin and Alain Peyraube, *Le Tremblement de Terre de Pekin* (Paris: Gallimard, 1991), pp. 335–341; quotation is on p. 336.

27. Xu's essay is discussed in Bodman and Wan, *Deathsong . . .*, pp. 72–73. Like many other translators of this discussion, Bodman uses the term "cultural luminary" instead of "enlightener." While literal, this does not convey quite the right sense. Xu and others were not speaking of being famous, a contemporary English implication of "luminary," so much as of bringing light. The Chinese term in question is the same used to refer to the eighteenth-century European Enlightenment, *qimeng*.

28. Quoted by Schwarcz, *The Chinese Enlightenment*, p. 33, following Sato Shin'ichi.

29. Quoted in Schwarcz, *The Chinese Enlightenment*, p. 20. Yet this is not altogether unique to China. Writing in the vernacular, rather than in Latin, was one of the crucial developments that paved the way for the European Enlightenment; it is worth reminding ourselves that a figure as modern as Hobbes was a pioneer in this regard. And in the European Enlightenment, and the development of modern consciousness more gener-

ally, literature played a central role. Similarly, in nationalist and other radical movements throughout the Third World, literary production may be *the* central means by which elite intellectual ideas are circulated and introduced into broader discussions creating a sense of nation (see Benedict Anderson, *Imagined Communities: Reflections on the Origin and Spread of Nationalism* (London: Verso, 1983).

30. Quoted in George Black and Robin Munro, *Black Hands of Beijing: Lives of Defiance in China's Democracy Movement* (New York: Wiley, 1993), p. 42; the poems were written by Huang Xiang, a former Red Guard and sent-down youth who was a member of the "lost" or "in-between" generation so prominent in China's cultural and political struggles. Huang Xiang later started a mimeographed magazine, called—like so many landmarks in the history of modern Chinese intellectuals—*Enlightenment*.

31. The "misty poetry" *(menglongshi)* was the most celebrated—and most widely attacked. There is discussion along with translations in Barmé and Minford, *Seeds of Fire*; see also Bonnie S. McDougall, "Bei Dao's Poetry: Revelation and Communication," *Modern Chinese Literature*, 1 (1985), pp. 225–252; William Tay, "Obscure Poetry: A Controversy in Post-Mao China," in J. C. Kinkley, ed., *After Mao: Chinese Literature and Society, 1978–1981* (Cambridge: Harvard University Press, 1983), pp. 133–157; and Michelle Yeh, "Debunking Official Ideology: The Controversy over Contemporary Poetry," a paper presented to the First Annual Conference of the American Association of Chinese Comparative Literature (Durham: Duke University, 1990).

32. Translation from Barmé and Minford, *Seeds of Fire*, p. 18.

33. Yeh, "Debunking Official Ideology," p. 6.

34. The 1978–79 "Democracy Wall" protests were the most important of the previous popular struggles of the reform era. They were mounted largely by intellectually alert young workers and veterans of the Cultural Revolution, including most famously Wei Jingsheng, Wang Xizhe, and Xu Wenli. One dimension of their protest was a call for China to live up to some of the democratic ideals that had been promulgated in the early years of the Cultural Revolution itself but that seemed betrayed by both the later history of the Cultural Revolution and successor regimes.

35. In Barmé and Minford, *Seeds of Fire*, p. 236. Bei Dao's poetry was only occasionally political, though its iconoclastic individualism made it nearly always fairly radical and moving to young people. Though he was not personally flamboyant in the same way and his style is not the same, his artistic stance is in some ways reminiscent of Xu Zhimo's seventy years before.

36. The story is translated in Barmé and Minford, *Seeds of Fire*, and the criticism reprinted on p. 29. The critic goes on to suggest that, in this story, Liu "has revealed that he lacks a firm basis in life and that he is out of step with the world around him."

37. Interview in Yuqian Guan, "Wang Ruowang Discusses Literary Policy and the Reform," *Chinese Law and Government*, 21, 2, (1988), pp. 35–38 (p. 44).

38. See Geremie Barmé, "Confession, Redemption, and Death: Liu Xiaobo and the Protest Movement of 1989," in George Hicks, ed., *The Broken Mirror: China After Tiananmen* (Chicago: St. James Press, 1990), pp. 52–99.

39. Barmé, "Confession, Redemption, and Death," p. 57.

40. Ibid., p. 76.

41. McDougall, "Bei Dao's Poetry," p. 238.

42. Yeh, "Debunking Official Ideology," p. 10.

43. Wang Qingpan quoted by Yeh, "Debunking Official Ideology," p. 12.

44. Su Shaozhi, *Democratization and Reform* (Nottingham: Spokesman, 1988).

45. Quoted in Perry Link, "The Chinese Intellectuals and the Revolt," *New York Review of Books*, vol. XXXVI, no. 11 (1989), pp. 38–41 (p. 40).

46. This is a point that Jürgen Habermas does not fully recognize in his classic *The Structural Transformation of the Public Sphere* (Cambridge: MIT Press, 1989). In his theory,

the combination of private life and identity formation in civil society provide for the formation of individuals as capable potential participants in the public sphere. See Nancy Fraser, "Rethinking the Public Sphere: A Contribution to the Critique of Actually Existing Democracy," in C. Calhoun, ed., *Habermas and the Public Sphere* (Cambridge: MIT Press, 1992), pp. 109–142.

47. "My Views . . ." in Han, *Cries for Democracy*, p. 94.

48. Charles Taylor, *Sources of the Self* (Cambridge: Harvard University Press, 1989), p. 211. Taylor emphasizes the importance of the Protestant Reformation, and, in a sense, his account of the affirmation of ordinary life is a reworking and expansion of themes treated by Max Weber in *The Protestant Ethic and the Spirit of Capitalism*, with less emphasis on "worldly asceticism." Praise for sober and disciplined production might have been the first prominent version of the new affirmation, but it was far from the only way the affirmation could find expression.

49. Orville Schell, "The Re-emergence of the Realm of the Private in China," in Hicks, ed., *The Broken Mirror*, pp. 419–427 (p. 420).

50. In the 1980s, any number of short stories, novels, and pieces of reportage explored the new themes of sexual fulfillment, marriage for love versus disastrous forced marriages, the acceptability of divorce, and similar themes. For discussion and a few samples in translation, see Barmé and Minford, *Seeds of Fire*, pp. 199–231, and Barmé and Linda Jaivin, *New Ghosts, Old Dreams: Chinese Rebel Voices* (New York: Times Books, 1992), pp. 293–311. This theme has a significant history and as so much else in the 1980s a resonance with the 1920s; see Margaret Decker, "Living in Sin: From May 4th via the Antirightist Movement to the Present," in Ellen Widmer and David Der-wei Wang, eds., *From May Fourth to June Fourth: Fiction and Film in Twentieth Century China* (Cambridge: Harvard University Press, 1993), pp. 221–248.

51. No works describe the immediate human quality of this new consumption better than Orville Schell's, especially *To Get Rich Is Glorious* (New York: Anchor Books, 1984) and *Discos and Democracy: China in the Throes of Reform* (New York: Pantheon, 1988).

52. The link between protest and the sense of relative deprivation amid rising affluence has been widely recognized, including in James C. Davis, "Toward a Theory of Revolution," *American Sociological Review*, 27 (1962), pp. 5–19.

53. Quoted by Schell in his article, "The Re-emergence of the Realm of the Private," p. 423, that gives a good brief introduction to this theme.

54. In Han, *Cries for Democracy*, p. 198.

55. See Li Qiao et al., "Death or Rebirth? Tiananmen: The Soul of China," trans. H. R. Lan and J. Dennerline, in Michel Oksenberg, Lawrence R. Sullivan, and Marc Lambert, eds., *Beijing Spring, 1989: Confrontation and Conflict* (Armonk, N.Y.: M. E. Sharpe, 1990), pp. 173–175.

56. This and other quotations without citation that follow come from my interviews with and survey of students involved in the occupation of Tiananmen Square.

57. Discussed in Leo Ou-fan Lee, "The Crisis of Culture," in A. J. Kane, ed., *China Briefing, 1990* (Boulder: Westview Press, 1990), p. 92.

58. Quoted in Lee, "The Crisis of Culture," pp. 93–94.

59. As Andrew Nathan notes, this is in accord with longstanding Chinese tradition. Nineteenth-century thinkers interpreted the Western notion of democracy initially through the Confucian-Mencian tradition of seeing "people-as-the-basis" (*minben*) of rule. "The people's only claim in the Mencian conception of government was for welfare, and even this was not a right they could demand but a responsibility the ruler was urged to shoulder for both moral and prudential reasons." Gradually, the notion of people-as-the-basis was supplemented by those of people's rights (*minquan*) and people's rule (*minzhu*). But the older heritage kept the focus (a) on the advantages popular participation could bring to public projects and (b) on rights of appeal or opportunities for

seeking correction of state policies—not on rights to run the state as such. "In short, democracy was seen as a highly efficacious means of tapping the vast energies latent in the masses to propel the country out of backwardness and into a position of world power fitting for a nation with rich natural resources and an enormous population." See Andrew Nathan, *Chinese Democracy* (Berkeley: University of California Press, 1985), pp. 127–128.

60. Mary S. Erbaugh and Richard Curt Kraus, in "The 1989 Democracy Movement in Fujian and its Aftermath," *The Australian Journal of Chinese Affairs*, 23 (1990), pp. 145–160, suggest that in Fujian (and perhaps more generally outside Beijing or the other major urban centers) the movement remained more narrowly elitist and self-interested, with less involvement of workers or other nonstudents. "Fuzhou students seemed mostly concerned with improving their own economic situations" (p. 153).

61. See Anderson, *Imagined Communities*.

62. From text in *Ming Pao News*, eds., *June Four: A Chronicle of the Chinese Democratic Uprising* (Fayetteville: University of Arkansas Press, 1989), p. 57.

63. I have argued this case at greater length in Calhoun, "The Problem of Identity in Collective Action," in Joan Huber, ed., *Macro-Micro Linkages in Sociology* (Beverly Hills: Sage, 1991), pp. 51–75.

64. Quoted in Black and Munro, *Black Hands of Beijing*, p. 231.

65. Translation in James Tong and Elaine Chan, "The Democracy Movement in Beijing," in a special issue of *Chinese Sociology and Anthropology*, 23, 1 (1990), pp. 15–17. The word 'elitist' may give an unfortunate impression in the translation and perhaps should be rendered simply as 'elite.' In any case, the students clearly meant to speak of themselves as an elite; they go on to repeat the term.

66. W. L. Chong, "Present Worries of Chinese Democrats: Notes of Fang Lizhi, Liu Binyan, and the Film "River Elegy," *China Information*, vol. III, 4 (1989), pp. 1–20 (p. 17).

67. Quoted in Schwarcz, *The Chinese Enlightenment*, p. 22.

68. This is equally true of rational choice theory and much traditional Marxism.

69. Doug McAdam has shown a similar process at work among participants in 1964's "Freedom Summer." More generally, he shows how participation in the longer-term civil rights movement nurtured an intense identification with that movement, supported by webs of relationships with fellow-activists. These, in turn, encouraged participation in the specific high-risk and high-cost actions of Freedom Summer. See McAdam, *Political Process and the Development of Black Insurgency, 1930–1970* (Chicago: University of Chicago Press, 1988); and McAdam, John D. McCarthy, and Mayer Zald, "Social Movements," in N. J. Smelser, ed., *Handbook of Sociology* (Newbury Park, Calif.: Sage Publications, 1986), pp. 695–737.

70. Qiu Jin's story is told in Mary Rankin, *Early Chinese Revolutionaries: Radical Intellectuals in Shanghai and Chekiang, 1902–1911* (Cambridge: Harvard University Press, 1971), and Jonathan Spence, *The Gate of Heavenly Peace: The Chinese and Their Revolution, 1895–1980* (Baltimore: Penguin, 1981).

71. Jane MacCartney, "The Students: Heroes, Pawns, or Power-Brokers?" In Hicks, ed., *The Broken Mirror*, p. 7.

72. MacCartney, "The Students," p. 10.

73. Ibid.

74. This is part of what Pierre Bourdieu evokes through the concept of "habitus." Bourdieu's use of the notion of "habitus" is an attempt to grasp this constant process of improvisation where conscious and unconscious strategizing is constant but the play of the game is more than merely strategy, and identity becomes an embodied sensibility as well as assumed social roles. See Bourdieu, *Outline of a Theory of Practice* (Cambridge: Cambridge University Press, 1976), and his *The Logic of Practice* (Stanford: Stanford University Press, 1990).

75. J. K. Campbell, *Honor, Family and Patronage* (Oxford: Oxford University Press, 1964); also see Taylor, *Sources of the Self.*

76. See Peter Berger, "On the Obsolescence of the Concept of Honour," in Michael Snadel, ed., *Liberalism and Its Critics* (New York: New York University Press, 1984), pp. 149–158 (p. 149).

77. Barmé, "Confession, Redemption, and Death," p. 78.

78. Montesquieu's *Spirit of Laws* is a classic locus for this argument. See also Louis Dumont, *Essays on Individualism* (Chicago: University of Chicago Press, 1982).

79. Black and Munro, *Black Hands of Beijing*, p. 25.

80. Ibid., p. 314.

81. A somewhat distinct account of selective pressures is needed to account for the preponderance of students from outside Beijing in the Square just before the crackdown. These students had overcome greater obstacles (e.g., long-distance travel) to participate. They had a special need to demonstrate their own radical commitment since their comrades from Beijing had already proved theirs through the hunger strike and other earlier actions (and in any case had the benefit of membership in more prestigious and traditionally radical universities). Perhaps most important, it was much harder for these non-local students simply to leave as danger grew.

5

GENDER AND THE CHINESE
STUDENT MOVEMENT

Lee Feigon

During the protests of 1989, Chinese students and intellectuals proclaimed themselves untainted by the wrongful doctrines of past feudal rulers as well as present Communist ones. Even when activists became confused and divided about how to carry out their movement, they retained the conviction that China's problems stemmed from a failure to break with repressive and outdated familial values and other features of the oldest of the "ancien régimes" Young discusses in Chapter 1. But did the students really escape the hold of "feudal" values? Were they in fact as "untainted" as they claimed to be?

My goal here is to examine these questions by focusing on one particular issue: patriarchal practices and ideas. Elsewhere in this volume, other authors highlight the role that various kinds of entrenched patterns of thought and action had upon those who sought to create yet another "new" China in 1989. Thus, for example, Perry draws attention to the assumption of cultural superiority that many intellectual and student activists exhibited when dealing with members of other social classes, and Esherick and Wasserstrom highlight the influence long-standing scripts for collective action and patterns of political behavior had upon the protesters of 1989. But what of the beliefs and modes of behavior relating to gender that the students inherited? Were students more or less successful in breaking with the past when patriarchal structures as opposed to democratic political procedures or social egalitarianism were at stake? Were they even interested in challenging the status quo concerning issues of gender and sexuality?

Despite the enormous amount that has been written about the events of 1989, questions such as these have rarely been asked. Standard works on the topic, such as the accounts discussed by Wasserstrom in Chapter 13, generally have little or nothing to say about the topic of gender. Rey Chow has written a provocative essay, "Violence in the Other Country: China as Crisis, Spectacle, and Woman," that uses concepts of "otherness" developed by feminist literary critics to look at the way foreign observers treated the bloodshed of 1989.[1] Dru Gladney has presented a conference paper on the symbolism of the protests, which has a good deal to say about the importance of gender and sexuality.[2] (And, of course, in the preceding chapter, Calhoun refers in passing to the ways in which protesters assumed that the national essence was male.) Works such as these are, however, rare indeed. This is unfortunate, if hardly surprising, because all of the various "anciens régimes" that the students claimed to be rejecting have been patriarchal in one way or another. Looking at student beliefs and practices relating to gender can thus tell us a great deal about the political and cultural assumptions they shared with the rulers whose authority they sought to undermine.

Breaking with the Past

There are some grounds for thinking that the students of 1989 were a good deal less patriarchal than the regime they challenged. It was, after all, a woman, Chai Ling, who spearheaded the protest movement during its final stages. Invariably described in both Western and Chinese accounts as frail-looking, Chai's role in the student movement belied the description. In early May, when the movement was flagging, she went to the campus of Beijing University Her passionate speech single-handedly convinced several hundred students to add their names to the list of those willing to begin a hunger strike in Tiananmen Square. Thanks in large part to this and other speeches, she became one of the top student leaders, sharing the spotlight with Wang Dan and Wuer Kaixi. Later she became commander-in-chief of the Tiananmen forces.

She remained in Tiananmen to the end. Not until the wee hours of the morning of June 4 did she lead the student out of the square. A few days after the massacre, Chai Ling, from her hiding place, taped a ringing and defiant condemnation of the government that her followers have listened to over and over again inside and outside China. Her words have served both as an inspiration to those who continue to struggle against the Chinese government and as a generally credible account of what happened on the evening of June 4.[3] Almost a year after the movement was crushed, she captivated Chinese audiences again. Her escape from China, long after most of the other well-known dissidents had exited the country, offered hope that the struggle for democracy in China would continue.

Chai Ling's prominence in the movement—as well as that of other female leaders, especially the older graduate student Wang Chaohua—could easily lead to the conclusion that in spring 1989, Chinese students attempted to redefine the status of women in modern China. Even for those not especially concerned with feminist issues, Chai Ling signified the possibility of opening a radical new chapter in Chinese history, one that would break with the chauvinist and patriarchal Han culture of China's past. The leadership role played by Chai Ling, not to mention Wuer Kaixi, a Uigher from China's northwestern Xinjiang Province, indicated student repudiation of China's traditional male Han ruling culture. This impression was reinforced because both Chai Ling and Wuer Kaixi often criticized traditional gender and family relationships in their discussions of the movement. Their emphasis on cultural and social issues set them apart from earlier activists, who stressed political and intellectual matters.

Safely in exile in the United States in fall 1989, Wuer Kaixi dramatically articulated this attitude at a scholarly conference in Boston called to celebrate the movement. At the conference, he sang a popular Chinese rock song and suggested that Chinese rock and roll influenced students' ideas more than any of the theories of aging intellectuals on democracy. A few weeks later in a conference in New York, Wuer Kaixi declared that democracy for Chinese students implied sexual liberation.[4]

Chai Ling has been less controversial but hardly less emphatic in her insistence that Chinese students struggled for changes in cultural and social relationships. Since her dramatic escape from China approximately a year after the June 4 massacre, Chai Ling has several times noted that what she saw in families throughout China while she was in hiding convinced her that democratic values would come to her country after changes occur in the authoritarian structure of the Chinese family. As she put it in an interview with *Ms.* magazine: "The government, the family, it's all connected. The Chinese family has an unequal structure. There is always a tyrant—sometimes the father, sometimes the mother. Sometimes it's the son, because the parents have no chance to succeed, so they put all their expectations on the son. And when he grows up, he doesn't know how to be equal or respect others. He builds another such family. And so on up through society, such relationships, such hierarchy."[5]

In exile, with her marriage to fellow activist Feng Congde threatened, she has related the lack of democracy in China to the inequalities between men and women in Chinese society. In the *Ms.* interview, she notes: "There are some men who work for the democracy movement in the daytime but beat their wives at night. If democracy is just a concept and not a style of living, it's useless." She also somewhat cryptically contends that: "In the movement, it's traditional wisdom that's represented by a woman, wisdom and love."

Power and Gender: Familiar Patterns

As important as Chai Ling was within the movement, both as a leader and as a symbol of changing gender relations, it should not be forgotten that she was one of only a very few female leaders of the Chinese struggle for democracy in 1989.[6] In spite of her prominence, males still dominated the upper levels of the movement, both in composition and tone. This situation may have been an improvement over the present Chinese government, where none of the 19-member Politburo and only 10 of the 175-member Central

Committee of the Chinese Communist Party are women, but it did not mark
a radical new chapter for gender relations in China. In short, to adopt the
dramatic metaphors Esherick and Wasserstrom and Perry use in their chapters, stars such as Chai Ling aside, in both the official and subversive acts of
political theater performed in 1989, women were relegated for the most part
to traditional kinds of supporting roles.

The men in the student movement, though enlightened about many of the
inequalities of Chinese society, were not particularly enlightened about the
role of women in society. There were two generations of student leaders, as I
have contended elsewhere.[7] The first generation, especially the graduate students from the Party History Department at People's University, launched
the initial demonstrations after the death of Hu Yaobang. They had thought
deeply about the difficulties of the movement and the problems of communi-
cating democratic ideals to a patriarchal Chinese society. These men, and
they were all males, proved remarkably prescient about the shortcomings of
their fellow students. But they did not see other issues as clearly: To the extent that gender issues even entered my conversations with them, they did so
in a few lighthearted, patronizing remarks about the number of "pretty girls"
taking part in the demonstrations. In the minds of these People's University
student leaders, like those of the former revolutionaries they opposed,
changes in gender relations would have to wait until they resolved what they
considered the more important and immediate problems affecting the Chinese people as a whole.

Surprisingly, few of the women leaders, either at People's University
or any other school, acted offended by this attitude. Under prodding from
Robin Morgan of *Ms.*, Chai Ling allowed: "Next time it's human rights for
women."[8] But as a number of recent studies have demonstrated, throughout
this century the Chinese women's movement has been told to wait until
"next time" to resolve its problems.[9] In Chapter 3, Perry has argued that Chinese intellectuals have a long tradition of identifying "closely with the regime in power." Women intellectuals do not differ from their male colleagues
in this regard. They have bought into a system in which it has been taken for
granted that one should not raise issues like gender discrimination while
supposedly more important issues are on the agenda. Talk of sexual discrimination, it has been alleged, would alienate worker and peasant allies. Because women intellectuals in China, like their male counterparts, have benefited from what seemed to be a special relationship between the government
and the intelligentsia, they have willingly put off gains in their own position
until "next time," accepting the government's or the Party's claim that "this
time" more pressing problems exist.

In spring 1989 not once did I see a poster or hear a speech discussing gender discrimination in China. Moreover, neither Chai Ling nor any of the other
women leaders at the time criticized the way virtually all the top male Chinese student leaders reveled in the sexual clout that went with their prestige
and power. Almost all the male leaders enjoyed the attentions of female
groupies. Wang Dan, identified as the "intellectual" of the movement and the
best-known leader in addition to Wuer Kaixi and Chai Ling, openly bragged

to at least one reporter about the love letters he received from admirers. Although some of the stories of Wuer Kaixi and women may perhaps be dismissed as government propaganda, his calls for breaking with old ideas of sexual chastity seemed more a reaction to social prudery than a sensitivity to women's issues. Wuer Kaixi had girlie pin-ups on the wall of his headquarters at Beijing Teacher's College. He boasted about his drinking ability and thought nothing about appointing his "girlfriend" as secretary to screen his calls.

Wuer Kaixi served as a particular target for government efforts to discredit student leaders as corrupt and decadent. He was labeled a "playboy." Numerous articles appeared in the Chinese papers about his supposedly corrupt and indecent behavior. Although some of these charges might have a factual basis, the government (and for that matter some rival leaders) may have found it easy to single him out for particular criticism because his Uigher heritage makes him susceptible to traditional Chinese stereotypes of so-called barbarian behavior.

In China barbarians have often been associated with a kind of eroticism and sexual vitality thought to be lacking in Han Chinese. Even contemporary artists and writers have used these stereotypes as a way of criticizing the dominant ethos in Chinese society. As Esther Yau has pointed out, for instance, the recent film *Sacrificed Youth* dwells on the supposed sexual vigorousness of Dai women as a way of challenging prim Han standards.[10] At a time when Chinese men have questioned their own virility as a result of their subordination to an oppressive authoritarian model, this proof of their sexual power can, as Yau argues, be an important way of establishing an identity independent of the government.[11] In this context, the flaunting of masculine sexuality by Wuer Kaixi and the other male student leaders may be interpreted as a political act, demonstrating their strength and independence from the restrictive values of the government. Similarly, as I have discussed elsewhere, the student fascination with *liumang* (hoodlum) elements and modes of behavior shows their defiance of the conventions of a society they oppose.[12]

But where does this leave the women of the movement? Many of the women activists also embraced their own sexuality and what some might consider a kind of frivolous femininity as a way of breaking with tradition. Early in the movement, even in the most dangerous and tiring marches and parades, women students wore high heels, tight T-shirts, and other attire obviously meant to make them appear sexually appealing. One young man grinningly informed me that the women were using their sexual lures to convince male students to join the demonstrations. His point was probably overstated; the women dressed so as to demonstrate their own sexual potency and beauty, not necessarily to entice men into the movement.

But it is true that the women's behavior was certainly open to differing interpretations. On the one hand there seemed to be the degrading notion that one role for women in the movement was to be sexually available to men. (This was implied in the remark mentioned in the paragraph above and in other comments I occasionally heard.) On the other hand, however, women also showed a sense of pride in their bodies and a liberation from the constraints of the old society, especially the traditional double standard for men and women.

Young argues persuasively that the "ancien régime" that both the students and the government claimed to oppose was, among other things, a combination of the supposed feudalism of the Qing and the austere communism of the Maoist era. For the students, one aspect of this "ancien régime" was the puritanical morality and isolationism associated with the first few decades of the revolution. Reacting against this order, students looked to the West, especially Western movies, pulp novels, and magazines, for an image of sensuality and liberation that they associated with democracy. After all, if, as the Deng regime has implied throughout much of the last decade, the austere poverty of the Chinese countryside has produced China's backwardness, then the apparent materialist sensuality of the West must mean modernization. In any event, it's fun, not least of all because their elders have been cautioning Chinese youth against this kind of decadence for years.

Before and during the movement, often somewhat shocking pornography sold openly on many campuses. During the movement, it became almost a formula for student leaders to proclaim their sexual prowess. In his speech in New York, Wuer Kaixi associated the movement with sexual liberation, and in his autobiography Shen Tong discusses his first sexual experiences, assuming that by doing so he shows himself to be modern and liberated.[13]

Similar attitudes prevailed among the women. For those raised in a society that had once recommended cold showers and loose underwear as a way of coping with teenage problems, this sensuality appeared a welcome change. However, it also often resulted in stereotypes of subordination as bad as or worse than those many women thought they were leaving behind.

The students were evidently attempting to define for themselves a realm of individual expression. This was particularly important for women because of the subordination they routinely experienced in both the public and private realms. The woman writer Wang Anyi has commented on this phenomenon, suggesting that in a society in which women have been compelled to work as well as to do their traditional household chores, they already feel they have been "made too equal." Wang Anyi's views are that "what women in China want is to have the freedom to express their femininity, including the freedom to wear skirts, put on make-up, and stay at home to take care of their child."[14]

This desire to dress up or stay at home and take care of their children, though certainly understandable, also demonstrates the way even modern and independent Chinese rebel women still often receive their cues from the official policies of the Chinese state. By the 1980s, a slew of articles and official pronouncements implied that problems of chronic unemployment could be eased if female workers who are "physically weaker than men" and pose "problems" for enterprises would stay at home to tend to household chores.[15] Rather than directly confront this concept, women students embraced an image of women as a gender more focused on personal, interior problems. To the consternation of even those in official circles, who generally endorse this view, they have shown their rebellion by pushing this self-image to an extreme. They have flaunted their sexuality and highlighted their physical differences from men.

Before the movement began, Wang Anyi, who generally sanctions what she considers the return to femininity, worried about the radicalness of this rebellion. "Nowadays," she complained to an interviewer, "university students are really wild, it's fashionable to be sexually liberated."[16] Pressured by changing government attitudes on the one hand and a desire to imitate what they believed to be the fashionable and independent Western woman on the other, many Chinese women became confused about the right behavior. A typical example presented itself to me in early 1989, when I went to the house of a friend, whose college-student daughter came in wearing tight leather hot pants of the sort worn by urban U.S. prostitutes. "Doesn't she look fashionable," her proud mother exclaimed. "She looks just like an American co-ed."

Unfortunately, by spring 1989 this misguided effort to make a modern feminine statement obscured the few genuinely revolutionary protests that had occurred in the months before the demonstrations. Women had begun to demand that the government do something about increasingly sexist job and wage discrimination. The campaign for a "one child per family" policy, many complained, had resulted in girl babies again being killed in the countryside by parents who wanted boys; women demanded that it be stopped. Why, some asked, were women in particular being urged to stay home and not work? In the universities, many grumbled that highly qualified women were dismissed from jobs to make way for men and that young women graduates had an impossible time finding good employment.

Not only did the mass protests of April–June subordinate these cries for gender equality, but for some urban intellectuals the macho aspects of the movement may have given them the freedom to express more blatant sexist sentiments than had been the case before. In the middle of the demonstrations, for example, an acquaintance sought my help in getting his new son-in-law into a graduate school in the United States. It puzzled me because his daughter seemed a better candidate than her husband. When I mentioned my concerns, suggesting at the same time that I would much rather help the daughter (whom I had known for a number of years) than the son-in-law (whom I didn't know), my friend laughed and admitted he would like his daughter to study some day in the United States, but then he also candidly acknowledged that he didn't want a wife to precede her husband to the United States.

Even Chai Ling sometimes appeared to see herself as simply a stand-in for the men who should have been in her position. During the movement, word circulated over and over that Chai Ling had assumed her role as a leader because she was seen as a kind of compromise candidate who could get the macho, quarreling men to put aside their arguments temporarily. The male leaders argued belligerently with one another over who had the final word in the movement, sometimes even engaging in physical struggles for control of the microphones at public news conferences. In distinction to this, Chai Ling pandered to an image of herself as a mother figure, calling the students her "children." In the *Ms.* interview, Chai Ling said that she "did not seek leadership. The group chose me. Maybe because they couldn't agree on anyone else and I had less ego than the men. Maybe they made a bad choice. . . . But if someone more suitable is found I would not mind stepping down."[17]

The idea that women are not suited for men's jobs has become commonplace again in Chinese society in recent years. It is a view sanctioned, as I have mentioned, by the official establishment. Not surprisingly, women activists in the movement accepted this idea—certainly not unique to Chinese society—even justifying it by claiming that although women are not particularly powerful within society as a whole, they rule the home. Chai herself suggests that women aren't like men, because "men become journalists, professors, politicians, and just work, work, work. They lose themselves. They know only power, knowledge, politics."[18] She does, it's true, then add that Chinese women are now beginning to fight for their own role within the society, but then she continues that "if Chinese men could realize women's love and wisdom in their actions, the world would be more balanced."[19]

Many of the men in the movement who were Chai's rivals for power dismissed her as someone who couldn't be taken seriously because of these "womanly" qualities. Shen Tong, for instance, whose own role in the movement did not become generally known either in China or abroad until he came to the United States and hired the William Morris Agency to represent him, dismisses her as "an idealist" but one whose "ideals were based very much on emotion and not on a real philosophy."[20] Wuer Kaixi describes her similarly. The insecurity of these male leaders was apparent from their constant need to brag about their ability and influence. Chai Ling had the opposite problem. In spite of her immense powers of persuasion and obvious intelligence, she spent much of her time bemoaning her powerlessness to affect what was happening. At times it almost appeared she felt more secure when she could think of herself as the traditional, helpless female, although that was clearly not what she was.

The Goddess as Symbol and Gesture

Both the strengths and difficulties that women like Chai Ling had in the movement are represented in the symbol of Chinese womanly values constructed by the students, the Goddess of Democracy statue that Tsao Tsingyuan treats in detail in Chapter 6. Its creators have acknowledged that their original intent was to copy the U.S. Statue of Liberty. But after considering it they decided that they needed to adapt it to the Chinese vernacular. They used as a model a preexisting figure of a Chinese peasant man grasping a wooden pole in both hands. The bottom part of the staff was cut off and the top part changed into a torch, so only the hand above the man's head grasped this symbol of freedom. The students then lengthened the hair, added breasts, and feminized the facial features, transforming the male figure into a woman.

By specifically changing a male figure into a female one, the students made it clear that it was important for them to have a woman as their image of defiance. As a "goddess," the statue resembled Chinese folklore figures. She was Chai Ling's idea of woman as "traditional wisdom." But at the same time, the statue was a representation of the U.S. symbol of liberty. As such, she personified the proud, independent Western woman many Chinese students wanted to imitate. And the significance of the statue didn't stop there since (as Tsao argues in the following chapter) the sculpture was also influenced in part by "the Russian school of revolutionary realism."[21]

This image of the goddess as a fecund and strong Soviet farm woman contrasts powerfully with the impotence of the feeble old men who ran the Chinese government. In their youth the present leaders of the Chinese government had also looked to Soviet models (indeed in this light the goddess appears a reincarnation of the poster art and sculpture of the 1950s and even, as Esherick and Wasserstrom argue in Chapter 2, the icons of the Cultural Revolution era), so the image of the statue was a particularly apt way of demonstrating the extent to which the old men had failed to live up to even their own measurements. The goddess exemplified the potency of students no longer cowed by that government. At a time when word of Gorbachev's reforms was sweeping China, she reminded the government of how far it was falling behind both the West and the Soviet Union.

The goddess also demonstrated the hollowness of this conception of feminine strength, however, and inadvertently highlighted the dependence of the student movement on the Chinese government. The students initially built the goddess for what they planned would be a departing gesture against a government that clearly had the upper hand. They intended to leave the statue behind when they bowed to the inevitable and vacated the square at the end of May. Then after the sculpture arrived in the square, the students changed their minds and remained in place. It appears that what was in reality a helpless although stirring symbol falsely heartened them; they waited immobilized in the square with their goddess as the government garnered its forces against them.

Perhaps it is unfair to say so, but in the end it appeared that the goddess emphasized student impotence against a government they had mocked for being run by feeble old men. The symbol, constructed from papier-mâché, offered nothing concrete for either women or democracy in China. Like the choice of Chai Ling, she was a "fragile" compromise decided upon because those who were running the revolution could agree on no other alternatives. The first tanks into the square easily toppled and beheaded the goddess. Like much else about the movement, the statue looked impressive but offered little resistance to the old order.

The weakness of their symbol may aptly demonstrate the ambivalence Chinese women intellectuals felt toward the government concerning gender issues as well as democracy. Although it is undeniably true that the status of women as a whole has been set back as a result of the reforms, women intellectuals have probably been affected less by this than most other elements in the society. Pressure on women graduates to accept jobs inferior to those of their male counterparts or not to work at all has mounted, but women intellectuals have generally done better than their worker or peasant counterparts, whose jobs in factories have been eliminated and whose freedoms and opportunities have been increasingly restricted throughout the period of reforms. Although women intellectuals may be angered by gender-based job discrimination and may shudder at the reemergence of female infanticide in the countryside, most women students have little incentive to make common cause with their less fortunate counterparts.

This lack of unity on gender issues is significant not only in and of itself but also because it helps explain why the movement failed. The failure to take a strong position on the issue of gender roles did not sink the movement. But the fuzzy thinking that characterized the student approach to gender issues also clouded their understanding of issues like democracy and economic reform. As was the case with gender issues, the students often struggled against a government whose authority and logic had a much greater hold on them than they admitted. On gender issues as on other matters, students allied themselves with workers but failed to appreciate their concerns; as Perry argues in Chapter 3, the gap between these groups weakened the movement.

In 1989, students did not comprehend the extent to which they had accepted governmental attitudes that men were strong in the world of government and politics and women in the household. They failed to appreciate the sufferings and concerns of peasant and worker women. But this may change, as the results of gender-based job discrimination hit the universities. However flawed, the examples of leaders like Chai Ling and Wang Chaohua send a powerful message to women about their potential as leaders. In light of the failure of the movement, some women have now begun to think about their place as women in the movement and may work more militantly on this in the future. The first step would be for male activists like Wuer Kaixi or Shen Tong to undergo the same kind of introspection. There is little evidence that any of them has begun to reconsider his own actions. But the revolution is still young, and the new generation may have a very different attitude.

Notes

1. Rey Chow, "Violence in the Other Country: China as Crisis, Spectacle, and Woman," in Chandra Mohanty et al., eds., *Third World Women and the Politics of Feminism* (Bloomington: Indiana University Press, 1991).

2. Dru Gladney, "Bodily Positions and Social Dispositions: Sexuality, Nationality and Tiananmen" (paper presented at the Institute of Advanced Study, Princeton, April 26, 1990).

3. For a translation of this statement, as well as transcripts of interviews with Chai Ling conducted during the month preceding June 4, see Han Minzhu, ed., *Cries for Democracy* (Princeton: Princeton University Press, 1990), pp. 197–199, 214–215, 327–328, and 361–366.

4. For further discussion of Wuer's activities and speeches in autumn 1989, see Richard Bernstein, "To Be Young and in China: A Colloquy," *New York Times*, October 7,

1989, p. 11, and Dru Gladney, "The People of the People's Republic: Finally in the Vanguard?" *Fletcher Forum of World Affairs*, 12, 1 (Winter 1989–1990), pp. 62–76.

5. Robin Morgan, "Chai Ling Talks with Robin Morgan," *Ms.* (September–October 1990), p.15.

6. One sign of this is that Chai and Wang Chaohua were the only two women included in the government's list of the twenty-one most-wanted protesters, the full text of which can be found in Wu Mouren et al., *Bajiu Zhongguo minyun jishi* (Annals of the 1989 Chinese democracy movement) (New York: privately published, 1989), pp. 833–835. There were female leaders in provincial student movements, as the picture of a Shanghai activist in Han, *Cries for Democracy*, p. 171, indicates. The caption to this photograph, however, reminds readers that "relatively few female students assumed leadership roles in student organizations."

7. Lee Feigon, *China Rising* (Chicago: Ivan R. Dee, 1989).

8. Morgan, "Chai Ling," p. 16.

9. Among the books that in one way or another discuss this problem are: Margery Wolf, *Revolution Postponed: Women in Contemporary China* (Stanford: Stanford University Press, 1985); Kay Ann Johnson, *Women, the Family and Peasant Revolution in China* (Chicago: University of Chicago Press, 1983); Judith Stacey, *Patriarchy and Socialist Revolution in China* (Berkeley: University of California Press, 1983); Patricia Stranahan, *Yan'an Women and the Communist Party* (Berkeley: Center for Chinese Studies, 1983); Phyllis Andors, *The Unfinished Liberation of Chinese Women, 1949–1980* (Bloomington: Indiana University Press, 1983); Elisabeth Croll, *Feminism and Socialism in China* (New York: Schocken Books, 1980); and Elisabeth Croll, *Chinese Women Since Mao* (Armonk, N.Y.: M. E. Sharpe, 1983). For a more positive assessment of the commitment Chinese revolutionaries have had toward eliminating patriarchy, see Ono Kazuko, *Chinese Women in a Century of Revolution, 1850–1950*, ed. Joshua A. Fogel (Stanford: Stanford University Press, 1989).

10. Esther C.M. Yau, "Cultural and Economic Dislocations: Filmic Phantasies of Chinese Women in the 1980s," *Wide Angle*, 11, 2 (1989), pp. 15–16.

11. Ibid., p. 18.

12. Feigon, *China Rising*.

13. See Shen Tong and Marianne Yen, *Almost a Revolution* (Boston: Houghton Mifflin, 1990).

14. W. L. Chong, "Love and Sexuality: Themes from a Lecture by Woman Writer Wang Anyi," *China Information*, 3, 3 (Winter 1988–1989), p. 65.

15. A comprehensive analysis of the (often mixed) messages Chinese women receive through the official press, as well as an important discussion of the way these same women use letters to the editor and other forms of writing to respond to these messages, can be found in Gail Hershatter and Emily Honig, *Personal Voices: Chinese Women in the 1980s* (Stanford: Stanford University Press, 1988).

16. Alice de Jong and Anne Sytske Keyser, "A Talk with Woman Novelist Wang Anyi," *China Information*, 3, 3 (Winter 1988–1989), pp. 67–68.

17. Morgan, "Chai Ling," p. 15.

18. Ibid., p. 14.

19. Ibid., p. 15.

20. Shen and Yen, *Almost a Revolution*, p. 276.

21. For other discussions of the symbolism of the goddess that highlight the implications of the statue's gender, see Gladney, "Bodily Positions and Social Dispositions," and Chow, "Violence in the Other Country."

Part Three

POPULAR CULTURE AND THE POLITICS OF ART

Each of the previous thematic parts has contained chapters that refer to the important roles that specific creative works, ranging from portraits of Chairman Mao to films such as *He Shang* (River Elegy), have played in recent Chinese political struggles. The two chapters in Part 3, the first contributions to this volume by scholars who specialize in the study of the arts, expand and enlarge upon this topic in important ways. Art historian Tsao Tsing-yuan's essay is an eyewitness account of the creation and display of one of the most famous symbols of the protests of 1989—the Goddess of Democracy statue— to which earlier chapters (such as Feigon's) have already referred. The second piece, by literary specialist Jones, focuses on the ways in which contemporary Chinese rock music can function as either a transmitter of dissent (a function that Calhoun has already highlighted in Chapter 4) or as a genre through which much more ambiguous political messages are voiced. When taken together, the two chapters in Part 3 draw attention not only to the politicized nature of artistic creation but also to the fascinating and often chaotic eclecticism of form and content that characterizes the Chinese art scene. The statue that Tsao describes, after all, was visually reminiscent of socialist realist icons, traditional representations of Chinese deities, and Western goddess figures such as the Statue of Liberty, and its display was an act of patriotic performance art that included the playing of a work by Beethoven. That a similar eclecticism can be found within the realm of popular music is illustrated by the references Jones makes to groups whose members alternate between strumming electric guitars and playing instruments associated with ancient China, and who combine an interest in contemporary styles with a penchant for historical allusions and group names (such as "Tang Dynasty") that are clearly meant to evoke memories of the distant past. The supplementary materials listed below range from case studies of other artistic genres, to works on the connections between art and politics under other state socialist regimes, to general collections of essays on Chinese popular culture.

Recommended Supplementary Materials for Classroom Use

Scholarship on China: Contemporary Politics

Barmé, Geremie. "Wang Shuo and Liumang ('Hooligan') Culture." *Australian Journal of Chinese Affairs*, vol. 28 (July 1992), pp. 23–64. An essay on the satirical dimensions of an iconoclastic contemporary writer, whose works of fiction are widely read in their original form and also have served as the basis for several popular films.

Davis, Deborah, et al., eds. *Urban Spaces in Contemporary China.* Cambridge: Cambridge University Press, forthcoming. A conference volume on city life, which includes several chapters on Part 3's theme of the role of art in politics and culture; these include essays that deal with the economic side of artistic creation, the avant-garde scene, contemporary poetry, and the usefulness of the concept of a "velvet prison" developed by Miklos Haraszti (whose work is hereinafter cited under "Comparative Works") for understanding the relationship between Chinese artists and the state.

Lee, Benjamin, and Leo Ou-fan Lee. "The Goddess of Democracy Deconstructed." *New Perspectives Quarterly*, vol. 6, no. 3 (1989), pp. 58–61. An essay that uses the famous statue as the starting point for a brief but wide-ranging discussion of the symbolism of the events of 1989.

Wu Hung. "Tiananmen Square: A History of Monuments." *Representations*, no. 25 (Summer 1991), pp. 84–117. A study of the architectural history and statuary of this famous square, which includes a discussion of the Goddess of Democracy that complements and builds upon Tsao's eyewitness account.

Yang, Mayfair. "Of Gender, State Censorship, and Overseas Capital: An Interview with Director Zhang Yimou." *Public Culture*, vol. 5, no. 2 (Winter 1993), pp. 297–313. A wide-ranging conversation between an anthropologist and the director of several widely acclaimed and controversial recent films.

Scholarship on China: Historical Perspectives

Chow, Rey. *Woman and Chinese Modernity: The Politics of Reading Between East and West.* Minneapolis: University of Minnesota Press, 1991. A work on literary and cinematic texts dealing with China, which draws upon theories associated with feminism and postmodernism to explore issues ranging from Western views of China to the way female writers such as Ding Ling deal with issues of gender and power.

Johnson, David, et al., eds. *Popular Culture in Late Imperial China.* Berkeley: University of California Press, 1985. A multidisciplinary collection of essays on topics ranging from the texts used by popular religious sects during the Qing era, to the rise of mass journalism just before and immediately after the 1911 Revolution.

Kraus, Richard C. *Pianos and Politics in China: Middle-Class Values and the Struggle over Western Music.* Oxford: Oxford University Press, 1989. A study that draws attention to the cultural and political connotations of imported musical genres in twentieth-century China.

Link, Perry, et al., eds. *Unofficial China: Popular Culture and Thought in the People's Republic.* Boulder: Westview Press, 1989. A multidisciplinary collection of essays on historical themes ranging from peasant operas of the pre-1949 era to Cultural Revolution fiction; also includes chapters on more contemporary themes.

Widmer, Ellen, and David Der-wei Wang, eds. *From May Fourth to June Fourth: Fiction and Film in Twentieth-Century China*. Cambridge: Harvard University Press, 1993. A conference volume that deals with aspects of two major genres of artistic creation during the period from 1919 to 1989.

Comparative Works and Case Studies of Other Countries

Burke, Peter. *Popular Culture in Early Modern Europe*. New York: Harper and Row, 1978. An influential introduction to the study of popular culture.
Chartier, Roger. "Texts, Printing, Readings." In Lynn Hunt, ed., *The New Cultural History*. Berkeley: University of California Press, 1989, pp. 154–175. An essay by a leading French historian who is concerned with elucidating the cultural contestations that affect the ways in which literary texts are created, distributed, and interpreted by readers; the article includes a critique of the tendency of scholars to draw sharp lines of demarcation between the "popular" and "elite" cultural realms.
Garofolo, Reebee, ed. *Rockin' the Boat: Mass Music and Mass Movements*. Boston: South End, 1992. A collection of essays on the political meanings of popular music in various countries.
Haraszti, Miklos. *The Velvet Prison: Artists Under State Socialism*. New York: Basic Books, 1987. A study of the limits placed on artistic endeavors in Soviet Bloc countries before the fall of the Berlin Wall; focuses on the deals struck between regimes and artists willing to forego public expressions of dissent in return for certain kinds of benefits.
Johnson, James. "Revolutionary Audiences and the Impossible Imperatives of Fraternity." In Bryant T. Ragan, Jr., and Elizabeth A. Williams, eds., *Re-Creating Authority in Revolutionary France*. New Brunswick: Rutgers University Press, 1992, pp. 57–78. Examines the politicization of various forms of artistic expression during the French Revolution.

Primary Sources

Barnstone, Tony, ed. *Out of the Howling Storm: The New Chinese Poetry*. Hanover, N.H.: Wesleyan University Press, 1993. Translations of poems by a variety of writers associated with the "misty" *(menglongshi)* school of poets and other groups.
Chen Kaige. *Yellow Earth*. A provocative and controversial film by one of China's leading directors (now living in exile); the film looks in part at the efforts the Chinese Communist Party (CCP) made before 1949 to adapt popular culture forms (in this case folksongs) to serve specific political goals.
Fraser, Stewart, ed. *100 Great Chinese Posters*. New York: Images Graphique, 1977. Color reproductions of propaganda posters from the first three decades of CCP rule; most might best be classified as works of "socialist realism" with Chinese characteristics.

6

THE BIRTH OF THE GODDESS
OF DEMOCRACY

Tsao Tsing-yuan

Nothing excites a sculptor so much, ordinarily, as seeing a work of her or his own creation take shape. This time, however, I was watching the creation of a sculpture that I had no part in making, and feeling the same excitement. It was the "Goddess of Democracy" statue that stood for five days in Tiananmen Square, from May 30 to the morning of June 4, 1989. I witnessed the making of it and want to put the story on record for the world to know.

I was, until recently, a graduate student at the Central Academy of Fine Arts in Beijing—where the sculpture was made—and was living there when these events took place. Since I was trained as a sculptor before becoming an art historian, I have been especially close to the faculty and students of the Central Academy's Sculpture Department and was looked on by the students as a kind of older sister. The reason I did not participate directly in the making of the statue was that my own status—I am now living mostly abroad with a foreign husband—might have made trouble for the students if I had taken part. I might even have been identified with the "small group of instigators" and "people with ulterior motives" whom the government was attempting to charge with responsibility for the demonstrations. So I avoided conspicuous involvement, adopting instead the role of observer and supportive friend.

By May 27, a week after the declaration of martial law in Beijing, the student movement seemed to be losing some of its momentum; the students suspected that the government was waiting for them to tire and leave the Square

---

A short, preliminary form of this essay was published in the *Los Angeles Times*, June 18, 1989, opinion page. A few minor errors in that version have been corrected here.

by their own choice. The word got around that on the evening of May 29 there would be an "important announcement" on the Central Broadcasting Station, and it was expected to be the resignation of Zhao Ziyang. The Federation of the Beijing University Students, which was coordinating the movement, decided that as a response to this broadcast they would stage the largest demonstration of all, involving students, workers, residents of Beijing—everyone—after which they would all return to their units. And they decided to leave behind in the Square, as a stand-in for themselves, a monumental work of art that would continue, so long as it was allowed to stand, to assert their symbolic presence and their ideals.

Students and faculty of the Central Academy of Fine Arts, which is located only a short distance from Tiananmen Square, had from the beginning been actively involved in the demonstrations. It was students in the Academy's Oil Painting Department who in the first days, when a major objective of the movement was to honor the recently deceased Hu Yaobang, had made a huge oil portrait of him and propped it against the Monument to the People's Heroes in the Square. On May 27, a representative of the Federation of Beijing University Students came to the Central Academy to ask that they produce another large-scale work of art, this time a statue, and that it be ready by the time of the great demonstration scheduled for May 30. That gave them three days in which to do it. The Federation offered them 8,000 yuan (more than US$2,000 by the official rate) for materials and other expenses. The undergraduate students in three of the four studios of the Central Academy's Sculpture Department agreed to take on the job. There were about fifteen of them, all young men in their early twenties.

The Federation suggested that the sculpture be a replica of the Statue of Liberty in New York, like the smaller one that had been carried in a procession by demonstrators in Shanghai two days earlier. But the Central Academy sculpture students rejected that idea, both because it might be taken as too openly pro-American and because copying an existing work was contrary to their principles as creative artists. They also rejected the suggestion of a "Chinese-style" work, because there is no tradition in China for sculpture that powerfully expresses a political concept. A statue in the manner of Buddhist cave sculptures might have been more pleasing to foreign viewers (such as the *Art News* critic who complained about the Goddess's Western style) but could not have achieved the emotional impact that the statue was to have on the great mass of people for whom it was made.

What was needed, the students felt, was a new work of universal appeal, Chinese only in the eclectic way that today's China sometimes borrows what it needs from foreign cultures. But apart from style, they had another problem: the short time in which they had to complete it. How could an original, monumental work of sculpture be finished in three days, even if they worked through the nights? Normally, much more time than that was spent on creating the model, and still more on making the finished work.

Their solution was ingenious and explains some features of the statue as it took shape—for example, its slightly off-balance look and its posture with two hands raised to hold up its torch (where the Statue of Liberty uses only one). The students, with the strong academic training that young artists receive in China, chose a thoroughly academic approach to their problem: they decided to adapt to their purpose a studio practice work that one of them (or perhaps it was several of them) had already made, a half-meter-high clay sculpture of a man grasping a pole with two raised hands and leaning his weight on it. It had been done originally as a demonstration of how the distribution of weight is affected when the center of gravity is shifted outside the body; it had been made first as a nude figure and later draped, with the organic body still perceptible under the drapery. The students knew from their training that a draped figure not based on a fully worked-out body underneath would be structurally unconvincing. This was the unlikely beginning from which the Goddess of Democracy was to be developed through a remarkable process of transformation. The students cut off the lower part of the pole and added a flame at the top to turn it into a torch; they leaned the sculpture into a more upright position; they changed the man's face to a woman's, and otherwise added feminine characteristics to make the him into a her.

I did not witness this transformation of the model myself but was told about it afterward by the sculptors. They were a bit embarrassed in relating how it happened; they thought of it more as an emergency expedient than as an ingenious or admirable solution. Their aim was to portray the Goddess as a healthy young woman, and for that, again, the Chinese sculpture tradition offered no models. What they turned to was the tradition favored within the Central Academy's Sculpture Department, the Russian school of revolutionary realism, and specifically the style of the woman sculptor Vera Mukhina, whose monumental statue of "A Worker and Collective Farm Woman," placed originally atop the Soviet Pavilion at the 1937 Paris World's Fair, is still much admired in China. As a comparison will quickly reveal (see, for example, Peter Selz, *Art in Our Times*, fig. 739), the head of the farm woman in this work was the principal inspiration for the face and head of the Goddess.

This transformed model was then made the basis for the ten-meter-high statue. It was divided (marked) into four horizontal sections, and teams of young sculptors transferred the measurements of these, by a process well known to academic sculptors, to the corresponding parts of the huge work that would be assembled on the Square. The main material was styrofoam plastic; this had not, so far as I know, been used before in China for monumental sculpture, but perhaps the idea had come from foreign sculptors who had used it or from the use of that material in advertising displays, store windows, and so forth. Large blocks of it were carved into rough approximations of the shapes desired and then wired together, with plaster added to the surface to join the pieces more strongly and to allow finer modeling. Constructed in this way, the four sections were fairly light: each could be lifted by five or six students.

It may be difficult for foreign artists and art scholars, with their strong feelings about originality and individualism, to accept the fact that there was no single artist for the Goddess of Democracy. It was as close to a true collaborative work as any project of this kind can be. Among the group of fifteen or so undergraduate students who made it, a smaller number emerged naturally in time as leaders to plan the operation loosely and coordinate the workshifts—some working while others slept. One of them, when it was all over, said to me, "If I had handled the project by myself, I could have arranged it much better—I would have divided the workers into three groups, for instance, and given them eight-hour shifts, around the clock. But we had no clear-cut leadership, no delegation of responsibility." Anyone who claims now to have been the artist or the organizer or the leader should be regarded with some suspicion: From the account I was given by the students themselves, that was not the way it happened.

One young Central Academy faculty member was openly supportive of the students and served as a go-between to help them get materials and access to facilities that they could not have obtained, even with money, without such help. Others on the faculty were certainly giving their support behind the scenes, persuading the political leaders in the Academy and protecting the students. Without their help, the sculpture could not have been made openly, as it was, in the Sculpture Department's outdoor workspace within the Central Academy compound.

I was not there through the whole making of the statue; no one was. Sculpture goes slowly and cannot hold the interest of a nonparticipant for long. I was on the Square much of the time the work was going on, doing what I could for the demonstrators and hunger strikers, talking with them, buying things to take to them—food, water, towels, flashlights, and other necessaries. But I would stop by often to see how the statue was progressing and to talk with the sculptors.

The work was done in the courtyard where large-scale sculpture was always made. Teachers living in the buildings surrounding it complained that they could not sleep because of the noise, since the work continued through the night, and there were always onlookers, commenting and talking. The Academy's overt attitude toward the making of the sculpture was one of passive toleration, not active sanction—that was impossible. But many of the faculty, perhaps most, approved quietly, and when the statue was moved to the Square, many of them came along to show support.

When the time came to transport the pieces of the statue to the Square, another problem arose: The students had intended to bring the pieces in one of the Academy's trucks, but the Security Bureau, hearing of this, sent word that any driver daring to take them would lose his license. In the end the students hired six of the familiar Beijing carts, made like a bicycle in front and a flat cart with two wheels behind; four of these carried the sections of the statue, with tools and materials on the other two. Students from the Central Academy, along with others from seven other academies of crafts, drama, music, dance, and so on who were cooperating, accompanied the carts to guard them. The procession was led by a bearer of the Central Academy's flag, followed by two ranks of strong young people (including myself for part of the way) for protection; then the six carts; and all of this was enclosed on every side by students, marching with us as an outer guard.

The route had been announced: turn left outside the Academy gate, then westward to the Donghua-men, the east gate of the Forbidden City, and so around the road between the wall and the moat to the Square. But this was to deceive the police, in case they were waiting to stop us; in fact, we turned right out of the Academy and followed the shorter route, down Wangfujing, the well-known shopping street, turning right along Chang'an Boulevard, past the Beijing Hotel.

The place on the Square where the statue was to be erected had been chosen carefully. It was on the great axis, heavy with both cosmological and political symbolism, that extended from the main entrance of the Forbidden City, with the huge portrait of Mao Zedong over it, through the Monument to the People's Heroes that had become the command headquarters of the student movement. The statue was to be set up just across the broad avenue from Mao, so that it would confront him face-to-face. When we arrived around 10:30 at night, a huge crowd, perhaps fifty thousand people, had gathered around the tall scaffolding of iron poles that had already been erected to support the statue. The parts were placed one on top of another, attached to this frame; plaster was poured into the hollow core, locking all parts onto a vertical iron pole that extended from the ground up through the statue's center to hold it upright. The exposed iron supports were then cut away, leaving the statue freestanding. It stood on a base covered with cloth. The statue was deliberately made so that once assembled it could not be taken apart again but would have to be destroyed all at once.

The work continued through the night. A ring of students joined hands around the statue so that those working on it would be undisturbed. I went back to the Academy to get some sleep, returning to the Square the next morning. By then it was difficult to get inside the circle of guards; many people had waited there all night, and too many of them wanted to watch the construction of the statue from close by. Only those involved with making it were to be allowed in; even students who were to perform music and dance at the unveiling ceremony had to wait outside. I showed my Central Academy of Fine Arts student badge, but the guards only pointed and said, "Central Academy students wait over there." I felt crestfallen, wishing I had not gone back to sleep; had I missed my chance? But then I waved and shouted to the sculptors working inside: "Hey, come and rescue me!" Three or four of them came over and told the guards: "She's special, let her in." So I got in.

By noon on May 30, the statue was ready for the unveiling ceremony. Actually, only the face was "veiled," by two long pieces of cloth, bright blue and red—the students could never have collected enough cloth to cover the whole figure. Journalists and others who were gathered there had become restless by mid-morning and were showing signs of leaving. I warned the students of this and advised them that they should announce the time of the ceremony over the loudspeaker to persuade people to stay. They said, "You speak English, why don't you make the announcement?" So I did, saying in my best English, "Ladies and gentlemen, please stay where you are, we will have the unveiling ceremony around twelve noon." Even that much public speaking left me embarrassed, and the students joshed me: only those few sentences and her face turns red!

The ceremony was simple and very moving. A statement had been prepared about the meaning of the statue, written on a long banner standing near the statue, and was read over the loudspeaker by a woman, probably a student at the Broadcasting Academy, who had a good Mandarin accent. Like the sculpture itself, the statement was a piece of passionately dedicated improvisation; it was written in rather crude calligraphy. Here is a rough rendering of it:

Dear compatriots and fellow students:

We, as proud citizens of China, have broken the autocracy of the government and now stand before the Democracy Movement of 1989. All the people are of a single mind; to combat bravely the feudal autocracy. Fighting tirelessly through the days and nights of the past weeks, we have achieved victories one after another, because the people are invincible.

Now this autocratic government, possessing only animal characteristics, lacking all human feeling, has used the most shameless and scurrilous methods, violence and cheating, in their attempt to kill the Goddess of Democracy as a newborn infant in her cradle. But this coming of darkness proves only that they have already reached the end of their road; the day of their doom has already arrived. They will be judged by all people.

At this grim moment, what we need most is to remain calm and united in a single purpose. We need a powerful cementing force to strengthen our resolve: that is the Goddess of Democracy.

Democracy, how long it is since we last saw you . . . !

You are the hope for which we thirst, we Chinese who have suffered decades of repression under the feudal autocracy!

You are the symbol of every student in the Square, of the hearts of millions of people!

You are the soul of the 1989 Democracy Movement!

You are the Chinese nation's hope for salvation!

Today, here in the People's Square, the people's goddess stands tall and announces to the whole world: a consciousness of democracy has awakened among the Chinese people! The new era has begun! From this piece of ancient earth grows the tree of democracy and freedom, putting forth gorgeous flowers and a bountiful harvest of fruit!

The statue of the Goddess of Democracy is made of plaster, and of course cannot stand here forever. But as a symbol of the people's hearts, she is divine and inviolate. Let those who would sully her beware: the people will not permit this!

We believe strongly that this darkness will pass, that the dawn must come. On the day when real democracy and freedom come to China, we must erect another Goddess of Democracy here in the Square, monumental, towering, and permanent. We have strong faith that that day will come at last. We have still another hope: Chinese people, arise! Erect the statue of the Goddess of Democracy in your millions of hearts!

Long live the people!

Long live freedom!

Long live democracy!

The statement was signed by the eight art academies that had sponsored the whole project: the Central Academies of Fine Arts, Arts and Crafts, Drama, and Music; the Beijing Film Academy; the Beijing Dance Academy; the Academy of Chinese Local Stage Arts; and the Academy of Chinese Music.

When the time came for the actual "unveiling," two Beijing residents, a woman and a man, were chosen at random from the crowd and invited into the circle to pull the strings that would remove the pieces of red and blue cloth. As these "veils" fell, the crowd burst into cheers, there were shouts of "Long live democracy!" and other slogans, and some began to sing the "Internationale." A musical performance was given by the students from the Central Academy of Music, choral renditions of the "Hymn to Joy" from Beethoven's Ninth Symphony, another foreign song followed by a Chinese one, and finally the "Internationale" again. A planned performance by students in the Central Academy of Dance had to be canceled, since with the pressure of the crowd there was not enough room for them to dance.

I stood there with the huge crowd gazing up at this ten-meter-high work. It was scarcely a masterpiece of world sculpture—made in three days and nights by a group of undergraduate students, it could hardly have been that. And yet it was the greatest sculpture I have ever seen, and the ceremony had been the greatest I have ever attended.

After the unveiling ceremony, we returned to the Central Academy. I invited all the young sculptors to lunch, but they said, "We still have a few hundred yuan"—from the money given them for the statue—and they treated me instead. At lunch I asked about their backgrounds and learned that several were children or nephews of older sculptors whom I knew—my colleagues. Hearing this, they asked me: Should we call you Auntie, then, instead of Older Sister?

The lunch was short because they soon left, one by one, saying that what they needed most was not food but sleep. They had not slept for four days. I thought: These young people are the future of China; why can't Deng Xiaoping appreciate the youth of this country? They had made themselves special T-shirts and caps as mementos, white with a red "V" for victory; the shirts were later reproduced in quantities and sold, but only fifteen or twenty of the caps were made, and they gave me one for being their older sister-companion and the one who would tell their story.

During the early evening on that day there was a strong wind and rainstorm, and we rushed to the Square afterward to see if the statue had been damaged. But it had endured this first serious test without harm. We took this as a good omen; we were wrong.

On the terrible night of June 3–4, I was out around the Square for some forty hours without sleep; that is another story. Afterward, I could no longer go on living at the Central Academy—it was too dangerous—and most of the students and faculty had fled when I returned there the day after the massacre. But I found a few of the sculpture students and quickly questioned them about matters to do with the planning and making of the statue that were not clear to me. Before, there had seemed no urgency about getting the whole story; now there was. That was the last I saw of them; they were frightened, with good reason, and dispersed to safer places. I have not heard anything about any of them since then.

The toppling of the Goddess of Democracy, the final heart-rending symbolic event, was seen by millions of TV viewers: pushed by a tank, it fell forward and to the right, so that its hands and the torch struck the ground first, breaking off. It must have been quickly and easily reduced to rubble, mixing with all the other rubble in the Square, to be cleared away by the Army as part of its deceitful show of cleanliness and order. The statue, however, could not be so easily destroyed. As the unveiling statement had said, it was intended from the beginning to be ephemeral and yet to endure as an image of the desire of the great mass of Chinese people for the ideals it symbolized, liberty and democracy. Replicas of it have already been made—or are planned—by Chinese student groups and others in the United States and elsewhere who want them to be lasting reminders. Like the writers of the statement, I myself envision a day when another replica, as large as the original and more permanent, stands in Tiananmen Square, with the names of those who died there written in gold on its base. It may well stand there after Chairman Mao's Mausoleum has, in its turn, been pulled down.

7

THE POLITICS OF POPULAR MUSIC IN POST-TIANANMEN CHINA

Andrew F. Jones

Popular music as propaganda—be it in support of resistance to Japanese aggression in the 1930s, anti-imperialism in the 1940s, Maoism during the Cultural Revolution, or economic modernization in the 1980s—has long been a fixture of modern Chinese political culture.[1] The extent to which popular music became a vehicle for *popular protest* during the Tiananmen movement of 1989, however, was unprecedented. Throughout the movement (as Craig Calhoun previously noted in Chapter 4), popular music—and in particular the rock music *(yaogun yinyue)* that emerged in Beijing in the late 1980s as an "underground" alternative to state-run popular music *(tongsu yinyue)*—served as a powerful means for the public expression of political and cultural dissent. Cui Jian's "I Have Nothing" *(Yiwu suoyou)* was adopted by students and workers as a marching anthem, several rock bands performed for hunger-striking students on the square, and satires of government corruption set to popular melodies were regularly broadcast over makeshift public address systems throughout Beijing. On a less overtly political level, the rock subculture's embrace of Westernization, antitraditionalism, and individualism had much to do with informing the sensibilities (and ultimately, the political behavior) of the students and workers who participated in the protests.[2] In the months after the crackdown, despite the suppression of rock music on the part of the Chinese Communist Party (CCP) and a barrage of *tongsu* songs intended to drown out any dissonance that might have lingered in the wake of the movement's demise, rock music performances continued to provide one of the few forums in which popular dissent could be safely enacted.

In the nearly five years that have elapsed since the crackdown, however, the politics of popular music have changed in ways that throw fascinating and complex light on the current political situation in China. Rock music, although it remains on the margins of state-sanctioned culture, can no longer be characterized as an unambiguously counterhegemonic form. Instead, rock music's gradual absorption into China's burgeoning market economy has defused much of its politically oppositional potential, while allowing for the music to extend its cultural influence well beyond the narrow confines of the Beijing subculture from which it originally arose. At the same time, the ideological agenda of rock music has increasingly less to do with its earlier advocacy of cultural and political democratization than as an (inherently problematic) embrace of market economics and nativist politics. In the work of youth cultural icons, such as the heavy metal rock band Tang Dynasty and the pop-rock singer Ai Jing, we see the beginnings of a kind of "commodity nativism" that—rather than providing a vehicle for popular protest—is in many ways *complicit* with the CCP's headlong rush toward the combination of economic liberalization and political authoritarianism that Nicholas Kristof has recently dubbed "Market-Leninism."[3]

Rock Music as Subculture

The emergence of a rock music subculture in China is, of course, a relatively recent phenomenon. Indeed, it could be argued that between 1949 and 1978, popular music as such simply did not exist in mainland China. In the years after the CCP's ascension to power, the mass-mediated popular music produced in the prewar years in urban centers like Shanghai was suppressed in favor of officially sanctioned mass music *(qunzhong yinyue)* and revolutionary song *(geming gequ)* that had less to do with commerce and popular leisure than the marriage of the CCP's ideological imperatives with its bureaucratic control of the mass media. With the institution of Deng Xiaoping's sweeping program of economic reform and "opening to the outside world" in the early 1980s, however, popular music in China underwent a remarkable renaissance. In the early 1980s, China began to import popular music from Taiwan and Hong Kong. By the mid-1980s, China had begun to develop its own state-run popular music industry in response to this influx. At the same time, the state-run song and dance troupes *(gewutuan)*, record companies, and television studios responsible for producing and disseminating what has come to be called *tongsu* music began to be weaned from their reliance on state subsidies. Inevitably, the monolithic dominance of ideological concerns began to be challenged by the imperatives of the market; the fledgling industry began to engage not just in "serving the people" *(wei renmin fuwu)* with propagandistic paeans to the socialist modernization plans but also in "serving the people's money" *(wei renminbi fuwu)* with love songs and dance music based on foreign models.[4] By 1988, the industry had grown strong enough to challenge the dominance of imports from Taiwan and Hong Kong with a new and wildly popular style called the "northwest wind" *(xibei feng)* that grafted a combination of Chinese folk music and disco with lyrical meditations on traditional Chinese culture and the dilemmas posed by China's new era of rapid modernization.

At the same time, a rock music subculture had begun to emerge in Beijing outside of the confines of the mainstream popular music industry. Excluded from the state-controlled mass media and subject to periodic suppression on the part of the CCP, rock musicians like Cui Jian had by 1988 nevertheless managed to establish a significant following among college students, intellectuals, and private entrepreneurs in Beijing, largely by virtue of an underground network of privately owned performance venues and foreign investors. In the liberal political climate of the months before the outbreak of the Tiananmen movement, rock music was allowed to make limited incursions into a wider public realm. Cui Jian's seminal first album, *New Long March Rock (Xin changzheng lushang de yaogun)*, was released by a state-run record company in March of that year and went on to serve as a kind of soundtrack for the Tiananmen movement.

The Tiananmen movement marked a major turning point in the development of rock music in China. Despite a government crackdown on rock music (itself precipitated by the active role many rock musicians had played in the movement), the number of rock bands active in Beijing increased exponentially. Cui Jian, in part because of the countercultural cachet conferred upon him by the association of his music with the student protest, found himself elevated to the status of a youth cultural icon. His fame was further increased by a 1990 national tour, underwritten by the CCP as a means of raising funds for the eleventh Asian Games in Beijing, that was canceled in mid-course when officials discovered that his performances had become volatile occasions for the direct expression of political dissent on the part of his predominantly college-aged fans.

Despite Cui Jian's widespread popularity, the rock scene as a whole remained an essentially subcultural phenomenon as of 1990, one similar in many ways to those common in industrialized Western states as well as Eastern Europe before the upheavals of 1989. Rock musicians and other participants in the rock scene formed a closely knit group of no more than several hundred people who shared a common commitment to the production, consumption, and discussion of music and identified themselves to each other and society at large through distinctive clothing styles, hairstyles, slang, and types of behavior (drug use, sexual activity) that deliberately transgress societal norms.

In the view of most theorists of subcultural phenomena, this sort of rebellion against established norms is largely of a "symbolic" nature.[5] Subcultural groups arise in order to confront socioeconomic problems faced by their participants. Their solutions to these problems, however, are largely of an expressive and symbolic nature; subcultures "provide a pool of available symbolic resources which particular individuals or groups can draw on in their attempt to make sense of their own specific situation and create a viable identity."[6] Rather than engaging in political activism, subcultures wage "semiotic guerilla warfare" at the level of music and fashion: their "rebellion seldom reaches [the level of] articulated opposition."[7]

The rock subculture in Beijing differed from this theoretical model in one important respect.[8] While rock musicians in Beijing disavowed the notion that their music constituted a form of political activism, their activities hinged on a clearly articulated, self-consciously held ideology of *cultural* opposition. The central concern of participants in the rock subculture—as expressed in song lyrics and a series of interviews I conducted in 1990—was the need to rebel against "oppression" *(yayi)*. *Yayi* was conceived of as a cultural problem, as the stifling of individual expression, liberty, and creativity brought about by what was seen as an authoritarian, conformist, and "feudal" cultural tradition. This repudiation of a (however imperfectly understood) Chinese "feudalism," of course, involved a concomitant embrace of nominally "Western" values. Accordingly, Gao Qi, a heavy metal guitarist, framed his discussion of rock music in terms of intergenerational conflict and the struggle of young people to create "viable identities" in an era of rapid modernization and social change:

> *Tongsu* music is written for an older audience. Rock is youth music. . . . Young people need to express themselves. They are in the process of developing their opinions, their identities. . . . In China, we have several thousand years of feudalism, which makes people's thinking all alike, conformist, without individualism. Now, after reform and liberalization, you have a generation of youth that are familiar with all sorts of Western things and Western literature...and this has resulted in a complete cultural transformation. . . . The younger you are, the greater the Western influence. . . . The changes have been so fast that the generation gap is like leaping over thousands of years. And rock belongs to this younger generation.[9]

Gao Qi's emphasis on an anti-traditionalist individualism (and its non-Chinese origins) was echoed by Zhu Xiaomin, lead singer of the (now defunct) Thump Band *(Tutu yuedui):*

> Rock has become an international phenomenon because it's a direct expression of basic human desires, of our unlimited capacities as human beings. Human personality is the same everywhere. Everyone needs to express themselves. . . I don't like Chinese folk songs or *tongsu* music that's based on Chinese folk. All it can express is a closed [*fengbi*], parochial nationalism. If you're singing about China, you can't sing about yourself, about your basic human desires.[10]

This sort of faith in individualism informed every aspect of the rock subculture. The sheer physicality of rock music (itself a form borrowed from the West) was seen as a means of effecting a visceral liberation from cultural norms and of asserting individuality.[11] Rock lyrics also echo this theme: many songs recount a kind of archetypal narrative in which the singers confront and ultimately deliver themselves from the oppression, hypocrisy, and alienation that characterize daily life to a new world of freedom and authenticity. Wei Hua's "Don't Try to Stop Me Again" *(Bie zai shitu zulan wo)* is a typical example:

Don't try to stop me again
Don't use lies to trick me
Don't try to hide the truth from me again
I'll struggle free of these fetters in the end
I don't need your promises, time would go by too slowly
Even if I've suffered, the sun's rays will shine on me in the end[12]

The rock performance, in turn, was conceived of as a space in which—in Cui
Jian's words—rock fans could "feel real freedom" as they came together to
enact a collective ritual of resistance against the "oppression" brought to
bear on them by society at large. These performances, which by 1990 took
place nearly every weekend in bars, hotels, and restaurants throughout
Beijing, afforded rock musicians and fans an opportunity to derive a sense of
affective empowerment in symbolic defiance of the "oppression" of the quo-
tidian social world in which they were embedded.

Rock Music and Youth Culture

This emphasis on rock music as a culturally oppositional subculture, however, is misleading in several different respects. First, in a social and cultural
context as heavily politicized as that of modern China, distinctions between
"symbolic," cultural activism and overt political activism tend to blur. Cui
Jian's claim that he is essentially an apolitical figure, for instance, may strike
many observers as disingenuous. Second, rock music has reached and influenced the political behavior of a far larger audience than its limited subcultural provenance might indicate.

The popularity of rock music (and particularly of Cui Jian) outside of its
subcultural milieu has been inextricably linked with a larger youth culture
centered around college campuses and the urban private sector.[13] When rock
music has been allowed to be featured at large-scale concerts (as with both
Cui Jian's Asian Games Tour and the Modern Music Festival held in Beijing
in March 1990), audiences have been composed largely of students and private entrepreneurs (*getihu*)—some of whom were instrumental in promoting
and financing the music in its earliest stages. Cui Jian has performed repeatedly at schools like Beijing University, and students often explore the bars
and restaurants where rock performances take place. Such excursions became one component of the intellectual ferment of college life in the years
before the Tiananmen uprising, as the student leader Shen Tong observes:

> The 1980s were probably the years when the Chinese people enjoyed the most
> intellectual freedom they had had since the founding of the People's Republic of
> China in 1949. I became more aware of this when I entered Beida [Beijing Univer-
> sity] and discovered that Western influences were everywhere. . . . When my
> friends and I went out to various bars in the city, we heard new bands experiment-
> ing with rock-and-roll.[14]

These kinds of contacts exercised considerable influence on the development of student activism (as well as the emergence of what Geremie Barmé has termed "*liumang* culture," a phenomenon that Saich analyzes in Chapter 12) in the late 1980s.[15] Indeed, the sensibilities and concerns of rock musicians and student activists involved in the Tiananmen democracy movement not only dovetail but are expressed through an almost identical rhetoric; one that takes as its focus the critique of feudalism in Chinese culture.[16] This is strikingly apparent in a speech delivered by one of the most prominent student organizers of the Tiananmen demonstrations, Wuer Kaixi, on the cultural background of the 1989 movement. His statements serve to illustrate the way in which students both used rock songs, such as Cui Jian's "I Have Nothing," as a focal point for their own affective investments and incorporated the insights into their condition gained from the experience of listening to rock into their rhetoric (and, in the case of Tiananmen, into their political activity):

> Chinese culture is feudalistic, despotic, closed [*fengbi*]; it negates the individual, and it has lasted for 5,000 years. . . . After 1949 and during the Cultural Revolution this feudalistic culture developed to such an extreme that it now absolutely and completely negates individuality. With reform and the open door policy, and liberalism in thought and culture under Deng Xiaoping, resistance [to feudalism] erupted with full force. . . . In recent years, Chinese college students have been stressing the individual, the self, and rebelling against all sorts of authority . . . but this idealism and the sense of the individual are contradictory to the reality of present society [so] young people have been left lost and disoriented. The people who are most influential among young people are not [the prominent dissidents] Fang Lizhi and Wei Jingsheng, but . . . singers such as Cui Jian. His "I Have Nothing" . . . serves to reflect the sense of loss and the disorientation of Chinese youth.[17]

This set of ideas appears to be nearly identical to those expressed by the keyboard player of the Breathing Band, Dong Dong:

> China is afflicted by feudalism, by conservatism and close-mindedness [*fengbi*]. The feudal powers [*fengjian shili*] oppose rock music. Feudal power comes out of blind obedience to Confucian ideals, and relationships between people in society. The open door policy is one way to solve this, but it has been only superficial. People have learned some foreign technologies, but they're still psychologically feudal, and their social circles are still feudal. Even some of the rock musicians' long hair is a sign of this superficial approach to Westernization. We don't want to change the world, but we do want to challenge feudalism with a kind of spiritual liberalization [*jingshen shang de kaifang*], to help each individual solve these problems on a psychological level, through individual freedom.[18]

Clearly, there is only a fine line between the rhetoric of Dong Dong's brand of cultural activism and the more explicitly politicized objectives of student activists. The political goals of student activists who took part in planning the Tiananmen movement echo the cultural critique of rock musicians and, especially, the sense of intergenerational conflict expressed previously by Gao Qi. Shen Tong relates a discussion held by a group of student activists several months before the outbreak of the Tiananmen movement that sheds light on this point:

China doesn't need a movement for national salvation ... what China needs
now is personal liberation. What our generation needs to do is push for individual
freedom.[19]

What, then, accounts for the similarity of the individualist, antifeudalist
rhetoric shared by rock devotees and college students? One important link
between the two groups is the mass media. College students and rock musicians have listened to the same *tongsu* music, watched the same films, and
read many of the same books, magazines, and newspapers. Each group acknowledges the influence of Western popular music, literature, and art on the
development of their generation's sensibilities. Perhaps the single most important link, however, was Su Xiaokang and Wang Luxiang's influential television miniseries, *He Shang* (River Elegy), which presented an attack on the
despotism and conservatism of Chinese culture through a "deconstruction"
of cherished national symbols—like the Great Wall—to a nationwide audience in 1988.[20] Su posits the Yellow River as a symbol of a culture that has
died young, arguing that China must abandon an irretrievably flawed tradition (embodied by the landlocked loess plains of northwest China at the
source of the river) and turn its attention outward to the economically vibrant, "seafaring" southeast coast, and by extension, the modern West. The
final scene of the series presents an image of the Yellow River pouring out
into the sea, as a narrator advocates continued economic reform, cultural
openness, and political democratization.[21]

Many analysts, including contributors to this volume such as Calhoun
(Chapter 4), draw attention to the impact that *River Elegy* had on the protesters in 1989. Dru Gladney has even argued, quite persuasively, that the film's
celebration of student activism, and its implicit advocacy of a political democracy characterized by dialogue and "transparency," had a formative influence on the way in which the Tiananmen movement unfolded.[22]

The influence of *River Elegy* on the ideological positions of rock musicians
was considerably less direct. Fittingly, *River Elegy* engaged the imagination of
rock musicians not as a political agenda but as a way in which to understand
and discuss the ostensible "feudalism" of Chinese culture and rock's own an-
tifeudal stance. Rock musicians often speak of their music in terms of the
temporal and geographical axes (from feudal Chinese tradition to Western
modernity—from the stagnant northwestern plains to the vibrant south-
eastern coast and the ocean) along which the writers of *River Elegy* structured
their critique of Chinese culture. When asked "How would you define
Chinese rock?" several interviewees unhesitatingly prefaced their responses
with, "China has a five-thousand-year-old tradition of feudalism. ... "[23] Each
interviewee went on to interpret rock music as a manifestation of a conflict
between feudalism and modernity. Again, their language echoed that of *River
Elegy*: Feudal culture is "landlocked/closed" (*fengbi*), while rock music is
"liberalized/open" (*kaifang*). Cui Jian's own assessment of the cultural function and value of rock music, for instance, relies on a metaphor that quite
obviously derives from the film:

Chinese history and Chinese culture are very long and very rich. But right now our culture is like a river without an exit, without a way out to the ocean. The river's moving, but we don't know where it's heading. What we want to do is find a way to release this river, to find an outlet for it, to let it flow into the ocean, and join with the world outside China. We want to create a new culture, a culture that isn't parochial and closed in on itself.[24]

Many rock musicians did actively support both this 'culturalist' agenda and the more explicitly political objectives of the student activists with whom they shared a common rhetoric through their participation in the Tiananmen movement. Even so, it is important to remember that their role in the protests remained peripheral. Rock musicians did not necessarily share the commitment of student activists to engage in direct political action.[25] Cui Jian claims that rock is a means to make people "*feel* real freedom," not to institute political reform.[26] The distinction is important, even when the realms of cultural and political activism did overlap, as when musicians like Cui Jian and the punk rocker He Yong performed protest anthems at Tiananmen Square to hunger-striking students.[27]

Political Uses of Rock

Meaning in popular music is mercurial. The ideological agenda of rock musicians, although certainly an important factor in shaping both the ways commentators have discussed the significance of the rock scene and the ways audiences have responded to it, can hardly be said to be decisive. Audiences are free to (mis) interpret, enjoy, and make use (political or otherwise) of a pop song in any number of different ways, regardless of authorial intent. Rock songs and rock performances have been utilized by students and other fans both as a means for affective empowerment, cultural critique, *and* as a conduit for explicitly political protest.

Cui Jian's "I Have Nothing" is a salient example, for it is the most popular song to have emerged from the rock subculture into a wider youth cultural realm. The song's lyrics are as follows:

I've asked tirelessly, when will you go with me?
But you just always laugh at my having nothing
I've given you my dreams, given you my freedom
But you always just laugh at my having nothing

Oh! When will you go with me?
Oh! When will you go with me?

The earth under my feet is on the move,
The water by my side is flowing on,
But you always just laugh at my having nothing
Why haven't you laughed your fill?
Why will I always search?
Could it be that before you I will always have nothing?

Oh! When will you go with me?
Oh! When will you go with me?

The earth under my feet is on the move
The water by my side is flowing on

I'm telling you I've waited a long time
I'm telling you my very last demand
I need to grab both your hands
Only then will you go with me
That's when your hands will tremble
That's when your tears will flow
Can it be that you're telling me you love my having nothing?

Oh, only then will you go with me
Oh, only then will you go with me[28]

"I Have Nothing," as with rock music in general, primarily works for its fans "on the affective level of [their] everyday lives, at the level of the strategies [they] use to gain some control over that affective life, to find new forms of pleasure and excitement, or to cope with new forms of pain, frustration, and boredom."[29] One college student at Cui Jian's Asian Games Tour concert in Xi'an expressed the song's power in this way:

When you sing it over and over again, you will learn how to be confident despite hard times, how to awaken yourself from stagnation. You will realize your self-worth after having followed a difficult road.[30]

Another concertgoer relates that, "when we sing this song, we don't feel ashamed of having nothing anymore."[31] This sort of reaction, of course, tallies with what rock musicians characterized as the central aim of their music.

The intensity of listeners' reactions to "I Have Nothing," however, often had less to do with individual empowerment than political protest. Interpretations of the lyrics, of course, inevitably vary from listener to listener. A Beijing city official may see the song as a mystifying and subversive denial of the benefits conferred upon China's youth by socialism. Others might hear the story of a love affair between a poverty-stricken young man and a snobbish, rich woman. Despite this ambiguity, or perhaps because of it, many listeners and critics read the text in terms of political allegory. Tim Brace has suggested that readers of the song lyrics try a simple test: for every "I" substitute a "we," and for every "you," think of the Communist Party.[32] Read in this light, the song becomes an ironic response to the Chinese lyrics of the "Internationale" (Guoji ge), a socialist anthem whose ubiquity in Chinese everyday life is second only to that of the national anthem:

Slaves rise up, rise up!
We cannot say that we have nothing [yiwu suoyou]
We will be masters of all under heaven[33]

The substitution of "we" for "I" makes implicit sense both in terms of the politicization that has surrounded Chinese popular music since its inception and in the way in which we enjoy pop music. Much of the pleasure of listening to popular music results from identifying our own passions with those of the singer. This identification, of course, links us not only with the performer but with the other members of the audience—with a community of shared feeling. The singer's "I" becomes *our* "I." Our "I's," in turn, merge with a collective "we." Cui Jian denies that the song addresses the government, that "I Have Nothing" is equivalent to "we have no freedom and democracy." On the streets of Beijing and Hong Kong, however, the use of the song as a marching chant in the spring of 1989 demonstrated that his objections may well have been beside the point.

In the months after the crackdown, moreover, rock music continued to serve as a rallying point for participants in China's urban youth culture. Audiences, cognizant of the music's oppositional cultural stance and its association with the democracy movement, often utilized rock concerts as an opportunity to publicly and vocally show their discontent with the regime. The following description of Cui Jian's 1990 Asian Games benefit show in Beijing, written by an anonymous rock music fan, is both a testament to the sense of political empowerment that fans derive from rock music performances and revealing of the political volatility that led the CCP to cancel Cui's tour. Much of the poignance of this particular performance lay in the fact that it took place only months after the crackdown at Tiananmen Square:

> In order to raise money for the 11th Asian Games, even this guy has been allowed to give a performance. Nowadays his songs are full of a kind of decadent mood, and he has been prevented from giving many concerts. But yesterday he challenged the authorities again. He sang a forbidden song when the audience encouraged him with passionate applause. He tied a red cloth over his eyes, and his guitarist gagged himself with a red cloth as well. What did this mean? Of course, everyone in Beijing knew exactly what it meant! Most of the audience of 15,000 people rose to their feet. It was so exciting, just like that *other* unbelievable day and night [that is, June 3–4, 1989].[34]

Rock After Tiananmen

In the five years since the crackdown, Chinese rock musicians have been engaged in a sort of ideological cat-and-mouse game with CCP authorities. Rock music remains largely excluded from television and radio. Restrictions on performance remain tight, especially in Beijing, where rock shows have been banned for the entire month of June every year since 1990, presumably because officials fear that they will provide audiences with an opportunity to commemorate the anniversary of the June Fourth Massacre. Even so, rock music cassettes (almost all of which have been produced by Hong Kong and Taiwanese record companies because of a lack of domestic support) are openly sold at state-run audiovisual outlets, largely because domestic record industry officials are eager to "serve the people's money" and capitalize on the market potential of the form. In addition, rock is increasingly disseminated throughout the provinces through media over which the authorities have little or no control. Rock music videos, produced by foreign investors, air on the Hong Kong based Star TV cable network, to which many urban households have access, either through satellite dishes or bootleg videotapes. Bootleg cassettes have also become common. Many rock bands, finally, have taken to circumventing performance restrictions in the capital by simply playing in provincial cities in which officials are less wont to enforce government sanctions against the music.

Perhaps the most significant change that has occurred, though, involves what Geremie Barmé has termed the "compradorization of the Chinese avant-garde."[35] In order to make a living and achieve commercial success in a restrictive and sometimes hostile domestic climate, rock musicians have been forced to rely almost exclusively on the financial support of offshore investors from Hong Kong and Taiwan. As a result, mainland rock music is both "imported home" by way of Star TV and companies like Taiwan's Rock Records *and* exported abroad to Hong Kong and Taiwan. Ironically though, the music's principal market is abroad, largely because the domestic market is saturated by Hong Kong and Taiwanese imports.[36] These economic circumstances, as I argue later, have had much to do with the gradual abandonment of an oppositional cultural politics on the part of many rock musicians in Beijing.

Subcultural expressions of dissent of the sort I outlined in the preceding sections do continue to play an important role in rock music. "Beijing Rock" *(Yaogun Beijing)*, a domestic compilation of rock music released in the summer of 1993, is a case in point.[37] Many of the values espoused by rock musicians in 1990 are in prominent evidence here: singers like Wei Hua, the Women's Band *(Nuzi dui)*, and Black Panther *(Heibao)* rebelliously call for individual liberty, attack hypocrisy, and sing of the virtues of authentic self-expression. Wang Yong, formerly a Cui Jian collaborator, contributes a song, "Requiem March" *(Anhun jinxingqu)*, that is a thinly veiled tribute to the victims of the democracy movement:

> . . . Tears of terror streamed from your frightened eyes
> Future ideals rang from your lips
> Now dead souls sing, awaiting your arrival
> And the living grieve as they see you off
> Rest in peace, come back to life . . .[38]

Commodity Nativism

The packaging notes for the cassette, however, reflect a new awareness of rock's status as a commodity pitted in direct competition with a massive influx of Hong Kong and Taiwanese imports. Its attempt to frame how consumers should react to the product at hand also reflects the ongoing commodification of the music: rather than emphasizing the potentially volatile realm of performance that was once the focal point of the rock subculture, the copywriter dwells on the pleasures of private consumption:

[This tape] will also answer a question you've probably never thought about before—where can I find music which fuses artistry, intelligence, and commercial
potential, and that's been created and produced by we mainland Chinese [*dalu ziji
chuangzao, ziji zhizuo*]? Flip open your tape player and let the forceful sound of
rock music reverberate through your personal space *(ni de kongjian)*.

This assertion of nativist sentiment ("we mainland Chinese")—itself quite
foreign to the kind of internationalist, individualist sensibility routinely
voiced by rock musicians in 1990—is echoed by several of the songs included
on the tape, both in terms of lyrics and musical style. Several songs incorporate traditional Chinese instruments into arrangements that in all other respects mirror those of their Anglo-American counterparts. Wang Yong's "Requiem March" concludes with a Buddhist chant recited by a local monk. The
heavy metal band Again sets a Song Dynasty song-lyric *(ci)* by Xin Qiji
to wailing electric guitars. Gao Qi, fronting a new band called Overload
(Chaozai), sings a paean to peasant revolt called "Ancestors."

These nods to traditional culture are part of a larger effort on the part of
many rock musicians in Beijing to create "rock and roll with Chinese characteristics" *(you Zhongguo tese de yaogun yue)*.[39] The rock subculture is closely
knit and characterized by a remarkably high degree of intellectual self-con-
sciousness. Musicians frequently discuss and debate the nature and function
of the "cultural phenomenon" that their music represents. Over the course of
a month I spent researching the rock scene in Beijing in June 1992, those informal debates repeatedly and urgently returned to the vexed question of how
(and whether) rock musicians could convey a distinctly Chinese sensibility
by way of a foreign musical form. Often, these discussions were framed in
terms reminiscent of the late Qing reformer Zhang Zhidong's argument that
China must pair *ti* (Chinese essence) with *yong* (Western practices) in order to
regain parity with the West:

A few years ago, everybody [in the scene] was excited by rock music, just by the
form *(xingshi)* itself. But now we need to discover how to use the form to create
something of our own. We're moving from form to content *(neirong)*. Instead of
just borrowing a Western form, we need to make music that's based on Chinese
life.[40]

These debates were undergirded by the notion that Chinese and Western culture are fundamentally and intractably different. Lao Wu, lead guitarist for
Tang Dynasty, explains the band's use of traditional Chinese instruments and
imagery in terms of cultural essentialism:

Rock is based on the blues, and we can never play the blues as well as an American. It's just not in our blood. We can imitate it, but eventually we'll have to go
back to the music we grew up with, to traditional Chinese music, to folk music.[41]

In some cases, finally, the desire to reclaim Chinese tradition was expressed in terms of a nativist cultural agenda that represents nothing less
than a negation of the *River Elegy*-esque rhetoric current in 1989. Although

the rhetorical vehemence with which Yang Jun, lyricist and artistic director for Tang Dynasty, advocates a nativist return to traditional roots is atypical, his ideas are instructive as to the kinds of dilemmas faced by Chinese rock musicians as a whole:

> I've been westernized almost my whole life. I spent twenty years absorbing any-thing Western that I could get my hands on. I never knew anything about my own tradition. And now I really hate anything from the West. I resent its influence . . . modern Chinese culture has never lived up to the tradition because it's been ruined by all the Western influence. We have to get back to our roots, "back to the Tang dynasty" [quoting from a song by Tang Dynasty]. That's the only way we can revitalize our nation and our culture. That's what the mission of this cultural phe-nomenon [rock music] should be all about.[42]

Yang Jun's comments, of course, reveal many of the paradoxes inherent to any such "mission." Chinese rock musicians are, almost by definition, a cre-ation of "Western influence," and Chinese rock is necessarily a hybrid form.

The rationale behind having named the band Tang Dynasty—as explained to me by Zhang Ju, the band's bass player—is itself an effort to symbolically reconcile these paradoxes. On the one hand, the Tang dynasty represents the apex of traditional Chinese civilization. On the other, its capital, Chang'an, was characterized by its cosmopolitanism and openness to cultural influ-ences (and particularly exotic new forms of popular music) arriving from Central Asia and the Middle East. These themes shape much of the band's work: its eponymous domestic debut fuses heavy metal, Xinjiangese folk har-mony, and traditional Chinese instrumentation. In songs like "A Dream Re-turn to the Tang Dynasty" *(Meng hui tangchao)*, nativist sentiments are con-veyed through lyrics written in a pastiche of ersatz classical and modern Chinese:

> Chrysanthemum, ancient sword, and wine
> Percolate like coffee into the hubbub of the courtyard
> The stranger from abroad pays homage to the moon at the Altar of the Sun
> The splendor of the ancients enchants us
>
> Wind—cannot blow away our grievances
> Flowers—cannot color over our longing for home
> Snow—cannot reflect the mountain stream
> Moon—cannot fulfill the ancient dream
>
> Following the patterns on my palm
> Branded there by fate
> Following fate I fall into a trance
> In dream I return to the Tang dynasty[43]

Here, the geographical axes of the *River Elegy* argument are reversed. Rather than a flawed and peripheral nation that must flow out to the sea in order to redeem itself, we are presented with a "central kingdom" to which foreigners "pay homage." This fantastic vision of Chinese dominance, however, is inev-itably disrupted by the specter of China's debasement at the hands of contemporary reality. The "splendor" of Tang times is only a dream, and the dreamer is left only with "grievances" and "longing."

Although "A Dream Return to the Tang Dynasty" can hardly be characterized as a coherent ideological message, the presence of nativist discourse in contemporary Chinese music may well indicate the emergence of, in Edward Friedman's phrase, "strong shoots of a new nationalism . . . breaking up out of the old discredited [anti-imperialist nationalism], producing a new identity holding the promise of a better future for all Chinese, though not necessarily a democratic future."[44]

The final point is an important one, for while the band strongly disclaims that their music has anything to do with politics, their cultural agenda is in many ways complicit with the CCP's post-Tiananmen market-oriented authoritarianism. As many commentators have noted, in the absence of the Maoist ideological glue that once supported the regime, the CCP has increasingly sought to mobilize the nationalistic sentiments of its citizenry in an effort to maintain a measure of legitimacy. This trend is perhaps most vividly exemplified by the massive propaganda campaigns and barrages of nationalist rhetoric accompanying both China's sponsorship of the Asian Games in 1990 and its (unsuccessful) campaign to win for itself the honor of hosting the 2000 Olympics in Beijing.

The extent to which commerce and nativism are intertwined in the work of Tang Dynasty is also emblematic of the politics of China's increasingly market-driven, export-oriented economy. The band is an avowedly commercial venture, and in this light, its nativism (displayed visually through videos filmed in traditional settings, cover art featuring traditional calligraphy, and even their penchant for wearing topknots and Tibetan jewelry onstage) is perhaps less an ideological stance than a marketing device, one designed to differentiate the band from its slick, eminently contemporary Hong Kong and Taiwanese competition both at home and abroad.[45] This interpretation is shored up by the kind of commercial discourse that has come to surround rock music in recent years. Barmé, for instance, cites a 1991 *China Youth News* article that implores the government to tolerate rock music, if only because it alone can prevent the inundation of the mainland market by Hong Kong and Cantonese pop.[46] There is not just a little irony here: an oppositional subculture based on an Anglo-American musical form that originally sprang from a repudiation of traditional Chinese culture is nationalistically invoked in the official press as a domestic alternative to foreign products.

Toward 1997

I want to close with a song that in many ways provides a complex summation of the politics of popular music in post-Tiananmen China. Ai Jing's "My 1997" was perhaps the most popular song to emerge from the rock subculture in 1993, selling well over 50,000 copies in the mainland alone within a month of having been released.[47] The song—like Cui Jian's "I Have Nothing" before it—is a remarkable example of the way in which a popular music fuses individual desires and national concerns, and in doing so, provides its listeners with opportunities for affective empowerment and (if only symbolic) political protest.[48] Ai Jing's song, though, is less a tale about having nothing than about *wanting everything.* Ai Jing's personal narrative—set to chiming, folksy guitars and the pluck of a three-stringed Chinese lute *(sanxian)*—is an ambiguous political act, one that both subtly impugns Chinese communism and satirically embraces Chinese nationalism as it (quite literally) maps the contours of a new China transfigured by rapid political change and commodity economics:

> My music teacher was my papa
> He's been working in a state-run factory for twenty years now
> My mother used to sing northern style opera
> She always sighs that she never saw good times
> When I was little I won prizes for singing
> My two sisters wanted to be just like me
> When I was seventeen I left my home town Shenyang
> Because I sensed that I wouldn't find my dreams there
> I came all alone to the unfamiliar city of Beijing
> And joined the famous Eastern Song and Dance Troupe led by Wang Hun
> Really, I loved those days in art school best of all
> But my teachers probably don't feel that way
>
> Making a living with my voice wasn't so bad
> I sang my way down to the Shanghai Bund
> And from Shanghai, I sang my way down to the South for which I had longed
> I spent a long time in Guangzhou
> Because my boyfriend lives in Hong Kong
>
> When will I get to go to Hong Kong? What are people like in Hong Kong?
> He can come to Shenyang, but I can't go to Hong Kong
>
> Hong Kong, Hong Kong, Hong Kong, Xiao Hou says I should check it out
> Hong Kong, Hong Kong, what's so fragrant about the fragrant harbor?
> I hear that it's Cui Jian's biggest market
> Let me go see that brilliant world, put a big red stamp on my passport
>
> Come quick 1997! What's it really like to shop at Yaohan?
> Come quick 1997! Then I can go to Hong Kong!
> Come quick 1997! Let me stand on the stage of Hunghom Auditorium!
> Come quick 1997! He'll take me to the night markets!
> Come quick 1997! What kind of clothes do they sell at Yaohan?
> Come quick 1997! Then I can go to Hong Kong . . .[49]

In closing, it is worth noting two things that illustrate how quickly artistic themes can be overtaken by events in contemporary China: Yaohan Department Store has recently opened branches in Beijing and Shanghai, and the cover art that accompanies Ai Jing's recording shows the singer enjoying the sights of Hong Kong's Lam Kwai Fong district.

Notes

1. By popular music, I indicate music that is disseminated through the mass media, sold as a commodity, and has its roots in the acculturation of Western musical forms. Liang Maochun provides an excellent summary of the development of popular music in China in his "Dui woguo liuxing yinyue lishi sikao" (Reflections on the history of Chinese popular music), *Renmin yinyue*, vol. 7 (1988), pp. 32–34. See also my own *Like a Knife: Ideology and Genre in Contemporary Chinese Popular Music* (Ithaca: Cornell East Asia Series, 1992), pp. 9–18.

2. The student leader Wuer Kaixi, as Lee Feigon has already noted (Chapter 5), claims that Cui Jian's influence on the students participating in the movement far outstripped that of political dissidents like Fang Lizhi. See "Chinese Writers Under Fire: The Struggle for Human Rights in China," in *PEN American Center Newsletter*, no. 70 (December 1989), p. 15.

3. Nicholas Kristof, "China Dumping Communism in Headlong Pursuit of Profit," *San Francisco Chronicle*, September 7, 1993.

4. Editors of *Yinyue Yanjiu*, "Tan liuxing yinyue" (Discussing popular music), *Yinyue yanjiu*, vol. 2 (1988), p. 23.

5. Dick Hebdige, *Subculture: The Meaning of Style* (London: Routledge, 1987), p. 92.

6. Michael Brake, *Comparative Youth Culture: The Sociology of Youth Culture and Youth Subcultures in America, Britain, and Canada* (London and New York: Routledge and Kegan Paul, 1985), p. 27.

7. Brake, *Comparative Youth Culture*, p. 8.

8. The following conclusions are based on a series of more than twenty interviews I conducted with participants in the Beijing rock scene in the summer of 1990.

9. Interview with Gao Qi, July 20, 1990.

10. Interview with Zhu Xiaomin, July 19, 1990.

11. Cui Jian makes this point in Ping Fang and Ma Mu, "Yiwu suoyou: Zhongguo yaogun gexing Cui Jian" (I have nothing: Chinese rock star Cui Jian), *Xiju shijie*, vols. 3–4 (1990), p. 6.

12. Wei Hua, lead singer of Breathing *(Huxi yuedui)*, is notable for the fact that she became a rock singer after having been fired from her post as an English-language newscaster at CCTV after having reported sympathetically on the student movement in 1989. Lyrics by Wei Hua and Gao Qi, included on Wei Hua, *Taiyang sheng* [The sun rises], RCA/BMG Pacific 8–280048, 1990. For more examples of rock lyrics, see Jones, *Like a Knife*, pp. 155–63.

13. By youth culture, I indicate the sensibilities and leisure patterns (consumption of music, literature, etc.) of young people who have not distanced themselves from the mainstream in terms of their institutional affiliations, lifestyles, or aspirations. Subculture is distinct from youth culture in that its participants have largely divorced themselves from the mainstream. Tom Gold discusses the culture of the urban private sector in his "Guerilla Interviewing Among the *Getihu*," in Perry Link, Richard Madsen, and Paul G. Pickowicz, eds., *Unofficial China: Popular Culture and Thought in the People's Republic* (Boulder: Westview Press, 1989).

14. Shen Tong and Marianne Ye, *Almost A Revolution* (Boston: Houghton Mifflin, 1990), p. 113.

15. *Liumang* literally means "hoodlum" but is used by Geremie Barmé as a kind of rubric for the culture of China's urban, Bohemian fringe (artists, unemployed youth, private entrepreneurs, rebellious students, etc.). See his "Wang Shuo and *Liumang* ('Hooligan') Culture," *Australian Journal of Chinese Affairs*, 28 (July 1992).

16. Unfortunately, I have been unable to find any materials that would confirm whether or not this is true of the *getihu* as well. As is well known, many private entrepreneurs played a role both in bankrolling the movement and in street protests.

17. Wuer Kaixi, transcript of panel discussion, "Chinese Writers Under Fire: The Struggle for Human Rights in China," in *PEN American Center Newsletter*, no. 70 (December 1989), p. 19.

18. Interview with Dong Dong, Beijing, June 21, 1990.

19. Shen Tong, p. 150.

20. Alice De Jong presents a detailed account of the film's production and reception in "The Demise of the Dragon: Backgrounds to the Chinese Film *River Elegy*," *China Information*, vol. 4, no. 3 (Winter 1989–90), pp. 28–43. A transcript of the program is contained in Su Xiaokang and Wang Luxiang, *Heshang* (Hong Kong: Joint Publishing Company, 1988) and translated into English by Richard W. Bodman and Pin P. Wan as *Deathsong of the River: A Reader's Guide to the Chinese TV Series* Heshang (Ithaca: Cornell East Asia Program, 1991).

21. Su and Wang, *Heshang* transcript, pp. 109–11.

22. Dru Gladney, lecture on "Tiananmen: Retrospection and Mediation," New England China Seminar, Harvard University, March 20, 1990. *River Elegy* included footage of the epochal May 4, 1919, student movement, as well as shots of the student demonstrations for democracy that swept across many major Chinese cities in the winter of 1986–87. In addition, the film included a short segment on the use of hunger strikes as a political weapon—a method that, before Tiananmen, had never been employed by activists in China.

23. As in interviews with Cui Jian, Dong Dong, Gao Qi, and Zhu Xiaomin in Beijing, June–July, 1990.

24. Cui Jian, as interviewed in the television documentary *China Rocks: The Long March of Cui Jian* (BBC–TV, dir. Greg Lanning, 1991).

25. Some—including several members of the heavy metal bands Tang Dynasty and Black Panther—claim to have been either indifferent or opposed to the movement. Personal interviews with Zhang Ju and Li Tong, Beijing, June 3 and 12, 1992.

26. BBC–TV interview with Cui Jian.

27. He Yong's most notorious song, "Garbage Dump" (*Laji chang*) likens Chinese culture to a garbage dump and a slaughterhouse and urges listeners to "tear it down!" Cui Jian performed a song called "Opportunists" (*Touji fenzi*) that was written on the occasion of the outbreak of the student movement and urges young people to "show our strength" and "voice our desires." Interestingly, one English-language article quotes a source suggesting that Cui Jian was "used as a pawn by student leaders" and abruptly cut short his performance at Tiananmen because he was disgusted "by all the bullshit that was going down." See Hans Ebert, "Cui Jian's Rock Resonates in Hearts of China's Youth," *Billboard*, May 9, 1991.

28. Cui Jian, *Xin changzheng lushang de yaogun*.

29. Lawrence Grossberg, "Rock and Roll in Search of an Audience," in James Lull, ed., *Popular Music and Communication* (Newbury Park, Calif.: Sage Publications, 1987), p. 186.

30. Ping Fang and Ma Mu, "Yiwu suoyou," p. 6.

31. Ibid. These comments reiterate almost verbatim those of Gu Tu in a *People's Daily* article of July 16, 1988. Whether Ping Fang and Ma Mu have simply plagiarized that article, or fans have internalized the critical discourse on Cui Jian, is unclear.

32. Tim Brace, "Popular Music in Contemporary Beijing: Modernism and Cultural Identity," *Asian Music*, 2 (Spring/Summer 1991), p. 63.

33. "Guoji ge," as performed by the China Broadcast Arts Troupe Symphony Orchestra, on *Zhonghua renmin gongheguo guoge, guoji ge* [The national anthem of the People's Republic of China and the Internationale], Zhongguo changpian gongsi HL–314, 1984.

34. Personal communication, March 1990. These comments were made "off the record."

35. See Barmé, "The Greying of Chinese Culture," in Kuan Hsin-chi and Maurice Brosseau, eds., *China Review 1992* (Hong Kong: Chinese University Press, 1992).

36. In 1989, for instance, nine of the ten top-selling records in Shanghai were imported from Hong Kong and Taiwan. For a detailed report of market conditions for Taiwan and Hong Kong singers in the mainland, see Gu Biling, Luo Rulan, and Zhou Ping'er, "Gang-tai qunxing shanyao Shenzhen: liang di yanyi wenhua fengmo dalu" [Hong Kong and Taiwan stars shine in the mainland], *Zhongguo shibao zhoukan*, February 16–22, 1992, pp. 66–67.

37. The cassette was produced and distributed by the Tianjin Audio-Visual Company (Tianjin yinxiang youxian gongsi), a state-run record company.

38. Music and lyrics by Wang Yong.

39. This effort was one of the primary concerns of many of the rock musicians (including Tang Dynasty and Dou Wei of the band Dreaming) I spoke with in Beijing in June 1992. The phrase itself is in common usage among rock musicians in Beijing and derives from the official CCP injunction that China must build a "modern socialist civilization with Chinese characteristics."

40. Interview with Dou Wei, June 8, 1992.

41. Interview with Lao Wu of Tang Dynasty, June 3, 1992.

42. Interview with Yang Jun, He Yong, and Li Tong, June 12, 1992.

43. The record was released simultaneously in Hong Kong, Taiwan, and the mainland by Taiwan's Rock Records in late 1992. Music and lyrics by Tang Dynasty. Translated by Kaiser Kuo.

44. Edward Friedman, "A Failed Chinese Modernity," *Daedalus* (Spring 1993), pp. 1–2.

45. This is seemingly not an isolated trend, but a consciously adopted marketing policy on the part of Rock Records. A recent compilation of Chinese rock—intended primarily for the Taiwan market—capitalizes on nativist images by billing itself as "China Fire" and featuring guitar-wielding Chinese swordsmen in traditional livery galloping across the cover.

46. Barmé, "Official Bad Boys or True Rebels?" Human Rights Tribune, vol. 3, no. 4 (1992), p. 20.

47. Tang Dynasty's debut, by way of contrast, has sold only ten thousand copies.

48. The song also provided an opportunity for outrage and alarm on the part of several Hong Kong newspaper columnists.

49. From Ai Jing, *Wode 1997* (My 1997) (Taipei: Rock Records RD 1187, 1992). Lyrics by Ai Jing, music by Ai Jing and Eddie Ramdriampionana.

Part Four

CULTURAL DILEMMAS AND POLITICAL ROLES OF THE INTELLIGENTSIA

The three contributors to this section are all historians whose work to date has tended to focus on three very different types of intellectuals. Schwarcz is best known for her studies of radicals who came of age during the May Fourth Movement but later had trouble reconciling themselves to ruling parties that claimed to be committed to the goals of that struggle. Cheek's previous publications have usually focused on the lives and activities of propagandists and other "establishment intellectuals" who have been ready and willing to serve the needs of Chinese Leninist regimes, at least up to a point. And MacKinnon has written a great deal about various Chinese and Western journalists whose lives became entwined with (and whose writings shaped popular images of) the Revolution. Building on their earlier studies, the chapters these three authors contribute here use discussion of the politics of public and private memory, the ties between intellectuals and the state, and the relationship between Chinese and foreign journalists, respectively, to place the contemporary predicaments of the intelligentsia into historical perspective. The supplementary materials in the list that follows range from works that examine the views of specific intellectual figures involved in the events of 1989 to theoretical and comparative works that focus on the central role that journalists and mass circulation newspapers have played in the rise of nationalism and the outbreak of revolution in various parts of the world.

Recommended Supplementary Materials for Classroom Use

Scholarship on China: Contemporary Politics

Barmé, Geremie. "Travelling Heavy: The Intellectual Baggage of the Chinese Diaspora." *Problems of Communism* (January–April 1991), pp. 94–112. A discussion of

1989 that highlights the views of Liu Xiaobo and other intellectuals who were critical of the Deng regime but were also wary of or explicitly criticized certain features of the mass movement.

Bonnin, Michel, and Yves Chevrier. "The Intellectual and the State: Social Dynamics of Intellectual Autonomy during the Post-Mao Era." *China Quarterly*, 127 (September 1991), pp. 569–613. An essay on the changing relations between the intelligentsia and the Deng regime up to and immediately after 1989.

Dirlik, Arif, and Maurice Meisner, eds. *Marxism and the Chinese Experience*. Armonk, N.Y.: M. E. Sharpe, 1989. A multidisciplinary collection that includes works on both historical and contemporary topics; some of the chapters most relevant to Part 4 include an essay on the work of a contemporary feminist literary figure (by Roxann Prazniak), and an essay that analyzes Fang Lizhi's conception of "democracy" (by Richard C. Kraus); different parts of the book could also be used effectively in conjunction with other thematic parts of this volume.

Link, Perry. *Evening Chats in Beijing: Probing China's Predicament*. New York: W. W. Norton, 1992. Based on extended conversations with a wide range of intellectuals, this work explores issues ranging from the most basic daily life concerns to conceptions of patriotism as seen through the eyes of Beijing academics and writers.

Schell, Orville. *Discos and Democracy: China in the Throes of Reform*. New York: Pantheon, 1988. A work of reportage and analysis that focuses much of its attention on the lives, writings, and public activities of prominent intellectual figures, such as Fang Lizhi, Liu Binyan, and Wang Ruowang.

Scholarship on China: Historical Perspectives

Lee, Leo Ou-fan. "Modernity and Its Discontents: The Cultural Agenda of the May Fourth Movement." In Kenneth Lieberthal et al., eds., *Perspectives on Modern China: Four Anniversaries* (Armonk, N.Y.: M. E. Sharpe, 1991), pp. 158–177. A reconsideration of the legacy of the New Culture Movement; this article was written by a leading literary critic who has done work on everything from journalism to the fiction of Lu Xun.

Lin Yutang. *A History of the Press and Public Opinion in China*. New York: Greenwood, 1968—reprint of 1936 edition. A work by a leading Chinese intellectual of an earlier era; Lin touches upon issues ranging from censorship during the Nationalist era to intelligentsia petition drives that took place centuries before the Qing dynasty came to power.

Rankin, Mary. *Early Chinese Revolutionaries: Radical Intellectuals in Shanghai and Chekiang, 1902–1911*. Cambridge: Harvard University Press, 1971. Rankin analyzes the political writings, organizational activities, and social networks of an important group of intelligentsia opponents of Qing rule.

Schwartz, Benjamin, ed. *Reflections on the May 4th Movement: A Symposium*. Cambridge: Harvard University Press, 1972. A collection of essays that explores different aspects of the New Culture Movement of the late 1910s and 1920s and the intelligentsia-led protests of 1919.

Spence, Jonathan. *The Gate of Heavenly Peace: The Chinese and Their Revolution, 1895–1980*. New York: Viking, 1981. A survey that weaves a series of life histories of prominent intellectuals into a narrative of modern Chinese history.

Comparative Works and Case Studies of Other Countries

Anderson, Benedict. *Imagined Communities: Reflections on the Origin and Spread of Nationalism*. London: Verso, 1983. A study of nationalism by a political scientist deeply concerned with cultural issues; Anderson stresses, among many other things, the important roles that intellectual elites and mass circulation newspapers play in the construction of modern forms of national identity.

Bourdieu, Pierre. "The Corporatism of the Universal: The Role of Intellectuals in the Modern World." *Telos* (Fall 1989), pp. 99–110. An essay on the political functions of the intelligentsia by a prominent French theorist.

Havel, Vaclav, et al. *The Power of the Powerless.* Edited by John Keane and introduced by Steven Lukes. Armonk, N.Y.: M. E. Sharpe, 1990. A series of essays by East European dissidents; many of the essays focus on the important roles that intellectuals can play in legitimating or undermining the legitimacy of state socialist regimes.

Popkin, Jeremy, and Jack Censer, eds. *Media and Revolution: Comparative and Historical Perspectives.* Lexington: University of Kentucky Press, forthcoming in 1994. A conference volume that includes chapters by scholars working on events ranging from the English Civil War of the seventeenth century to the Eastern European events of 1989.

Ramet, Sabrina. *Social Currents in Eastern Europe: The Sources and Meaning of the Great Transformation.* (Durham, N.C.: Duke University Press, 1991. Ramet includes extended discussion of intelligentsia activism in various countries during the 1980s; the book also contains chapters on topics such as rock music and feminism that could usefully be paired with chapters in other parts of this volume.

Primary Sources

Barmé, Geremie, and Linda Jaivin, eds. *New Ghosts, Old Dreams: Chinese Rebel Voices.* New York: Times Books, 1992, Section IV: Wheels, pp. 321–410. This work includes short essays by many of China's most important contemporary intellectual figures, ranging from astrophysicist Fang Lizhi to journalist Dai Qing, as well as a short story by novelist Chen Ruoxi.

Liu Binyan. *People or Monsters? and Other Stories and Reportage from China After Mao.* Edited by Perry Link. Bloomington: Indiana University Press, 1983. A collection of pieces by China's most famous contemporary journalist.

Yue Daiyun and Carolyn Wakeman. *To the Storm: The Odyssey of a Revolutionary Chinese Woman.* Berkeley: University of California Press, 1985. The autobiography of a Chinese intellectual who lived through some of the most harrowing phases of the Chinese Revolution.

8

MEMORY AND COMMEMORATION: THE CHINESE SEARCH FOR A LIVABLE PAST

Vera Schwarcz

The great events, they are not our loudest but our stillest hours. Not around the inventors of new noises, but around the inventors of new values does the world revolve. It revolves inaudibly.

—Friedrich Nietzsche

China today is in danger of losing its past. Like a snail robbed of its shell, it has nothing to pull back into, little to carry forward with certainty. No homecoming to memory is allowed: The mass movement of 1989 did not happen. The government claims it was nothing but "counterrevolutionary turmoil" instigated by a handful of "hooligans." The authorities have honored the soldiers who died during the repression of June by calling them "revolutionary martyrs" (see Chapter 13 for more details), but the students and ordinary citizens killed in Beijing, Chengdu, and other cities may not be mourned publicly. On the first anniversary of the June Fourth Massacre, in fact, even to wear white (the traditional Chinese color of mourning) or black (its Western equivalent) was forbidden. Remembrance of the dead—which has long been the anchor of personal, familial, and to a certain extent national identity in China—is crushed under the weight of officially mandated amnesia. To compensate for the stifling of personal memory, China has gone through a period of loud, official commemorations and spectacles. First came the 1989 celebrations of the seventieth anniversary of the May Fourth Movement and the for-

An earlier version of this essay appeared in the *Wilson Quarterly* (Fall 1989); it is reprinted here with that journal's permission.

tieth anniversary of the founding of the People's Republic on October 1, and then a year later came a new round of state rituals associated with the Asian Games, which were designed to convince the world that life had returned to normal in Beijing. In all of these ceremonies, the CCP tried to use or disguise the meaning of the past, never to encourage historical remembrance. . . . But can commemoration replace memory?

This question was not as stark nor as urgent during the celebrations, discussions, and demonstrations I witnessed in Beijing during April and May 1989. I had gone to China to attend two conferences dealing with the May Fourth Movement. One took place at the Sleeping Buddha Temple on the outskirts of Beijing from April 30 to May 3. The second took place in the downtown of the capital from May 5 to May 8 and was sponsored by the Chinese Academy of Social Sciences (CASS). In both settings Chinese scholars from the mainland, Hong Kong, Taiwan, Singapore, and the United States gathered to celebrate an earlier student-led movement for democracy. For a few days in early May, it seemed as if the present had overtaken the past. It seemed as if public commemoration of the event of 1919 could be expanded to accommodate the dreams of a new generation of Chinese intellectuals.

During the May Fourth Movement of 1919, students and teachers of Beijing University had taken to the streets to protest China's mistreatment at the Versailles peace conference. They started out to express anger about the warlord government's acquiescence to a treaty that threatened China's national integrity. In the end, they developed an encompassing critique of the traditional values that underlay corrupt warlord politics. Their vision of an alternative "New Culture" was summed up by the two slogans: "science" and "democracy." In 1919 these were urgent, emotional ideals that promised to liberate China from centuries of Confucian autocracy. These ideals were personified as "Mr. Science" (*Cai xiansheng*) and "Mr. Democracy" (*De xiansheng*) by young intellectuals who longed to be saved from bureaucratic politics, from arranged marriages, and from the burden of formulaic learning. By spring 1989 a new generation of Chinese students was demonstrating in the streets of Beijing. It also marched under the slogans of "science" and "democracy." This generation now quarreled with corruption inside the Communist Party. For a tragically short interval these idealistic students were convinced they could change old habits of mind. The seventieth anniversary of the May Fourth Movement gave them a dramatic opportunity to see themselves as heroes on a world stage. On the Chinese government's commemorative stamps, as well as on U.S. television, young intellectuals proclaimed fidelity to the goals of the New Culture Movement. In both settings the background is Tiananmen Square. In both, young intellectuals make speeches, distribute pamphlets, carry flags. In both a look of fierce determination is carved onto the faces of those whose modern education endowed them with an ancient responsibility.

It was Mencius, Confucius's disciple, who first codified the Chinese intellectual's duty to society in the famous adages, "Those who work with their minds are meant to rule; those who work with their brawn are meant to be ruled" and "Those who know are the first to awake; the enlightened awake the others." In spring 1989, however, neither the ancient nor the arrogant echoes of this definition of the intellectual were much noticed on the streets of Beijing. Instead, millions of ordinary citizens swelled the ranks of student demonstrators—further convincing them that this indeed was the fruition of the earlier May Fourth Movement of 1919. In the heat of the mass movement of May 1989, it was possible to ignore—momentarily—the social isolation of Chinese intellectuals. It was possible, also, to overlook for a while the echoes of the Cultural Revolution of 1966–1969. That mass movement, too, had started with millions of young people on the streets of Beijing. But then, unlike in 1989, they had been called forth by one man, Mao Zedong, and, unlike this later May, students had been impatient, even cruel to the "unbelievers." The result of that earlier frenzy of mass action, however, was the same as today: The voices of the young were drowned out, their dreams swallowed by a struggle for power among the old men of the party.

Historical memory did not fare well in the midst of mass action and dramatic commemorations. Neither the Cultural Revolution nor Mencius had much to say to a student movement wrapped up in its conviction that history was starting anew. They did not have time to take notice of the heavy burden of the past that hung over the sea of red flags in Tiananmen Square. But it was there, gloomy and ominous like the solitary black flag used to proclaim the hunger strike on May 13, 1989. It was there also even earlier—in the conference halls where older intellectuals gathered for scholarly conferences on the May Fourth Movement. These scholars were intensely aware of the burden of the past. They had known its imprint on their own lives. They had spent decades analyzing the unfinished legacy of the May Fourth Movement. And yet these seasoned academicians, too, got caught up in the passions of the student movement. The seventieth anniversary of the event of 1919 made them intensely sympathetic to the hopes embodied in the student movement of 1989. On the actual day of May 4, 1989, most of us were to be found in and around Tiananmen Square. Chow Tse-tsung, veteran U.S. scholar of the May Fourth Movement, was hoisted high on the shoulders of a new generation of students clamoring for science and democracy. It was as if history had really come full circle and a new era was about to dawn. This vision, this exhilaration was carried by the scholars into the conference halls. It is ironic that the prodemocracy demonstrations of 1989 consummated what Mao Zedong had begun in the 1950s: They made the past into a mirror for the present. Mao had placed Chinese historiography into a straitjacket using the slogan *gu wei jin yong* (use the past for the sake of the present). In spring 1989, Chinese intellectuals themselves rushed to extract didactic lessons and inspiring messages for the present out of the complex, even troubling, legacy of May Fourth. Many, to be sure, were painfully aware of the unresolved questions left over from the May Fourth era. They noted the ambivalence toward enlightenment that lingered on from the May Fourth Movement through the reforms of Deng Xiaoping. They knew that for most of the past seventy years, Chinese history belonged to men whom Nietzsche might characterize as "inventors of new noises" and not "inventors of new values." In 1989, however, the rising tempo and decibel of the prodemocracy movement promised to fulfill and to carry forward the agenda of May Fourth. For a few weeks it looked as if the distinctions between noisy and inaudible events might vanish. Today, when the divide between these two kinds of history gapes huge once again, we might well ask what would have been the fate of May Fourth if tanks had not rolled into Tiananmen Square on June 4,1989? What if there had been no student movement at all? What if China's historical studies could have developed unaffected by this season of loud commemorations? This is the question I posed to Zhang Zhilian, eminent historian of the French Revolution at Beijing University shortly before he was to leave China to attend commemorations of the bicentennial of the event of 1789. His answer was: "Big, public occasions are good business for historians, but are not always beneficial for the development of historical scholarship. . . . Maybe history is best off when allowed to be simply historical."

Historic Commemorations

History has been wrenched out of the past throughout twentieth-century China. It has been used over and over again to explain a century of massive convulsions, a century riddled by revolution. "Revolution" is a new phenomenon in Chinese political culture that is still called by an old name: *geming*. Literally "broken mandate," this is a traditional appellation for the break of the mandate of heaven that leads one dynasty to give way to another. By 1989 China had gone through several revolutions, including the Republican revolution of 1911; the New Culture revolution of May 4, 1919; the establishment of the People's Republic in 1949, and the Cultural Revolution of 1966–1969.

With all this upheaval, one might imagine China was tired of revolution. One might imagine China ready for the language and the social experiment of reform. Instead, however, the student movement of 1989 reconsecrated the metaphor of the broken mandate. The movement had started out calling for political reforms, but it ended up as "revolutionary," first in its own eyes and later in the view of the government that condemned it as "counterrevolutionary." It was as if no other word but *geming* was available to China's political activists, the very situation Liu Xiaobo laments in Chapter 14. It was as if everyone had forgotten the ancient Chinese curse "May you live in interesting times." History had to be historic, or of no use at all in this year of momentous commemorations. The 1989 movement was seen as fulfilling not only the "mandate" of 1919 but also the "mandate" of 1949.

Throughout spring 1989, the seventieth anniversary of May Fourth fueled talk of a new, "more revolutionary May Fourth." In 1919, 3,000 students had marched the short distance from the old, downtown campus of Beijing University to Tiananmen Square. On May 4, 1989, hundreds of thousands of students marched for eight hours from the outskirts of the city where Beijing University and other institutions of higher learning are now located. The students of 1989 marched in full view and with full support of the citizens of the capital. The momentous scale of the 1989 demonstrations led to a hyperbolic evocation of the past. Commemorations of May Fourth now had to accommodate not only the intellectuals' aspirations for science and democracy, not only the students' grievances about lack of freedom of the press and bureaucratic corruption, but also the hopes of millions of ordinary citizens aroused by activists in Tiananmen Square. In this process, the anniversary of the event of 1919 became identified with a promise left unfulfilled from China's "liberation" in 1949.

On May 12, 1989, this vision of historic commemoration was explicitly proclaimed at a "democracy salon" held on the campus of Beijing University. This "salon" (translated into Chinese as *shalong*, or sand dragon) was the seventeenth in a series of student-sponsored discussions about political reform. On this day, 500 undergraduates crowded around the grassy patch in front of a statue of Cervantes. They came to hear Bao Zongxin, a well-respected scholar of Qing intellectual history. But Bao did not speak about the past. Instead, he fired up the crowd with a series of impassioned statements: "You, your movement, has finally made China stand up! On October 1, 1949, Mao proclaimed in Tiananmen Square that China has stood up. But that was propaganda. You have made those words real."

"Liberation" became more than a metaphor in spring 1989. In the fervor of commemoration, an intellectuals' movement became linked to—and in the end, swallowed by—the language of political revolution. Time to recall the political atrocities that had surrounded the revolution of 1949, or the naive cultural radicalism of the student movement of 1919, ran out as yet another mass movement engulfed China's capital. Especially after millions took to the streets in support of students who had called for a hunger strike in Tiananmen Square, there was little room left in Chinese public life for the ambiguities of historical memory.

That spring the past had to lead straight to the present—with an inspiring message, whenever possible. Official government newspapers like the *People's Daily* commemorated the anniversary of May Fourth with bombastic editorials about the "praiseworthy patriotism" of the students of 1919. Decoded, the message to the present generation of students was simple: Be loyal to the Party, dedicate yourself to the nation's modernization program, and forget about Western ideas that only aggravate the economic crisis at hand. Students responded with a fervent defense of the right to think critically. They insisted that the contemporary economic crisis must be blamed on the Party's own corruption. They, too, asserted that the past leads up to the present as they marched under banners reading "Seventy Years Already!" and "We have waited too long for Mr. Science and Mr. Democracy!"

In the heat of the confrontation between the government and the students, the seventy-year-old May Fourth Movement could not be consigned to the past. It had to provide usable slogans in spite of warnings by a few middle-aged scholars who tried to stem the tide of present-oriented commemoration. At the Sleeping Buddha Temple conference, especially, there was a noticeable effort to take a longer view of the problem of Chinese intellectuals. Several participants sought to place the event of 1919 into a context that was quite different from that of 1989. Chen Fangzhen (from the Chinese University of

Hong Kong), for example, reminded his compatriots that the original May Fourth had been the product of an extreme sort of political crisis. China in the late 1910s was in danger of disintegration at the hands of rapacious warlords and aggressive imperialists. China faced no such crisis in 1989. And yet the drama of a life-or-death crisis was reenacted with tragically augmented consequences.

At the conference sponsored by the Chinese Academy of Social Science, Chen Fangzhen went one step further. He told his fellow intellectuals that they were a transitional force, a group brought into existence by the social turmoil of twentieth-century China. Those who called themselves *zhishi fenzi* (intellectuals or, literally, knowledgeable elements), Chen argued, have a temporary mission: to voice criticism until other social groups find and express their own voice. Later, when others can speak for themselves, when the educated need no longer to be *daiyan ren* (carriers of the word for the wordless masses) then intellectuals will be superfluous. They will have no special calling in a truly modern society.

But Chinese intellectuals were not prepared to hear about their demise in the heady days of May 1989. Too much of what was going on in the streets of Beijing promised them a greater role in Chinese politics. They had every reason to hope for more public visibility as their activities drew more and more coverage from newly emancipated newspapers and television stations. This optimism was present in remarks made by the prominent philosopher Li Zehou. At both conferences, Li argued that the May Fourth promise of democracy could be fulfilled provided it became more grounded in philosophical reason and in political institutions. His new slogan, *minzhu yao kexuehua*—democracy must be more scientific—reordered and reinvigorated the old May Fourth ideals. At the same time, Li called attention to the insufficient legal foundation for democracy in China, to the absence of any constitutional guarantees for dissent.

But Li Zehou's effort to talk about the process of democratization, about its institutional prerequisites, was cut short by contemporary events. The prodemocracy movement in the streets of Beijing developed faster than middle-aged intellectuals could fathom in conference halls. Students on the streets augmented the hope and the sense of crisis. With the beginning of the hunger strike on May 13, 1989, the movement was brought to the brink of despair. Wang Dan, the student leader from Beijing University, advocated a "fight to the end" for science and democracy. Students were preparing to die. They started to write last wills and testaments, just as older intellectuals were beginning to talk about legal guarantees for dissent.

With the declaration of martial law on May 20, 1989, history appeared to have come full circle. The future of China's youth now appeared as grim as it had been in the worst nightmares of May Fourth activists. Old warnings, old pleas were now revived on the streets of Beijing. The closing lines of a 1918 story by China's foremost modern writer, Lu Xun, now echoed with a new sense of urgency. In "Diary of a Madman," Lu Xun had closed his scathing indictment of traditional autocracy with the cry: "Save the children!"[1] At the end of this May, students—the "children" from Lu Xun's bleak story about youth consumed by cannibalistic elders—roamed the faulty neighborhoods pleading: "The soldiers are coming! Teachers, teachers, please come out and save the children! Save your students!"

The teachers, now, as on the eve of the May Fourth Movement, came out in full. Nobody on the campus of Beijing University was immune to the powerful echoes of the event of 1919. Seventy years earlier, Lu Xun's generation of Beijing University teachers helped set in motion a student movement through publications such as *New Youth* magazine. They had started the assault on Confucian values that the student movement of 1919 then propagated through society as a whole. In 1989, students called out their teachers by reminding them of Lu Xun's commitment to "save the children." But the battle now was not against Confucian dogma but against the armed force of the People's Liberation Army. However "revolutionary" the meaning of May Fourth might have been, it was tragically impotent against the tanks that invaded Tiananmen Square on June 4, 1989.

By that time, May Fourth had been used too much. It was, in dark of night, used up. Young and middle-aged intellectuals alike faced a grim reality disrobed of illusions about the power of historic commemorations. They stood on the verge of a precipice described forty years earlier by the literary scholar Luo Changpei. On the eve of "liberation" in 1949, he, too, had tried to grapple with the lessons of 1919. Forty years before tanks rolled in to crush the largest movement for civil disobedience in twentieth-century China, Luo Changpei had a premonition. He voiced it mutedly in a Communist Party–sponsored volume of essays commemorating the thirtieth anniversary of May Fourth: "The old tune of May Fourth cannot be replayed. Without May Fourth, we would not have the present. If we continue to grasp forever the spirit of May Fourth, we will have no future."

The Problem of Chinese Intellectuals

The literary critic Luo Changpei did not live to see the seventieth anniversary of May Fourth. He did not have a chance to comment on the fate of Chinese intellectuals forty years after the founding of the People's Republic. But his younger colleagues did gather in early May of 1989 to assess their past and their future in light of the "old tune" of May Fourth. The most explicit statement of their concern was inscribed on the banner that hung above the conference at the Sleeping Buddha Temple: "May Fourth and the Problem of Chinese Intellectuals."

Those speaking beneath the banner were all survivors. They were victims of various criticism campaigns directed against China's educated elite from the 1950s onward. Some of the participants of the 1989 conference had been labeled "rightists" in 1957, after Mao found their expression of critical thought intolerable during the short-lived Hundred Flowers Movement. Many more had suffered when intellectuals became labeled members of the "stinking ninth" category during the Cultural Revolution. The "crime" of this group (deemed more odious than landlords, capitalists, Kuomintang sympathizers, etc.) was simply higher education. Having made a living with their minds, intellectuals were excommunicated from the sacred community of peasants and workers.

Thrown out of jobs, publicly humiliated, incarcerated in "cow pens" (as holding cells for intellectuals were known during the Cultural Revolution), these scholars had paid dearly for Mencius's ancient claim that those who labor with their minds are to rule over those who labor with their brawn. Mao had willfully, cruelly reversed the traditional Chinese veneration of the educated. By the time of his death in 1976, intellectuals had lost almost all of their former social status and much of their self-confidence as well. Rehabilitation began slowly and, predictably, from the top: Deng Xiaoping, a survivor himself, declared at the 1978 National Science Conference that the overwhelming majority of the intellectuals were indeed part of the working class. Like those who engage in physical labor, those who engage in mental labor are all socialist workers. Once renamed as workers (*gongzuo zhe*), intellectuals could hope for a little better housing, a little better pay. But their social calling—especially their right to comment critically about urgent political issues facing China in the age of reform—remained suspect in the eyes of Communist Party rulers.

In April 1986, a new one appeared on new fifty-yuan notes issued by the China People's Bank. It showed an intellectual with gray hair and tie alongside a worker and a peasant. The intellectual had replaced the soldier in the previous trinity. This was a symbolic step forward in the public rehabilitation of intellectuals. It was also a symbolic concession to the Confucian worldview that held the educated elite to be the foundation of Chinese society— along with peasants and, to a lesser extent, artisans. Soldiers, according to tradition, were the lowest, most ill regarded rung of the social hierarchy.

And yet the rehabilitation of Chinese intellectuals did not go far beyond the realm of the symbolic. Less than a year after the intellectual appeared on a bank note, China was once again in the throes of an anti-intellectual campaign. The attack mounted in early 1987 was nominally against "bourgeois liberalism," but its targets were the same critical thinkers whom Mao had sought to silence in 1957, and then again during the Cultural Revolution. The 1987 campaign followed closely on the heels of an earlier attempt to intimidate intellectuals during the 1983 campaign against "spiritual pollution." Over and over again, intellectuals were criminalized for their interest in ideas from abroad. These ideas about democracy, science, and freedom of speech had been used by Chinese intellectuals to quarrel with entrenched habits of thought on native ground. That quarrel was repeatedly squelched: in 1957, in the 1960s, in 1983, in 1987, and, most recently, with the armed assault against demonstrators on June 4, 1989.

And still the commitment to critical thought endures. In early May 1989, intellectual survivors gathered to commemorate 1919 and to ask themselves: What had gone wrong? Conversation at conferences returned to this subject over and over again: How are intellectuals to account for their repeated victimization and powerlessness in modern Chinese history? The May Fourth Movement offered these scholars a refuge in the past. The event of 1919 anchored them in a historical moment in which teachers and students had been able to speak their minds. During the May Fourth Movement, ideas about cultural and political reform had aroused the nation as a whole. An understanding of this history promised to heal the wounds of the more recent past. It also seemed to rekindle hope for the future. The student movement exploding on the streets of Beijing accelerated this optimism. More than proclamations from Deng Xiaoping or a new face on bank notes, the confluence of a contemporary social movement and the seventieth anniversary of May Fourth offered China's battered intellectuals a genuine opportunity for self-rehabilitation.

Most of the discussions at the academic conferences sought to deepen the question of what had gone wrong between intellectuals and politics in modern China. In light of the student activism flowering on the streets of Beijing, the question became: Why have intellectuals been prevented for so long from becoming an autonomous force in Chinese society? To the intellectuals' credit, they did not simply blame Mao Zedong or Deng Xiaoping for the short-sighted policies of the Chinese Communist Party. Rather, they took this as an opportunity to examine those aspects of the Chinese intellectuals' own tradition that had kept its modern heirs from finding and expressing an autonomous voice in public life.

In seminar rooms, in hallways beyond the reach of microphones and public lectures, intellectuals dissected the ancient burden of political responsibility. Politics, in one form or another, has consumed the life of Chinese scholars from Confucius onward. Unlike European intellectuals, who had first used religion and then science as an alternative to political authority, Chinese *wenren* (literally, people of the word) had little to shield from the claims of rulers who owned both words and swords. In the midst of May Fourth commemorations, conversation drifted back to intellectual ancestors who first muted their voices for the sake of official position—or, less selfishly, for the sake of national salvation. In these conversations, it was impossible to overlook the concrete benefits that had befallen scholar-bureaucrats from the Han dynasty onward, provided they buckled down and accepted state orthodoxy. At the same time, there was also plenty of historical evidence to suggest that Chinese intellectuals had served as the moral conscience of society for centuries. Long before modern events such as the May Fourth Movement of 1919, members of the educated elite had sought to distinguish between rule by force (*zhitong*) and rule by ethical ideals (*daotong*). But for centuries as well, they have been powerless to close the gulf between the two.

Now, with a new generation of students out on the streets, the question became more urgent: Can intellectuals find and maintain a critical voice in the midst of political corruption? Will they be able to develop the seeds of a new culture sown in the May Fourth Movement and thereby edge China closer to science and democracy? In both conferences commemorating 1919, the answer was far from certain. In both settings, participants noted that the idea of enlightenment, of *qimeng*, had been overpowered repeatedly by the exigencies of national salvation (*Jiuguo*). If intellectuals had been willing to forsake—or had been forced to abandon—their own ideas about political and cultural reform before 1949, what was to ensure the success of the current student movement?

Tragically, the answer from Tiananmen Square was: nothing. Without institutionalized autonomy, without legally safeguarded dissent, the current generation of students stood as naked in the face of arbitrary political authority as Chinese scholars buried in 212 B.C. by China's first emperor, Qin Shihuangdi. Unlike the ancient scholars, however, the contemporary generation of Chinese students received massive popular support. Before the tanks rolled on June 4, 1989, ordinary citizens had given students money, food, and water. Millions demonstrated in the streets, day after day, in support of hunger strikers in Tiananmen Square. They even tried to shield the demonstrators with their bodies during the first few days of martial law.

But, in the end, something overcame the students' idealism as well as the citizens best intentions. It was not only the force of guns. The politics of crowd action, too, helped crush the student movement. This has always been the fate of intellectuals consumed by mass movements. In China, the impotence of individuals, of institutionalized groups has been reflected by millions gathered on the streets of Beijing during the Cultural Revolution, as well as in 1989. In the course of this latest movement, students repeatedly pleaded for "dialogue" with the government. But the more they pleaded, the deafer the authorities appeared to become. And as the students became more desperate, their tactics as well as their slogans became more simplistic. From beginning to end, the tragedy at Tiananmen Square was cast in terms of an old drama: injured subjects pleading for a hearing from supposedly benevolent rulers. In mid-April, for example, students kneeled for hours on the steps of the Great Hall of the People with a petition describing their grievances. And, as so often before, the rulers proved uncaring. Even before the shooting of June 4, one could foresee the tragic end to these rituals. The echoes of the Cultural Revolution were amply evident on the streets of Beijing. The government used this historical precedent to attack the students' "turmoil," to fuel popular fear of chaos. But that was not the real danger. Rather, the Cultural Revolution loomed large as a warning about how student idealism can be used and abused in the course of crowd politics. During the commemoration of May Fourth, the echoes of the Cultural Revolution could already be heard as students roamed the campus chanting ever more ardent, ever more simplistic slogans. But no one was really listening.

In the conference halls, too, commemoration displaced historical memory. At one point during our discussion at the social science academy conference, I asked: "What is the connection between the May Fourth Movement, the current student protest, and the Cultural Revolution?" Dead silence surrounded me in this seminar room filled with middle-aged intellectuals who had been victimized as members of the "stinking ninth" less than twenty years ago. A few minutes later, an old gentleman from Shanghai leaned over and whispered to me:

Maybe there is a link after all. Maybe it is to be found in the way that both democracy and intellectuals have been ridiculed for so long. Remember the cultural conservative Gu Hongming, who was so outspoken in the late 1910s? He wore a long pigtail down his back, wrote good English, and mocked May Fourth activists by calling the proponents of democracy "demo-crazy." That is what Mao thought about intellectuals as well—crazy and dispensable. Maybe our fate is no different today. . . .

Memory in the Interstices of Commemoration

The question about the Cultural Revolution was not the only one to be met with silence around the conference table. Another concerned the intellectuals' historical memory more directly. On May 6, at the social science academy gathering, we had been talking about recent memoirs by May Fourth participants published on the mainland and in Taiwan. Scholars from both sides agreed that these personal narratives provided a meaningful alternative to politically mandated histories of the event. I asked aloud: "What about the distortions at work in personal memory as well?" Embarrassed glances crossed the small seminar room. But I went on because the issue of historical memory is a sore and important subject—at least for me: "What about the internalized censors who adjust an individual's recollections in keeping with the changing requirements of political history? What about ninety-eight-year-old Xu Deheng? This veteran of May Fourth has written a commemorative essay about May Fourth at each major anniversary for the past fifty years. Each time he has corroborated whatever version of May Fourth the Communist Party needed at the moment. What about his recollection of May Fourth printed just the other day in the *People's Daily*? As often before, he dwells on the May Fourth students' patriotism. As before, he slights their aspirations for a more democratic political culture."

The silence deepened around the conference table. Xu Deheng is an important figure in Chinese public life. He has served as head of the National People's Congress after joining the Communist Party in 1979. To call into question the veracity of his historical memory is almost as risky as to challenge the politics of Deng Xiaoping. I did not press my Chinese colleagues further. Nonetheless, the old gentleman from Shanghai again leaned over: "Xu is really too senile to write anymore, you know. His secretaries now publish stuff in his name. . . . He sounds like a windbag . . . not what you might call genuine historical memory."

What constitutes genuine historical memory in China today? I tried to ask my neighbor, but he pulled away and moved our whispering onto safer subjects. Nonetheless, this gentleman from Shanghai helped me better understand the difficulties faced by Chinese intellectuals who try to stretch the parameters of historical memory. He enabled me to better appreciate the papers presented at the conference that managed to accommodate large chunks of materials from a more genuinely remembered past. Unlike Xu Deheng, the authors of those papers wrestled with the full complexity of May Fourth. In re-remembering the event of 1919, they managed to give it a second chance, a second life as it were. This has made it possible for their colleagues to envisage a version of May Fourth that breaks through the constraints of party historiography.

One essayist, for example, dealt with the love life of Hu Shi—a major figure in the New Culture Movement of the May Fourth era. Hu became the champion of liberalism in China and a symbol of political error on the mainland after 1949. Though he lived in Taiwan, his colleagues, students, and ideas were put on trial during several campaigns directed against intellectuals. After 1979 the political venom against liberalism subsided somewhat, and Hu Shi could once again be talked about in terms of the "revolutionary literary theories" he put forth. By 1989 it was possible to explore something deeper, more personal, more complicated—Hu Shi's friendships with female intellectuals (Chinese and American) during the course of his old-fashioned marriage to an uneducated woman with bound feet.

The essay dealing with Hu Shi's inner life stretched the parameters of the remembered past, not only through new documentation from Hu Shi's letters but by going beyond the pale of political history altogether. A similar effort was palpable in an essay about Zhang Ruoming, a prominent woman student of the May Fourth era who became a major scholar of French literature. Zhang Ruoming has been more or less forgotten in Chinese public memory, but for her briefly noted political association with Zhou Enlai, the man who became premier in the People's Republic after 1949. Little else was known about Zhang Ruoming until her son began to recollect his mother's scholarly life. On the occasion of the seventieth anniversary of May Fourth, it became possible to write about Zhang Ruoming's cosmopolitanism in a way that went beyond the canons of party history.

Again, the subject and the documents brought to life details overlooked in official versions of May Fourth. The bulk of the essay about Zhang Ruoming focused on her study of André Gide—not on her role in the demonstrations of 1919, not even on her short career as a Chinese communist in France in the 1920s. It detailed her effort to interpret Gide's work according to the central theme of "narcissism"—which Zhang Ruoming wrote about with distinct appreciation. Her appreciation, in turn, evoked a positive response from Gide himself, who wrote to Zhang Ruoming in 1931: "It seemed to me in traversing your pages that I have regained consciousness of my existence. I do not think I have ever felt so well understood." Zhang Ruoming herself might have written the same thing about this May Fourth commemoration, if she had been alive in 1989. In her absence, her son's essay managed to expand public remembrance. In the interstices, as it were, he placed a recollection that did not dwell on his mother's communism in the 1920s, nor on her obsessive loyalty to the Party during the 1957 campaign against "rightist" intellectuals, nor even on her suicide out of fear and despair a year later. Instead, he used the anniversary of May Fourth to augment his contemporaries' understanding of a uniquely cosmopolitan generation of Chinese intellectuals.

Commemoration thus did not fully displace historical memory in 1989. Rather, it offered Chinese intellectuals an opportunity to tell parts of their own story in their own terms. Even as a momentous new student movement arose in Beijing, even as the passions of crowd action were engulfing the intellectuals' agenda in Tiananmen Square, recollection received its due. Far from the noise of the streets, the muted voice of memory kept history alive. Nowhere was this more apparent to me than on May 20, when I attended a

ceremony commemorating the fifty-sixth anniversary of an eminent philosopher's scholarly career.

This was the day after martial law was declared in Beijing. A large lecture
hall on the Qinghua University campus had been set up to accommodate
hundreds of guests. Now it looked cavernous around the forty or so intellectuals who managed to get there. They had come by bicycle from universities
nearby, unlike their colleagues from the social science academy downtown—
whose buses were canceled at the last minute. At the center of the ceremony
stood Zhang Dainian, the renowned scholar of classical Chinese thought. Everyone knew that the ceremony had been planned by former students to
mark the master teacher's eightieth birthday. But such personal occasions
still have to be clothed in public significance in China. Hence, the disciples
fastened upon the anniversary of Zhang Dainian's teaching career at Qinghua University. The large red banner over the head table proclaimed the odd
number "56" in contrast to the round, recognizably momentous "70" that
had graced commemorations of May Fourth. The awkward banner and the
rows of empty chairs, however, were not the only features that distinguished
this gathering from those other commemorations. The whole mood had
changed in the past three weeks. Now the student movement on the streets
had been crushed. To be sure, no tanks yet rolled in Tiananmen Square, but
an ultimatum had been given. Fear of persecution and arrest was thick
among the intellectuals gathered to pay homage to Zhang Dainian.

Behind the head table hung scrolls traditionally used to honor master
teachers. Classical couplets recalled the integrity of Zhang Dainian's scholarly career. A large painting portrayed an aged crane standing tall and proud
on a gnarled pine branch. The bird and the pine, too, were traditional symbols for an outstanding intellectual of high moral character. These symbols
were further elaborated during speeches that paid tribute to Zhang Dainian's
work in classical philosophy. Several former students got up in turn to talk
about the enduring influence of Zhang Dainian on their own lives. One described the lasting impression he had of Zhang's *wei ren*—his way of being
fully human in a world that often denied the intellectual's humanity. This
"moral achievement," his student argued, is more important than all of
Zhang Dainian's considerable scholarly accomplishments. Another student
emphasized his teacher's *zi zai*—his inner peace maintained through fidelity
to classical moral ideals. All the speakers alluded to Zhang Dainian's suffering after he was labeled a "rightist" in 1957. All praised his ability to survive,
to remain productive, to be truthful to himself under conditions that repeatedly thwarted and threatened his self-esteem.

On this day, when martial law reigned in Beijing, there was little doubt that
Zhang Dainian's students were also speaking about themselves. Praising
their teacher's endurance, they were trying to encourage one another to outlast yet another crackdown. None of this was explicit, of course. The symbols
and the rituals of recollection sufficed for the moment. This was an intensely
personal occasion. The odd setting of a fifty-sixth commemoration combined
with the new situation of martial law made it more poignant.

Zhang Dainian's own speech on this occasion was subtle as well as truthful. Moved by his student's tributes, he responded with simple, modest words: "I have done nothing special over these fifty-six years. I just went on living and somehow managed to reach eighty—that is something auspicious just by itself. Throughout my life I have tried to bring together Marxism and Chinese philosophy, but I have not done it yet. . . . After 1979 [the year of Zhang's political rehabilitation], I have regained my courage and my energy. I have tried to think more independently after I turned seventy. But it has been too little, too late. Most of my life I have spent obeying and so did not accomplish enough. Still, I expect to go on with my work." As a foreign observer of this commemorative occasion, I was deeply moved by the tenacity of the bond between these intellectuals and their work. In one of the bleakest days of their shared history, they managed to come together and to hearten one another by paying tribute to the moral fortitude of one of their aged mentors. If Zhang Dainian could endure and still make significant contributions to China's understanding of truth, beauty, morality, and tradition (all major themes reflected in the titles of his recent books), others, too, might outlive the present nightmare. The key to Zhang's survival with integrity lay in his commitment to the past. It was this commitment that he had passed down to his students through his teaching and, now, through the gathering on May 20, 1989. In the very midst of what Nietzsche might have decried as loud, noisy history, Zhang Dainian and his disciples managed to recover an hour of stillness. Even as martial law was enforced outside of the gates of Qinghua University, inside intellectuals reminded themselves that the world revolves not around the inventors of new noises, but around the inventors of new values—or, as it was apparent now, around the guardians of values. Foremost among the values that Chinese intellectuals have treasured for centuries is that of historical recollection itself. In the excitement of the seventieth anniversary of May Fourth, in the heat of the passions evoked by the student movement of 1989, this treasure was almost overlooked. But never completely, never for long. The tragic end of the protests on the streets of Beijing has made historical recollection all the more precious. Now that enforced amnesia rules over Chinese public life, Confucius—the arch rememberer— becomes ever more compelling. It was this ancient master who first encouraged intellectuals by saying "I am not someone who was born knowing the past. I love the past and am someone who seeks for it earnestly." To love the past (*hao qu*) is to hold out for the possibility that it may yet be known. To seek for it (*qiu zhi*) is to commit oneself to outlast commemorations, to outwit crackdowns, to live another day in the pursuit of truth. This remains the mission of Chinese intellectuals today.

Notes

1. Lu Xun, "Kuangren riji" (Diary of a madman), in *Lu Xun quanji* (The complete works of Lu Xun) (Beijing: People's Literature Publishers, 1981), p. 432.

9

FROM PRIESTS TO PROFESSIONALS: INTELLECTUALS AND THE STATE UNDER THE CCP

Timothy Cheek

The image the West has had of China has changed from time to time, and no doubt will change again. Of course an image to some extent reflects the viewpoint of the observer, thus distorting the reality that lies behind it. First impressions, however, are usually correct, and this holds true when two civilizations first come into contact just as much as when two people meet for the first time.... The first image of China formed in the West, if we discount the rationalist wisdom with which the eighteenth-century "philosophers" clothed it, was that of a mandarinate.
                                        —Etienne Balazs, "China as a Permanently Bureaucratic State"[1]

Balazs's reflections from 1959 are a helpful reminder as Western scholars reassess their understanding of China and changes within China since the cataclysmic events of May and June 1989. The "mandarinate" does not include all Chinese intellectuals, and intellectuals are only part of the organizational and attitudinal structures that make up the mandarinate. Nevertheless, Balazs's point stands: The close relationship between members of the educated elite and the state has been a constant feature of Chinese history, including the revolutionary era, and continues to help shape the post-Tiananmen period, despite the traumatic events of 1989. We should not mistake the very real disgust individual Chinese intellectuals have expressed with the end of a *system*—that combination of ideas and institutions that make up the unwrit-

I would like to thank Tony Saich for giving an earlier version of this chapter a tough, critical reading. I would also like to thank the editors of this volume for their suggestions and (even more importantly) their patience.

184

ten contract between intellectuals and the state.[2] If, as China watchers, we misread conditions in China in the 1980s, it was by extending our hopes that Chinese intellectuals in significant numbers were leaving their priestly vocations in the mandarinate and demanding a new (what some would call "modern") relationship with the state—as professionals who earn their keep in some way fundamentally separate from the government. The irony of the popular movement of 1989 and its suppression is that the wishful image of increasing professional autonomy many of us thought we saw before June has, in fact, become more of a reality precisely because of the suppression of traditional forms of loyal remonstrance (such as the petition presentations described in Chapter 3). As Esherick and Wasserstrom argue in Chapter 2, the 1989 popular protests were not a "democracy movement" for most of the participants in any sense that resembles democracy in the United States or Europe.[3] Few Chinese intellectuals argued for a fundamental restructuring of the political order before May 1989; many dissidents simply demanded the right to fulfill the kind of mandarin role that Chinese states (imperial, nationalist, and communist alike) have promised the intelligentsia: that of acting as advisers to those who govern.

The crackdown changed this situation. Although many still serve or hope to serve the current government, a significant group has been disestablished, forcibly alienated from the regime by its leaders, and has thus moved closer to professional autonomy. Losing one's position in the state bureaucracy does not make one instantly an independent professional. Indeed, the tragedy of mainland China's intellectuals is, as David Kelly notes, that they "remain, as a stratum, an artifact of the system they oppose."[4] However, combined with the social forces unleashed by a decade of reform—a new class of entrepreneurs, the return of inflation along with government corruption, the increased contact with foreigners and travel outside China, the increased translation of a variety of foreign books on social, economic, and literary topics—the violent reaction of the government in 1989 (and its continued repression of enemies, real and imagined) marks a major step in the punctuated evolution of China's educated elite.

Intellectuals have made a further step in the movement from priest-rentiers serving the cosmic state (Confucian or Leninist) to professionals salaried in a bourgeois society They are not there yet, and that is one of the reasons why the popular protests of 1989 in China did not result in the dramatic change of regimes we saw in Eastern Europe (a phenomenon Chirot's chapter elucidates so well). The significance of Tiananmen is that this critical "event" has pushed that process forward. However, the mandarin vocation—which calls for a generalist serving the state through a central bureaucracy and with a unified ideology, rather than professional specialists serving the nation through a variety of separate institutions within a pluralistic range of ideologies—has not yet disappeared in China today. It is the purpose of this chapter to suggest that a greater appreciation of the "establishment" role of intellectuals will help us better understand the events of 1989 and the likely future contribution of intellectuals to China's unfinished revolution.

It is true that the CCP lost the "silent majority" of China's establishment intellectuals in 1989.[5] But if the "moral rot" (to use Chirot's term) has become increasingly apparent to leading intellectuals—starting at least in the late 1980s, with the crescendo in spring 1989, and the bitter continuing proof through repression of government critics since then—why has the "moral bankruptcy" of the regime in Beijing not become broadly apparent in China in a way sufficient to bring the regime's collapse (Chirot's thesis for Eastern Europe)? We can say that the state has lost the allegiance of many of those who are expected to staff it and propagate its policies and ideals and that alterative ideas, such as liberal democracy, are moving from the fringe of Chinese society—where such ideas certainly lay before 1989—to capture the attention of more than a few malcontents and idealists (such as the student protesters and dissident intellectuals treated in Chapters 4 and 8). Bookstores in the West are full of books on Tiananmen and especially writings by leading Chinese participants in the 1989 popular movement—from students such as Shen Tong and Li Lu to older intellectuals such as Liu Binyan and Yan Jiaqi. These valuable records, however, reinforce our propensity to overestimate the reform spirit in China. To understand the relative balance of intellectual forces for a return to full Party dominance, relaxation, or fundamental reform in China, we must see major intellectual groupings in relation to each other—students, "democratic radicals," apolitical professionals, and today's mandarins. The comparison with Eastern Europe is particularly helpful because, as Chirot describes it, three factors led to the collapse of those regimes: a loss of faith among the educated "middle classes" (which he quite helpfully describes in "cultural and educational" rather than purely economic terms) to the point that they ignored the Party-state; some range of organizational and propaganda outlets (often literature) for disaffected intellectuals to reach that audience; and, third, enough information about the outside world to enable leading intellectual speakers and the "middle-class" audience to know the state has lied to them. The power of speakers, the range of audience, and the access to examples from the outside world were all severely limited in the case of China by the nature and continuing power of the "deal" between intellectuals and the state.[6]

The Deal Between China's Intellectuals and the State

The aftermath of Tiananmen has demonstrated that the old intelligentsia-based mandarinate, its institutions and attitudes in Leninist incarnation, still exists in China today. It still attracts talented intellectuals, still has the massive support of the Party, state, and army. It will be with us for a while longer, and we would be wise, if we pretend to understand China, to familiarize ourselves with the intellectual establishment and its establishment intellectuals. As Perry points out in Chapter 3, the job allocation system in the PRC gives the state today even more control over meaningful employment opportunities for intellectuals than did the famous imperial examination system that for millennia tied Confucian elites to the state. Additionally, the work unit (*danwei*) holds sway over the lives of individuals in China, particularly urban professionals. The work unit not only dispenses one's salary, but housing, health care, and needed authorizations for travel, children's schooling, and job transfers. Despite a decade of reform, local party chiefs still control the work units of China.[7] In addition to such institutional realities, attitudes and values bind China's intellectuals to the state.

Chinese intellectuals' attitudes about their relationship to political power can be categorized on three levels: attitudes toward the state, their group, and themselves. Key attitudes shape intellectuals' behavior at each of these levels. Intellectual attitudes toward the state have been characterized by fierce *patriotism;* their behavior with superiors, peers, and subordinates reflects an acceptance of *patronage;* and their self-expressions reflect a profound elitism and sense of *paternalism.* The content of these attitudes has varied among individuals, naturally, and has changed on critical points over the past thirty years (for example, on whether the nation, the state, or the Party is most deserving of patriotic loyalty).

There have remained the three core aspects of an informal and unwritten deal between the CCP and intellectuals in the PRC.[8] This deal, which is a "social contract" in the sense that it is based on tacit understandings and shared assumptions between the Party leadership and leading intellectuals in the establishment, is fairly straightforward in principle: In return for obedient service to the Party, establishment intellectuals are promised the opportunity to serve China and to engage in intellectual pursuits. It is clear from the activities and writings of a number of the founding generation of establishment intellectuals between the 1930s and 1950s that they found the "sinification of Marxism" developed in Yan'an and embodied in Mao Zedong Thought to be not only an acceptable but actually a desirable revision of the old "contract" between intellectuals and the state under the new historical conditions of the twentieth century.[9] The praiseworthy contributions of these intellectuals during these decades shows that the deal clearly had a good side, and it was faith in the value of the contract that allowed early generations of CCP establishment intellectuals, including what Li Zehou calls the "1950s generation," to keep faith with the Party through the disasters of the 1960s and 1970s.[10] This is particularly significant in the case of the 1950s generation, as so many of those in power today (from technocrat politicians like Li Peng to heads of major academic institutions) belong to this cohort.

Under this deal with the CCP, the educated elite gave up claims to the wealth and political power of their scholar-gentry ancestors to serve what they felt was a more egalitarian and socially just government. They rejected the status of landlord and scholar-elite (*shenshi*) and accepted the status of intellectual (*zhishi fenzi*) and cadre (*ganbu*). They honored the common people (the worker, the peasant, the soldier) as never before in history and gave of their talents to raise the cultural and economic level of every Chinese. In essence they sought to select the good of the literati past and to discard the bad.

Important sociological changes also made the new establishment intellectuals serving the Communist mandarinate different from the Confucian literati. Although these intellectuals wished to continue the former role of censors (i.e., to act as loyal critics of the state), the CCP did not create an institutional equivalent to the imperial censorate.[11] In addition, intellectuals under socialism do not have the local power (i.e., lineage and local kinship organizations) that the traditional scholar-gentry had. That is, they have no estate, no monastery, no mountaintop to which to retreat when out of favor in court. This change has had ideological as well as organizational ramifications: Because the CCP does not consider passive acceptance of policy decisions a sufficient proof of loyalty, one now must speak out in favor of the state and its policies when asked to do so by the state's representatives. Intellectuals can no longer safely draw back into silence. In 1955 this was not important for Party intellectuals. In 1966 it was a matter of life and death. In the 1980s it has been a stumbling block and bone of contention for reformist intellectuals.

Generational differences have changed and will continue to change the nature and strength of the deal (first forged during the Party's Yan'an period) that binds establishment intellectuals to the Communist state, and cataclysmic events (such as those of June Fourth) have the potential to destroy the very foundation upon which the social contract is built. Nonetheless, the stability of China following the turmoil of 1989 (which contrasts so markedly with the situation in eastern Europe) demonstrates that some sort of deal between intellectuals and the state (not to mention the state and the army) still holds force. Even before June Fourth, not all intellectuals were full-fledged participants in this deal, because (as Bonnie McDougall rightly points out) throughout the Communist era there have always been members of the Chinese intelligentsia who have shied away from being "politically active." Among artists and writers (groups that have traditionally produced state ideologues and critics), for example, there have consistently been professionals who would rather steer clear of public policy issues and stick to less overtly political versions of their art.[12] However, for at least some of the politically active members of the intelligentsia, even the brutality of the crackdown of 1989 was not enough to trigger a complete repudiation of their contract with the state, in part because of the limited options available to intellectuals unprepared to take the personal and career-related risks associated with pursuing change through extralegal channels. Whether or not they felt betrayed by June Fourth and related events, establishment intellectuals in summer 1989 were faced with an unavoidable fact: There was (and still is) no functional alternative to the "Communist state" in China for the present, no nationwide, legal organization through which political alternatives could develop to parallel the Catholic church in Poland or the Lutheran church in what used to be East Germany.[13]

Although some kind of contract remains in force, the events of 1989 clearly transformed the character of the relationship between intellectuals and the state. Just how this relationship has and has not changed of late is difficult to assess with any precision at present. The rest of this chapter is devoted to putting the issue in perspective and highlighting some of the key features of the post-June Fourth contract between the intelligentsia and the state.

The Post-Tiananmen Establishment

In the months leading up to June 1989, no scholar or journalist (including myself) adequately communicated the staying power of the establishment, the limited reform goals of most reformers and students, and the profound vulnerability of all demonstrators. We ignored the power of the establishment, of the deal between intellectuals and the Party-state.[14] Nobody was running to interview General Yang Shangkun in spring 1989 or discredited "conservative" propaganda chief Deng Lichun in 1988, and only Roderick MacFarquhar wanted to talk to Peng Zhen (and that was about the Cultural Revolution). Mostly, we mistook *remonstrance* for *fundamental opposition*. But they were far from equivalent. Wei Jingsheng and many other heroes of the Democracy Wall Movement of the late 1970s were (and to a certain extent remain) marginal figures—of great moral significance, reflecting considerable personal courage and insight, but on the fringe of Chinese society and intellectual life.[15] For all the exciting changes in the literary world, the image McDougall has shown—that most artists and writers avoided dissent in favor of politically safe topics or cautiously remonstrated and advised the government—had not significantly changed by the end of the 1980s.[16] Among politically active intellectuals, some were drawn into a variety of think tanks and research groups under Premier Zhao Ziyang's state council and, of course, the Chinese Academy of Social Sciences.[17] Even the extreme reformers, such as Su Shaozhi (who headed the Marxism-Leninism Institute at CASS), Yan Jiaqi (who headed the Institute of Political Science at CASS), Wang Ruoshui (who remained at *People's Daily* and, though in limbo, was able to travel overseas), and even the highly critical astrophysicist Fang Lizhi (vice-president of the Science and Technology University until his purge in 1987) all tried to work through the system.[18] Wang Ruoshui is also a leading member of what Kelly calls the "counter-elite" in China—reformist theoreticians who confronted the "abyss" of moral bankruptcy of the regime and over the past ten years sought to "rebuild the Marxist edifice step by step, concept by concept."[19] One goal these different groups of intellectuals shared: to revise the deal between intellectuals and the state, not to reject it.

When the crunch came and the lack of continued popular resistance (in the face of tanks) became clear, we were shocked. In retrospect we may have expected more of the popular movement than had most of its participants and then blamed its leaders for failing to live up to our exalted expectations. Western journalistic accounts of the events of 1989 and after have placed equally unrealistic expectations upon Chinese intellectuals. The unstated assumption about conditions in China today in most of these accounts is that no self-respecting intellectual would freely serve masters who called in tanks on unarmed students and citizens. Nonetheless, many intellectuals who have remained in China (including some who think of themselves as committed reformers) have been struggling to make their peace with the government. It is as mindlessly cynical to call all of these people opportunists as it is to assume that every "leader" of the popular movement is a saint. All this suggests two things: Some kind of deal between intellectuals and the state is, as I have argued above, still in force; and in order to understand this deal we may have to abandon or at least refine some of the analytical paradigms conventionally used to study politically active members of the Chinese intelligentsia.

One place to begin trying to make sense of the post-June Fourth deal between intellectuals and the state is with the pronouncements that current members of the mandarinate made in the press in 1990. These reveal a continuity of many of the features of the old deal between intellectuals and the state and also shed light on the problematic of that service. In what will strike most Western readers as a near Orwellian case of doublespeak, Su Shuangbi, an editor of *Qiushi* (the successor to *Red Flag* as the CCP's leading theoretical journal), and the theorists Ru Xin and Xing Fensi (all proponents of fundamental reform a few years ago) appeared in the June 20, 1990, issue of *Guangming Daily*, the leading newspaper for intellectuals, in an extended interview discussing, "Continuing the Policy of Letting a Hundred Flowers Bloom and a Hundred Schools of Thought Contend."[20] The life histories of these three intellectuals, as well as the ideas and issues they raise can help us understand how and why the "priestly" role of administrative generalists rather than the secular role of professionals still attracts some Chinese intellectuals.

Su Shuangbi was a student of Wu Han, the famous historian, and in the post-Mao period he has been a spokesman for rehabilitating his mentor (and similar colleagues, such as the Party editor-theorist, Deng Tuo) and attacking their critics, the Gang of Four.[21] Su is a product of the 1950s generation, and as he explained to one visitor, the Party gave this working-class kid the chance for education and advancement. Like Xing and Ru, Su's public announcements on reform have swung back and forth through the 1980s, following the shifts in central Party pronouncements. Thus, in spring 1986 Su was speculating—under the very same rubric of "the Hundred Flowers"—that Marxism would have to be modified and the system open for total reform, and that non-Marxist views should not be attacked as anti-Marxist ones.[22] Ru Xin, a theorist in the Institute of Philosophy at CASS, more closely follows the career pattern of the famous "humanist" theorist Wang Ruoshui, at least up to the mid-1980s. Prominent critics of "humanism" in the early 1960s, both Ru and Wang emerged in the post-Mao period as devotees of the idea. But when "humanism" was again attacked in 1983–1984, Ru Xin caved in, criticizing himself and others in typical rectification fashion.[23] Unlike Wang Ruoshui, Ru could not bring himself to risk a break with the establishment. Xing Fensi falls somewhere between the Su's apparent acceptance of the Party line and Ru's apostate humanism.

All three strike a similar tone in the June 1990 *Guangming Daily* interview.[24] The question of the day is, says Su for the group, "How should China build socialism?" Ideology is an important arena in that effort, and the three men address the question on many intellectuals' minds: "How should we provide correct guidance for the struggle in the ideological field?" That is, what are the rules of the game now? The overt answers are not encouraging: The words of Deng Xiaoping, enunciated by Party resolutions and the new, post-

Tiananmen general secretary, Jiang Zemin, provide the guidelines. Early in the piece the three denounce both the "leftist" errors of (unnamed) earlier periods and the "rightist" errors of bourgeois liberalization.

On second reading, however, the interview is not so depressing. These men are participating in the negotiation of a revised deal between intellectuals and the state in post-Tiananmen China. These intellectuals are not free agents with many viable alternatives, but neither are they helpless. Although they make their peace with the system, they make several assertions at the same time. Repeatedly each man says there is a need for *explicit standards* as to what is or is not legitimate debate: The Party should announce and stick to such standards. Arbitrary political attacks on intellectuals is the underlying criticism of the interview. "It is necessary," says Ru Xin, "to formulate policies to protect and encourage those who are willing to study new problems." The three offer this solution to the problem: Separate academic from political debate and acknowledge and protect a separate class of theoreticians who should not be held to the more disciplined standards of publicists (i.e., propaganda work). "Theoretical study is different from publicity work," says Xing Fensi; "in theoretical study we have to proceed from what is known to what remains unknown. . . . You take risks when you make explorations. . . . We have to protect those comrades who make mistakes in making explorations . . . [otherwise] science and culture will be unable to develop." Indeed, despite the nods to current Party policy, Su Shuangbi maintains precisely the themes of his more reformist writings of 1986: Exploration and development (used to replace the now dubious "reform" in 1990) are needed and intellectuals must be free to explore (though in 1990 the limits are more clear), and non-Marxism should not be equated with anti-Marxism. What was less clear in 1986, however, was much clearer by 1990: There is but one truth, and that truth is Marxism. Su Shuangbi here demonstrates rhetorical skill worthy of his mentor, Wu Han. Su shows the dexterous flexibility of Party intellectuals that so enraged Mao. Although "upholding" Deng Xiaoping's four principles of Party dictatorship and "attacking" bourgeois liberalization, Su maintains the heart of his reform goals from 1986.

Nonetheless, these goals are limited. What these intellectuals demand are instrumental reforms, not fundamental ones. "We can only distinguish correct ideas, which conform to Marxism," says Su, "from erroneous ones, which run counter to Marxism, through calm discussions." Ru Xin tosses in the exception clause (to be utilized when conditions allow): "Marxism itself should be an open-ended theory . . . [able] to absorb useful research results of other non-Marxist schools of thought." These are precisely the ideas pushed in the 1980s by Su Shaozhi (now living in exile) when he was director of the Marxism-Leninism Institute of CASS.

The ideas and values, as well as the role for leading intellectuals, assumed in this interview maintain the priestly (read "theoretical") role for intellectuals, or that subgroup that wishes to attend to national ideological policy. By way of metaphor, we can call it Vatican II Maoism, with the socialist equivalents of folk masses and the vernacular liturgy. There is instrumental latitude, but the underlying dogma is not changed. This was first broached in the post-Great Leap period of 1961–1962 (by, among others, Wu Han). Democracy, pluralism, a release of key moral and political questions to a wide range of social groups—none of these are suggested (in fact they are rejected as "bourgeois liberalization"). Instead, instrumental themes are addressed (indeed the whole "Hundred Flowers" policy is instrumental: to "bring their [intellectuals'] enthusiasm and creativity into full play"). Su and his colleagues accept that there is one truth, but they are concerned that only imperfect humans are available for the task of revealing that liberating truth. The goal of philosophical inquiry, true since the days of Confucius himself, is good government policy. Intellectuals, particularly theorists, are qualified (by what certification is left unstated) to speak for the people on these questions in the traditional Maoist paradigm of collecting and synthesizing the ideas of the masses. "We can make a success of formulating policies," says Su, "if we pool the wisdom of the masses, hold conscientious discussions, and adopt a scientific approach." Given the lack of a viable institutional alternative to the Party, the deal outlined by Su, Xing, and Ru will likely be sufficiently attractive to a number of intellectuals to keep the system bumbling along.[25]

These values echo those expressed by an earlier generation of Party intellectuals in the aftermath of the debacle of the Great Leap Forward. Yang Xianzhen, the head of the Party School (the national cadre-training institute), clearly enunciated a version of these values by 1964, and Deng Tuo, a high official in Peng Zhen's Beijing Municipal Party organization, gave a very literate expression of these values in *Evening Chats at Yanshan* in the Beijing press during 1961 and 1962. Carol Hamrin and I have called these values "Chinese Leninism," which articulated itself in contradistinction to "Maoism" in the wake of the Great Leap. Both variants of Marxism had been integrated in the earlier, Yan'an orthodoxy.[26] The Chinese Leninism of the early 1960s is worth summarizing here because it appears to be the root set of values among the post-Tiananmen intellectual establishment, such as presented in the *Guangming Daily* interview. These values can also provide a ground for comparing and assessing the values of intellectual dissidents. It is worth remembering that the surviving elder leaders of today, such as Deng Xiaoping, Peng Zhen, and others, were closely associated with Chinese Leninist views in the past.

There are five salient aspects to the Chinese Leninist approach to political life.[27] First, in the realm of *theory* or ideology, acceptance of Marxism meshed with ancient Chinese attitudes about orthodoxy: the need for one absolutist moral ideology and the need to assert publicly its infallibility. The Chinese Leninist approach has come to rely on a relatively orthodox version of Marxism-Leninism in comparison with Mao's voluntarism. In the realm of *political organization*, Chinese Leninists, like most of the Chinese leadership, have assumed the traditional statist belief that political institutions should dominate culture and society. They have accepted the Leninist concept of the Party as the vanguard and have viewed its domination of all aspects of Chinese society as a good and necessary thing. However, Chinese Leninists have placed a premium on Party discipline and social order. They have been painfully aware of human imperfection, technical limitations, and the probability of error in the process of social transformation. Thus they support differences of opinion within the Party in the name of scientific experimentation.

In *social policy*, Chinese Leninists have had little tolerance for criticism from the larger society. Subgroup interests are to be taken into account by realistic investigation, strict discipline, strong moral training, and rational decision-making by Party officials acting on behalf of the people—not by non-Party organizations. In the realm of *professional activity*, Chinese Leninists have relied on specialists and technocrats. Leading intellectuals have been well recompensed for their efforts. The general population is assumed to be the passive recipients of their ministrations. In the realm of *private life*, this approach has acknowledged the legitimacy of personal interests and family concerns, so long as they do not interfere with the broad social policies of the Party. This personal latitude is granted not on pluralistic grounds but from a somewhat deterministic social philosophy that posits that ownership and control over the means of production (now in the hands of the vanguard Party) automatically determines the future of China's political institutions, culture, and thought. The Chinese Leninist approach acknowledges the importance of individual thinking, particularly the role of "thought reform" (*sixiang gaizao*), as an indispensable companion of economic development in the achievement of socialism. However, thought reform has been seen as a rational transformation based on an appreciation of scientific history, not as a cataclysmic emotional experience.

This excursion into the values of the post-Tiananmen establishment and its antecedents has sought to demonstrate that the establishment is alive and well, having survived the trauma of spring 1989. In exchange for the yoke of orthodoxy, intellectuals are offered a kinder and gentler plower and once again the opportunity to till the fields of history. It is, on the intellectual and moral level, a "velvet prison" as appealing to intellectual idealism as the velvet prison described by Miklós Haraszti for Hungary.[28] If we find it incredible for intellectuals to explain away the tragedy of June 1989, we need only recall how quite respectable intellectuals such as Wu Han, Deng Tuo, or Yang Xianzhen explained away a much greater tragedy twenty-five years ago after the Great Leap Forward.[29]

Returning to Chirot's model for intellectual change in Eastern Europe, we can say that the continued attractiveness of the priestly vocation in China's socialist state has limited (not eradicated) the loss of faith in the system and the growth of alternate organizations that contributed to the collapse of Communist regimes in Europe in 1989. However, what of the *audience* (Chirot's cultural and educational middle class) that serves as a sort of social base for radical ideas and invidious foreign comparisons with the native regime? There are still enough priests, like Su, Ru, and Xing, and there are new deacons and acolytes (He Xin, for one, has volunteered), but is there still a congregation of the faithful among China's intellectuals?

The answer to this question lies outside the scope of this chapter and has yet to be studied in great depth. There are some indications, though, and the prognosis is sobering. The forces that delimit reform activities of top intellectuals (or opinionmakers), such as the constraints of patriotism or loyalty to the Party and patronage, also affect lower-level "audience" intellectuals. Additionally, preliminary research shows a great diversity among Chinese intellectuals—not only by generation but by occupation, gender, attitude toward Westernization, personal political history, income, and the much-noted technical-humanist divide.[30] One empirical study of political attitudes of Chinese intellectuals was made in 1987 by the Public Research Institute at the Chinese People's University. Analyzed by expatriate Chinese in the United States, this detailed survey of some 1,200 Beijing urban residents tested respondents on their attitudes toward, knowledge of, and participation in reform. The results showed "radical" reform intellectuals to be but 7 percent of this already politically active base population. The majority were "emulators" of current policy (34 percent) or less informed but economically well-to-do "optimists" (13 percent).[31] That the majority of respondents were reformists of one sort or another suggests guarded optimism that some time in the future there may be an audience in China to parallel the one that served Eastern European reformers so well in 1989.

Intellectuals: Types, Roles, and Spheres of Activity

It is now time to turn more explicitly to the issue of conventional paradigms raised earlier and ask: Is there a better way to conceptualize intellectual activity in the public arena that might help us understand the relationship between intellectuals and the state in China? Over the past twenty years, there has been a cottage industry devoted to typologies of Chinese intellectuals—radicals (Maoists) vs. liberals (and later reform radicals), Marxian-Confucians vs. establishment radicals, establishment intellectuals vs. Maoists, and, more broadly, typologies such as inquisitors, technocrats, critical intellectuals, and dissidents.[32] Our inability to comprehend fully the role of China's intellectuals in the popular movement of 1989 and our failure to predict events, before, during, and since highlight the weaknesses in our understanding of current intellectual activity in China. I am no more likely than the next student of Chinese intellectual life to provide insightful and accurate typologies of key kinds or groups of Chinese intellectuals. What I can offer from my experience is the suggestion that it may be more fruitful to think of various Chinese intellectuals not in terms of types, but in terms of their *roles*, and furthermore in terms of *spheres of activity*.

Many of the intellectual types scholars identify can more usefully be seen as roles individual intellectuals may occupy serially or concurrently. In 1987 Merle Goldman and I suggested three such roles: as ideological speakers for the state, a role that dominated the career of the Party theoretician Ai Siqi, for example; as academic and professional elites, roles a number of Chinese intellectuals have endeavored (with mixed success) to separate from political life in the PRC; and as critical intellectuals, that dangerous modern role of Confucian censor and May Fourth iconoclast.[33] The focus on roles was an improvement over static "types," but our categories only concentrated on the politically relevant activities of Chinese intellectuals.

If we follow the career of one of China's modern mandarins—be it that of the former literary czar Zhou Yang or humanist theorist Wang Ruoshui or the infamous astrophysicist democrat Fang Lizhi or less extreme characters such as the economist Sun Yefang or Party propagandist Deng Tuo—we find that our concern with their political views and activities blots out large sections of these people's lives. In addition to seeing these people in terms of their political roles, we must attempt to account for *all* their activities, not just their overtly political ones. A focus on key realms or spheres of intellectual activity may help us to understand the various roles intellectuals play in Chinese politics. Such a concentration produces a more inductive study of intellectual behavior, demanding that a researcher gather information on all domains of public (and, if possible, private) activity in order to frame the significance of the political portion of an intellectual's career. My research on Deng Tuo introduced me to this reality—large amounts of his time were taken up in aesthetics, poetry writing, antique collecting, and Ming and Qing social history. Colleagues researching other Party intellectuals, such as Mary Mazur on Wu Han, report a similar breadth of activity.[34] Although we are a long way from a complete picture of these circles of activities in the lives of leading intellectuals, not to mention statistical data on large numbers of intellectuals, we can still identify three important areas of public activity generally undertaken in greater or lesser degree by all Chinese intellectuals.

Tu Wei-ming has suggested that we think of the behavior of Chinese intellectuals in terms of three overlapping spheres of activity: the realms of *zheng* (politics or governance), *xue* (learning or study), and *dao* (an almost untranslatable ethical and religious term often rendered as the "Way," but which I prefer to think of as the search for "transcendence").[35] The value of Tu's distinction among the spheres of *zheng, xue,* and *dao* stems not only from the rootedness of these concepts in Chinese culture and the models of intellectual activity available to current Chinese intellectuals (Tu developed his analysis from the ideas of his teacher, Confucian scholar Tang Junyi), but also from the ability of these spheres of activity to relate seeming opposite "types." Thus, both establishment intellectuals, like Su Shuangbi, and current dissidents, like Yan Jiaqi, operate primarily in the "political" sphere. Similarly, autonomous professionals and dependent state advisers are types found active in the "academic" sphere. In the "transcendent" sphere we find not only those engaged in public ethics and propaganda work (which, as we recall from the ancient injunction "wen yi zai dao" [literature carries the *dao*], includes most fiction and film) but also those engaged in religion, a fairly dormant activity until recently. It is fruitful to think about the ways in which Su Shuangbi and Fang Lizhi (normally seen as government spokesman and heroic dissident, respectively) are similar; how state planner and private economic consultant share professional skills; and how state propaganda and religious ceremonies parallel each other.

The real strength of this focus on the spheres of activity is that it calls on us to recognize the breadth of intellectual activity behind politically active intellectuals and requires us to contextualize activities in each arena for individual intellectuals. The results can add depth to our understanding of intellectual life and politics in China and can occasionally change our basic view of some intellectuals. I offer two examples, one from the past and one from the present.

Deng Tuo was a politically active intellectual in the CCP from 1930 (when he joined the Party) until his suicide under political duress in 1966, in the early months of the Cultural Revolution. He is famous in China as an intellectually talented, level-headed, and moderate Communist official. He is noted in Western and Japanese studies of China as a "liberal" or "Marxian-Confucian" who had the courage to denounce the errors of the Party after the failures of the Great Leap Forward. The key data for this picture are Deng's own set of over 150 essays from 1961–1962, *Evening Chats at Yanshan*.[36] However, sustained research on the totality of Deng's life (his historical writings in the 1930s and 1950s, his service as editor of leading CCP newspapers in the 1940s and 1950s, and his political falling out with Mao in the late 1950s) and the range of his intellectual activities in the years around 1960 greatly modify this picture. Not only are implications that Deng rejected the CCP (strongly made in earlier studies) simply not true, but it is apparent that Deng perceived himself to be a true, loyal Communist. His criticisms were given to improve, not remove, the Party. More fundamentally, his own perception of authority turns out to have been grounded not in his administrative rank (though he respected due rank and position) but in his *aesthetics*. Activities that at first seemed irrelevant, or tangential, to his political work now seem central to his identity as a "culture bearer." His historical forays into the niceties of Chinese history, culture, poetry, and art (which make up the bulk of Deng's *Evening Chats*, far outnumbering the overtly political essays that had formed the basis of Western views of his ideas) are blatant demonstrations of his qualifications for this literatus (*wenren*) status. Rootedness in the wisdom of Chinese culture not only suited the times (resurgent national pride to compensate for the depressing results of the Great Leap and the anxiety of the emerging Sino-Soviet split) but provided a fulcrum outside Mao Zedong Thought on which to lever the Party and China toward the goals of wealth and power and human dignity for the individual. This is nothing short of an attempt to "re-sinify" Marxism-Leninism in an elitist, intellectual, and rationalist manner in explicit contradistinction to the populist, anti-intellectual, and charismatic "re-sinification" of the Leap itself. It was an attempt, supported by a segment of the Party (especially Peng Zhen), to revive an attractive deal for intellectuals to participate in the government (or to serve its policies directly) following the dispiriting attacks on intellectuals since 1957. It was the Chinese Leninist deal, described earlier in this chapter.[37] Attention to the other circles in Deng Tuo's life—his academic and transcendent activities—has brought the political role of his aesthetics starkly into view.

Fang Lizhi is an example well known to most Westerners. An outspoken critic of the current regime, Fang has been called both "China's Tom Paine" and "China's Andre Sakharov."[38] He was purged from the CCP in January

1987 for "promoting bourgeois liberalization" among students. His case became famous when he took refuge in the U.S. embassy in Beijing shortly after the 1989 massacre. Fang has rightly been viewed as a critic of the regime, as one advocating fundamental democratic reform. But how he came to his views and what he hoped to achieve before he was dismissed from his post are less clear.

Sustained research on Fang's life by James Williams, who devotes much of his attention to Fang's activities in the seemingly "nonpolitical" spheres of physics and astrophysics, has refined our understanding of the scientist-dissident in important ways.[39] First, Fang came to his "radical" democratic ideas based on his experience as a scientist in the 1960s and early 1970s, with little reference to Western political theory. He was originally interested in laser physics but withdrew from any applied science in the wake of the Cultural Revolution. He turned to the theoretical field of astrophysics and cosmology. His hopes for academic autonomy were dashed in 1972 when his innocuous-sounding article "A Solution of the Cosmological Equations in Scalar-Tensor Theory, with Mass and Blackbody Radiation" became the object of heated political attack. Williams explains Fang's fateful error: By following the standard big bang model of cosmic evolution accepted by international physics circles, Fang and his colleagues had violated a basic tenet of dialectical materialism in that they proposed the universe may be finite in space and time. Insofar as Engels had declared the universe to be spatially and temporally infinite, and that the assertion of a finite universe provided arguments for the existence of that opiate of the masses, a God, such a proposition was tantamount to idealist heresy.

Throughout the 1970s and 1980s, Fang was periodically attacked for his calls for "science over politics." In *response* to these attacks, particularly by propaganda chief Hu Qiaomu, Fang extended his defense of professional autonomy to a critique of CCP science policy and from there to a general critique of CCP rule and the political order in China. In this he took advantage of the greater space for professional work outside the "sphere" of politics, as the three spheres of activity spread out, away from the extreme overlap of the Cultural Revolution years. Thus, Fang's famous democratic ideas evolved out of his mundane commitment to his profession and his defense of it from political attacks. The focus on the changing relationship of the three spheres of activity between 1967 and the 1980s helps draw our attention to these factors.

The fight between Fang and more conservative Party reformers can be seen as a fight over the role of intellectuals: Fang wants politically independent critical intellectuals, the Party leaders want politically engaged advisers. Fang explicitly rejects the idea that democracy, or any other social good, can be "bestowed" by the Party or government, and he advocates the basic values of a democracy based on humanism and individual rights and responsibilities. Fang's role as democrat is not limited to ideas. He represents an important sociological development in the PRC—the rise of autonomous professions. As a critic, Fang presents himself as a citizen, not as a politician or government official. His authority for speaking, he claims, is his education in *science*, not "philosophy" (by which he means orthodoxy, Marxism–Leninism–Mao Zedong Thought). His failure, as of this date, to find an audience inside China powerful enough to maintain a public profile in opposition to the current regime indicates that the social base for a polity in which an authority other than the Party and Marxism-Leninism is publicly legitimate has not yet emerged.

It is important to see Fang's efforts as an emerging democrat in the five-decade-long tradition of Party intellectuals pushing for greater individual autonomy and humanism within the corporatist polity of the Party-state. Since the establishment of state power by the CCP in the Yan'an area in the late 1930s, Party intellectuals have sought to negotiate and revise the deal offered by the CCP (the deal being to advise, staff, and propagandize). Each new set of "troublemakers" (who, like Fang, were all Party members) sought a degree of *autonomy* in their service to the state. Each sought that fulcrum in a different sphere of intellectual activity outside the political sphere.

In the early 1940s, Wang Shiwei and other left-wing writers claimed the right to criticize policy in public based on the romantic inspiration of the revolutionary artist. Literature that was, in essence, transcendent of the mundane reality of political bickering, said Wang Shiwei, gave the artist the moral authority to monitor and criticize politicians.[40] In the early 1960s, Deng Tuo, among others, sought such leverage in the moral cultivation derived from the study and practice of China's traditional arts and culture. This role as "culture bearer" drew from an intersection of the academic and transcendent spheres of activity. In the 1980s Fang, drawing purely from the academic sphere, made his fulcrum science, the rational and incremental thinking of the scientific method as embodied in twentieth-century international physics. With the claim of science, Fang could maintain his establishment stance (as vice-president of Science and Technology University and member of several government advisory committees) yet use a more effective pivot than his forebears of the 1940s and 1960s: Scientific method remains both more central to the current orthodoxy and less subject to dismissal (as "foreign" or "feudal") than claims to artistic insight or aesthetic moral cultivation. The sorry fact of the matter is, of course, that none of the three fulcrums has served to shift the Party-state very far in the desired direction.

Fang's efforts to influence politics add another important development in the tradition of Party intellectuals who push for reform. He does not presume to speak "for" or "to" the "people." If Fang appears arrogant when he calls intellectuals the vanguard of the proletariat, his stance is, in fact, more humble than previous establishment reformers or current incumbents, such as Su Shuangbi. He claims to speak only for his own group, intellectuals. He addresses them and calls on them to act. He is not an "interest politician" in the U.S. sense; he speaks for what he sees is the public good: fair government, individual freedom, public responsibility. He cares about other groups in China but is content to let them speak up for themselves. Because he is in a privileged position, Fang feels he and other intellectuals should speak first (especially when such outspokenness is dangerous), but that is all. This is a form of democratization new among Chinese intellectuals who have, otherwise, continued the traditional Confucian pretense to minister to and speak for the "people."[41]

Finally, the political context in which the three spheres of intellectual activity reside is not static. The Chinese "political order" has changed markedly in the course of the past several decades. During the first years of CCP rule, it became harder and harder to separate *xue* and *dao* activities from politics. By 1967, at the height of the Cultural Revolution, the concern with orthodoxy became so great that there was virtually no space left for autonomous scholarly and religious or ethical pursuits. As Mao put "politics in command," the *zheng* sphere swallowed up *xue* and *dao* activities.

In the 1980s, however, the centrifugal forces of the "four modernizations" and de-Maoification triggered a move in the opposite direction: Political concerns still shaped all others, but autonomous space for *xue* and *dao* pursuits gradually grew. The picture resembled that of the 1950s in many ways. There was certainly some integration of academic activity in politics (as in Zhao Ziyang's think tanks), but the boundaries of the three spheres were not coterminous. The key difference between the 1950s and 1980s was the direction of change. In the former decade, the realms of intellectual activity were moving toward a *zheng*-dominated "unity," whereas in the latter period the shift was toward diversity, especially in the provinces.

It is too soon to tell whether or not the trend toward comparatively autonomous *xue, dao,* and *zheng* spheres seen in the 1980s will continue in the 1990s. This will certainly be important to watch, for a continuation of this trend could play a key role in fostering the growth of the kind of "civil society" to which the authors of other chapters in this volume direct our attention. The conceptualization of intellectual activity sketched above, besides letting us put the issue of "civil society" into a slightly different perspective, can also help us minimize our misperceptions of changes in two significant domains: the institutionalization of knowledge and the creation and dissemination of ideology. Intellectuals are key, but not sole, actors in both domains. If we can place *individuals* into a detailed context of their political, academic, and transcendent activities (not to mention private concerns, which in the case of Chinese intellectuals, sadly, remains for the most part out of our sight), and if we can situate individuals' roles in a historical context (identifying the integration or conflation of the three spheres)—then we might move a step closer to figuring out what is going on in China.

Priests, Professionals, and the Price of Autonomy

To be of use, the three circles of intellectual activity that Tu Wei-ming has suggested should help us understand the conundrum that permeates this essay: Are intellectuals in China moving from the "priestly" deal of the early PRC to a "professional" contract in China's polity, or not? I think the answer is yes, but that the going will be painfully slow, much slower than Poland's thirty-year rise from reassertion of Party-state authority in 1956 to a demo-cratically elected government today. Still, when the circles of activity are as disassociated as they are now, intellectuals are confronted with de facto "sec-ularization" of academic and transcendent activities (and "demoralization" of political activity) by dint of the disbelief of political assertions on the part of the intended audiences. The circles, then, simply help us keep in focus the *contexts* of intellectual endeavor both at the individual and (by specific period) polity level. In the shift toward disengagement from the priestly mandarin role, context is important: 1967 would have been a terrible time to try it, the social anomie of the 1930s made it a frustrating time to try it, and the 1990s look to be a promising time to push ahead.

More than propitious circumstances are necessary to make this change, however. Chinese intellectuals will need to conceptualize their separation from the state, the end of their mandarin role. They must articulate, and then fight to protect, their *autonomy* from political direction. Among Chinese crit-ics I have seen numerous expressions of the latter, but only fitful expressions of the former, with Fang Lizhi being a key example. According to George Konrad, Hungarian intellectuals by the late 1980s had made this shift, choos-ing to speak for their own group rather than continuing the seductive role as voice of the people.[42] They have accepted liberal democratic electoral institu-tions as the imperfect but preferable mechanism for articulating the will of the masses. "The price of autonomy" for Chinese intellectuals will be not only to let go of their priestly vocation as have their Eastern European col-leagues, but to become as irrelevant as Western intellectuals in their nations' politics. Late Qing intellectuals like Liang Qichao inadvertently handed away their traditional Confucian role as legitimators of the state to a new and ill-defined political entity, the *qun* (masses).[43] The founding generation of es-tablishment intellectuals in the PRC recaptured the role of state legitimators, but ever since the antirightist movement of 1957, they paid "the price of engagement."[44]

It remains to be seen if intellectuals will be ready to pay the "price of au-tonomy" in the 1990s. Will they be willing to forgo their role as interpreters of Communist orthodoxy, or even of its reform into something else, and once again hand authority back to "the people" (now *renmin*) in practice as well as in theory, via the institutions and values of a free society? The search for "so-cialism with Chinese characteristics" would seem to have failed. Can China's intellectuals now contribute to the complex process of creating a workable "democracy with Chinese characteristics"? Can they resist the siren calls of participation as mandarins in an unelected bureaucratic state and instead ac-cept the less august role of opinion makers in an open market of ideas in which other groups can make key political and administrative decisions? The lesson from Tiananmen, for me, is that this transformation will have to be undertaken on the basis of reforming the still very powerful intellectual establishment in the PRC—both the political institutions of the state and the mental attitudes of the intellectuals. As ever, China's hope will have to be found within itself.

Notes

1. Etienne Balazs, *Chinese Civilization and Bureaucracy*, ed. Arthur F. Wright, trans. H. M. Wright (New Haven: Yale University Press, 1964), p. 13.

2. On the traditional pull of state service on Chinese intellectuals (and its limitations during an era of weak government), see Jerome Grieder's discussion of the Republican era (1911–1949), in *Intellectuals and the State in Modern China* (New York: Free Press, 1981); on this pull over five generations, see Wang Gungwu, *The Chinese Intellectual— Past and Present* (Singapore: Graham Brash, 1983).

3. Thus, to speak of the events of 1989 as a "democracy movement" reflects the wishful thinking of Western observers and the sloganeering of some Chinese activists. For this reason I prefer the term "people's movement," which Tony Saich adopts in his edited volume, *Perspectives on the Chinese People's Movement: Spring 1989* (Armonk, N.Y.: M. E. Sharpe, 1990), or the still more neutral terms such as "1989 protest movement" that contributors to the present volume use. For further discussion of the limits of democracy as a motivating force behind the protest movement, and descriptions of specific ways in which calling the events part of a "democracy movement" can obscure key differences in the political agendas of students and other social groups, see Lee Feigon, *China Rising: The Meaning of Tiananmen* (Chicago: Ivan R. Dee, 1990); Jane MacCartney, "The Students: Heroes, Pawns, or Power-Brokers?" in George Hicks, ed., *The Broken Mirror: China After Tiananmen* (London: Longman, 1990), pp. 3–23; and, in this volume, Elizabeth Perry's essay (Chapter 3) on the elitist "casting" of the political theater in and around Tiananmen Square. For a contrary view that articulately defends the use of the term *democracy* in this context and, more importantly, stresses the need to study the spiritual as well as economic factors involved (on this point I agree), see David Kelly, "Chinese Intellectuals in the 1989 Democracy Movement," in Hicks, *The Broken Mirror*.

4. Kelly, "Chinese Intellectuals," esp. pp. 46–47.

5. We see this in part in the personal memory of Chinese intellectuals sprouting in the cracks of the official Party-directed commemoration of the May Fourth anniversary in 1989, as recounted by Vera Schwarcz in this volume. Most China scholars have also seen it in the personal comments of our Chinese colleagues in the year since the crackdown. A small, but telling, example is the mailing of *neibu* books. *Neibu* books are ostensibly "internal circulation" books that foreigners are not supposed to see (because the books contain more frank information that our bourgeois ideology is bound to distort to China's detriment). Although many such books are simply academic studies or document collections with little security value and can easily be purchased in China by foreigners, it has been illegal to mail them out of China. Since June 1989, the number of *neibu* books received from the Chinese post by scholars I know in the United States and Europe has increased dramatically. I cannot but conclude that the flaunting of this petty regulation (in the spirit of disseminating information) is an indicator of general distaste for the government among clerks and office workers. Indeed, even a senior cadre known for his "leftist" views (supportive of the policies of the general current regime) refused a request to return from retirement after June 1989, so strong was his disgust with the military crackdown. My thanks to Tony Saich for raising this example.

6. Naturally, service in the establishment institutions of the PRC does not by itself demonstrate that an intellectual has *actively* consented to such a "deal." We can imagine a range of participation extending from tacit consent to active negotiation.

7. For an insightful analysis of the role of such "basic units" in relation to other control mechanisms in PRC society, see Lowell Dittmer, *China's Continuous Revolution: The Post-Liberation Epoch, 1949–1981* (Berkeley: University of California Press, 1987), pp. 53–57ff.

8. This analysis is pursued in Timothy Cheek, "Habits of the Heart: Intellectual Assumptions Reflected by Chinese Reformers from Deng Tuo to Fang Lizhi," in Shaochuan Leng, ed., *Changes in China: Party, State, and Society* (Lanham, Md.: University Press of America, 1989), pp. 117–143. Studies of lower-level institutions, such as factories, suggest that similar understandings (about expressions of patriotism, or loyalty to the Party, and patronage) extend to the working classes. See Andrew G. Walder, *Communist Neo-Traditionalism* (Berkeley: University of California Press, 1986). Thomas Gold follows similar themes in his study of daily life in post-Mao China, "After Comradeship: Personal Relations in China Since the Cultural Revolution," *China Quarterly*, no. 104 (December 1985), pp. 657–675.

9. This is my conclusion based on the biographies of numerous leading Party intellectuals, including Yang Xianzhen, Deng Tuo, Wu Han, Jian Bozan, Sun Yefang, and Wang Ruowang, as well as a younger generation: Bai Hua, Liu Binyan, and Wang Ruoshui—all of whom have biographies in either Carol Lee Hamrin and Timothy Cheek, eds., *China's Establishment Intellectuals* (Armonk, N.Y.: M. E. Sharpe, 1986), or in Merle Goldman, with Timothy Cheek and Carol Lee Hamrin, eds., *China's Intellectuals and the State: In Search of a New Relationship* (Cambridge: Harvard Council on East Asian Studies, 1987).

10. I follow the general definition of political generation (based on the formative political experiences of individuals between age seventeen and twenty-five) used by Michael Yahuda, "Political Generations in China," *China Quarterly*, no. 80 (December 1979), pp. 796–805. Li Zehou's valuable depiction of revolutionary generations has been expanded in English in Li Zehou and Vera Schwarcz, "Six Generations of Modern Chinese Intellectuals," *Chinese Studies in History*, 17, 2 (Winter 1983–1984), pp. 42–56. See also Wang, *The Chinese Intellectual*. I am fully aware that later cohorts (such as the generations of the Cultural Revolution and post-Mao reform period) have greatly different mixes of values compared to the two eldest generations. Nonetheless, for reasons elaborated below, the *institutional* realities of China today limit the younger generations, who have moved beyond their elders in the "alienation" process, whereas the mental constructs of the deal that the intellectuals and the state struck in the 1940s and 1950s continue to limit the actions of the older intellectual generations and those younger folk who adopt similar attitudes. Chirot, in Chapter 11 (on Eastern Europe), also notes the faith in the Communist system held by intellectuals of the 1940s and 1950s.

11. The profound dangers involved in trying to play the role of censor between the 1930s and 1950s are well documented in Merle Goldman, *Literary Dissent in Communist China* (Cambridge: Harvard University Press, 1967).

12. This point is made emphatically in Bonnie McDougall's conclusion, "Writers and Performers, Their Works, and Their Audiences in the First Three Decades," in Bonnie S. McDougall, ed., *Popular Chinese Literature and Performing Arts in the People's Republic of China, 1949–1979* (Berkeley: University of California Press, 1984), pp. 269–301, esp. pp. 270–271.

13. See for example, Tony Saich, "The Chinese Communist Party and the Future," *China Information*, 4, 4 (Spring 1990), p. 29.

14. Some did take note of this, at least in passing. See, for example, Carol Hamrin's 1987 conclusion to Goldman, *China's Intellectuals and the State*, pp. 275–304, esp. pp. 285ff. Nonetheless, those of us who study "establishment intellectuals" from the 1950s and 1960s used to joke in 1988 and early 1989 that our subjects were finally historical. We no longer think so. Interestingly, Chirot's chapter concludes in an analogous (but reverse) fashion, declaring that specialists on communism failed to predict events of 1989 in Eastern Europe because they focused too much on the power of the Communist establishment and did not consider the moral and ideological power of intellectual discussions popular in those countries.

15. Many reformist intellectuals have made denigrating remarks to Western scholars about these working-class activists as "unlettered boat rockers" upsetting the emerging reform deal for intellectuals. A public example is the famed translator Yang Xianyi, who quickly recanted his public dismissal of Wei Jingsheng at a conference in Britain after shocked protests from scholars there.

16. Perry Link's collections of literature and debates from the post-Mao period give me this impression. See particularly his introduction, which covers the continuing Party controls on literature in the 1980s, in *Roses and Thorns* (Berkeley: University of California Press, 1984). The same limitations can be seen in philosophical debates, as reflected in the *Chinese Philosophy Yearbook;* see Bill Brugger and David Kelly, *Chinese Marxism in the Post-Mao Era* (Stanford: Stanford University Press, 1990), p. 18. There have certainly been trenchant criticisms of the status quo in Chinese periodicals and books. My point is: How much of an audience did such critics have before 1989 and what could those who might agree with fundamental criticism of the system do? See the excellent collection of critical Chinese writings from the 1980s, Geremie Barmé and John Minford, eds., *Seeds of Fire: Chinese Voices of Conscience* (New York: Hill & Wang, 1988).

17. The key reform think tank was the Development Center (short for the State Council Research Center for Economic and Technological and Social Development) headed by Ma Hong. This and other groups, such as the Reform Institute and Rural Development Center, were organized under Zhao's reform-minded state council and offered intellectuals the opportunity to directly influence state policy. See Carol Lee Hamrin, *China and the Challenge of the Future Changing Political Patterns* (Boulder: Westview, 1989), esp. pp. 231ff.

18. All four men have been expelled from the Party, alienated by the regime from the deal. Still, as late as winter 1990, both Su Shaozhi and Liu Binyan, who are now in exile, maintained (much to the chagrin and anger of the expatriate Chinese student movement) that the Party will likely continue and that reformers will have to work through it if China wishes to avoid a period of bloody confusion (personal communications with Su and Liu). Both men have stuck their heads out to change the current system, so I take these comments as an indication of their reading of the institutional realities of China today.

19. See Brugger and Kelly, *Chinese Marxism*, esp. p. 3. The ideas of counterelite and the "abyss" come from Kelly's earlier essay, "The Emergence of Humanism," see note 23, below.

20. Translated in Foreign Broadcast Information Service: China (FBIS-CHI), 90–134 (July 12, 1990), pp. 25–29. The title of the monthly central Party theory journal, *Qiushi*, is literally "seek truth," just as *Pravda* means "truth."

21. See for example his collection of essays, Su Shuangbi, *Jieji douzheng yu lishi kexue* (Class struggle and historical science) (Shanghai: Shanghai Renmin chubanshe, 1982).

22. Su Shuangbi, "Guanyu kaizhan 'baijia zhengming' de jige wenti" (Several questions on the promotion of "A Hundred Schools of Thought" contend), *Guangming Ribao*, April 30, 1986, p. 3; translated in FBIS-CHI (May 19, 1986), pp. K7–11.

23. See David Kelly, "The Emergence of Humanism: Wang Ruoshui and the Critique of Socialist Alienation," in Goldman, *China's Intellectuals and the State*, esp. pp. 164 and 178. The classic model of rectification (*zhengfeng*) criticism and self-criticism in historical and political context is analyzed in Frederick Teiwes, *Politics and Purges in China: Rectification and the Decline of Party Norms*, 2d ed. (Armonk, N.Y.: M. E. Sharpe, 1992).

24. Quotations taken from translation in FBIS-CHI-90-134 (July 12, 1990), pp. 25–29.

25. Geremie Barmé gives the controversial example of He Xin, who went back into government service after June 1989; see Barmé's introduction to "A Word of Advice to the Politburo—Text by He Xin," *Australian Journal of Chinese Affairs*, no. 23 (January

1990), pp. 62–63. He's and Barmé's conversation continues in the next issue of that journal, no. 24 (July 1990), pp. 337–345.

26. See Carol Lee Hamrin, "Yang Xianzhen: Upholding Orthodox Leninist Theory," in Hamrin and Cheek, *China's Establishment Intellectuals*, pp. 51–91; and Timothy Cheek, "Deng Tuo: A Chinese Leninist Approach to Journalism," in ibid., pp. 92–123.

27. This analysis is fully developed in Timothy Cheek and Carol Lee Hamrin, "Collaboration and Conflict in the Search for a New Order," in Hamrin and Cheek, *China's Establishment Intellectuals*, pp. 6–11.

28. Miklós Haraszti, *The Velvet Prison: Artists Under State Socialism* (New York: Basic Books, 1987).

29. See Hamrin and Cheek, *China's Establishment Intellectuals* and Goldman, *China's Intellectuals and the State*. These volumes document elder intellectuals' criticism of the Great Leap, in Chinese Leninist fashion, behind closed doors in various Party meetings and indirectly through Aesopian language in the press.

30. See Lynn T. White III, "Thought Workers in Deng's Time," in Goldman, *China's Intellectuals and the State*, pp. 253–274; and Lynn T. White III and Cheng Li, "Diversification Among Mainland Chinese Intellectuals," in King-yuh Chang, ed., *Mainland China After the Thirteenth Party Congress* (Boulder: Westview, 1990), p. 466.

31. Jianhu Zhu, Xinshu Zhao, and Hairong Li, "Public Political Consciousness in China," *Asian Survey*, 30, 18 (October 1990), pp. 992–1006.

32. In order, types put forward by: Merle Goldman, *China's Intellectuals: Advise and Dissent* (Cambridge: Harvard University Press, 1981); Peter J. Moody, *Opposition and Dissent in Contemporary China* (Stanford: Hoover Institution Press, 1977); Hamrin and Cheek, *China's Establishment Intellectuals*; and a thoughtful paper by Frederic Wakeman, Jr., "Chinese Intellectuals Since the Cultural Revolution" (presented at the New England China Seminar, Harvard University, March 7,1983).

33. Goldman, *China's Intellectuals and the State*, pp. 3–10.

34. Timothy Cheek, "Broken Jade: Deng Tuo and Intellectual Service in Mao's China" (manuscript); Mary Mazur's study of Wu Han's life can be found in her forthcoming University of Chicago Ph.D. dissertation.

35. Tu has often mentioned the three circles in his public lectures. I had an extended conversation with him on this topic in December 1981 at Harvard.

36. Analyses by Moody, *Opposition and Dissent*, and Goldman, *China's Intellectuals*.

37. Such is the argument I seek to defend in *Broken Jade*. See also, Cheek and Hamrin, "Collaboration and Conflict."

38. "China's Tom Paine Speaks Out on Democracy," *Washington Post*, November 19, 1987, pp. C1 and C4; Orville Schell, "China's Sakharov," *Atlantic Monthly*.

39. The following discussion on Fang draws from the research and translations of James H. Williams. See his "Fang Lizhi's Expanding Universe," *China Quarterly*, no. 123 (September 1990), pp. 459–484; his translations and analysis of Fang's scientific writings in "The Expanding Universe of Fang Lizhi: Astrophysics and Ideology in People's China," *Chinese Studies in Philosophy*, 19, 4; and Fang Lizhi, *Bringing Down the Great Wall: Writings on Science, Culture, and Democracy in China*, trans. and ed. James H. Williams (New York: Alfred A. Knopf, 1991).

40. See Wang Shiwei, "Statesmen and Artists" (1942) translated as "Politicians, Artists" by Gregor Benton in *Wild Lilies—Poisonous Weeds: Dissident Voices from People's China* (London: Pluto Press, 1982), pp. 175–178; and Timothy Cheek, "The Fading of Wild Lilies: Wang Shiwei and Mao Zedong's 'Yan'an Talks' in the First CPC Rectification Movement," *Australian Journal of Chinese Affairs*, no. 11 (January 1984). For more details on the Wang Shiwei case and its continuing relevance to Chinese intellectuals today, see Dai Qing, *Wang Shiwei and "Wild Lilies": Rectification and Purges in the Chinese Communist Party, 1942–1944* (Armonk, N.Y.: M. E. Sharpe, 1991).

41. For an articulately argued contrary view that sees Fang as a self-interested speaker on behalf of a disgruntled elite only, see Richard C. Kraus, "The Lament of Astrophysicist Fang Lizhi: China's Intellectuals in a Global Context," in Arif Dirlik and Maurice Meisner, eds., *Marxism and the Chinese Experience* (Armonk, N.Y.: M. E. Sharpe, 1989), pp. 294–315, esp. p. 306. In "Habits of the Hearts," pp. 131–132, I also argued that Fang reflected nondemocratic paternalistic values. In view of Williams's research, I no longer hold that view.

42. Conversation with George Konrad during his stay at Colorado College, Colorado Springs, fall 1988.

43. Frederic Wakeman, "The Price of Autonomy: Intellectuals in Ming and Ch'ing Politics," *Daedalus*, no. 2 (1972), pp. 67ff.

44. This is what I argue in the revision of my dissertation on Deng Tuo; see Cheek, *Broken Jade.*

10

THE ROLE OF THE CHINESE
AND U.S. MEDIA

Stephen R. MacKinnon

In scholarly analysis of the events of spring 1989, the Chinese press is usually discussed as a tool manipulated by factions within the CCP and the student movement, whereas the U.S. press is pictured as swayed by familiar sympathetic symbols like the goddess of democracy. So far, serious historical analysis of the political role of either country's media has been lacking. In the case of the Chinese press, there is acknowledgment of its importance as a hesitant cheerleader of the democracy movement, having given the signal (by publication of Zhao Ziyang's May 4 speech and coverage of student marches) that sparked two weeks of mass demonstrations involving entire urban populations. Suppression of the Chinese press after May 20 is said to have prefigured the tragic outcome of June 4. Yet the place of journalism in the history of twentieth-century Chinese protest is underanalyzed. Likewise, media analysts often depict U.S. coverage in 1989 as naive, skillfully manipulated by the demonstrators, and having failed to probe the systemic forces that produced the tragedy.[1] As I argue in this chapter, the intertwined histories of both the Chinese press and U.S. reporting on China are directly relevant to an understanding of the political forces that led up to the Tiananmen incident.

In reconstructing Chinese political history since June 4, 1989, scholars have focused on the underdevelopment of a civil society in relation to the state's domination of the public sphere of political discourse.[2] How popular protest movements of the twentieth century were ritualized and ultimately controlled by the state has held center stage, with the history of the modern Chinese press treated as a sideshow. Similarly, U.S. coverage of China in the 1930s and 1940s is seen as censored and manipulated by those in power—or by their opponents, as in the case of Edgar Snow, Nym Wales, Harold Isaacs, Agnes Smedley, and others, who are portrayed as having been won over by student protestors and communist guerrilla leaders.³ Yet it was the forceful persistence of an outspoken, Chinese-language, treaty-port press during the 1930s and 1940s under editors like Zou Taofen, Cheng Shewo, and Chen Bosheng that brought a mass following to the student demonstrations of the mid-1930s. Likewise in the 1980s, without such publications as *World Economic Herald* (Shijie jingji daobao), *Scientific and Technology Daily* (Keji ribao), or the muckraking reporting and sophisticated political analysis of Liu Binyan and Wang Ruoshui, the mass movements of 1989 would have been unlikely. In the same way, U.S. reporting on China in the 1930s laid the groundwork for the emotional, contradictory U.S.-China relationship of the 1940s, just as the China-lobby journalism of Henry Luce in the 1940s laid the groundwork for the Asian cold war relationships of the 1950s and later. Today it is hard to overestimate the effect in political terms of U.S. media penetration of Chinese cities, as reflected in the present regime's concerned (albeit inept) attempts to counter such influence.

Since Deng Xiaoping initiated reforms in the late 1970s, the Chinese press had been liberalizing rapidly. *Xinwen gaige* (journalism reform) was the catchall phrase for reforms running from technical changes like the introduction of computers to structural changes in press financing, advertising, and censorship.⁴ The growth in the number of officially sponsored publications through the 1980s makes the point statistically. By 1987 2,578 newspapers of many varieties were being published, in contrast to the low of 46 during the depths of the Cultural Revolution (1966–1969). Tone and content changed, with prominence given to readers' letters, investigative reporting, and human interest stories. Behind all this was a new professionalism tied directly to the rapid expansion of journalism training and the ideas of Western journalism educators (particularly Americans). The latter saturated Chinese media institutions with U.S. definitions of objectivity, curriculum, critical analysis, textbooks, writing techniques, and so on. By spring 1989 the Chinese press was in the midst of a flowering of free expression the likes of which had not been seen since the 1930s and 1940s. Not surprisingly, the continuing political crackdown since June 1989 has been aimed at controlling the press and limiting U.S. influence. In future political struggles a critical battleground undoubtedly will be issues of a free press and Western (mainly U.S.) models.

Available works in English on the history of the Chinese press in the twentieth century are few. The most important is *Chinese Democracy* (1986), in which Andrew Nathan ties the Chinese press to the theory and practice of democracy in China.⁵ Nathan focuses first on the roots of the modern press during the early 1900s by discussing the polemical writings of figures like Liang Qichao. Then he leaps to the Democracy Wall episode of the late 1970s, skipping the period in between almost altogether. Yet the 1930s and 1940s were the most creative and courageous decades in the history of the Chinese press. The fluidity and freedom of the times were comparable to that of the 1980s for the Chinese press in Taiwan, Hong Kong, and mainland China. A key link between the two periods, the 1930s to 1940s and the 1980s, is the symbiotic relationship between the U.S. and Chinese press at both times.

The best-known aspect in the history of the Chinese press in the 1930s is its sometimes lethal restriction—or censorship—by Chiang Kaishek's government.[6] But official censorship was not a constant. It varied in strength from year to year and region to region. From 1930 to spring 1933, Shanghai was a freer place for journalists than during the following three years. Although publishers and writers were arrested and assassinated, the pattern was erratic and seemingly arbitrary. Leading figures such as Zou Taofen and Cheng Shewo saw papers shut down but usually escaped arrest. In 1936 Xi'an was an island of relatively free expression—especially about the need for a war with Japan—because of the presence of Zhang Xueliang and the Manchurian army. Two years later, when Hankou was the wartime capital, the Chinese press was freer and more vibrant than at any other time before or since. Communist, Kuomintang, Trotskyist, and independent publications proliferated.[7] In subsequent years, Japanese censorship blanketed the coastal cities and was complete by the time the Pacific War broke out in 1941. Likewise, after Chiang Kaishek moved to Chongqing, his regime became progressively more repressive of the press (both Chinese and Western). He virtually closed down the Communist press after the New Fourth Army incident during winter 1942.

Chiang's chief censor and sometime minister of information through much of the 1930s and 1940s was Hollington Tong (Dong Xianguang).[8] Tong was a University of Missouri journalism school graduate who prided himself on an American approach to journalism and good rapport with U.S. journalists. In the early 1930s he had worked closely on Shanghai English-language publications with the young journalists Harold Isaacs, Tilman Durdin, and Edgar Snow. He understood the importance of image making, applying U.S. media techniques to information control in China.[9] Between 1937 and 1945, Hollington Tong frustrated the U.S. reporters, whom he censored heavily, precisely because of his strong Western credentials.

As Chiang's chief censor, Hollington Tong was outmaneuvered at times by courageous editors. When their papers were closed down by the authorities in Nanjing or Beijing, these editors founded new publications in the foreign concession zones of Shanghai and continued their defense of civil liberties of intellectuals as well as criticism of the Nanjing government's reluctance to confront the Japanese. The most widely known among those who dodged official censorship was Zou Taofen, who was educated at the U.S. missionary college of Yanjing University—an outpost of the journalism school of the University of Missouri. Through publications like *Xin shenghuo* (New life), he mobilized people for the anti-Japanese street demonstrations of the mid-1930s. Moreover, Zou personally led the assault of a new "civil society" on the public sphere. In 1935 he founded the National Salvation Association (Jiuguo Hui), resulting in his arrest—along with five other notables—in the "six gentlemen incident." The event sparked national demonstrations of protest that in turn led to Chiang Kaishek's being kidnapped and turned over to the CCP during the Xi'an incident of December 1936. The experience radicalized Zou, who thereafter developed close ties to the Chinese Communist Party.[10]

Cheng Shewo was more of a political maverick and is less well known today than Zou Taofen. But in the 1930s, Cheng's papers had a wider circulation. He represented a prototype of the scrappy, entrepreneurial editor-publisher whom one finds today in Hong Kong, Taiwan, and overseas Chinese communities. In 1930 Cheng toured the United States. The highlight of his visit was a long stay at Hollington Tong's alma mater, the University of Missouri School of Journalism, where Cheng attended lectures and gave talks on Chinese journalism. The U.S. experience seemed to embolden Cheng. He was one of five founders in 1932 of the League of Civil Rights (Zhongguo Minquan Baozhang Tongmeng) and almost lost his life because of it. In 1934 Cheng was arrested and his papers shut down. Cheng moved his papers from Nanjing and Beijing to Shanghai (and in 1938 to Hong Kong). In the pages of the *Li Bao* (1935–1940), he challenged the Kuomintang on Japanese policy and continued to defend civil liberties. The key to Cheng Shewo's survival as a publisher was consistent patronage from individuals or factions (whom he paid off financially) within the ruling party. During most of the 1930s, Cheng was protected by Ye Chucang and Li Shizeng, cabinet-level officials in the Nanjing government. Yet at the same time, Cheng's papers were staffed by talented young Communists like Sa Kongliao and Zhang Youyu. Like Zou Taofen, Cheng was much more than a mouthpiece or tool. Through their publications and actions in the public sphere, these editors led the challenge to Kuomintang or Communist monopoly of political dialogue.[11]

The historical literature on U.S. press coverage of China in the twentieth century is sparse, consisting mostly of memoirs and a sprinkling of analytical studies. U.S. reporting about the Chinese Communists has received most of the attention, no doubt because of the controversies in the early 1950s concerning "who lost China." In conducting research for an oral history of reporters who covered China for major U.S. dailies during the 1930s and 1940s, I found that the connection between reporters and their Chinese colleagues was crucial to an understanding of the larger context or network within which the U.S. journalist operated.[12] Chinese journalists served in major staff positions and as chief sources for U.S. journalists: Teddy White of *Time* relied upon Cheng Defang; Peter Rand of the *New Yorker* depended upon Yang Chao; Hank Lieberman of the *New York Times* turned to Gong Peng and Qiao Guanhua. Of course the urban elite backgrounds and politically leftist sympathies of their Chinese colleagues and staff colored the kinds of stories U.S. reporters filed during the 1930s and 1940s. There was one place and year when the Chinese influence was especially pronounced: the wartime capital of Hankou in 1938. This was a crucial period in shaping positive first impressions of Chinese Communists and reinforcing the strong anti-Japanese and pro-Chinese nationalist sympathies of U.S. reporters who became the major interpreters of events in China from 1938 to at least 1947. Moreover, views developed in the crucible of Hankou affected the military as well as diplomats like Joseph Stilwell and John Davies, whose subsequent policy actions would shape the postwar debate on U.S.-China policy.

The symbiotic relationship between the Chinese and U.S. press of the 1930s and 1940s is illustrated further by the intertwined careers of F. McCracken ("Mac") Fisher and Liu Zunqi. Fisher studied journalism and Chinese at

Yanjing University in Beijing from 1931 to 1933. In 1935 Fisher participated with Edgar Snow in the December 9 demonstrations over Chiang Kaishek's Japan policy. By 1938 Fisher was in Hankou as United Press International bureau chief covering the war against Japan. In 1941 he moved to Chongqing, Chiang's wartime capital, and after Pearl Harbor became head of the Office of War Information (OWI), where he recruited and trained most of the U.S. journalists who would cover China for the next twenty years. Fisher's Chinese chief of staff in Chongqing was Liu Zunqi, arguably one of twentieth-century China's most important journalists.[13]

A fluent speaker and writer of English, Liu Zunqi was also a graduate of the journalism school at Yanjing. After graduation in 1932, Liu worked closely in Shanghai with Harold Isaacs and Agnes Smedley on the *China Forum*, a path-breaking, English-language anti-KMT weekly. Liu had been a secret member of the CCP since the late 1920s. Eventually he was arrested in the mid-1930s but managed to escape and make his way to the guerrilla areas in the northwest. In 1941 the party sent him to Chongqing, where he was recruited by Fisher, who had known him at Yanjing but was unaware of Liu's Party membership. From the key position as chief of the Chinese staff, Liu oversaw and facilitated the work of U.S. journalists in China during the war. It was Liu, for example, who arranged for the visits to Yan'an by U.S. journalists in 1944. Like Hollington Tong on the Kuomintang side, Liu applied U.S. techniques and know-how behind the scenes to improve the image of and contact with the Chinese Communists. After the war Liu worked in Shanghai and Hong Kong for the Chinese press. In the 1950s he was one of the founders of the *Guangming ribao* (a national daily) in Beijing. Then in 1957 he was branded a rightist because of his outspokenness and U.S. connections. Not until the late 1970s did Liu resurface as the founding father of China's only English-language daily, *China Daily*, recruiting staff heavily from those who had been rightists in the 1950s and who had worked earlier with U.S. reporters in Shanghai, Hankou, Chongqing, Yan'an, and elsewhere. (It is ironic that Fisher suffered a parallel fate to Liu at the time: Fisher's career was effectively derailed by McCarthyism and questions about earlier familiarity with Liu Zunqi.)[14]

In the 1980s the Sino-U.S. relationship in journalism became close again. With the revival of pre-Cultural Revolution schools at Fudan (Shanghai) and the People's University (Beijing) and the creation of new graduate schools, notably the institutes of journalism at the new Chinese Academy of Social Sciences and Xinhua News Agency, U.S. textbooks and foreign experts were heavily relied upon in the classroom. Extensive exchanges were conducted with major journalist training programs in the United States, beginning with the University of Missouri's journalism school. A national foundation was created to honor the memory and work of journalists Agnes Smedley, Edgar Snow, and Anna Louise Strong. Chinese bookstalls were flooded with translations of U.S. works in all fields—from mysteries, romances, and science fiction to more serious works on psychology and history, and biographies of major journalists like Walter Lippmann. A best-seller was Alvin Toffler's *Future Shock*. The response in the United States was similarly enthusiastic.

Deng Xiaoping was named *Time* magazine's man of the year twice (1979 and 1986)—a distinction he shares with Chiang Kaishek. Leading Chinese journalists were invited to study and lecture under the sponsorship of newspapers, universities, and foundations like Luce. Satellite news-report exchanges were instituted, and the number of correspondents in each country (with restrictions relaxed) annually increased until 1989.

A major result in terms of the Chinese press was the sweeping reforms described earlier, most of which went in a Western direction. These reforms, however, never broke the Communist Party's monopoly of the media. Prominent anti-rightist campaign victims of the 1950s, like Liu Binyan, were restored and able to publish penetrating exposés of the extensive corruption, political and otherwise, of the Party-run bureaucratic system. But by the middle of the decade, Liu was criticized and, when he refused to recant, dismissed from the Party and forced into exile by 1988. Media reform thus paralleled the ups and downs of the popular movement for democracy, from the Democracy Wall demonstrations of 1978–1979 to the Beijing uprising of May 1989.[15]

As in the 1930s, the key to survival in the 1980s for a Chinese journalist or editor was patronage within the ranks of the Party elite. A major figure in the liberalization of the *People's Daily* (for whom Liu Binyan worked) was vice-editor An Gang, who had a direct line to Party Secretary Hu Yaobang. An Gang's Party pedigree ran back to Communist-led New Fourth Army units in his home province of Anhui during the war against Japan (1937–1945). An Gang spearheaded the application of high technology (computerization and new presses) to production at the *People's Daily* as well as the creation of its overseas edition. He founded the paper's most profitable ancillary publications: two weekly magazines focusing on the marketplace and political cartoons, respectively. An Gang also played a major role with Liu Zunqi in the establishment of the *China Daily*, which became a pacesetter in the use of photocopy and computerized production.

In the end, however, An Gang went too far too fast. In 1985 he headed a team that financed the preparation of a two-hour video documentary that contrasted China's economic backwardness to the development of Japan and the West—exactly the same theme as that of *He Shang* (River Elegy), which would scandalize the Party elders during summer 1988. After Hu Yaobang fell from power in January 1987, An Gang was mysteriously beaten up on the street. He retired from the leadership of the new commercially successful and self-sufficient newspaper *Jingji ribao* (Economic Daily), of which he had been editor-in-chief and founder. By 1989 An Gang had virtually disappeared from the scene.[16]

The major difference between the 1980s and the 1930s–1940s, of course, is the effectiveness of Communist Party controls over the media in the later period. There have been no treaty-port alternatives to state publications in the People's Republic of China; underground opposition media never developed as in Eastern Europe. Journalists like Liu Binyan and An Gang chose to dissent within the system as "establishment intellectuals" (see Chapter 6).[17] Yet in the long run, given the growing fragility of the Communist state in China, this distinction may not be so important. Like Zou Taofen and Cheng Shewo in the 1930s, Liu Binyan and An Gang in the 1980s were perceived by the government as having challenged the state's monopoly over political discourse in the public sphere. Despite setbacks, the confidence-building experience and examples of Liu and An, as well as the plethora of semi-independent publications that flowered for a time in the 1980s, may well do more to transform Chinese politics by the end of the twentieth century than have street demonstrations.

The travails and growing sophistication of the Chinese press during the 1980s was reflected in improving U.S. coverage of China. At the beginning of the decade, U.S. reporting was remarkably homogeneous and derivative of the Chinese view, blaming the Cultural Revolution for all of China's contemporary ills.[18] As in the 1930s and 1940s, U.S. reports on China retained a strong urban bias (in the overestimation of success in population control efforts, for example). By the end of the decade, however, sustained access to reliable sources and experience gave greater variety and depth to the coverage, notably in the work of Orville Schell (feature writer mostly for the *New Yorker* and *Atlantic*), Frank Ching *(Wall Street Journal)*, Mike Chinoy (Cable News Network), Nicholas Kristoff and Sheryl WuDunn *(New York Times)*, and Jonathan Mirsky (U.S. writer for British publications). Thus, taken as a whole, even television reporting of the events of spring 1989 was comparatively sophisticated. Teams of academic and diplomatic analysts were enlisted for interpretation of events on an unprecedented scale. The results compared favorably, for example, with reporting on Indochina from 1965 to 1975 or coverage of the Persian Gulf crisis in 1990 and 1991.

Finally, just as during the late 1940s, serious divisions over U.S. policy have opened up between Washington policymakers and reporters covering China. Following the events of June 4, 1989, the more experienced journalists in the field have reported more hostilely and cynically on policy paralysis in Beijing and the obsession with security and control of Deng's regime. Their empathy for the suppressed Chinese intellectual resembles that of counterparts like Theodore White and Anna Lee Jacoby in the 1940s. A major diplomatic figure like the U.S. ambassador to China, Winston Lord, has risked a career by breaking with the president over policy. Splits in Congress over most-favored-nation trading status for China and the Chinese government's human rights violations reflect mixed editorial opinion in the regional press. But as Harry Truman reluctantly supported Chiang Kaishek in the late 1940s, George Bush continued lukewarm backing of an unpopular Deng Xiaoping for global geopolitical reasons.

On balance U.S. influence on the Chinese press may be greater than the reverse, given the importance of the ideal of a free press to the Chinese democratic movement since the turn of the century. But it is worth remembering that the U.S. journalists covering China inevitably reflect the prejudices and concerns of their Chinese co-workers. Current features of U.S. press reporting in some ways resemble those of the 1940s: poor coverage of rural conditions, strong coverage of the urban-educated elites, and genuine empathy for political dissenters. What may be more important by the end of the century is the leading contribution of both media to the creation of a civil society in China or a political dialogue and legitimacy outside a state-dominated public sphere. In the 1980s the Chinese and U.S. press demonstrated that the struggles for press freedom in China of the 1930s and 1940s had not been an empty exercise.

The liberalization of the Chinese press in the 1980s and its interaction with U.S. media had a dual effect: It provoked a crackdown yet demonstrated the potential of an unbridled press to mobilize the urban masses against the state and give form to a new body politic. By 1989 even more threatening to the Communist Party's domination of the media was the renewed and growing Chinese journalistic commitment to a higher kind of loyalty: to truth outside the state. Exercise of such rights had led in the United States to Richard Nixon's impeachment in the mid-1970s. For two momentous weeks in mid-May 1989, the Chinese press pursued their Fourth Estate rights—with sadly different results. Tragic as the outcome was in the short run, however, this flexing of journalistic muscle may well have prefigured an even more critical role for the media in the years ahead.

Notes

1. Seth Faison, "The Changing Role of the Chinese Media," in Tony Saich, ed.,*Perspectives on the Chinese People's Movement: Spring 1989* (Armonk, N.Y.: M. E. Sharpe, 1990), pp. 144–162; Michael J. Berlin, "Chinese Journalists Cover (and Join) the Revolution," *Washington Journalism Review* (September 1989), pp. 33–37; James C. Thomson, "Jilted Again: The U.S. Media's Courtship with Democracy in China," *Gannett Center Journal* (Fall 1989), pp. 91–103; and Yi Mu and Mark V. Thompson, *Crisis at Tiananmen* (San Francisco: China Books, 1989), esp. pt. 3 on the press.

2. David Strand, "Protest in Beijing: Civil Society and Public Sphere in China," *Problems of Communism*, 29, 3 (May–June 1990), pp. 1–19; and Andrew Nathan,*China's Crisis: Dilemmas of Reform and Prospects for Democracy* (New York: Columbia University Press, 1990). See also Esherick and Wasserstrom (Chapter 2) in this volume.

3. Kenneth Shewmaker, *Americans and Chinese Communists, 1927–45: A Persuading Encounter* (Ithaca: Cornell University Press, 1971).

4. Judy Polumbaum, "Tribulations of China's Journalists After a Decade of Reform," introduction to Chin-Chuan Lee, ed., *Voices of China: Politics and Journalism* (New York: Guilford Press, 1990); Won Ho Chang, *Mass Media in China: The History and the Future* (Ames: Iowa State University Press, 1989).

5. Andrew Nathan, *Chinese Democracy* (Berkeley: University of California Press, 1985).

6. Lee-hsia Hsu Ting, *Government Control of the Press in Modern China, 1900–1949* (Cambridge: Harvard University Press, 1974).

7. Chinese sources summarized in *Wuhan kangzhan shiyao* (Important events in Wuhan during the War of Resistance) (Hubei, 1985). See also Guo Moruo, *Hong Boqu* (Tianjin, 1959), a book of poems celebrating the Hankou spirit.

8. On Hollington Tong and his U.S. background, see his memoir,*Dateline China* (New York: Rockport Press, 1950).

9. An interesting parallel is the strong U.S. influence on Chiang Kaishek's reformed police structure under Dai Li; see Frederic Wakeman, "Policing Modern Shanghai," *China Quarterly* (September 1988), pp. 408–440.

10. Parks Coble, "Chiang Kaishek and the Anti-Japanese Movement in China: Zou Taofen and the National Salvation Association, 1931–37, *"Journal of Asian Studies*, 44, 2 (February 1985), pp. 293–310.

11. Cheng Shewo, *Baoxue Zashu* (Journalism miscellany) (Taipei, 1957); *Xinwen Yanjiu Ziliao* (Materials on the study of journalism), vols. 26–29 (Beijing, 1985); *Zhongguo Minquan Baozhang Tongmen* (The Chinese League of Civil Rights) (Beijing, 1979); and Wesley S. Palmer, "Cheng Shewo and Chinese Journalists in the 1920s and 1930s" (M.A. thesis, Arizona State University, 1988).

12. Stephen R. MacKinnon and Oris Friesen, *China Reporting: An Oral History of American Journalism in the 1930s and 1940s* (Berkeley: University of California Press, 1987).

13. MacKinnon and Friesen, *China Reporting;* and F. McCracken Fisher Papers, Arizona State University, Hayden Library.

14. MacKinnon and Friesen, *China Reporting*, pp. 196–199; Harold R. Isaacs, *Reencounters in China: Notes of a Journey in a Time Capsule* (Armonk, N.Y.: M. E. Sharpe, 1985), pp. 95–110; and E. J. Kahn, Jr., *The China Hands: American Foreign Service Officers and What Befell Them* (New York: Penguin, 1976).

15. Liu Binyan, *A Higher Kind of Loyalty* (New York: Pantheon, 1990).

16. I worked for *People's Daily* for two years (1979–1981) and at the Chinese Academy of Social Sciences in 1985, during which time I had close contact with An Gang. Thereafter I followed An Gang's career through students who worked under him at the *Economic Daily*.

17. Literature on this subject is abundant; the best recent work is Timothy Cheek and Carol Lee Hamrin, eds., *China's Establishment Intellectuals* (Cambridge: Harvard University Press, 1986).

18. The first wave of reporters after 1979 produced books that were remarkably similar in terms of viewpoint and conclusions about China. Two even have the same title. See Fox Butterfield *(New York Times), China: Alive in the Bitter Sea* (New York: Times Books, 1982); John Fraser *(Toronto Globe), The Chinese: Portrait of a People* (New York: Summit, 1980); David Bonavia *(Times of London) The Chinese* (New York: Penguin, 1980); Jay Mathews and Linda Mathews *(Los Angeles Times), One Billion: A China Chronicle* (New York: Random House, 1983); and Richard Bernstein *(Time), From the Center of the Earth: The Search for Truth About China* (Boston: Little, Brown, 1982).

Part Five

STATE POWER AND LEGITIMACY

The two chapters in this thematic part were written by scholars who have quite different academic backgrounds and research interests: Chirot is a sociologist whose work tends to focus on regions other than East Asia; Saich is a China specialist whose training is in political science. Their contributions to this volume also concentrate on different periods: Chirot's chapter is mainly concerned with the events leading up to 1989; Saich's pays particular attention to political and cultural developments since the early June massacres that took place in Beijing and Chengdu. Despite these differences, both authors share a common interest in the methods state socialist regimes use to legitimate one-party rule, and each of their chapters argues that contests for power can only be understood if we pay close attention to factors that defy simple quantification, such as (in Chirot's case) a growing sense of moral outrage among key segments of the populace, and (in Saich's case) a change in the ruling elite's ability to control public discourse. Each author suggests in his own way that one of the most important things to watch for is signs that the regime in power is running low on what Pierre Bourdieu refers to as "symbolic capital" (a term that Saich uses and explains in his chapter and that Bourdieu himself defines clearly in his piece cited in the supplementary materials list accompanying Part 2). In addition, both Chirot and Saich are concerned with identifying the conditions that allow subordinated groups to act publicly upon the shared grievances that James Scott refers to as subversive "hidden transcripts" (see his book in the following supplementary materials list). Then, finally, the chapters here in Part 5 each contain arguments that have relevance for ongoing debates within the field of revolutionary studies, because (as the collections of essays edited by Nikki Keddie and Jack Goldstone in the following list illustrate) participants in these debates have recently begun to pay a great deal of attention to the relative importance of state structures and symbolic struggles in precipitating or shaping the course of social revolutions.

Recommended Supplementary Materials for Classroom Use

Scholarship on China: Contemporary Politics

Anagnost, Ann. "Socialist Ethics and the Legal System." In the first edition of Wasserstrom and Perry, *Popular Protest and Political Culture in Modern China*. Boulder: Westview Press, 1992, pp. 177–205. A study of the power of the Chinese state; the study uses discussion of village compacts to analyze ideological practice and the control of discourse in the era of Deng Xiaoping.

Brook, Timothy. *Quelling the People: The Military Suppression of the Beijing Democracy Movement*. Oxford: Oxford University Press, 1992. A detailed account of the activities of the People's Liberation Army during the period leading up to and including the Beijing and Chengdu massacres of early June.

Friedman, Edward, et al. *Chinese Village, Socialist State*. New Haven: Yale University Press, 1991. A study of rural politics by a multidisciplinary team of scholars; Friedman et al. emphasize the process through which local inhabitants came to lose faith in and feel victimized by the state apparatus controlled by the CCP.

Nathan, Andrew J., Lowell Dittmer, and Andrew G. Walder. "Tiananmen 1989: A Symposium." *Problems of Communism* (September–October 1989). Essays on 1989 by three prominent American China specialists, each of whom is concerned with issues of state power and legitimacy.

Shue, Vivienne. *The Reach of the State: Sketches of the Chinese Body Politic*. Stanford: Stanford University Press, 1988. A series of interconnected essays on the contours of state power in contemporary China.

Scholarship on China: Historical Perspectives

Duara, Prasenjit. *Culture, Power, and the State: Rural North China, 1900–1942*. Stanford: Stanford University Press, 1988. Duara argues that, despite the chaos that has generally been seen as characterizing the era, this period was one of state-building as well; the work also includes discussion of the "cultural nexus of power" that empowered local elites within their home villages and connected them to central authorities.

Esherick, Joseph W., and Mary B. Rankin, eds. *Chinese Local Elites and Patterns of Dominance*. Berkeley: University of California Press, 1990. A conference volume containing detailed case studies of a wide variety of locations and periods; introductory and concluding essays by the editors take pains to place these findings into the broadest possible comparative and theoretical perspectives, highlighting issues relating to hegemony and the cultural dimensions of political power at both regional and national levels.

Watson, James L., and Evelyn S. Rawski, eds. *Death Ritual in Late Imperial and Modern China*. Berkeley: University of California Press, 1988. This work contains several chapters that are relevant to the arguments presented here in Part 5 and includes essays by Evelyn Rawski and Frederic Wakeman, Jr., that focus on the legitimizing functions of state funerals held to honor high-ranking political figures.

Woodside, Alexander. "Emperors and the Chinese Political System." In Kenneth Lieberthal et al., eds., *Perspectives on Modern China: Four Anniversaries*. Armonk, N.Y.: M. E. Sharpe, 1991, pp. 5–30. Woodside focuses on the roots of legitimacy in the imperial era and compares the symbolic position of Chinese emperors to that of European kings.

Zito, Angela. "Grand Sacrifice as Text-Performance: Writing and Ritual in Eighteenth-Century China" (unpublished doctoral dissertation, University of Chicago, 1989). Zito's anthropological study of the symbolism and meaning of a key state ritual of the imperial era.

Comparative Works and Case Studies of Other Countries

Geertz, Clifford. "Centers, Kings, and Charisma: Reflections on the Symbolics of Power." In Sean Wilentz, ed., *The Rites of Power*. Philadelphia: University of Pennsylvania Press, 1985, pp. 13–38. Geertz analyzes the crucial role that public rituals play in legitimating the power of ruling elites, even in the most seemingly secular of states.

Goldstone, Jack, ed. *Revolutions: Theoretical, Comparative, and Historical Studies*. San Diego: Harcourt Brace Jovanovich, 1994. This second edition is a wide-ranging collection of readings, which includes essays by prominent contemporary theorists (including the editor and Theda Skocpol) whose models of revolution emphasize the importance of social structural factors in triggering state crises; the book contains several chapters on China and some discussion of 1989.

Keddie, Nikki, ed. *The Debate on Revolutions: Theory and Practice*. New York: New York University Press, forthcoming in 1994. A volume that brings together essays on revolution that first appeared in the journal *Contention* during the early 1990s; several of these pieces assess the extent to which various events that took place in 1989 can be interpreted as either confirming or contradicting social-structural/state-centered theories.

Scott, James C. *Domination and the Arts of Resistance: Hidden Transcripts*. New Haven: Yale University Press, 1990. Scott argues that even the most oppressed groups have the symbolic and tactical resources to carry out effective struggles for change, especially when a weakening of the forces of hegemony allows these groups to bring into the open and to act upon their subversive "hidden transcripts" that are kept alive in more oppressive times through secretive and often satirical forms of communication.

Sewell, William H., Jr. "Ideologies and Social Revolution: Reflections on the French Case." *Journal of Modern History*, vol. 57, no. 1 (1985), pp. 57–85. A critique of the materialist emphasis in Theda Skocpol's work on social revolutions; stresses the important role that symbolic and discursive struggles play in the fall of old regimes and the rise of new ones.

Primary Sources

Barmé, Geremie and John Minford, eds. *Seeds of Fire: Chinese Voices of Conscience*. New York: Hill & Wang, 1988, second edition. Selected writings by Chinese dissidents.

Gao Yuan. *Born Red: A Chronicle of the Cultural Revolution*. Stanford: Stanford University Press, 1987. A memoir by a former Red Guard; Gao illustrates quite effectively how the state and its policies has affected even the most private aspects of life in the People's Republic of China.

Koppel, Ted (and ABC News). "The Koppel Report: Tragedy at Tiananmen—the Untold Story." A documentary that highlights issues relating to political legitimacy and power struggles within the Chinese elite; this report could also be used in conjunction with Part 6 of this book, because it illustrates many of the themes Wasserstrom refers to (in Chapter 13) in his discussion of the Western media's treatment of the events of 1989.

11

WHAT HAPPENED IN
EASTERN EUROPE IN 1989?

Daniel Chirot

The world knows that in Eastern Europe communism collapsed in 1989, and that the USSR set out on a path that not only promises the end of socialism but threatens its very territorial integrity. But knowing this does not explain why it all happened. Nor are the implications of all these revolutionary events as clear as the immediate, short-run strategic effects that follow from the dissolution of the Warsaw Pact and the Council for Mutual Economic Assistance.

There are many ways of looking at the "revolution of 1989." As with other great revolutionary events—the French Revolution of 1789, the European revolutions of 1848, the Bolshevik Revolution of 1917, or the Chinese Revolution of 1949—economic, political, cultural, and social analyses offer only partial insights because everything was interconnected. Yet no single analysis can entirely absorb all aspects of such cataclysmic events. Even after 200 years, the French Revolution is still a subject for debate, and novel interpretations remain possible. And if the political controversy generated by that revolution two centuries ago has cooled somewhat, for well over a century and a half it remained a burning issue at the center of European and world politics.[1] We should not be surprised, then, if over the next several decades the events of 1989 form the basis of much passionate political and scholarly debate.

Having said this, I should add that for those of us interested in social

This essay was originally prepared for inclusion in Daniel Chirot, ed., *The Crisis of Leninism and the Decline of the Left: The Revolutions of 1989* (Seattle: University of Washington Press, 1991). It is reprinted here with the permission of the University of Washington Press. The author would like to thank Tim McDaniel for his helpful comments on the chapter.

change, revolutionary periods offer the most important fields of observation. We cannot, of course, conduct controlled laboratory experiments that suit the needs of our research. But in fact revolutions are large-scale social experiments. Though they are neither tailored to scholarly ends nor by any stretch of the imagination controllable, they are the closest we can come to those major scientific experiments that have shaped our understanding of the physical world. Great revolutions, then, are better windows into how societies operate in the long run than almost any other type of historical event. So, aside from being immediately and keenly interested in the events that have taken place in Eastern Europe in 1989 because these are reshaping the international political order, we also have a fascinating, unexpected, revealing glimpse into how seemingly stable, enduring social systems fail and collapse.

The Underlying Causes

Economic

There is no question that the most visible, though certainly not the only, reason for the collapse of Eastern European communism has been economic. It is not that these systems failed in an absolute sense. No Eastern European country, not even Romania, was an Ethiopia or a Burma, with famine and a reversion to primitive, local subsistence economies. Perhaps several of these economies, particularly the Romanian and to a more limited extent the Polish one, were headed in that direction, but they had very far to fall before reaching such low levels. Other economies, in Hungary, but even more in Czechoslovakia and East Germany, were only failures by the standards of the most advanced capitalist economies. On a world scale these were rich, well-developed economies, not poor ones. The Soviet Union, too, was still a world economic and technological power despite deep pockets of regional poverty and a standard of living that was much lower than its per capita production figures would indicate.[2]

There is no need to go over the defects of socialist economies in detail. These have been explained by the many excellent economists from these countries, particularly the Poles and Hungarians, the two most famous of whom are Wlodzimierz Brus and János Kornai.[3] The main problem is that investment and production decisions were based largely, though not entirely, on political will rather than on domestic or international market pressures. In order to overcome the force of the domestic market, which ultimately meant consumer and producer wishes and decisions, the quantities and prices of goods and services were fixed by administrative order. To exclude external market forces, which might have weakened domestic guidance of the economy, foreign trade with the advanced capitalist world was curtailed and strictly controlled, not only by fiat but also by maintaining nonconvertible currencies. The aim of curtailing the power of market forces was achieved, but an inevitable side effect was that under these conditions it became impossible to measure which firms were profitable and which production processes were more or less efficient. There were no real prices.

As the inefficiencies of socialist economies became evident, it proved impossible to reform them largely because the managers were so closely tied to the ruling political machinery. They were able to lobby effectively to steer investments in their direction, regardless of the efficiency of their enterprises. Success as a manager was measured by the ability to produce more, maintain high employment, and attract politically directed investment, not by producing more efficient, more marketable goods. Equally important was that the very concept of profit as a measure of efficiency was foreign to these managers.[4]

Such systems developed inevitable shortages of desired goods. This was partly because production was so inefficient that it kept the final output of consumer goods lower than it should have been at such high levels of industrialization. It was also because the crude ways of measuring success, in terms of gross output, slighted essential services and spare parts, so that the very production process was damaged by shortages of crucial producer goods and services.

But whereas in some cases it was possible to carry out reform, most notably in agriculture and some services (the outstanding successes were the Chinese decollectivization of agriculture after 1976 and the Hungarians' ability to privatize some services and small-scale agricultural production), in industries the power of the Communist Party and its managers was simply too strong to effect real change. The sincere commitment to full employment and the maintenance of low food prices further damaged efficiency.[5]

None of this would have made the slightest sense without the ideological base of communism. Some critics of Communist economic arrangements have argued that the system was simply irrational. In strict economic terms, it may have been, but that hardly explains its long life. The key is that political will was ultimately the primary determinant of economic action, and this will was based on a coherent worldview developed by Lenin, Stalin, and the other Bolshevik leaders. This view then spread to other Communist leaders and was imposed on about one-third of the world's population.

Lenin was born in 1870, and Stalin in 1878 or 1879. They matured as political beings in their teens and early twenties, when the most advanced parts of the world were in the industrial heartland of Western Europe and the United States—in the Ruhr or in the newly emerging miracles of modern technology in the U.S. Midwest, from Pittsburgh and Buffalo to Chicago. It is not mere coincidence that a century later these areas and others like them, including the major steel and shipbuilding centers of Britain or the coal and steel centers of northern France and Belgium, became giant rust belts with antiquated industries, overly powerful trade unions, and unimaginative, conservative, bureaucratic managers. It has been in such areas, too, that industrial pollution has most ravaged the environment, and where political pressures resistant to free trade and the imposition of external market forces were the fiercest in the advanced countries. But in 1900 these areas were progressive, and for ambitious leaders from a relatively backward country like Russia, they were viable models.

Lenin, Stalin, and all the other Bolshevik intellectuals and leaders (Leon

Trotsky, Lev Kamenev, Grigory Zinoviev, Nikolay Bukharin, and so many others) knew that this was what they ultimately had to emulate. They felt, however, that they could make it all happen more quickly and more efficiently by socialist planning than by the random and cruel play of market forces. Despite the inherent inefficiencies of socialism, these astonishing, visionary men—in particular Stalin—actually succeeded. The tragedy of communism was not its failure but its success. Stalin built the institutional framework that, against all logic, forced the Soviet Union into success.[6] By the 1970s the USSR had the world's most advanced (late nineteenth-century) economy, the world's biggest and best, most inflexible rust belt. It was as if Andrew Carnegie had taken over the entire United States, forced it to become a giant copy of U.S. Steel, and the executives of the same U.S. Steel had continued to run the country into the 1970s and 1980s.

To understand the absurdity of this situation, it is necessary to go back and take a historical look at the development of capitalism. There have been five industrial ages so far. Each was dominated by a small set of leading high technology industries located in the most advanced parts of the industrial world. Each has been characterized by a period of rapid, extraordinary growth and innovation in the leading sectors, followed by slower growth, and finally a period of relative stagnation, overproduction, increasing competition, declining profits, and crisis in the now aging leading sectors. It was precisely on his observations about the rise and fall of the first industrial age that Karl Marx based his conclusions about the eventual collapse of capitalism. But each time, one age has been followed by another as unexpected new technologies have negated all the predictions about the inevitable fall of profits and the polarization of capitalist societies into a tiny number of rich owners and masses of impoverished producers.

The ages, with their approximate dates, have been:

1. the cotton-textile age, lasting from about the 1780s into the 1830s and dominated by Great Britain;
2. the rail and iron age, which went from the 1840s into the early 1870s and was also dominated by Britain;
3. the steel and organic chemistry age, from the 1870s to World War I, during which new industries based on the production and utilization of electrical machinery were developed and in which the U.S. and German economies gained the lead;
4. the age of automobiles and petrochemicals, from the 1910s to the 1970s, *consumer goods* during which the United States became the overwhelmingly hegemonic economy;
5. the age of electronics, information, and biotechnology, which began in the 1970s and will certainly run well into the first half of the twenty-first century; in this last age, it is not yet certain which economies will hold sway, though certainly Japan and the European Community are well on their way to replacing the United States.[7]

Transitions have been difficult. Depressions and political turmoil from the

1820s to the 1840s, in the 1870s and 1880s, and in the 1920s and 1930s can be explained, at least in good part, by the difficult effects of the passage from one age to another. World War I—or, more precisely, the mad race for colonies in the late nineteenth century and the European arms race (especially the naval competition between Germany and Britain)—was certainly a function of the shifting economic balance within Europe. World War II resulted from the unsatisfactory outcome of the first war and from the Great Depression of the 1930s. The shocks from the latest transition to the fifth industrial age have been mild by comparison, but the difficulties that attended past transitions produced many predictions about the imminent collapse of capitalism that seemed reasonable at the time.[8] This brief bit of economic history has to be connected to the events of 1989.

The Soviet model, that is, the Leninist-Stalinist model, was based on the third industrial age, the one whose gleaming promises of mighty, smoke-filled concentrations of chemical and steel mills, huge electric-generating plants, and hordes of peasants migrating into new factory boomtowns mesmerized the Bolshevik leadership. The Communist Party of the Soviet Union found out that creating such a world was not easy, especially in the face of stubborn peasant and worker refusal to accept present hardships as the price for eventual industrial utopia. But Stalin persuaded the Party that the vision was so correct that it was worth paying a very high price to attain it. The price was paid, and the model turned into reality.[9]

Later, the same model was imposed on Eastern Europe. Although sheer force ensured that the East Europeans accepted the model, it must also be said that the local Communists, many of whom were only a generation younger than Stalin, had faith in Stalin's vision, particularly those who came from more backward countries. In Romania Nicolae Ceausescu held on to it until his last day in power. It was based on his interpretation of his country's partial, uneven, and highly unsatisfactory drive for industrialization in the 1930s, when he was a young man just becoming an active Communist.[10] To a degree we usually do not realize because the country remained so heavily agricultural, this was Mao's vision for China, too.[11] In 1991 the last practitioner of the Stalinist plan was Ceausescu's contemporary and close ideological ally, Kim Il-Sung of North Korea.

In the Soviet Union, the more backward areas of Eastern Europe, the already partly industrial areas of China (especially on the coast and in Manchuria), and North Korea, the model worked because there were numerous peasants to bring into the labor force; because this type of economy required massive concentrations of investments into huge, centralized firms; and because, after all the technology was pretty well worked out. Also, producer goods were more important than consumer goods at this stage. It is worth remembering, too, that these were all areas where industrialization had begun before communism, either because of local initiatives, as in Russia or most of Eastern Europe, or because of Japanese colonial investments, as in North Korea and Manchuria. (I should note, in passing, that the model is particularly harmful for very backward economies that have no industrial base to begin with. Thus, whatever successes it may have had in East Asia and Europe, it has produced nothing but disaster when tried in Africa or Indochina.)

But if the Stalinist model may be said to have had some success in creating third-age industrial economies (based on steel, organic chemistry, and electricity), it never adapted well to the fourth age of automobiles, consumer electrical goods, and the growth of services to pamper a large proportion of the general population. This is why we were able to make fun of the Soviet model, even in the 1950s and 1960s, because it offered so few luxuries and services. But the Soviets and those who believed in the Stalinist-Leninist model could reply that though they did not cater to spoiled consumers, the basic sinews of industrial and military power, the giant steel mills and power-generating plants, had been built well enough to create an economy almost as powerful as that of the United States.

Alas for the Soviet model, the fifth age turned out to be even more different. Small firms, very rapid change, extreme attention to consumer needs, reliance on innovative thinking—all these were exactly what the Stalinist model lacked. Of course, so did much of the United States' and Western Europe's rust-belt industry (chemicals, steel, autos), but even as they fought rearguard actions to protect themselves against growing foreign competition and technological change, these sectors had to adapt because market pressures were too intense to resist. Their political power was great but, in capitalist societies open to international trade, not sufficient to overcome the world market. In the Soviet case, such industries, protected by the Party, and viewed as the very foundation of everything that communism had built, were able to resist change, at least for another twenty years. That was what the Brezhnev years were—a determined effort to hold on to the late nineteenth-century model the Bolsheviks had worked so hard to emulate. So in the 1970s and 1980s, their relative backwardness went from being amusing to being dangerous. The Soviets and East Europeans (including the Czechs and East Germans) found themselves in the 1980s with the most advanced industries of the late nineteenth and early twentieth centuries: polluting, wasteful, energy intensive, massive, inflexible—in short, huge rust belts.[12]

Of course, it was worse than this. It was not just the adherence to an outdated, rigid model, but all of the well-known failures of socialism that prevented adequate progress. The strains of keeping out the world market, of excluding knowledge about what was going on in the more successful capitalist world, became more and more difficult. It also threatened to intensify backwardness. What had been possible in the early stages of communism, when the leadership was fresh and idealistic about the possibilities of creating a more perfect world, became increasingly problematic with the growing awareness and cynicism about the model's failure.

But the Soviet and East European leaders in the Brezhnev years were very aware of their mounting problems. Much of their time was spent trying to come up with solutions that would nevertheless preserve the key elements of Party rule, Soviet power, and the protection of the new ruling class's power and privilege. The Soviets urged their East European dependencies to overcome their problems by plunging into Western markets. That was the aim of détente. China, of course, followed the same path after 1978. This meant borrowing to buy advanced technology and then trying to sell to the West to repay the debts. But as we now know, the plan did not work. The Stalinist systems were too rigid. Managers resisted change, using their political clout to force ever greater investments into obsolete firms and production processes. In some cases, most notably Poland and Hungary, foreign loans started to be used simply to purchase consumer goods to make people happier, to shore up the crumbling legitimacy of regimes that had lost what youthful vigor they had once possessed and were now viewed simply as tools of a backward occupying power. This worked until the bills came due and prices had to be raised. Societies with little or no experience with free markets responded to price increases with political instability. This was truest in Poland, but it became a potential problem in Hungary (and China) because it created growing and conspicuous social inequities between the small class of new petty entrepreneurs and the large portion of the urban population still dependent on the socialist sector.[13] (Kornai and others have explained why the partial freeing of the market in economies of shortage creates quasi-monopolistic situations favoring the rapid accumulation of profits by those entrepreneurs able to satisfy long-repressed, immense demand.)[14]

What had seemed at first to be a series of sensible reforms proved to be the last gasp of European communism. The reforms did not eliminate the rigidities of Stalinism, but they spread further cynicism and disillusionment, exacerbated corruption, and opened the Communist world to a vastly increased flow of Western capitalist ideas and standards of consumerism. They also created a major debt problem. In this situation, the only East European leader who responded with perfect consistency was Ceausescu: He reimposed strict Stalinism. But neither Romania's principled Stalinism, Hungary's semi-reformism, nor Poland's inconsistency and hesitation worked.[15]

Political and Moral Causes of Change

Although economic problems certainly contributed to the downfall of communism, the changing moral and political climate of Eastern Europe was the primary catalyst of the destruction. There is no better way to approach this topic than by using the old concept of legitimacy. Revolutions only occur when elites and some significant portion of the general population—particularly intellectuals, but also ordinary people—have lost confidence in the moral validity of their social and political system.

Never before in advanced industrial countries, except at the end of major, catastrophic wars, has the basic legitimacy of the system collapsed. And if some serious questions were raised in Germany after World War I, France in 1940, or Germany and Japan in 1945, no successful revolutions occurred there. It would be laughable to claim that Eastern Europe's economic crisis in the 1980s approached such levels of massive crisis as those brought about by utter defeat in international war. In times of peace and relative stability in societies with a strong sense of their nationhood and with functioning infrastructures, police forces, armies, and governments, to have had such revolutionary situations developing in the absence of foreign invaders or international crises and without precipitating civil wars, famines, or even depressions would be unprecedented. No mere recitation of economic problems can provide sufficient explanation.

To see how this loss of legitimacy occurred, it is necessary to go back to the beginning. In the mid- to late 1940s, at least among cadres and a substantial number of young idealists, communism had a considerable degree of legitimacy, even where it had been imposed by force, as in all of Eastern Europe. After all, capitalism seemed to have performed poorly in the 1930s, the liberal European democracies had done little to stop Hitler until it was too late, and Stalin appeared to be a leader who had saved the Soviet Union. The claim that Marxism-Leninism was the "progressive," inevitable wave of the future was not so far-fetched. In fact, many intellectuals throughout Europe, East and West, were seduced by these promises.[16] In the Soviet Union itself, as in China after 1949, communism benefited from the substantial nationalist accomplishments it had to its credit. Foreigners had been defeated, national greatness reasserted, and for all of the problems faced by these regimes, there was clear economic growth and extraordinary progress.[17]

The repressions, terror, and misery of life in the early 1950s soured some believers, but after Stalin's death, reform seemed possible, and after all, the claims made about rapid urbanization, industrialization, and the spread of modern health and educational benefits to the population were true. Not 1956, when the Hungarian revolution was crushed, but 1968 was the decisive turning point. That was when the implications of the Brezhnev policy became clear: Fundamental political reform was not going to be allowed. It must be said in Brezhnev's defense that what happened in 1989, both in Eastern Europe and in China, has proved that in a sense he and his policy of freezing reform were perfectly correct. To have done otherwise would have brought about an earlier demise of communism. Economic liberalization gives new hope for political liberalization to the growing professional and bureaucratic middle classes and to the intelligentsia. It further increases the appeal of liberal economic ideas as well as of democracy. The demand for less rigid central control obviously threatens the Party's monopoly on power.

Whatever potential Communist liberalism may have had in the Prague spring of 1968, the way in which it was crushed and the subsequent, gradual disillusion with strictly economic reform in Hungary and Poland in the 1970s brought to an end the period in which intellectuals could continue to hope about the future of communism. But this was not all. The very inflexibility of Communist economies, the unending shortages, the overwhelming bureaucratization of every aspect of life created a general malaise. The only way to survive in such systems was through corruption, the formal violation of the rules. That in turn left many, perhaps almost all, of the managerial and professional class open to the possibility of blackmail and to a pervasive sense that they were living a perpetual lie.[18]

Then, too, the original imposition of the Stalinist model had created tyranny, the arbitrary rule of the few. One of the characteristics of all tyranny, whether ideological and visionary, as in this case, or merely self-serving and corrupt, is that it creates the possibility for the dissemination and reproduction of petty tyranny at every level. With tyrants at the top, entire bureaucracies become filled with tyrants below, all behaving arbitrarily and out of narrow self-interest. The tyrants at the top cannot hope to enforce their will unless they have subservient officials, and to buy that subservience they have to allow their underlings to enjoy the fruits of arbitrary power. In any case, such tyranny becomes the only model of proper, authoritative behavior.

This is one of the recent explanations given for the widespread, almost uncontrolled spread of purges in the USSR in the 1930s and of course for the ravages of the Chinese Cultural Revolution decade from 1966 to 1976. Once the model is set from the top, imitating that behavior becomes a way of ensuring survival for officials. But even beyond this, a tyrannical system gives opportunities for abuse that do not otherwise exist, and lower-level officials use this to further their own, narrow ends. (This is not meant to suggest that in some way the tyrants who ruled such systems, and their immediate followers, can be absolved of responsibility for the abuses; it does imply that the way in which tyrannies exercise power is necessarily deeply corrupt.)[19]

Daily exposure to petty tyranny, which at the local level rarely maintains the ideological high ground that may have inspired a Lenin, Stalin, Mao, or even a Ceausescu, also breeds gradual disgust with corruption and the dishonesty of the whole system. In the past, peasants subjected to such petty tyranny may have borne it more or less stoically (unless it went too far), but educated urbanites living in a highly politicized atmosphere where there were constant pronouncements about the guiding ideological vision of fairness, equality, and progress could not help but react with growing disgust.[20]

In that sense, the very success of communism in fostering a more urban, more educated, more aware population also created the potential for disintegration. The endless corruption, the lies, the collapse of elementary social trust, the petty tyranny at every level—these were aspects of life less easily tolerated by the new working and professional classes than they might have been by peasants. (This remains, of course, the advantage of the Chinese Communists; they can still rely on a vast reservoir of peasant indifference and respect for authority as long as agriculture is not resocialized.)[21]

The whole movement toward the creation of alternate social institutions, free of the corruption and dishonesty of the official structures, was the great ideological innovation of what began to emerge in Poland in the 1970s and 1980s as the movement toward the creation of a "civil society." Traditional revolutionary resistance, taking to the streets, planning covert military actions, and assassinations might be fruitless because they could only bring down a heavy military intervention by the Soviets. But simply by beginning to turn away from the state, by refusing to take it seriously, Polish and then other Central European intellectuals exposed the shallowness of communism's claims and erased what little legitimacy Communist regimes still had. It is because of his early understanding of this fact and his excellent descriptions of how this new ideology grew in Central Europe that Timothy Garton Ash has justly earned his fame.[22]

Certainly, in the Soviet Union all these forces were at work, too, but the patriotism engendered by superpower status (though it has turned out that this was largely Russian, not "Soviet," pride and patriotism), the sheer size of the military, and the long history of successful police terror and repression kept the situation under better control than in much of Central Europe. Yet combined with the slow erosion of legitimacy, there was also the fundamental economic problem alluded to above, namely, the failure to keep up with the rapidly emerging fifth industrial age in Western Europe, the United States, and, most astonishingly for the Soviets, in East Asia.[23]

There is no doubt that in the mid-1980s, after Solidarity seemed to have been crushed in Poland, with the Soviets massacring Afghan resistance fighters, with Cuban troops successfully defending Angola, with Vietnam controlling all of Indochina, it seemed to the rest of the world that Soviet military might was insurmountable in countries where the Soviet system had been imposed. But underneath, the rot was spreading. So the question is not, "What was wrong with Eastern Europe?" or "Why was communism so weak?" Every specialist and many casual observers knew perfectly well what was wrong. But almost none guessed that what had been a slowly developing situation for several decades might take such a sudden turn for the worse. After all, the flaws of socialist economic planning had been known for a long time. Endemic corruption, tyranny, arbitrary brutality, and the use of police force to maintain Communist parties in power were hardly new. None of these answers the question, "Why 1989?" Almost all analysts thought that the Soviet system would remain more or less intact in the USSR itself and in Eastern Europe for decades more. To understand why this was not to be requires a shift in analysis from a discussion of general trends to a review of some specific events in the 1980s.

The Events of the 1980s

No single event can explain what happened, but if there was a series of developments that began to unravel the entire system, it has to be located in the interaction between events in Poland in the early 1980s and a growing perception by the Soviet leadership that their own problems were becoming very serious.

As late as 1987 and throughout most of 1988, most specialists felt that the Soviet elite did not understand the severity of their economic situation. Although Gorbachev and many of the Moscow intellectuals almost certainly did, there was some question about the lesser cadres and even many of the top people in the government. But as Gorbachev's mild reforms failed to have a beneficial impact, as the original influence of his policy of openness, encouragement, and anti-alcoholism ran into sharply diminishing returns, the Soviet economy began to slip back into the stagnation of the late Brezhnev years.[24]

Serious as rising discontent in the Soviet Union might have seemed to Gorbachev, this would not have been enough had it not been for the direct military implications of the Soviets' inability to keep up with the developments of the fifth industrial age. If the Soviet nuclear deterrent was unquestionably safe and effective in preventing any possibility of a frontal attack by the United States, the growing gap between Western and Soviet computer and electronic technology threatened to give NATO (and ultimately Japan) a striking advantage in conventional weapons. This is almost certainly why the Soviets were so worried about the "Star Wars" antiballistic missile system not simply because the illusion of an effective defense was likely to unbalance the nuclear arms race. Pouring billions into this kind of research was likely to yield important new advantages in lesser types of electronic warfare that could be applied to conventional air and tank battles. This would nullify the Soviets' numerical advantage in troops and machines and would threaten Soviet military investments throughout the world.[25]

Given the long-standing recognition by the major powers that nuclear war was really out of the question, a growing advantage by the capitalist powers in electronic warfare had the potential to transform any future local confrontation between Western and Soviet allies into a repetition of the Syrian-Israeli air war of 1982. From the Soviet point of view, the unbelievable totality of Israel's success was a warning of future catastrophes, even if Israel's land war in Lebanon turned out to be a major failure.[26]

There was one other, chance event that encouraged change in the Soviet Union by revealing to the leadership the extent of the country's industrial ineptitude: the 1986 nuclear plant accident at Chernobyl. Unlucky as the catastrophe was, it served to confirm what was already suspected. Many such massive industrial and environmental accidents had happened before in the Soviet Union, with little effect on Soviet policy. But on top of everything else in the late 1980s, Chernobyl served to galvanize Gorbachev and his advisers.[27]

Meanwhile, in Eastern Europe, the Communist orthodoxy imposed under Brezhnev was seriously threatened in Poland. Rising discontent there had made Poland ungovernable by the mid-1980s. It seemed that Hungary would soon follow. Economic reforms were not working, the population was increasingly alienated, and though there was no outward sign of immediate revolt, Wojciech Jaruzelski's regime had no idea of how to bring the situation back under sufficient control to be able to carry out any measures that stood a chance of reversing the economic decline and regaining the trust (rather than the mere grudging and cynical acceptance) of the population.[28]

In retrospect, then, the events in Poland in the late 1970s, from the election of a Polish pope, which galvanized the Poles and created the massive popular demonstrations that led to the creation of Solidarity, to the military coup that seemed to destroy Solidarity, had set the stage for what was to happen. But the slow degeneration of the situation in Poland, or in all of Eastern Europe, would not have been enough to produce the events of 1989 had it not been for the Soviet crisis. Nonetheless, had there been no breakdown of authority in Poland, and a looming, frightening sense of economic crisis and popular discontent in Hungary and probably in the other Eastern European countries, too, the Soviets would certainly have tried to carry out some reforms without giving up their European empire. The two aspects of the crisis came together, and this is why everything unraveled so quickly in the late 1980s.[29]

Gorbachev must have realized that it was only a matter of time until there was an explosion—a bread riot leading to a revolution in Poland or a major strike in Hungary that would oblige the government to call out the army. The problem was that neither the Polish nor Hungarian army was particularly reliable. The special police could always be counted on, but if they were overwhelmed, it would be necessary to call in Soviet troops. This the Soviet economy could not bear if it was also to reform itself enough to begin to meet the challenges of the fifth industrial age, especially if this involved increasing trade and other contacts with the advanced capitalist countries.

I believe that some time in 1988 Gorbachev decided that it was necessary to head off the danger before it was too late to prevent a crisis.[30] I cannot prove this because the documentation is not available, but I am almost certain that because of this decision, in discussions with the Poles there emerged the plan to allow partially free elections and the reopening of talks with Solidarity. The aim would be to relegitimize the regime and give it enough breathing room to carry out economic reforms without risking strikes and massive civil disobedience. The idea of roundtable talks between Solidarity and the regime were proposed in a televised debate between Lech Walesa and a regime representative on November 30, 1988. The talks themselves began on February 6, 1989.[31] They did not work. Everyone—Gorbachev, the Communist parties of Eastern Europe, foreign specialists, and intelligence services in NATO and the Warsaw Pact—vastly underestimated the degree to which the moral bankruptcy of communism had destroyed any possibility of relegitimizing it.

There was something else, too, an event whose import was not fully appreciated in the West and that remains almost unmentioned. In January 1989, Gorbachev tried an experiment. He pulled almost all of the Soviet army out of Afghanistan. The United States and the Pakistani army expected this to result in the rapid demise of the Communist regime there. To everyone's surprise, it did not. I think that this might have been an important card for Gorbachev. He could point to Afghanistan when his conservative opponents, and especially his military, questioned his judgment. Afghanistan was proof that the Soviets could partially disengage without suffering catastrophe, and that in some cases, it might even be better to let local Communists handle their own problems. I suspect that a rapid victory by the anti-Communist guerrillas in Afghanistan would have slowed progress in Eastern Europe, if not ended it entirely.[32]

We know how rapidly event followed event. Despite the patently unfair arrangements for the Polish election designed to keep the Party in power, the electorate refused to tolerate Communist control any longer, and Party rule collapsed. Because the Soviets had agreed to the process and wanted at almost any cost to avoid a war of invasion, they let Poland go. Once it became obvious that this was happening, the Hungarians set out on the same path.[33]

Then, partly out of a well-timed sense of public relations, just before George Bush's visit, the Hungarians officially opened their border with Austria. In fact, the border had no longer been part of any iron curtain for a long time, but this move gave thousands of vacationing East Germans the idea that they could escape to the West. We know that this set off a mass hysteria among East Germans who had given up hope of reform and whose demoralization and disgust with their system led hundreds of thousands to want to flee. They rushed to West German embassies in Budapest and Prague and began demonstrating in East Germany, particularly in Leipzig and Dresden.[34]

The failure of communism in East Germany, in many ways, represents the ultimate failure. Here was a country that was not poor, where there were 200 automobiles for every 1,000 inhabitants, and where for years Western, particularly West German, sympathizers had said that communism was working by producing a more communal, more kindly Germany than the harsh, market-driven, materialistic West German Federal Republic. It was just wishful thinking.[35]

It is known that head of state Erich Honecker ordered repressive measures. During summer 1989, Chinese officials had visited East Berlin to brief the East Germans on how to crush prodemocracy movements. But during his early October visit to East Germany, Gorbachev had publicly called for change and let it be known that the Soviets would not intervene to stop reform.[36]

By October, ambulances were readied to cart away the thousands of dead and injured in Leipzig and perhaps Dresden that were sure to be produced by the crackdown. This was prevented. Most accounts credit a local initiative in Leipzig led by the conductor Kurt Mazur, though the central Party machinery, taken in hand by Egon Krenz, also played a pacifying role. It is likely that an appeal was made to the Soviets and that the local Soviet military commander said he would not intervene. Knowing this, the East German Communist Party simply overthrew Honecker rather than risk physical annihilation.[37]

East Germany was no China, despite Honecker's claim that it would be. It had no reserve of ignorant, barely literate peasant boys to bring into the breach, and its economy was far too dependent on the West German connection to risk a break. So once repression was abandoned, the system fell apart in a few weeks. With East Germany crumbling, the whole edifice of Communist rule in Eastern Europe simply collapsed. On November 9 the Berlin Wall was opened. It was no longer possible to maintain it when the government of East Germany was losing control over its population, and the rate of flight was increasing at such a rapid rate.

East Germany was always the key Soviet position in Europe.[38] It was on the internal German border that the cold war began, and it was there that the military might of the two superpowers was concentrated. When the Soviets abandoned the East German hard-liners, there was no hope anywhere else in Eastern Europe. The Bulgarians followed in order to preserve what they could of the Party, and the day after the Berlin Wall was opened, Todor Zhivkov resigned after thirty-five years in power. This was surely no coincidence. A week later, demonstrations began in Prague, and within ten days, it was over. Only Ceausescu resisted.[39]

Enough is now known about Ceausescu's Romania so that it is unnecessary to give much background. Only three points must be made. Ceausescu himself still held on to the Stalinist vision. Aside from the possible exception of Albania (which began to change in spring 1990),[40] there was only one other Communist country in which the model was so unquestioned: North Korea. In fact, Ceausescu and Kim Il-Sung long considered themselves close allies and friends, and their style of rule had many similarities. Yet in Romania, and probably in North Korea as well, this model turned sour about two decades ago, and pursuing it meant economic stagnation, a growing gap between reality and ideology, and the progressive alienation of even the most loyal cadres.[41]

Second, Romania was the most independent of the Warsaw Pact European countries and so felt itself less dependent on Soviet support. But though this brought considerable legitimacy to the Romanian regime in the 1970s, when partial independence was thought to be grounds for hope, by the late 1980s that hope had failed, and intellectuals and a growing number of ordinary urban people alike had noticed that the Soviet Union had become more progressive than Romania.[42] In southern Romania, they listened to Bulgarian television and radio, and when they heard that even there (for the Romanians, Bulgaria has always been a butt of jokes as a backward, thick-headed, peasant nation) there were reforms, it must have had a considerable impact. In the north and west, Romanians could pick up the Hungarian and Yugoslav media and so be informed about what was going on elsewhere. In the east, of course, they had the example of the Soviet Union and of Romanian-speaking Soviet Moldavia, where, for the first time since the 1940s, people were freer to demonstrate than in Romania itself. I should add that aside from broadcasts from these neighboring countries, Radio Free Europe, too, played a major role in educating Romanians about what was going on elsewhere in Eastern Europe. The point is that, again unlike China, it proved impossible to keep the news about the world out of the reach of the interior.

Finally, and this is much less known than other aspects of Romania's recent history, even at its height, the Ceausescu regime relied very heavily on the fear of Soviet invasion to legitimize itself. There was always the underlying assumption that if there were too much trouble, the Soviet tanks would come in, and was it not better to suffer a patriotic Romanian tyrant than another episode of Soviet occupation? Once it became clear, in 1989, that the Soviets were not going to march, the end was in sight. It was only because Ceausescu himself was so out of touch with reality, and because he had so successfully destroyed his Communist Party by packing it with relatives and sycophants (like Kim Il-Sung) that no one told him the truth, and he was unable to manage the more peaceful, gradual, and dignified exit of his Bulgarian colleague, Zhivkov.[43]

So in the end communism collapsed. The ramifications are far from clear, and there is no way of knowing how things will develop in the Soviet Union. But come what may in the USSR, it is certain that the Soviet empire in Eastern Europe is dead and that there are almost no foreseeable circumstances that would make the Soviet army invade any of its former dependencies. We cannot be sure what directions the various revolutions of Eastern Europe will take, though it is safe to predict that there will be important differences from country to country. On the whole, it is also possible to be somewhat optimistic about the future of Eastern Europe, or at least its northern, "Central European" parts, if not necessarily of the Balkans and the Soviet Union. Why this is so I leave to my concluding remarks, in which I try to draw together some of the lessons Eastern Europe has taught us about revolution and social change in general.

On the Causes of Revolution in Advanced Societies

Eastern Europe and the Traditional Causes of Revolution

Most widely accepted sociological models of revolution provide limited help in explaining what happened in Eastern Europe in 1989. There was no sudden fall in well-being after a long period of improvement. If the Polish, Hungarian, and Romanian economies were deteriorating (at very different rates), the East German and Czechoslovak ones were not yet causing immediate problems. People felt deprived when they compared their lives to those available in Western Europe, but this had been true for well over three decades. In Poland, as a matter of fact, the sharpest period of economic deterioration was in the early 1980s, and though the situation had not improved much since then, it could be assumed that people were getting used to it.[44]

In Poland there was a prolonged period of protest marked by open explosions in 1956, 1968, 1970, 1976, and of course 1980–1981. As time advanced, Poles learned to organize better and more effectively. But this gradual mobilization and organization seemed to have been decisively broken by the military seizure of power. In fact, there is good evidence that the Communist Party and police had learned even more from the long series of protests than the protesters themselves and had become very adept at handling trouble with just the right level of violence. Certainly in the early 1980s, the Jaruzelski regime was able to impose peacefully a whole series of price increases that in the past had provoked massive, violent uprisings.[45]

Only in Hungary was there much open mobilization of protest in the late 1980s, and that only in the last couple of years. Much of it was over ecological and nationalist issues that did not take the form of direct anti-regime activity. In fact, the Communists even supported some of this activity.[46] None of the other countries had much open dissent. At most, in Czechoslovakia a few, seemingly entirely isolated intellectuals had organized themselves, but they had no followers. In East Germany the Protestant churches had supported some limited draft protests and a small peace movement, but the regime had never been directly threatened. In Bulgaria only a tiny handful of intellectuals ever made any claims to protest. In Romania there had been some scattered outbreaks of strikes in the late 1970s and a major riot in one city, Brasov, in 1987, but there, even intellectual protest was muted, rarely going beyond certain restricted literary activities.[47]

The international position of the East European countries was not at stake either. Although in the Soviet Union it is clear that key elites, particularly in the KGB, saw the impending danger to the USSR's international strength, in Eastern Europe no one cared about this kind of issue. None of the elites saw their countries as potentially powerful nations, nor was their national existence threatened by any outsiders except the Soviets. And that threat, present since 1945, was now so highly attenuated as to be almost absent. That the Soviets were unpopular in Eastern Europe was a given, and a very old one, but there was no new risk of further intervention or damage because of these countries' weakness.[48]

Perhaps, however, the debt crisis in Poland and Hungary (and in Romania, because it had provoked such harsh and damaging countermeasures by Ceausescu) was the equivalent of visible international failure that exposed the incapacity of the regimes. But though this remained severe in Poland and Hungary in the late 1980s, elsewhere the problem was not particularly acute.[49]

Nor can a very strong case be made for the rise of an economically powerful new class that was fighting to gain political power. Political and economic power was firmly in the hands of what the Yugoslavian critic Milovan Djilas had called the "New Class," but that class, the professional party cadres, had been in charge for four decades, and it seemed neither highly dissatisfied nor in any way revolutionary. The leadership of the revolutions, if there was any, was in the hands of a few intellectuals who represented no particular class.[50]

Poland, of course, was different. There, an alliance between the Catholic church, the unionized working class, and dissident intellectuals was very well organized, and it had almost taken power in 1980. But the days of Solidarity seemed to have passed, and the regime reasserted visible control. Virtually none of the Polish opposition thought it had much chance of success in an open, violent confrontation. So even in Poland, this was not a traditional revolution. The opportunity for that had passed with the successful imposition of martial law.[51]

What happened was that the moral base of communism had vanished. The elites had lost confidence in their legitimacy. The intellectuals, powerless as they seemed to be, disseminated this sense of moral despair and corruption to the public by their occasional protests and veiled commentaries, and the urban public was sufficiently well educated and aware to understand what was going on. The cumulative effect of such a situation, over decades, cannot be underestimated. Those who had had hope in the 1940s or 1950s were replaced by those who had never had hope and who had grown up knowing that everything was a lie. Educated youths, not just in the universities but those who had only gone through high school, knew enough about the rest of the world to know that they had been lied to, that they had been cheated, and that their own leaders did not believe the lies.[52]

What took everyone by surprise was the discovery that the situation was not all that different in the Soviet Union. Nor could anyone foresee the kind of panicked realism, combined with astounding flexibility and willingness to compromise, shown by Gorbachev. In the end, this was the reason that all of this happened in 1989 rather than in the 1990s, but sooner or later, it would have happened anyway.

Eastern Europe Compared to Other Modern Revolutions

This brings up a serious issue. It has long been assumed that modern methods of communication and the awesome power of tanks, artillery, and air power would prevent the kind of classical revolution that has shaken the world so many times since 1789. Even relatively inefficient regimes, such as the Russian autocracy or the KMT in China, fought successfully against revolution until their armies were decisively weakened by outside invaders. In China's case, it took the Communists two decades to build the strong army that finally won power for them, and they probably would have failed had it not been for the Japanese invasion.[53]

Many utterly corrupt, weak African, Asian, and Latin American regimes have held on to power for a long time with little more than mercenary armies whose loyalties are purchased by allowing them to loot their own countries. This is what goes on in, for example, Burma, Guatemala, and Zaire. Cases where such regimes were overthrown show that it takes long years of guerrilla organization and warfare to carry out revolutions, and then the chances of success are slim. If revolutions occurred in Fulgencio Batista's Cuba and the Somozas' Nicaragua, in Uganda Idi Amin held on until he foolishly provoked Tanzania into attacking him. If "Baby Doc" Duvalier was frightened into leaving office in Haiti, even by 1991 it was not clear that the Duvalier system had been removed.[54]

Finally, even anticolonial wars, when the overwhelming majority of populations have sympathized with revolutionary movements, have been long, bloody events when the colonizers have chosen to fight back, as did the Dutch in Indonesia, the French in Indochina and Algeria, or the British in Kenya and Malaya (where, however, the Malay population rallied to the British side against the Chinese revolutionaries). A particularly startling case was the Bangladesh war, when massive popular opposition to Pakistani rule still needed help from an Indian military invasion to get rid of the Pakistani army.[55] Only internal military coups, as when the Ethiopian or, much earlier, the Egyptian monarchies were removed, seem to make for relatively easy revolutions.[56]

But none of these types of revolutions fit what happened in Eastern Europe. Even if the Romanian case is included, the total level of bloodshed was minuscule compared to other revolutions. There were certainly no military coups. In Romania there was almost certainly cooperation between the army and the population but no direct coup, and that was the only case where the army was involved at all. But compared to any African, Latin American, or almost any non-Communist Asian dictatorship, the East European Communist regimes were overwhelmingly strong. They had large, effective, loyal secret police forces; an abundance of tanks and soldiers led by well-trained (though not necessarily enthusiastic) officers; excellent internal communications; and no threat of external, hostile invasion. Only in Romania was the army thoroughly alienated. Again, we are left with the same explanation: utter moral rot.

Few observers have noticed a startling parallel between events in Eastern Europe in 1989 and in Iran in 1979. There, too, the shah should have been stronger. But despite numerous deaths in the final days, and months of rioting before the shah's departure in January, many were taken by surprise by the overwhelming lack of legitimacy of the regime. Even the newly prosperous middle classes and the young professionals, who had much to lose if the shah were overthrown, failed to back him.[57] Although this is not a suitable place to discuss Iranian society and politics in the 1960s and 1970s, it is evident that the rapid modernization and urbanization of the society helped its intellectuals disseminate their feelings of disgust about the shah's regime, with its empty posturing, lies, torturers, corruption, and lack of redeeming moral values.

We can wonder, of course, to what extent the rising intellectual and professional classes in urban France in 1787 to 1789 felt the same way about the French monarchy, church, and aristocracy, and the extent to which such feelings played a decisive role in unleashing that revolution. We know that in Petrograd and Moscow from 1915 to 1917, whatever the level of popular misery, the professional and middle classes felt a good bit of disgust at the corruption and lack of morality at the imperial court.

The lesson may be that we need to combine some Marxist notions of class with an understanding of John Rawls's theory of justice as fairness in order to understand what happened in Eastern Europe. Economic modernization did, indeed, produce a larger middle class (not in the sense of bourgeois ownership, of course, but in the cultural and educational sense, as well in its style of life). That class was in some ways quite favored in Communist regimes. But because of the flaws of the socialist system of economic management, it remained poorer than its west European counterpart and even seemed to be falling further behind by the 1980s. This is the Marxist—or class and material basis—of what happened.

But what is more important is that, almost by definition, the educated middle classes are well informed and can base their judgments about morality on a wider set of observations than those with very limited educations. The artistic and literary intellectuals who address their work to these middle classes in a modern society helped them understand and interpret the immorality of the system and so played a major role. They needed receptive audiences, but it was their work that undid Eastern European communism.

Without the social changes associated with the economic transformations that took place in Eastern Europe from 1948 to 1988, these revolutions would not have taken place. But it was not that new classes were striving for power so much as that a growing number saw through the lies on which the whole system was based. That is what utterly destroyed the will to resist on the part of those in power. Once these conditions were set, the massive popular discontent with material conditions, particularly among the working classes in the giant but stagnating industries that dominated Communist economies, could come out into the streets and topple these regimes.

Models and Morals

In exploring the revolutions in Eastern Europe, we should keep three points
in mind. First, the fundamental reason for the failure of communism was that
the utopian model it proposed was obviously not going to come into being.
Almost everything else could have been tolerated if the essential promise
were on its way to fulfillment. But once it was clear that the model was out of
date and its promise increasingly based on lies, its immorality became
unbearable. Perhaps in the past, when other ideologically based models
failed to deliver their promises, systems could still survive because the middle classes and the intellectuals were present in smaller numbers. But in
advanced societies, the original economic problems spelled out above, the
absurdity of basing a whole social system on an outdated industrial age, was
more than an economic mistake. It undermined the whole claim to scientific
validity that lay at the very heart of Marxism-Leninism.

Second, much of the standard of morality that created such a revolutionary
situation in Eastern Europe was based on the middle classes' interpretation
of what was going on in Western Europe. This is one reason why, despite all
the economic and political troubles that are sure to accumulate in the near
future in Eastern Europe, there is some reason for optimism. Western Europe
is no longer the warlike set of competing imperialistic powers it was when
the Eastern Europeans first began to look at the West as their model in the
nineteenth century and through 1939. All of Western Europe is democratic,
its various countries cooperate well with one another, and on the whole they
have abandoned their imperialistic pretensions. This means that, as a model,
Western Europe is a far healthier place than it was in the past. It does not
mean, however, that all future revolutionary intellectuals and scandalized
middle classes will look to Western Europe or to the United States as their
model. After all, the Iranians looked to Islam, and it is only because Eastern
Europe has long been so close to Western Europe that it automatically looks
in that direction.

Third, we must come to realize that in the twenty-first century there will
still be economic problems, political instability, and revolutions. But more
than ever, the fundamental causes of revolutionary instability will be moral.
The urban middle and professional classes, the intellectuals and those to
whom they most directly appeal, will set the tone of political change. Regimes to which they do not accord legitimacy because these regimes are seen
as unfair and dishonest will be shaky. When these classes can be persuaded
to defend their own narrow material interests, when they accept immoral
and unfair behavior, then regimes, no matter how corrupt, will be safe. But it
would be foolish for regimes that are defending essentially unjust social systems to rely too much on the continued acquiescence of their middle classes
and intellectuals.

But many of us who study social change must be reminded that we barely
know how to study moral perceptions and legitimacy. We have been so busy
observing material changes—which are, after all, more easily measured and
perceived—that we do not know where to look to sense the moral pulse of

key classes and intellectuals. In some ways, the lesson of Eastern Europe has this to offer, too: Sometimes literature written for what seems to be a handful of people is a better measure of the true state of mind of a society than public opinion polls, economic statistics, or overt political behavior.

An alternative "civil society," places where people could interact freely and without government interference, where they could turn their backs on the Party-state's corruption, was in the making in Eastern Europe before 1989. This alternative civil society was the creation of intellectuals, novelists, playwrights, poets, historians, and philosophers like Vaclav Havel, Miklós Haraszti, Adam Michnik, György Konrad, and hundreds of other, less famous ones. In a sense, in their literature and pamphlets, in their small discussion circles, they imagined a future that most of their people could only dimly perceive and that hardly anyone believed possible.

Vladimir Tismaneanu, in an article entitled "Eastern Europe: The Story the Media Missed," points out that most Western observers never grasped the significance of this creation of an alternative "civil society."[58] That is not quite correct because even before 1989 those most closely following the intellectual life of East-Central Europe were aware of what was going on and were writing about it. Garton Ash was the best known, but a few other scholars saw it, too.[59] On the whole, however, most of the specialists on communism were too hard-headed, too realistic, and even too dependent on social science models to take such highly intellectualized discussions seriously. After the fact, it is easy for us to say this. Before the fact, almost none of us saw it.

Notes

1. Because of its second centennial anniversary in 1989 this has been a particularly busy period for the publication of new works on the French Revolution. That the event still generates considerable excitement is shown by the controversies about Simon Schama's hostile critique of the revolution, *Citizens: A Chronicle of the French Revolution* (New York: Knopf, 1988). A more positive evaluation is Eric J. Hobsbawm's *Echoes of the Marseillaise: Two Centuries Look Back on the French Revolution* (New Brunswick: Rutgers University Press, 1990). A lively review essay about recent books on the revolution is Benjamin R. Barber's "The Most Sublime Event," *Nation*, March 12, 1990, pp. 351–360.

2. A review of the condition and prospects for the East European economies can be found in John R. Lampe, ed., "Special Issue on Economic Reform," *Eastern European Politics and Societies*, 2, 3 (Fall 1988). Though the articles in this issue emphasize the region's economic problems, not all are pessimistic, and none predicted the astounding political changes that were to begin within months of publication. The same is true of a slightly older but still recent review of Eastern Europe's economies, with some comparative chapters on other socialist economies in Ellen Comisso and Laura Tyson, eds., *Power, Purpose, and Collective Choice: Economic Strategy in the Socialist States* (Ithaca: Cornell University Press, 1986). A surprisingly positive account of the Soviet economy published a few years ago by Ed A. Hewett also seemed to soften the nature of the crisis, even though Hewett gave an excellent account of the many problems facing the Soviets. See his *Reforming the Soviet Economy: Equality Versus Efficiency* (Washington, D.C.: Brookings Institution, 1988).

3. Janos Kornai, *Economics of Shortage*, 2 vols. (Amsterdam: North Holland, 1980), and Wlodzimierz Brus, *Socialist Ownership and Political Systems* (London: Allen and Unwin, 1977).

4. The popular resistance to accepting capitalist profits should not, after all, be surprising. Karl Polanyi's seminal work, *The Great Transformation* (Boston: Beacon Press, 1957), showed how difficult it was for the British to accept the notion that market forces should regulate the economy in the early nineteenth century. By now, the capitalist West has had almost two centuries to get used to this dramatic change in the organizing principles of society, and it has only been in the last few decades that resistance to the market has waned in Western Europe. That Eastern Europe, especially the Soviets, should view markets with suspicion is understandable. Among the many discussions of this, Geoffrey Hosking's new book, *The Awakening of the Soviet Union* (Cambridge: Harvard University Press, 1990), is particularly good. He writes, "How many times over the last year or two have I heard Soviet citizens use the word 'speculator' to disparage private traders or co-operatives providing at high prices goods and services seldom available at all in the state sector? This sullen egalitarianism dovetails neatly with the interest of the party-state apparatus in retaining their network of controls and hence their grip on the economy" (p. 132).

5. On China, see Nicholas Lardy, *Agriculture in China's Modern Economic Development* (Cambridge: Cambridge University Press, 1983), pp. 190–221. On Hungary, see Tamas Bauer, "The Hungarian Alternative to Soviet-Type Planning," *Journal of Comparative Economics*, 7, 3 (1983), pp. 304–316. See also Ellen Comisso and Paul Marer, "The Economics and Politics of Reform in Hungary," in Comisso and Tyson, *Power, Purpose, and Collective Choice*.

6. Though the story is now well known, it is worth reviewing the nightmarish quality of this success. For a good account, see the essays in Moshe Lewin, *The Making of the Soviet System* (New York: Pantheon, 1985).

7. The attempt to fit the industrial era into such straightforward stages oversimplifies its economic history. Walt W. Rostow identifies nine "trend periods" in his *World Economy: History and Prospect* (Austin: University of Texas Press, 1978), pp. 298–348. My industrial ages group together his first and second periods (1790–1848); take his third period (1848–1873) as a distinct age; group together his fourth and fifth periods (1873–1920) and his sixth, seventh, and eighth periods (1920–1972); and consider his ninth (starting in 1972) as the beginning of a new industrial age. I rely more on the history of technology provided by David S. Landes in his *Unbound Prometheus: Technological Change and Industrial Development in Western Europe from 1750 to the Present* (Cambridge: Cambridge University Press, 1969), and by the various authors in Carlo M. Cipolla's edited series, *The Fontana Economic History of Europe*, vols. 4–6 (Glasgow: Fontana/Collins, 1973–1976), than on price data and business cycles. I explain my reasoning more fully in Daniel Chirot, *Social Change in the Modern Era* (San Diego: Harcourt Brace Jovanovich, 1986), pp. 223–230. The point, however, is not to argue about precise periodization but to recognize that there are different technologies, different types of social organization, and different models of behavior at different stages of the industrial era. The forceful maintenance of an outdated model is one of the main reasons for the backwardness of Soviet-type economies.

8. Polanyi's *Great Transformation* was one such prediction. So was Lenin's in *Imperialism, the Highest Stage of Capitalism* (New York: International Publishers, 1939). For an account of the ideological effects of the Great Depression of the 1930s on Eastern Europe, see Daniel Chirot, "Ideology, Reality, and Competing Models of Development in Eastern Europe Between the Two World Wars," *Eastern European Politics and Societies*, 3, 3 (1989), pp. 378–411.

9. Alexander Erlich, *The Soviet Industrialization Debate* (Cambridge: Harvard University Press, 1960). Whether or not this strategy was necessary remains a subject of debate in the Soviet Union, where Stephen F. Cohen's book on Bukharin has been greatly appreciated by the Gorbachev reformers because Bukharin was the most important ideological opponent of the Stalin line. See Cohen's *Bukharin and the Bolshevik Revolution: A Political Biography, 1888–1938* (Oxford: Oxford University Press, 1980). For Eastern Europe, however, the issue is moot.

10. Vladimir Tismaneanu, "The Tragicomedy of Romanian Communism," *Eastern European Politics and Societies*, 3, 2 (1989), gives the most recent, and best short account of the origins and development of the Romanian Communist Party from the prewar period until 1989 and explains Ceausescu's role in determining its fate.

11. Lardy, *Agriculture in China's Modern Economic Development*, pp. 130, 155, 158, and 165.

12. Hosking quotes the Soviet reform economist Otto Latsis, who put it this way: "They build irrigation channels which bring no increase in agricultural production. They produce machine tools for which there are no operators, tractors for which there are no drivers, and threshing machines which they know will not work. Further millions of people supply these superfluous products with electricity, ore, oil, and coal. In return they receive their wages like everyone else, and take them to the shops. There, however, they find no goods to buy, because their work has not produced any." And Hosking also quotes Soviet Premier Nicolai Ryzhkov: "We produce more tractors in this country than all the capitalist countries put together. And yet we don't have enough tractors" (*Awakening of the Soviet Union*, p. 134).

13. Kazimierz Poznanski ascribes the failure of the Polish reforms in the second half of the 1970s to political pressure rather than to economic mismanagement, but it would be fruitless to argue about which came first. See his "Economic Adjustment and Political Forces: Poland Since 1970," in Comisso and Tyson, *Power, Purpose, and Collective Choice*.

14. Comisso and Marer, in their article "The Economics and Politics of Reform in Hungary," cover this and the other major contradictions in the Hungarian economic reforms, pp. 267–278.

15. On the debt crisis and Eastern Europe, see Laura D'Andrea Tyson, "The Debt Crisis and Adjustment Responses in Eastern Europe: A Comparative Perspective," in Comisso and Tyson, *Power, Purpose, and Collective Choice*. On Romania, see Ronald H. Linden, "Socialist Patrimonialism and the Global Economy: The Case of Romania," in Comisso and Tyson, *Power, Purpose, and Collective Choice*.

16. Jan Gross stresses this in "Social Consequences of War: Preliminaries to the Study of Imposition of Communist Regimes in East Central Europe," *Eastern European Politics and Societies*, 3, 2 (1989), pp. 213–214. There is no way of quantifying the extent to which youthful enthusiasm helped Communist cadres take power and effectively transform their societies in the late 1940s and early 1950s, but the phenomenon is attested to by numerous literary sources describing the period. Even such bitter anti-Communists as Milan Kundera in *The Joke* (New York: Harper & Row, 1982) verifies this. Had there never been a substantial body of energized believers, it is unlikely that the sheer force of Soviet military could have held all of Eastern Europe in its grip. Yet as Gross and others—for example, Elemér Hankiss, "Demobilization, Self-Mobilization, and Quasi-Mobilization in Hungary, 1948–1987," *Eastern European Politics and Societies*, 3, 1 (1989)—have pointed out, Communist regimes worked hard to destroy social cohesion and any type of genuine solidarity, so that in the long run it was inevitable that the enthusiasm of the early intellectual believers would be curbed and debased. As for Western, particularly French, Marxism, Tony Judt believes that it also contributed to the legitimacy of Eastern European Communist regimes. See his *Marxism and the French Left* (Ox-

ford: Oxford University Press, 1986), pp. 236–238. Thus, the rise and demise of Marxism in Eastern and Western Europe are not wholly separate phenomena but fed on each other.

17. The best-known explanation of communism as nationalism is Chalmers Johnson, *Peasant Nationalism and Communist Power: The Emergence of Revolutionary China, 1937–1945* (Stanford: Stanford University Press, 1962), esp. pp. 176–187. Johnson explicitly compares Yugoslavia to China. To varying degrees, but most strongly in Poland, Czechoslovakia, and Albania, the Communists were able to make similar claims as national saviors after 1945 elsewhere in Eastern Europe. In East Germany, Hungary, Bulgaria, and Romania, they could at least claim to represent the substantial leftist nationalist sentiments that had been silenced during the period of Nazism or the German alliance.

18. Again, it is difficult to quantify feelings of moral revulsion. But the sense of all-pervasive corruption and self-disgust can be grasped in all of the literature of Eastern Europe, starting in the 1950s and becoming ever more obvious with time. A particularly somber view is given by Petru Dumitriu's *Incognito* (New York: Macmillan, 1964).

19. Though he certainly exaggerates the role of local officials, this is a central theme in J. Arch Getty's revisionist view of the Stalinist purges in his *Origins of the Great Purges: The Soviet Communist Party Reconsidered, 1933–1938* (Cambridge: Cambridge University Press, 1985). On the Chinese Cultural Revolution, see Hong Yung Lee, *The Politics of the Chinese Cultural Revolution* (Berkeley: University of California Press, 1978). Although such events could not have begun without central direction, they could not have been carried out without local officials trying to ingratiate themselves by imitating the top. But this very process led to widespread cynicism and corruption, and so had to undermine the long-term legitimacy of communism.

20. James C. Scott's argument about how the violation of a "moral economy's" sense of justice leads to revolts is based on observations of peasants, but it actually applies even more to urban intellectuals and professionals. It is now evident that they also have a "moral economy," though one tied to their own sense of self-worth rather than to their subsistence. See *The Moral Economy of the Peasant: Rebellion and Subsistence in Southeast Asia* (New Haven: Yale University Press, 1976), particularly pp. 157–192.

21. Yet it is difficult to believe that China will not follow the same course as Eastern Europe in future years. The crisis of the Democracy Movement in spring 1989 was caused by all the same factors that led to the collapse of communism in Eastern Europe: the contradictions of economic reform in a system still run by Communist officials, growing corruption, loss of faith in the official ideology, and increasing disgust with the endless hypocrisy of those in power. The main difference, of course, was that China in 1989 was much less developed, much less urbanized than the Eastern European countries and also much more insulated from the effects of the economic and political crisis in the Soviet Union. For a brief review of the events in China and their causes, See Jonathan D. Spence, *The Search for Modern China* (New York: Norton, 1990), pp. 712–747.

22. His major essays from the late 1980s have been collected in Timothy Garton Ash, *The Uses of Adversity* (New York: Random House, 1989).

23. Kazimierz Poznanski, *Technology, Competition and the Soviet Bloc in the World Market* (Berkeley: Institute of International Studies of the University of California, 1987).

24. Each new report from the Soviet Union makes the picture of the Brezhnev years and the prognosis for the future seem bleaker. For years, the CIA reports painted a bleaker picture than the official Soviet reports, but recently Soviet economists have said that even the CIA reports were too optimistic. As an example of what is now known about the state of the Soviet economy and how it reached its present crisis, see Bill Keller, "Gorbachev's Need: To Still Matter," *New York Times*, May 27, 1990, section 1, pp. 1, 6. None of this is new to academic specialists such as Marshall Goldman, who discusses it in *USSR in Crisis: The Failure of an Economic System* (New York: Norton, 1983).

25. That scientists did not believe the extravagant claims made by the proponents of

the "strategic defense initiative" is clear. See, for example, Franklin A. Long, Donald Hafner, and Jeffrey Boutwell, eds., *Weapons in Space* (New York: Norton, 1986), particularly the essay by Hans Bethe, Jeffrey Boutwell, and Richard Garwin, "BMD Technologies and Concepts in the 1980s," pp. 53–71. Yet the Soviets were very troubled by it, and it was Gorbachev's political genius that figured out that U.S. funding for military research could only be reduced in the context of a general move toward disarmament, and this necessitated a reversal of traditional Soviet foreign policy that would reassure the West. For an appreciation of Gorbachev's policy in an otherwise harshly critical article, see Elena Bonner, "On Gorbachev," *New York Review of Books,* May 17, 1990, p. 14. In general, it seems to me that the Soviets' fear that their conventional warfare capabilities would be undermined by the West's technological superiority has been relatively neglected in most of the discussion about arms control. It has, however, been noted by experts. See Alan B. Sherr, *The Other Side of Arms Control: Soviet Objectives in the Gorbachev Era* (Boston: Unwin Hyman, 1988), pp. 38 and 63.

26. Chaim Herzog, *The Arab-Israeli Wars* (New York: Random House, 1982), pp. 347–348. That the Soviets remained concerned by this is shown by statements in Alexei Arbatov, Oleg Amirov, and Nikolai Kishilov, "Assessing the NATO-WTO Military Balance in Europe," in Robert D. Blackwell and F. Stephen Larrabee, eds., *Conventional Arms Control and East-West Security* (Durham, N.C.: Duke University Press, 1989), pp. 78–79.

27. Hosking, *Awakening of the Soviet Union,* pp. 56–60.

28. The desperate and almost comical attempts made by the Jaruzelski regime to create new organizations and institutions that would reimpose some sort of political and social coherence and bring society back into the system are explored very well by George Kolankiewicz in "Poland, and the Politics of Permissible Pluralism," *Eastern European Politics and Societies,* 2, 2 (1988), pp. 152–183. But even Kolankiewicz thought that the attempt to include broader segments of the population, and particularly the intellectuals, in officially defined institutions might meet with partial success. In the event, it turned out that these desperate inclusionary policies failed, too.

29. Timothy Garton Ash, "Eastern Europe: The Year of Truth," *New York Review of Books,* February 15, 1990, pp. 17–22. A collection of Garton Ash's new essays on 1989 appears in *We the People: The Revolution of '89, Witnessed in Warsaw, Budapest, Berlin and Prague* (Cambridge: Granta/Penguin, 1990).

30. In summer 1988 it certainly became obvious that the forces of political and social disintegration in the Soviet Union were starting to get out of hand, too, and this no doubt influenced Gorbachev greatly. See the essays of Boris Kagarlitsky in *Farewell Perestroika: A Soviet Chronicle* (London: Verso, 1990), particularly "The Hot Summer of 1988," pp. 1–29.

31. The whole process is well documented by the Polish publications, particularly, issues of *Rzeczpospolita, Polityka, and Trybuna Ludu.* I thank Dieter Bingen of Cologne's Bundesinstitut für Ostwissenschaftliche und Internationale Studien for helping me understand the sequence of events in Poland during this period.

32. Bill Keller, "Getting Out with Honor" (February 2, 1989), in Bernard Gwertzman and Michael T. Kaufman, eds., *The Collapse of Communism* (New York: New York Times, 1990), pp. 10–12. This book is a collection of relevant articles published in the *Times* during 1989.

33. In Gwertzman and Kaufman, *Collapse of Communism,* see John Tagliabue, "Solidarity May Win 40 Percent of Parliament" (February 19, 1989), pp. 20–21; "Stunning Vote Casts Poles into Uncharted Waters" (June 5, 1989), p. 121; "Warsaw Accepts Solidarity Sweep and Humiliating Losses by Party" (June 8, 1989), pp. 121–123; and "Jaruzelski, Moved by 'Needs and Aspirations' of Poland Names Walesa Aide Premier" (August 19, 1989), pp. 130–132. To this must be added the August 17, 1989, article from Moscow by Bill Keller, "In Moscow, Tone Is Studied Calm," pp. 132–133.

34. In Gwertzman and Kaufman, *Collapse of Communism,* see Henry Kamm, "East Germans Put Hungary in a Bind" (September 1, 1989), pp. 154–156; and Serge Schmemann, "East Germans Line Émigré Routes, Some in Hope of Their Own Exit" (October 4, 1989), p. 158, and "Security Forces Storm Protesters in East Germany" (sent from Dresden, October 8, 1989), p. 159.

35. Thomas A. Baylis "Explaining the GDR's Economic Strategy," in Comisso and Tyson, *Power, Purpose, and Collective Choice,* esp. the optimistic conclusion, pp. 242–244. A conventionally favorable summary of how East German Communist labor relations worked is found in Marilyn Rueschemeyer and C. Bradley Scharf. "Labor Unions in the German Democratic Republic" in Alex Pravda and Blair A. Ruble, eds., *Trade Unions in Communist States* (Boston: Allen and Unwin, 1986). Judging by the comments from these and other similar studies, East Germans should not have behaved the way they did in 1989.

36. In a speech on October 7 in the GDR, Gorbachev said, "Life itself punishes those who delay." Quoted in Timothy Garton Ash, "The German Revolution," *New York Review of Books,* December 21, 1989, p. 14. Then, on October 25 in Helsinki, he said that the Soviet Union did not have the moral or political right to intervene in the affairs of Eastern Europe. This was interpreted by his spokesman, Gennadi I. Gerasimov, as the replacement of the Brezhnev Doctrine by the "Sinatra Doctrine" (after the song, "I Did It My Way"). Bill Keller, "Gorbachev in Finland, Disavows Any Right of Regional Intervention" (October 25, 1989), in Gwertzman and Kaufman, *Collapse of Communism,* pp. 163–166.

37. Garton Ash, "The German Revolution," p. 16.

38. Christopher Jones, "Gorbachev and the Warsaw Pact," *Eastern European Politics and Societies,* 3, 2 (1989), pp. 215–234.

39. Serge Schmemann, "East Gerrnany Opens Frontier to the West for Migration or Travel; Thousands Cross," *New York Times,* November 10, 1989, p. 1. Clyde Haberman, "Bulgarian Chief Quits After 35 Years of Rigid Rule," same issue of the *Times,* p. 1. Timothy Garton Ash, "The Revolution of the Magic Lantern," *New York Review of Books,* January 18, 1990, pp. 42–51. The Czech Communist regime fell on November 24.

40. Louis Zanga, "Albania Decides to End Its Isolation," *Soviet/East European Report* of Radio Free Europe/Radio Liberty, May 1, 1990, p. 4. Then, after partial liberalization was announced in Albania, and a *New York Times* reporter was allowed in, there was this story by David Binder, "Albanian Youths Split on Pace of Change and Leader's Sincerity," *New York Times,* May 27, 1990, section 1, p. 9.

41. The Ceausescu regime began to move in this direction in the early 1970s, though the full ramifications of the return to autarkic Stalinism did not become entirely obvious until the early 1980s. For an explanation of the changes in the early 1970s, see Ken Jowitt, "Political Innovation in Rumania," *Survey,* 4 (Autumn 1974), and Daniel Chirot, "Social Change in Communist Romania," *Social Forces,* 57, 2 (1978), pp. 495–497. Jowitt noted Ceausescu's references to his "beloved friend" Kim Il-Sung and to the sudden demotion of a young reform Communist who had built up well-educated, technocratic cadres and who was expected to become increasingly important. That was Ion Iliescu, the man who was to become the first post-Communist president of Romania. Jowitt again emphasized the similarity of the North Korean and Romanian regimes in "Moscow Centre," *Eastern European Politics and Societies,* 1, 3 (1987), p. 320. For a brief description of what Romania was like by 1988, see Daniel Chirot, "Ceausescu's Last Folly," *Dissent* (Summer 1988), pp. 271–275. In North Korea, despite the many similarities with Romania, decay was not as advanced in the late 1980s, perhaps because, as Bruce Cumings has suggested, Kim's autarkic Marxist patrimonialism was more in tune with Korean historical and cultural tradition than Ceausescu's was with Romania's past. See Bruce Cumings, "Corporatism in North Korea," *Journal of Korean Studies* 4 (1982–1983), particularly p. 277, where Cum-

ings quotes Ken Jowitt's quip about Romania and North Korea being examples of "socialism in one family." Since then, that quote had been widely repeated without being attributed.

42. One of the best accounts of what was going on in Romania was written by the Romanian dissident Pavel Campeanu, "Birth and Death in Romania," *New York Review of Books*, October 23, 1986, That article was written anonymously. His "Revolt of the Romanians," *New York Review of Books*, February 1, 1990, was signed. See also, Daniel N. Nelson, *Romanian Politics in the Ceausescu Era* (New York: Gordon and Breach, 1988), pp. 213–217.

43. There could hardly be a better demonstration of how removed Ceausescu had become from reality than the way in which he was overthrown. The shock on his face as the crowd he was addressing began to jeer him on December 21,1989, was captured on television. More than this was the unbelievable ineptitude of his attempt to escape. Some highly placed Romanians have told me that Ceausescu realized in the last few days that changes had to be made, and that he was hoping to reassert his full control before starting to reform. But it is quite clear that despite the years of growing misery and the alienation of all Romanians outside the Ceausescu family, he still believed he had enough legitimacy to carry on. His surprise may have come about because the demonstration against him was probably instigated by elements in the army and from within the Securitate itself. The reports in the *New York Times* on Romania from December 22 to December 25, 1989, give the essence of the story without, however, clarifying what still remains, much later, a murky sequence of events.

44. The famous J-curve theory of James Davies predicted that a growing gap between rewards and expectations would lead to revolutions; see his article, "Toward a Theory of Revolution," *American Sociological Review*, 27, 1 (1962). Ted Gurr expanded on this and other "psychological explanations" of revolution in *Why Men Rebel* (Princeton: Princeton University Press, 1970). These would be, at best, weak explanations of what happened, except, of course, for the obvious point that many people must have been dissatisfied for regimes that were essentially intact to fall so quickly. There is no obvious reason why discontent should have been any higher in 1989 than five, ten, or twenty years earlier.

45. Michael Bernhard has shown that in fact the Party-state machine in Poland learned from the events of the 1970s and of 1980, and that Jaruzelski was able to impose martial law, raise prices repeatedly, and avoid the political turmoil that had occurred earlier. "The Strikes of June 1976 in Poland," *Eastern European Politics and Societies*, 1, 3 (1987), pp. 390–391. Both the opposition and the regime became more sophisticated with time, but by the mid-1980s the regime had won. The prevailing political attitude, according to many and on the whole fairly reliable surveys done in Poland, was growing apathy toward all political issues. See Jane L. Curry, "The Psychological Barriers to Reform in Poland," *Eastern European Politics and Societies*, 2, 3 (1988), particularly p. 494. David S. Mason's *Public Opinion and Political Change in Poland, 1980–1982* (Cambridge: Cambridge University Press, 1984) consistently shows this, but also that the turn in the J, that is, the growing gap between a deteriorating reality and high expectations created by the growth of the early 1970s, took place in the late 1970s and in 1980. As the 1980s unfolded, peoples' expectations fell into line with reality, the excitement of 1980–1981 replaced by the apathy and hopelessness of martial law. See particularly pp. 42–53 and 222–232.

46. Hankiss, "Demobilization, Self-Mobilization, and Quasi-Mobilization," pp. 131–139.

47. Vladimir Tismaneanu, quoting Vaclav Havel, points out that the dissidents in these countries made up a "minuscule and rather singular enclave." *The Crisis of Marxist Ideology in Eastern Europe: The Poverty of Utopia* (London: Routledge, 1988), p. 166. In his chapter on intellectual dissidents (pp. 160–182), however, Tismaneanu is prophetic in noting that the refusal of the intellectuals to accept the lies of communism can destroy

these systems precisely because they are ultimately based on ideas. This, in fact, was the entire premise of the dissident intellectuals, particularly in Poland, Czechoslovakia, and Hungary.

48. The analysis of conflicts between states trying to reform in order to keep up their power in the international arena and obstructionist traditional elites makes up an important part of Theda Skocpol's theory of revolution in *States and Social Revolutions* (Cambridge: Cambridge University Press, 1979). Classes more committed to reform, then, play an important role in conducting revolutions. But however much merit this argument has in explaining the classical French, Russian, and Chinese revolutions, it seems to have little bearing on what happened in Eastern Europe in 1989. It may, however, have considerable bearing on the future of politics in the Soviet Union.

49. Przemyslaw T. Gajdeczka of the Word Bank claimed in 1988 that the debt problem was more or less under control and that international lenders gave only three countries poor ratings: Poland, Romania, and Yugoslavia. "International Market Perceptions and Economic Performance: Lending to Eastern Europe," *Eastern European Politics and Societies*, 2, 3 (1988), pp. 558–576.

50. That rising classes cause revolutions is at the heart of the Marxist theory of revolution. An interesting twist to this was suggested by György Konrad in *Intellectuals on the Road to Class Power* (Brighton: Harvester Press, 1979). Intellectuals were identified as the rising class that helped put the Communists into power and were becoming the ruling class. But intellectual dissidents in Eastern Europe represented no class, were not numerically large, and were held together by a common moral position, not their position in the economic structure. Zygmunt Bauman identified their role more correctly by pointing out that they were more the carriers of national consciousness and morality than a class as such. "Intellectuals in East-Central Europe: Continuity and Change," *Eastern European Politics and Societies*, 1, 2 (1987), pp. 162–186.

51. Only in Poland could it be said that Charles Tilly's theory about revolutions, that organization of the revolutionary groups counts most, works at all. But even in Poland, the height of organizational coherence in Solidarity was reached in 1980. To the limited extent that Poland fits Tilly's theories about mobilization, that cannot explain the loss of nerve and collapse in the other Communist regimes. See Tilly's *From Mobilization to Revolution* (Reading: Addison-Wesley, 1978).

52. Thus, the first step of what Jack A. Goldstone has called the "natural history" approach to the study of revolutions, based largely on the 1938 work of Crane Brinton, turns out to describe some of what happened in Eastern Europe, too: "Prior to a great revolution, the bulk of the 'intellectuals'—journalists, poets, playwrights, essayists, teachers, members of the clergy, lawyers, and trained members of the bureaucracy— cease to support the regime, writing condemnations and demanding major reforms." Goldstone, "The Comparative and Historical Study of Revolutions," *Annual Review of Sociology*, 8 (1982), pp. 189–190. See also Cane Brinton, *The Anatomy of Revolution* (New York: Vintage, 1965). But most recent theorists of revolution have not taken this observation as anything more than a symptom of deeper class and structural conflicts, and none seems to have believed it could be the prime cause of revolutions. Goldstone's own theory that rapidly rising demographic pressures explain revolutions has much validity in premodern history (pp. 204–205); it has no bearing on Eastern Europe.

53. See Johnson, *Peasant Nationalism*, pp. 31–70.

54. It would be pointless to extend the number of examples because there are so many. For some African cases, see Robert H. Jackson and Carl G. Rosberg, *Personal Rule in Black Africa: Prince, Autocrat, Prophet, Tyrant* (Berkeley: University of California Press, 1982), particularly chapter 6, "Tyrants and Abusive Rule," about the incredible misrule of Idi Amin of Uganda and Macias Nguema of Equatorial Guinea. For Haiti, Robert I. Rotberg's classic study, *Haiti: The Politics of Squalor* (Boston: Houghton Mifflin, 1971)

remains excellent. The tyranny in Burma and the revolution of 1988 (the ultimate effects of which are still pending, despite the repression that took place during that year) are discussed by Bertil Lintner in *Outrage: Burma's Struggle for Democracy* (Hong Kong: Review Publishing, 1989).

55. Leo Kuper, in *Genocide* (New Haven: Yale University Press, 1981), estimates that up to three million Bengalis were killed as the Pakistani army tried to reverse the overwhelming electoral victory of the independence-minded Awami League (pp. 78–80). Of course, it was not just the army but a general collapse into anarchy and interethnic warfare that contributed to the high death toll, but the point is that despite all this, as in Cambodia in 1979 or Uganda also in 1979, the nightmare perpetrated by the government in control against the wishes of the large majority of the population could only be overthrown by outside military intervention (p. 173). By these standards, the European colonial powers, however brutal they may have been, seem to have been more prone to give in to a combination of moral arguments against what they were doing and simple calculations of the costs and benefits of their colonial wars. None of these cases shed much light on what happened in Eastern Europe. After all, the last case of large-scale killing in Eastern Europe was by the Soviets in Hungary in 1956.

56. Ryszard Kapuscinski's *The Emperor* (London: Picador/Pan, 1984), about the fall of Haile Selassie, makes that emperor seem very much a Ceausescu-like figure—out of touch with his population and with his own elite. But some have pointed out that Kapuscinski's book may have been as much about his native Poland under Edward Gierek as about Ethiopia. The violence that followed the first, peaceful stage of the Ethiopian revolution, however, is unlikely to be repeated in Eastern Europe, though it is a chilling reminder of what happens when a disintegrating multiethnic empire tries to hold itself together at any cost.

57. Tim McDaniel has pointed out the extraordinary analogy between the Russian Revolution of 1917 and the Iranian one of 1978–1979. In both cases, autocratic modernizing regimes, despite some real successes, managed to alienate almost all elements in the society. In the case of Iran, this was even more startling because, as in Eastern Europe, there was no major defeat, just a collapse. See McDaniel, *A Modern Mirror for Princes: Autocratic Modernization and Revolution in Russia and Iran* (Princeton: Princeton University Press, 1991).

58. Vladimir Tismaneanu, "Eastern Europe: The Story the Media Missed," *Bulletin of the Atomic Scientists* (March 1990), pp. 17–21.

59. For example, Tony R. Judt in a paper delivered at the Woodrow Wilson Center in Washington, D.C., during summer 1987 and published as "The Dilemmas of Dissidence: The Politics of Opposition in East-Central Europe," *Eastern European Politics and Societies*, 2, 2 (1988). The journals *Telos* and *Cross-currents*, run by scholars from Central Europe, were aware of what was going on, as were some other equally specialized publications in Europe. But before the events of 1989, very few scholars or intellectuals paid much attention to such publications, and even most specialists, especially those in the policy-related fields, hardly took them seriously.

12

DISCOS AND DICTATORSHIP: PARTY-STATE AND SOCIETY RELATIONS IN THE PEOPLE'S REPUBLIC OF CHINA

Tony Saich

During the late spring and early summer . . . a tiny handful of people exploited student unrest to launch a planned, organized, and premeditated political turmoil, which later developed into a counter-revolutionary rebellion in Beijing. . . . Their purpose was to overthrow the leadership of the Chinese Communist Party and subvert the socialist People's Republic of China.

—Chen Xitong

Now, this is what I call turmoil. Can anyone really describe just how fuckin' good this feels? This is, like, the longest kiss I've ever had in my whole life. It's even longer than the Avenue of Eternal Peace. It knocks my soul right out of my ears and sends it flying into the ozone. I relax and feel something totally wild sprouting in every cell of my body.

—Liu Yiran

That's right, enjoy your life, that will really piss them all off.

—Yu Guan in Wang Shuo, *Wanzhu*[1]

The gap between official Party rhetoric and social practice widened significantly during the 1980s. By 1989, the gap appeared as large as a chasm into

This chapter was originally presented as an inaugural lecture at the University of Leiden on March 12, 1993. I would like to thank Jeffrey Wasserstrom and Elizabeth Perry for suggesting that I might include it in this second edition. My thanks go to the members of the University of California–Los Angeles China Seminar, who raised a number of key issues when I presented the ideas there, and also to those responsible for the International Studies and Overseas Program, UCLA, where I spent a most agreeable academic year (1992–1993) as a Senior Visiting Fellow. Finally, I would like to thank especially Sue Tuohy, who subjected an earlier version of this paper to a very vigorous reading. Her comments have improved both the style and contents greatly.

which the Party-state apparatus would fall. Yet, the Chinese Communist Party (CCP) has not gone the same way as its brothers and sisters in Eastern Europe and the Soviet Union. The veteran revolutionaries were able to make one last effort to rally the People's Liberation Army to cow the urban population. From the outside, the Party seems in control; its leaders congratulate themselves on avoiding the fate of their Romanian friend Ceausescu and the "socialist traitor," Gorbachev. Yet, anyone who has visited China recently sees another picture—one that is perhaps confused but that certainly does not conform to the official view. It is this situation that is forcing the Party to push ahead with reforms over the short term while threatening its structure over the long term.

The three introductory quotes highlight two key questions concerning Party-state and societal relations in contemporary China. The two different perceptions of turmoil (the first by the then Mayor of Beijing; the second by a writer in the People's Liberation Army) highlight this growing gap between the official rhetoric and that of those living in the Party-penetrated society. The fact that the second "voice" exists and can be articulated prompts the question—How can the Chinese Party-state appear both strong and weak at the same time? Or to put it another way, how can discos and dictatorship coexist?[2] The third quote, from a character in a work by popular writer Wang Shuo, raises the question—What will be the consequences for a generation that is committed to individualism and self-gratification and that pays scant, if any, attention to official Party-state definitions of what is correct, socially defined behavior, or *orthopraxy* (to use a term of James Watson's that Esherick and Wasserstrom discuss in Chapter 2).[3]

Specifically, I will discuss three major topics: (1) how the reforms have affected the ideological self-definition of the Party-state and have led to both a decay in the strength of the legitimating ideology and to the search for alternatives within the ruling elite; (2) how the reforms have affected the Party-state's relationship to society in terms of the structure of representation; and (3) this Party-state relationship to society in terms of control over discourse, which combines the study of the system with that of practice and accepts that society and the Party-state interact and interpenetrate and that the Party-state can powerfully constrain society. This system taken as a whole can be simultaneously constructed or deconstructed through human action, interaction, and even inaction.

Changes in the Ideological Self-Definition of the Party-State

The reforms introduced by senior leader Deng Xiaoping and his supporters since 1978 marked a significant liberalization of previous regime practice in terms of Party control over the economy, society, and ultimately over public discourse. However, it was not the intention that this liberalization should lead to democratization; but once social spaces were opened up by the Party-state's tactical withdrawal, it did lead to both the pressure for additional opening up of space and the filling of the space that was opened with unorthodox ideas. As the events of 1989 revealed in most spectacular fashion, the Party-state cannot remain immune to the process of liberalization that it sets in motion. A number of consequences have arisen, and these have resulted in a shift in ideological self-definition of the Party-state to accommodate the changing realities.[4]

In particular, the Party changed its self-definition in new statutes adopted in 1982 that refer to the Party as the "vanguard of the Chinese working class" rather than as the "political Party of the proletariat and its vanguard." The term "working class" is more neutral than that of "the proletariat" (the latter term evokes visions of class struggle). Similarly, the 1982 State Constitution defines the nature of the state as a "socialist state under the people's democratic dictatorship," a concept similar to the 1954 definition of China as a "people's democratic state." The 1954 and 1982 State Constitutions were adopted during periods when the emphasis in policymaking was on economic development. Clearly, the intention is to use a definition that incorporates as many people as possible—thus limiting the number of those who can be considered as enemies of the Party-state. As a result of the focus of policymaking on economic modernization since 1978 and a concurrent downgrading of class struggle, the fiercer definition used in the 1975 and 1978 Constitutions—of China as a "socialist state of the dictatorship of the proletariat"—was no longer deemed suitable.

This move to class conciliation and away from class conflict was apparent at the Party's Fourteenth Congress (October 1992). General Secretary Jiang Zemin, when presenting the "Work Report" to the Congress, implied that the new program developed under Deng Xiaoping's guidance amounted to "another great revolution" (*you yici weida geming*) that could be compared to the "New Democratic Revolution" led by the first generation of revolutionaries with Mao Zedong as the central figure. The message is clear: While Mao knew how to bring the classes together to liberate China from Japanese invasion and imperialist aggression, Deng knows how to put together a new coalition of classes to modernize China's backward economy.[5]

This shift is also reflected in the ideological reorientation of the Party-state. With the Party bankrupt in terms of traditional ideological leadership and no longer able to call on traditional notions of class warfare and the like, Deng Xiaoping and his supporters know that the Party's legitimacy to rule will be dependent on its capacity to deliver the economic goods. This knowledge explains their persistent efforts to remove ideological issues from economic debates by blurring the distinctions between socialist and capitalist techniques and their attempt at both the Thirteenth and Fourteenth Party Congresses to shut out debate on the issue for 100 years.

The definition of socialism offered at the Fourteenth Party Congress amounted to no more than a vague commitment to some capacity for the state to iron out problems created by unfettered market forces and, more significantly, to preserve Party rule. The newly revised Party statutes define socialism in the following way:

> The essential nature of socialism is to liberate and develop the productive forces, to eliminate exploitation and polarization, and ultimately to realize common prosperity *(gongtong fuyu)*.[6]

This definition is not unique to socialism and could be applied equally to a whole range of systems from authoritarian to democratic. Such statements confirm the view that socialist ideology—as genuinely *socialist*—is no longer relevant to China's development. The continued use of "socialism" is tied to the Party's self-prescribed legitimacy to rule. Unless the Party claims that the road to prosperity is a socialist one, there is no real reason for the Party's monopoly on power. Thus, "socialist" in Party practice has come to mean authoritarian rule by the CCP.

This process resembles that identified by Vaclav Havel in Eastern Europe with the degradation of ideological discourse and the emergence of a cynical pseudo-morality. Marxism as an official language in China has degenerated into a sterile ritual. Yet the Party-state sees it as a necessary ritual and requires all to abide by it. The obvious utilitarian role of ideology and the linking of legitimacy to economic performance has desanctified the Party and its supreme leaders. The Party has begun to appear mortal and members of society have become more inclined to judge it on earthly, performance-based criteria. This process was speeded by the Party's own admission of past failures during the Great Leap Forward and the Cultural Revolution. Despite the attempts to blame such follies on individuals, the Party's mask of infallibility has slipped and cannot be put back in place. The Party is no longer perceived to be in possession of a higher truth that will guide China to the distant nirvana of communism.[7]

The desanctification of the Party and its supreme leaders was encapsulated for the television audiences of China and the world when Premier Li Peng was obliged to meet with the hunger strikers' representatives in mid-May 1989. While politically and morally necessary, this meeting stripped away the aura of impenetrability that had always surrounded the Party's senior leaders. This aura-stripping process was further evidenced by the way that Li Peng was so obviously out of touch and out of his depth when trying to patronize student leaders Wuer Kaixi and Wang Dan. With the Party stripped of its mythic powers, veteran Party leaders chose to resort to naked force to restore their power.

However, while many Party members have gone along with the repudiation of class war on society, not so many have been willing to give up their privileged political position and have dug in their heels.[8] This retention of political power—when combined with the effects of partial economic reform—has resulted in a corrupted formation within which some Party cadres appear parasitic in using their public function for private gain.

The Party is aware of the public's concern about the official corruption and speculation that arises from this system. How could they not be, given the powerful resonance that the student slogan—"oppose official speculation" *(dadao guandao)*—found among the people in 1989? However, the Party finds it very problematic to do anything serious about the corruption, because the degradation of the official ideology has made it difficult for the Party to portray itself as a moral force in society. Although what remains of the morality of Leninism compels those who produce Party publications to rail against such activities, the existing economic and political structures make it impossible for Party officials to reverse the trend. Indeed, many Party members are rushing to get on the moneymaking treadmill.[9]

The situation where economic riches are pursued without genuine marketization and democratization and where power remains hierarchically structured with information dependent on position is causing corruption to become institutionalized. A system of state, society, Party, and bureaucratic reciprocities based on networks of favor, kinship, friendship, and association is the operational norm. Many public enterprises controlled by the state have become, in practice, fiefdoms—more or less plundered by those who run them—and a market system has emerged in which goods and services are less important than power and prestige. The genuine good of value in this form of market is information that can be traded for money or, more often, for further power.[10]

Both the decay of official ideological discourse and the fact that many, including Party members, see Marxist explanations as irrelevant to China's future have caused some within the Party to explore different theories to legitimize continued CCP rule.[11] The increase in interest in theories of neo-authoritarianism and neo-conservatism will be considered here.[12] This interest derives from the Party's overwhelming desire for stability while implementing economic reforms and the wish of some Party officials to retain a centralized political structure to ensure the continued generation of "private" profits. While neo-authoritarianism was associated with think-tank members close to former General Secretary Zhao Ziyang, neoconservatism is associated with a group of younger leaders and scholars clustered around the children of certain senior Party officials, such as Chen Yuan (son of Chen Yun).[13] These theories—with their appeals to authoritarian government and "strongman" rule—have come under attack not only from more "liberal" reformers but also from orthodox Party members who appear to be worried about certain implications of the theories.

Both theories share a rejection of the Marxist-Leninist mode of discourse; indeed, it is difficult to find any intellectual in Beijing who will spontaneously talk about Marxism. Although the theories' use of foreign models—such as the "Four Little Dragons" and Latin-American types (such as Brazil and Argentina)— might leave much to be desired, the arguments are couched in terms familiar to Western (or Western-trained) social scientists. Instead of invoking Marxism, China's "next generation of leaders" use arguments about economic development to justify their future authoritarian rule. The problem with their argumentation—as far as orthodox Party members are concerned—is that while such theories outline the need for a strong central political authority, they dispense with the explicit need for a Communist Party to rule the system. This conflicts with the demand for unchallenged Party rule as enshrined in Deng Xiaoping's "Four Cardinal Principles."[14] In

fact, it has been reported that Deng supported the view that the modernization process in a backward country needed "strongman politics," rather than
Western-style democracy, as a driving force. However, he had reservations
about the term 'neo-authoritarianism' and suggested that another term might
be found.[15] Such concerns partly explain both the failure of Party members
associated with neoconservatism to be elected to the Fourteenth Central
Committee in 1992 and the rejection of the neoconservatists' policy program
in favor of Deng Xiaoping's call for rapid economic transformation combined with strong, centralized *Party* rule as enshrined in the Four Cardinal
Principles. Despite orthodox Party members' unease with neoauthoritarian
and neoconservative theories, the degradation of official discourse permits
such theories to play an important part in future debates about the nature of
political power during China's economic transformation phase.

Ideas supporting neo-authoritarianism began to appear in 1986, but the
theory became more important as a justification for holding power in late
1988 as the reforms began to falter. From the examples of the swiftly developing economies of both Southeast and East Asia, CCP supporters drew the
conclusion that China's drive for economic modernization required a strong
centralized political structure, especially in the early, start-up phase, in order
to prevent social divisions from undermining the process. The regime believes that this will help push through unpopular measures without the consequences of mass protest. Quite simply, the Party equates democratization
with chaos, and chaos with underdevelopment.

Key proponents of the regime's reforms, such as the scholars Zhang Bingjiu and Wu Jiaxiang, were alarmed by critics who claimed that such views
were essentially antidemocratic and who sought to portray those who held
such views as "moderate democrats." Zhang proposes that the gradual extension of market mechanisms will create the necessary basis for democracy
and thus justifies the measures as a means for producing democracy.[16] Zhang
and like-minded intellectuals argue that, at present, China does not possess
the necessary cultural conditions for democracy. Thus, for the foreseeable future, a central authority is necessary to push through the policies that will
create the basis for change.

This projected development has a distinct appeal for many in the Party-
state system. The call for authoritarian rule by core Party groups in Beijing is
translated into centralized rule at the provincial and local levels. It also has a
certain appeal to moderate reformers who do not want to risk a complete
breakdown in China that would leave a dangerous political void. These reformers see—in the examples of East and Southeast Asia—the growth of a
more affluent middle class that can gradually establish an economic and social structure independent of the Party-state. They believe that this structure
will lead to demands for more meaningful participation in the political
process that they argue will, in turn, roll back the boundaries of Party-state
power. This argument is similar to that of reformers previously in Hungary.
In both cases, what is proposed is a process of *embourgeoisement* that is econ-
omy-centered, nonconfrontational, and elite-centered. At the same time,
this process offers the intellectuals continuation of their privileged position

within regime patronage and holds out a more extensive role for engineers and scientists.

Similar themes run through the approach of the neoconservatives, but their approach draws more consciously on traditional values within Chinese political culture.[17] With the collapse of the Soviet Union, one of the key documents of neoconservatism argues that China can rely on traditional arguments for centralized rule rather than rely on Marxist principles. This would allow China to pursue its own national interest instead of adopting a foreign policy that was overly influenced by ideological analyses of the world situation.[18] Party supporters accept the neo-authoritarian thesis that stability is the overriding concern during the economic transformation phase, and some propose that the Party take control of China's economic assets. Further, neo-conservatives argue for the cultivation of a modernizing elite within the existing structure of the CCP. To date, unlike with the defenders of neo-authoritarianism, there has been little attempt by the Chinese media to portray the theory of neoconservatism as leading to a more democratic state and societal structure in the mid- to long term.

Impact on the Organizational Structure of Representation

The intention of China's leaders, such as Deng Xiaoping, has been to create the necessary conditions to provide the information and expertise needed for the ambitious programs of economic modernization rather than to make the Party-state genuinely accountable to the citizens of China. It is a tricky policy to follow, and it has been impossible for Party members to remain immune from the influence of different social groups and for the Party organs to channel entirely the activities of the organizations that have developed in recent years toward the state's program of economic reform.

The tacit recognition by the Party of the existence of other groups in society should not be interpreted as the emergence of a "pluralist" political system. It is an attempt to finesse self-regulated and autonomously defined political organizations by incorporating those groups that the Party leadership sees as important into the existing modified power structures and spaces. In this attempt at "revolution from above" groups are "created" by the Party-state rather than being "recognized." Thus, as Jowitt has noted in the context of Eastern Europe, the move of the Party from insulation from society to integration within it can be interpreted as an attempt to prevent an arising plurality of definitions by revising the structure of the regime and the Party's relationship to the state and to society.[19] The Party moves to accommodate the increasingly wide range of articulate audiences to thwart or limit the possibility of alternate political-ideological definitions.

The reforms introduced under Deng Xiaoping's leadership since 1978 have changed the function of a number of existing organizations and have created new social groups and organizations. The redistribution of power has changed the institutionalized patterns of interaction among members of Chinese society and between them and the Party-state. Despite the Party's attempts to prevent a genuine democratization, inevitably this process has made Chinese society more complex and dynamic.

Since the 1980s, official Party policy has tried to influence key groups in society more indirectly by binding them into organizations that become dependent on regime patronage. To head off mass opposition, the Party will seek to extend its organization, coordination, and supervision of as much of the population as possible. Traditionally, the Party has relied on what it terms "mass organizations," such as the Trade Unions and the Women's Federation; such reliance has been a two-edged sword as the Party provides a mechanism of participation to officially sanctioned groups but makes the formation of autonomous union organizations or women's organizations impossible. By subjugating sectoral interests to general Party policy, the Party allows such organizations the autonomy to organize their own activities, within a broadly defined framework, and to support the pursuance of legitimate rights of their members insofar as they do not override the common good, as defined by the Party. In return, the Party expects unconditional support for its broader political, economic, and social programs. The structures that emerge and their interrelationships begin to resemble Schmitter's definition of "state corporatism."[20]

The unions, for the most part, have been engaged in conflict avoidance (conflict management) and in mobilizing support for Party policy. Even before the events of 1989, however, there was frustration with these officially sponsored trade unions and pressure built up for the unions to take up a more active promotion of their members' interests. In a July 1988 symposium sponsored by the official union, it was proposed that the unions should play down their political role as a conduit of Party policy and concentrate on protecting the workers' economic and welfare interests.[21] Evidence suggests that this process has been continuing with the official unions since 1989. The All China Federation of Trade Unions has taken up workers' demands for a five-day workweek to replace the current six-day system and has tabled motions to this effect to the last two sessions of the National People's Congress (1992 and 1993).[22]

In 1989, two things in particular shook the orthodox Party members and made them fear that they might be confronted by a Solidarity-type situation in China. The first was the donation given by the official trade union to the students and its calls for senior leaders to enter into dialogue with the students. But the fact that the official trade union was going over to the opposition was outdone by the establishment of an independent workers' organization that rejected Party rule entirely. The foundation of the Capital [or Beijing] Workers' Autonomous Federation, independent of the official workplace-based unions, was a direct affront to the Party's claim to be the sole representative of the working class, and the Federation was interpreted by orthodox Party members as a "counterrevolutionary" organization.

The Party focus on economic modernization has resulted in attempts by the leadership to draw key groups of experts into the decisionmaking process on a more systematic basis and in the upgrading of the position of intellectuals in ideological and material terms. Gone are the references to the "stinking ninth category," a term that Party propagandists once used to raise doubts about the patriotism and revolutionary zeal of members of the intelligentsia as well as to denigrate them. Intellectuals are now defined as an integral part of the working class. This "ideological upgrading" has been accompanied by attempts on the part of intellectuals to improve their work, housing, and salary conditions, and intellectuals have been given greater freedom within their fields of professional competence. There has been an explosion of professional journals and convenings of congresses to enable the exchange of views. Professional societies have been mushrooming as a further forum for the exchange of ideas and as organizations on which Party-state organs can draw for expertise. Many of these newly formed organizations have been drawn into inner-Party debates through their provision of advice to different policymakers within the top leadership. Other organizations have used the newly granted public space to challenge the boundaries of acceptable discourse.

The revival of the "united front" approach and the increased reliance on experts has led to a revitalization of the eight other political parties in mainland China. Contrary to the view that these parties would pass away with the generation that spawned them, they have flourished and have begun to recruit growing numbers of members. The CCP sees these other parties as providing a useful link to the intellectuals whom the CCP cannot draw directly under its own influence and as playing a pivotal role in mediating with influential Chinese abroad. For example, the *Jiusan Society* is composed mainly of intellectuals from scientific and technical circles, and the CCP has sought to take advantage of those connections.

It appears that, with Deng Xiaoping's approval, Zhao Ziyang and his advisers had set up an *ad hoc* group in January 1989 to draft a plan to expand the role of these parties. According to American political scientist James Seymour, by May the proposals were ready and they included the following: a greater role for these parties in the organs of state power; the suggestion that these parties be consulted on the choice of state leaders; and participation of these parties in the formulation of state principles, policies, laws, and decrees. Non-Communists were to be included in government and judicial work.[23]

Many in China see these parties as merely subservient lackeys of the CCP who meekly do its bidding. As one wall poster in 1989 noted: "It is better to get divorced than to be a concubine of the other Party. Democratic parties, become independent while it is still not too late to speak for the people."[24] While they may not have spoken for the people, these parties have used the new opportunities to press the interests of their own members. The Democratic National Construction Association—composed mainly of people from financial and business circles—even contemplated the possibility of setting up a genuine opposition political party rather than forming another party that operated under the tutelage of the CCP.

Since the repression of the student movement in June 1989 and the changes in Eastern European politics that Chirot has surveyed in the preceding chapter, which have resulted in many cases in the emergence of multiparty systems, the CCP has taken pains to stress the unique nature of its own multiparty system to forestall any moves toward genuine independence by the pre-existing parties. Articles in the official media have stressed the acceptance by the other eight parties of the CCP's leadership.[25] In an interview, the Chairman of the Democratic National Construction Association, Sun-Qimeng, stated that CCP leadership was the prerequisite and guarantee for multiparty cooperation. Contrary to views expressed by his association a year or so before, Sun noted that his party was not a "party out of office or an opposition party."[26]

Not only has there been a revival of activity in these more traditional organizations, but also new organizations have been brought into existence—ranging from philately associations to China's first private commercial law firm. The *China Daily* estimated that there were some 1,000 autonomous organizations operating at the national level and 100,000 locally.[27] In April 1988, the first trade union for the private sector was set up. This was formed by 200 workers (out of a total workforce of 240) in the Shenyang Xigui Transportation Company and was affiliated with the official All China Federation of Trade Unions.[28] While orthodox Party members tried to reign-in the activities and expansion of such organizations after 1989, the effect has been limited. As marketization and privatization proceeds, China is becoming a patchwork of private, collective, state, and hybrid organizations.

Education provides a good example of how marketization is forcing the Party-state to yield control over the process of socialization of the young. Private universities have already been established, the first being Ningbo University financed by the wealthy Hong Kong businessman, Y. K. Pao. The State Education Commission has accepted that it cannot continue to adequately fund all those institutions of higher education within its jurisdiction. (Local authorities had already abandoned their commitment to primary and senior schools, especially in the rural areas). As a result, many institutions will have to resort to charging fees, raising funds from commerce or abroad, and deriving revenues from research or the sale of assets. These trends will make higher education less amenable to centralized political control.

The creeping privatization of education has already made its effects felt in several parts of the country. By 1992, there were already 20,000 private schools operating in China, including a Sichuan institution named the Guangya Primary School (the first such school since 1949). While schools in many rural areas close through lack of funds, Guangya charges a one-time enrollment fee of 180,000 *yuan* and an annual tuition fee of 4,200 *yuan* to educate the children of entrepreneurs, senior government officials, and private businesspeople.[29]

It would be wrong, however, to see these developments as necessarily marking a collapse of Party rule, and chances exist for the Party to retain its dominant position within a dramatically changed economic and social landscape. These developments do, of course, make the practice of Party rule much more difficult. As I suggested earlier in this chapter, the distinction between public and private is often blurred. One of the largest state-owned enterprises in Beijing has already set up some forty to fifty companies that are nominally private, collective, or joint ventures. Some private companies (the briefcase companies—*pibao gongsi*) and service organizations are staffed by state employees who are moonlighting. Within the private sector there is ambivalence on the question of reform, and most would favor a regime that can provide stability even if this might mean a more authoritarian power structure. In theory, they should have a vested interest in supporting further development of the program for economic and political change, which would not only provide them with a greater opportunity for expansion but also would lend their activities legitimacy. Further, the increased use of market forces and a decrease in administrative regulation of the economy would give private enterprises greater freedom from being "squeezed" by local officials. As Dorothy Solinger notes, however, the picture is less clear-cut than some have suggested. The hybrid economic structure means that the officials and the merchants have become "dependent, mutually interpenetrated semi-classes, even as both share a new kind of dependence on the state." This causes some merchants to be wary of further reform to a pure market system—because it would deprive them of their special inside tracks that they have established with Party-state officials.[30]

Gordon White's research on Xiaoshan City in the province of Zhejiang reveals this ambiguity. He focuses on the organic accompaniment of the spread of market relations with the consequent emergence of a new realm of social organizations—based on voluntary participation—that enjoy some autonomy from the state. White concludes that while social space has opened up, the state has continued to retain a great deal of its power and has moved to occupy this space and organize the newly emergent, dispersed sources of economic power by encouraging the establishment of societal organizations to act as intermediaries. These new social organizations, in White's view, do not reflect a clear distinction between "public" and "private" spheres but rather a mixture of public and private in which the public continues to dominate.[31] It is not surprising that, as noted above, a younger generation of well-connected Party members is interested in the statist ideologies of neo-authoritarianism and neoconservatism.

The Decline in Control over Public Discourse

The reforms in China during the 1980s have not only been accompanied by sharp debates among the Party leadership but also by the public expression of quite unorthodox ideas. The Party has met with difficulties in maintaining its regime patronage for certain intellectual groups and social organizations, and it is slowly losing control over the discourse that is filling the public spaces. Increasingly, public discourse is breaking free of the codes and linguistic phrases established by the Party-state. Examples such as these highlight the weakness of the Party-state and display how its authority is gradually being undermined.

The hostility of many veteran Party members to an independent public discourse stems from their Leninist heritage, from their post-1949 experi-

[handwritten annotations in top margin: "Something greatly detested; a thing or person accursed" and "curse"]

ences, and, more particularly, from their memories of pre-1949 Yan'an, where the Party's strategies for legitimating its authority were first articulated fully and implemented on a small scale. Quite simply, the idea that a civil society could arise is an anathema that would portend an anarchistic individualism that would undermine the Party's "universalizing we." While Marx saw the proletariat as the universalizing force that would bring unity through the destruction of bourgeois civil society, it was Lenin who later substituted the Party as the universalizing agent. The model of the Party-state structure that was offered to China was thus elitist in nature, and this gelled well with China's own imperial tradition. The suspicion of particular interest and political activity outside of direct Party control seemed to be reinforced by events in the chaotic world of the young Republic. It certainly seemed to be the case after 1949 when the Party was opened up to criticism by outside forces, such as during the "Hundred Flowers" campaign of the late 1950s (which began with top officials encouraging people to voice complaints about the political status quo) and the Cultural Revolution.

It was in Yan'an that Mao gave the Leninist heritage its Chinese characteristics and defined the basic elements of his discourse community.[32] Under Mao's direction, the now veteran revolutionaries set out deliberately and explicitly to change the world by reinterpreting it, and they were remarkably successful in realizing this objective. Yan'an provides a prime example of how power is generated by an inversionary discourse community that constructed its own language of belief. This discourse community constituted itself in terms of a primary affiliation. Affiliation to the Party replaced affiliations to family and friends and offered an equivalent intimacy. It was conceived of initially as a miniaturized version of the society that was to be or was in the process of being formed. Commitment to the organization was crucial and no matter how personalized the leadership, the organization claimed a higher truth and demanded devotional conduct. The realization of this truth was to be obtained by means of collective action. This process of creation in Yan'an provided Mao and the veteran revolutionaries with the symbolic capital of their revolution.[33]

However, the symbolic capital created in this situation could not last. It had to give way when political priorities shifted from moral moments and exceptional events to the duller slogging of generating economic capital. Yan'an could never serve as the design for a modern industrial society. For modernization and development, models were required invoking discourse based on systemic relationships between needs, wants, priorities, preferences, and interests rather than principles. This discourse "community" has constantly struggled to be heard in China since 1949. Individuals increasingly believe that they have more to gain through the pursuit of their own self-interests and everything to lose if they try to draw down benefits from the collective. Revolutionary goals have disappeared and behavior has gradually become separated from the erstwhile norms and principles of the revolution.

Like many revolutionary or even messianic movements before them, the Party's veteran revolutionaries have discovered that it is one thing to build up symbolic capital in movements against domination and hegemonic power but that it is another to use that capital as a basis for exercising such power after the threat has subsided. As Geertz has noted, once there is a local state rather than the mere dream of one, the task of radical ideologizing changes dramatically. It is no longer sufficient to construct symbols for the demise of an alien order and to rally around symbols of its demise; now the task is to define a collective subject to whom the actions of the state can be internally connected—the creation of an experimental "we" from whose will the activities of government seem spontaneously to flow.[34] It is in this respect that, over the long term, the CCP has conspicuously failed.

The Party-state in power lost its previously privileged role as the opposition Party—as the agent of the progressive forces in history. In its new situation, slowly but surely the Party-state loses out because it becomes victimized by its own power. Whereas the veteran revolutionaries formerly knew "realities" better than their opponents, they now know it only through information passed upward by subordinates. With increasing coercion, subordinates only pass up what leaders want to hear, while negative information is suppressed and its agents repressed. The Party has invariably punished the messenger that has not provided the "truth" the Party wants to hear.

To deal with this situation, the Party needs to introduce genuine political reforms—but orthodox Party members resist them, as they fear that sectoral groups will pounce on such reforms to pursue their own individual agendas that diverge radically from those of the Party-state. What they see lurking in the shadows are revivalism, religion, linguistic division, and regional and non-Han ethnic loyalties. They are right, of course; but although they might send the People's Liberation Army to Tibet, Xinjiang, and Tiananmen Square, their authority erodes as naked force becomes increasingly necessary to retain their power. Orthodox Party members seek continually to close down public spaces, believing that a docile population will meet only under very controlled and ritualized circumstances.

However, the system of regime patronage that I previously discussed is breaking down; the Party's foundational myths are being eroded and discourses are being increasingly heard that do not share the Party-state's code—thus making even a "shared discourse of antagonistic classes impossible."[35]

The late-1980s exposed problems with the system of regime patronage for intellectuals. As the CCP leadership divided over fundamental issues, the parameters of debate were continually redrawn in such a way that many of the "loyal intellectuals" fell outside of the realms of the acceptable. Especially after the removal of Hu Yaobang in January 1987, many of the harsh judgments that had been reserved for private discussion were thrown into the public domain. The disillusionment with incomplete reform in the political sphere caused critical intellectuals to question both the validity of working within the constraints laid down by Deng Xiaoping and the feasibility of "revolution from above." While mobilized participation and Party-guided political study sessions declined, genuine politics began to emerge. This process was not depoliticization as some have referred to it but a real politicization of Chinese society. Demands were made to place issues of accountability, subgroup autonomy, and self-determination on the political agenda.

While the "voice" of alternative discourses was heard most strongly in 1989, it has not gone away; the events of 1989 were themselves a result of the gradual erosion of belief in Party-state-determined symbols and rituals. While these also were challenged in the "Hundred Flowers" campaign, the origins of rejection lie in the Cultural Revolution and became increasingly apparent during the reform period. As one poster put up in mid-May at the Chinese People's University stated, loyalty to the Party equaled "subservience and blind faith as a result of [intellectual] castration and loss of the ability to have any independent thought."[36]

The search for alternative agendas and identities has not stopped—as anyone who has visited China recently can verify. Urban China is awash with the kinds of jokes, mockery, and cynicism that continue to erode the legitimacy of the Party-state. While Premier Li Peng boldly claims that "only socialism can save China," the students whisper "only China can save socialism." Students at Beijing University talk of two factions, the *ma pai* and the *tuo pai*; they are not referring to the Marxist and Trotskyite factions of Party hagiography but to those who play mah-jongg and those who want to pass the TOFL test in order to go abroad.

Even the singing of official, patriotic songs is used to mock the authorities. Immediately after the suppression of the demonstrations in 1989, academics at the Chinese Academy of Social Sciences were encouraged to sing patriotic songs. The choice by a group of elderly women of the children's song "I love Beijing Tiananmen" was not only a poignant reminder of what had happened in the nation's capital, but the sight of grown women marching singing a children's song critiqued the infantalization of the adult population that the Party has sought to bring about. A Party that bans satirical T-shirts, as the Beijing Party Committee did in the summer of 1991, and even bans laughter in Tiananmen Square on the 1992 anniversary of June 4, does not inspire confidence as being in control of a strong Party-state.[37]

While these anecdotes may not be overwhelming evidence of Party-state weakness, they do point the way to a partially submerged discourse that is clearly at odds with the official one.[38] As in many other authoritarian regimes in the throes of transition, it is the writers and other creative intellectuals who have been at the forefront in bringing this discourse to the public and who have opened up another world for us to see in China. Here, I will just mention two categories: (1) works that challenge the official metanarrative of the Party-state (a metanarrative in which the kinds of specifically historical narratives that Wasserstrom discusses in the following chapter play a key role)[39] and (2) works that ignore the discourse of the Party-state and attempt to map out a new form of language and communication.

Official histories and accounts of key events are a key element of CCP rule. These provide the metanarrative to legitimize the hegemony of the ruling Party. This metanarrative is to be received by all and the idea of a community with its own historical memory is to be destroyed and alternative narratives are to be eradicated. The official metanarrative is intended to show the historical inevitability of the Party's rise to power and that its removal from power would mean chaos. Underground literature during the Cultural Revolution, much of which was made public during the Democracy Wall Movement (1978–1979), comprised attempts to "deconstruct" the Party's metanarrative. In the mid-1980s, "roots literature" *(xungen wenxue)* involved the creation of a community distinct from the sterile narratives of official Party writing. As Leo Ou-fan Lee has noted, "Han [Shaogang] and the other *xungen* writers would argue, the present reality as defined by the Party culture is a dead 'crust' overlaid on the seedbed of a vibrant mixture of several ancient and unorthodox cultures."[40] What these and other literatures in the 1980s and 1990s reveal are "heroes" who are not necessarily Party members, colorful local histories, and vibrant sexuality that proves to be just as much a driving force as the ideological favor displayed in official Party writings.[41]

The film *Yellow Earth (Huang tudi,* 1984) angered many Party veterans, particularly vice-President Wang Zhen, with its portrayal of conditions in a village on the shores of the Yellow River in Northwest China before the Communist victory. This film damagingly exposed a number of the basic myths of the Party's metanarrative about its rise to power. The village is portrayed as having a continuing history only broken by the changing seasons and whatever ills nature may inflict upon it. The struggle is against nature, not a class struggle against landlords as portrayed in official Party history.

If such revelations in the film were not enough, the Japanese invasion is made to seem irrelevant to village life and (most damningly of all) the Party is portrayed as being remote. Yan'an, the center of the revolution, is most notable by its absence. The only trace of the Party is Gu Qing, a soldier in the Eighth Route Army, who is on an expedition to gather folksongs (in 1939). Indeed, as illustrated in the following narrative, where the Party does intervene in the persona of Gu Qing, it proves disastrous even though the intention is benevolent if paternalistic.

Arriving in the village, Gu finds it hard to square his idealized image of the peasantry with the harsh realities that confront him. He is shocked further when he asks the young goatherder, Hanhan, to sing one of his peasant songs—a song that Gu presumably expects will celebrate peasant survival in the midst of such harsh nature. Instead, Gu hears the following:

> When the pomegranate flowers, the leaves start showing,
> My mother sold me off to him, without me knowing.
> All I ever asked for, was a good man to wed,
> But what I ended up with was a little piss-in-bed.
> When you piss, I'll piss along,
> Curse you, you can piss with me.
> In spring next year, when flowers blossom red,
> Frogs will start croaking, under the bed.
> Right to the East Ocean, flows a river of piss,
> To the Dragon King's palace, under the sea.
> The Dragon King laughs, as he hears the piss:
> This little piss-in-bed is in the same line as me.[42]

The perplexed soldier replies with a song typical of the sterile eulogies of the CCP.

Cuiqiao, the sister of Hanhan, having heard of the new world being created in Yan'an, demands to be taken back with Gu to the revolutionary heartland. The soldier is incapable of making the decision, but he promises "to reflect her opinions to the leadership," a phrase familiar to all victims of bureaucratic vacillation in China. The girl is devastated and decries this new world order for replicating the old order—with its lack of spontaneity, its rules, regulations, and what appears to be a patriarchal hierarchy. Hearing nothing, Cuiqiao strikes out on her own, but she drowns in her attempts to cross the Yellow River. The remote, absent, unreachable Yan'an interferes in her life to produce disaster.

The film has a number of subtexts. One is the complete disappearance of symbolic capital. It renders it an illusion. The film casts doubt on the whole Yan'an enterprise and undermines it as the legitimizing myth of Communist rule; the film implies that it never had any real relevance in the lives of ordinary people except by imposition.[43]

While Chen Kaige (director of *Yellow Earth*) seems to offer us a romantic vision of the noble peasant, other artistic works have offered us heroes that turn the Party's world upside down. Xie Jin's film *The Legend of Tianyun Mountain* (*Tianyunshan Chuanqi*, 1980), has as its main theme the view that the difficulties that plagued China as it entered the 1980s stemmed not just from the Cultural Revolution, as the 1981 official Party history would have it, but from the 1950s and especially the antirightist campaign in which Deng Xiaoping played a prominent role.[44] The film also provides us with an antihero to contrast with the positive role models provided by official Party literature. The film highlights the fact that many of those restored to positions of authority after the Cultural Revolution, such as Song Wei and her husband Wu Yao, were precisely those who had persecuted others a decade before in the antirightist campaign. As a result, they resisted the rehabilitation of other more deserving victims, such as Luo Chun, who had suffered previously for their honesty. What emerges from this is not identification with the "good" cadres who had been harshly treated during the Cultural Revolution; instead, the director encourages us to view those persecuted a generation before as the real heroes.

The inversion of Party heroes is taken one step further by other writers who do not engage with the Party's discourse at all—even though their heroes are products of the reforms introduced by the Party-state. They seek their heroes from the underside of Chinese society—from the fixers and streetwise dealers of a generation spawned by the reforms. Perhaps one of the best examples of this kind of writing is found in the works of Wang Shuo—who, as Geremie Barmé has pointed out, is one of a new generation of the "financially independent unemployed."[45] This independence from state patronage for writers is a relatively new phenomenon in China and has clearly led to a more independent, critically minded form of literary expression. These writers' works show an interest in the private sphere of emotions rather than in the collective sphere and a more independent, carefree approach than the *danwei* (work unit) regulated life of the Party-state.

More threatening than the ridicule such writings (or their televised series) often heap on the bureaucratism of everyday life is the fact that these writers refuse to engage the Party on its own turf. By displacing the terrain of the discourse, they present a fundamental challenge to the Party's hegemony over the arts. If the Party ideologues and writers such as Wang Shuo are not talking about the same things anymore, what hope is there for Party control over the arts and literature? Perhaps it is more threatening for the Party-state to be ignored rather than to be met head-on. As Wang Shuo is reported to have said in early 1993: "I just thumb my nose at these people [Party critics]. If they had the power to put me in jail, then I might listen to them, but they're just a bunch of dusty, out-of-touch old bores and they can't hurt me. If they don't like what I write, they can just turn their televisions off."[46]

Many works of modern Chinese literature are characterized by the attempt to emerge from the linguistic and encoded discipline imposed by the Party-state and to develop a language and communication form that expresses the feelings of the younger generation growing up in urban China today. Perhaps the most important medium to which these youths have turned is popular music of the sort that Calhoun and Jones discuss in Chapter 4 and Chapter 7, respectively. The fact that rock music has found an enthusiastic audience among Chinese youth shows that it is giving "voice" to a new generation in much the same way as Richard Pryor did for a new generation of African-Americans that tested the limits of the First Amendment.[47]

Not surprisingly, a strong trend in contemporary literature is to dwell on the expression of private emotions. This terrain is denied existence by the official Party-state or, if recognized, is denounced as representing "petty bourgeois individualism." In general, before the outbreak of this new experimentalism with the emotions, when one cried it was because of the terrible deeds wrought by class enemies or imperialists on the proletariat and their class allies, the peasantry. I always remember watching in amazement films such as *The Guerrilla Detachment of the Plains (Pingyuan youjidui)*. In this film, the heroine stoically watched her family being butchered by invading tyrants without any flicker of emotion apart from deepening her belief in the correctness of the CCP. Now emotions are as liable to be expressed over broken love affairs and because individual objectives have been thwarted. Even if the Party-state could not expect orthodoxy on behalf of China's urban inhabitants, the younger generation has even rejected *orthopraxy*. Many revel in jokes that undermine Party credibility and wear clothes or sport hair fashions that shock not just the Party elders but also many of their family elders.

Since 1989, there has been a notable trend in the performing arts (and in jokes) that combines satire with an anarchic sense of boredom with life in urban China. The search for roots as a part of a moralistic critique found in the works of many in the 1980s has been abandoned by many writing in the 1990s. This trend is reflected in the films beginning to be made by the "sixth generation" of filmmakers who graduated from the Film Academy in 1989. In contrast with the "fifth generation" of filmmakers, such as Chen Kaige and

Zhang Yimou, who took up a moralistic and usually aesthetically pleasing critique of Party metanarrative in their works, the new filmmakers reject moral solutions and show very little faith in politics as providing the solution to anything.[48] They feel that the documentary style is more suitable to the "realistic" world they seek to portray, and their films, such as Zhang Yuan's *Beijing Bastards* (*Beijing zazhong*, 1993), are peppered with earthy street language.

However, this more free-for-all urban society has produced a number of negative effects. Perhaps the most disconcerting is the degradation of personal relationships. Most visitors to China's cities quickly become aware of the commercialization of interpersonal relationships, that is, of a situation in which people are continually calculating the material benefits and less-tangible perks (such as access to formally off-limits documents, and introductions to government officials able to help with exit visas) that might come from developing a friendship. One can be quickly sized up in terms of use value, and returning citizens often use the phrase "no morality" (*meiyou daode*) to describe the shock they feel at the pace of change.

The emergence of the individual as focus is impossible for the veteran Party members to contemplate. It means that the Party's symbolic capital—no matter how brightly it may have burned in its moral moment—for the younger generation at least, is a rather bad, as well as irrelevant, joke. There is no psychological benefit to be drawn by the Party from the collective—only fear or a certain passive acquiescence. The veteran revolutionaries had promised the citizens of the People's Republic that the collective would generate more benefits for society than the summation of all individuals acting on their own behalves or pursuing their own self-interests. Perhaps in the moral moment of the revolution that was true, but today such a notion has dissipated entirely and cannot be regenerated.

Of course, many Party members know that they have no more symbolic capital in reserve—despite what the dreaming veteran revolutionaries may think. They know that the campaigns both to study the selfless Maoist heroes, such as Uncle Lei Feng, and to be on the guard against the ravages of "spiritual pollution" have little effect on an urban population that is busy making money, listening to Hong Kong and Taiwan pop songs (or those of Beijing antihero, Cui Jian), and reading the novellas of Wang Shuo. This knowledge lies behind their attempts to shift the basis for legitimacy of the Party-state to performance-based criteria and, in particular, to management of the economy. However, this opens up the Party-state to completely different sets of criteria for evaluation. In terms of self-legitimation, a younger generation of potential leaders is beginning to use the kinds of arguments to justify authoritarianism that are familiar to students of Third World politics.

The arguments that I have presented in this chapter do not mean that the Chinese Party-state is liable to immediate collapse, but events in Eastern Europe and in the Soviet Union have revealed regime fallibility once its moral authority begins to slide. My arguments do mean that those who run the Party-state in the future will have to become more flexible and sophisticated in order to retain their dominant position. Many of the reforms that they will have to undertake will gnaw away at the legitimacy of the Party-state over the long term. In fact, the Party-state—although appearing strong—is weak in certain fundamental respects. It has shown that it can use the continued threat of force to gain compliance. It does not have either the respect or the support that might seem to be expressed through voluntary citizen participation in Party-state-run or Party-state-authorized institutions. Most of these institutions are ships of convenience that are shown to be leaking. If the Party-state is to survive, its future leaders need to devise institutional mechanisms to deal with the newly emerging interests that have arisen as a result of the program of economic reform. Much political activity that takes place does so outside of the official institutions and channels of the Party-state and has become increasingly antisystemic. Finally, as I demonstrated in the last section of this chapter, the Party-state is denied legitimacy by much of its urban population. There is no acceptance and certainly no appropriation of the Party-state's rules of the game, a factor that severely undermines its moral authority.

Notes

1. The quotes are from Chen Xitong, "Mayor Chen Xitong's Report on Putting Down Anti-Government Riot," *Information Bulletin of the Embassy of the People's Republic of China*, 1990, delivered on June 30, 1989, to the Eighth Meeting of the Standing Committee of the Seventh National People's Congress; Liu Yiran, translated in Geremie Barmé and Linda Jaivin, eds., *New Ghosts, Old Dreams: Chinese Rebel Voices* (New York: Random House, 1992), p. 5; and Wang Shuo, *Wanzhu* (The Dealers); in *Wang Shuo xiequ xiaoshuo xuan* (Selected comic fiction of Wang Shuo) (Beijing: Zuojia chubanshe, 1990), p. 59.

2. The use of the words discos and dictatorship is obviously a play on the title of Orville Schell's excellent book, *Discos and Democracy: China in the Throes of Reform* (New York: Doubleday, 1989). The point here is that what needs to be explained is not how the apparently freewheeling atmosphere of the disco accompanies the democratization of the Party-state but how it can coexist within an authoritarian political setting. A disco itself is not an entirely free setting; it can offer wild abandon for the dancers but only within a well-organized and usually controlled setting. If the Party could control the setting, it could provide citizens with the chance to let off steam without risking a direct challenge to its continued rule. Yet, as I will discuss in the section that follows, this is a risky exercise, because the boundaries of control are continually challenged and new organizations might provide alternative, structured spaces.

3. See James L. Watson's chapter, "The Renegotiation of Chinese Cultural Identity in the Post-Mao Era," in the first edition of Wasserstrom and Perry, *Popular Protest and Political Culture in Modern China* (Boulder: Westview Press, 1992).

4. Clearly, there has been widespread debate within the Party and sharp differences of opinion exist concerning issues such as the correct terminology to be used and the relationship of the Party to the state and to society. For a review of these differences, see Tony Saich, "Much Ado About Nothing: Party Reform in the Eighties," in Gordon White, ed., *China Under Economic Reform* (Basingstoke: Macmillan Press, 1992). The sources used in this section are official Party documents that are, of course, compromises often presenting little more than the lowest common denominator between different major viewpoints. However, they are crucial documents inasmuch as they contain official portrayals of the Party not only for members but also for the public at large.

5. See Tony Saich, "The Fourteenth Party Congress: A Programme for Authoritarian Rule," *China Quarterly*, 132 (December 1992), pp. 1142–1144.

6. The new Party Statutes can be found in *Renmin ribao* (People's Daily), overseas edition, October 22, 1992, pp. 1–2.

7. For a view that moral failure played an important part in the collapse of Eastern European regimes in the late-1980s, see Chapter 11 by Daniel Chirot in this volume, "What Happened in Eastern Europe in 1989?"

8. For a similar phenomenon in the Soviet Union under Krushchev, see Ken Jowitt, "The Leninist Extinction," in Daniel Chirot, ed., *The Crisis of Leninism and the Decline of the Left* (Seattle: University of Washington Press, 1991).

9. A *Xinhua* report claimed that 733,543 cadres had been punished for engaging in corruption but, of these, only 154,289 had their Party membership withdrawn and 42,416 had criminal proceedings brought against them. *Xinhua*, October, 22 1992; reported by *Japan Economic Newswire*, October 22, 1992.

10. See David E. Apter and Tony Saich, *Discourse and Power: The Revolutionary Process in Mao's China* (Cambridge: Harvard University Press, 1994).

11. The decline in the importance of Marxism is best shown by the fact that the People's University in Beijing, a top Party training institution, has dropped courses on Marxism, scientific socialism, and the scientific nature of national economic planning from its 1993–94 academic program. Dropped courses will be replaced by courses on international trade and business management, and marketing. Similarly, mid-level and senior Party cadres attending programs at the Central Party School in 1992 and 1993 were being instructed on how to deal with the intricacies of a market economy.

12. On "neo-authoritarianism," see Barry Sautman, "Sirens of the Strongman: Neo-Authoritarianism in Recent Chinese Political Theory," *China Quarterly*, 129 (March 1992), and Ma Shuyun, "The Rise and Fall of Neo-Authoritarianism in China," *China Information*, vol. 5, no. 5 (Winter 1990–1991). Translation of key articles in the debate can be found in the four issues of *Chinese Sociology and Anthropology* edited by Stanley Rosen and Gary Zou (Winter 1990 to Fall 1991). For "neoconservatism," see Gu Xin and David Kelly, "New Conservatism: Intermediate Ideology of a 'New Elite'?" in David S. G. Goodman and Beverly Hooper, eds., *China's Quiet Revolution: New Interactions Between State and Society* (forthcoming). Key articles concerning neoconservatism can be found in David Kelly, ed., "Realistic Responses and Strategic Options: An Alternative CCP Ideology and Its Critics," *Chinese Law and Government*, forthcoming.

13. The children of senior leaders are often referred to collectively as the "princelings party" *(taizi dang)*. For a description of their activities, see He Ping and Gao Xin, *Zhonggong "taizi dang"* ("The Princelings Party" of the CCP) (Taipei: Mingbao shudian, 1992).

14. These four principles are adherence to the leadership of the Communist Party, to Marxism-Leninism–Mao Zedong Thought, to democratic centralism, and to the socialist road.

15. Deng was reported to have said this on March 6, 1989, in a discussion with Zhao Ziyang. *Zhongguo tongxun she*, April 7, 1989, in Michel Oksenberg, Lawrence R. Sullivan, and Marc Lambert, eds., *Beijing Spring 1989: Confrontation and Conflict* (Armonk, N.Y.: M. E. Sharpe, 1990), p. 125.

16. Zhang Bingjiu, "Radical of Moderate Democracy," in Liu Jun and Li Lin, eds., *Xinquanwei zhuyi dui gaige lilun gangling de lunzheng* (Neo-Authoritarianism: A Debate of the Theoretical Program of Reform) (Beijing: Beijing jingji xueyuan chubanshe, 1989). See also Wu Jiaxiang, "Democratization Through Marketization," *Shijie jingji daobao* (World Economic Herald), April 10, 1989.

17. The term "neoconservatism" was first used by Xiao Gongqin, an Associate Professor at Shanghai Normal University, at an informal conference on "China's Traditional Culture and Socialist Modernization" in December 1990. Xiao had been a key figure in

the earlier debates on neo-authoritarianism and his views at that time are said to have influenced the then Party Secretary of Shanghai, Jiang Zemin.

18. China Youth Daily Ideology and Theory Department, "Realistic Responses and Strategic Options for China After the Soviet Events," translated in David Kelly, ed., "Realistic Responses and Strategic Options."

19. See Ken Jowitt, "Inclusion and Mobilization in European Leninist Regimes," *World Politics*, vol. 28, no. 1 (1975).

20. See Philippe Schmitter, "Still the Century of Corporatism?" in F. Pike and T. Stritch, eds., *The New Corporatism* (Notre Dame: University of Notre Dame Press, 1974), and idem., "Democratic Theory and Neo-Corporatist Practice," *Social Research*, vol. 50, no. 4 (Winter 1983).

21. I am grateful to Mr. Lin Qi for providing this information.

22. Tianjin, "Caifeng ribao," reported in *Japanese Economic Newswire*, January 8, 1993.

23. James D. Seymour, "China's Minor Parties and the Crisis of 1989," *China Information*, vol. 5, no. 4 (Spring 1991), p. 3.

24. Translated in Suzanne Ogden, Kathleen Hartford, Lawrence Sullivan, and David Zweig, eds., *China's Search for Democracy: The Student and Mass Movement of 1989* (Armond, N.Y.: M. E. Sharpe, 1992), p. 135.

25. See, for example, Liu Lantao, "Stability and Multi-Party Cooperation," *Renmin ribao*, April 23, 1990.

26. Lu Yun, "Democratic Party Leader on Multi-Party Cooperation," *Beijing Review*, vol. 33, no. 2 (January 8–14, 1990).

27. *China Daily*, September 2, 1989, p. 4.

28. *Xinhua* in English, April 27, 1988, in *Summary of World Broadcasts: Far East*, 0139 B2/1, April 30, 1988.

29. On Guangya, see Kevin Murphy, "China's Cash Crisis Opens School Door to Private Sector," *International Herald Tribune*, October 5, 1993.

30. Dorothy Solinger, "Urban Entrepreneurs and the State: The Merger of State and Society," in Arthur Lewis Rosenbaum, ed., *State and Society in China: The Consequences of Reform* (Boulder: Westview Press, 1992), pp. 121 and 130.

31. Gordon White, "Prospects for Civil Society in China: A Case Study of Xiaoshan City," *The Australian Journal of Chinese Affairs*, 29 (January 1993), pp. 85–86.

32. These comments draw on Apter and Saich, *Discourse and Power*.

33. On symbolic capital, see Pierre Bourdieu, *Outline of a Theory of Practice* (Cambridge: Cambridge University Press, 1977).

34. Clifford Geertz, "After the Revolution: The Fate of Nationalism in the New States," in Clifford Geertz, *The Interpretation of Cultures* (New York: Basic Books, 1973), p. 240.

35. See Fredric Jameson, *The Political Unconscious: Narrative As a Socially Symbolic Act* (London: Metheun, 1981).

36. Translated in Ogden et al., eds., *China's Search for Democracy*, p. 227.

37. As Andrew Jones points out in Chapter 7 in this volume, "The Politics of Popular Music in Post-Tiananmen China," rock performances are banned by the Beijing authorities during each month of June. The authorities clearly fear that rock performances could provide the opportunity for the individualistic disposition of the younger generation to spill over into antiregime demonstrations.

38. On the role that public and hidden transcripts play in helping us understand the political process, see James C. Scott, *Domination and the Arts of Resistance: Hidden Transcripts* (New Haven: Yale University Press, 1990).

39. See Jerome Bruner, "The Narrative Construction of Reality," *Critical Inquiry*, vol. 18, no. 1 (Autumn 1991).

40. Leo Ou-fan Lee, "Afterword: Reflections on Change and Continuity in Modern Chinese Fiction," in Ellen Widmer and David Der-Wei Wang, eds., *From May Fourth to June Fourth: Fiction and Film in Twentieth-Century China* (Cambridge: Harvard University Press, 1993), p. 376. Han is one of the Hunan writers whose work has developed in the style of Shen Congwen.

41. In Mao Yan's story, "Red Sorghum" *(Hong gaoliang)*, the resistance to the Japanese invaders is organized not by the Party and the Red Army but by the narrator's ancestors; the films of Tian Zhuangzhuang on China's non-Han ethnic groups *(On the Hunting Ground [Liechang zhasa]* and *Horse Thief [Daoma zei])* provide a stark contrast to official films of the "national minorities" and even exclude the presence of the Han Chinese; and Liu Heng's "Fuxi, fuxi" (filmed as *Judou*) presents the reader with awesome sexual power.

42. Adapted from the translation in Geremie Barmé and John Minford, eds., *Seeds of Fire: Chinese Voices of Conscience* (New York: Hill & Wang, 1986), pp. 256–257.

43. See Apter and Saich, *Discourse and Power.*

44. See Paul G. Pickowicz, "Popular Cinema and Political Thought in Post-Mao China: Reflections on Official Pronouncements, Film, and the Film Audience," in Perry Link, Richard Madsen, and Paul G. Pickowicz, eds., *Unofficial China: Popular Culture and Thought in the People's Republic* (Boulder: Westview Press, 1989), p. 46.

45. Geremie Barmé, "Wang Shuo and *Liumang* ('Hooligan') Culture," *Australian Journal of Chinese Affairs*, 28 (July 1992), p. 28.

46. Carrie Gracie, "Cokes All Round in Chinese Soap," *The Manchester Guardian*, February 19, 1993.

47. For more on rock music, see Woei Lien Chong, "Young China's Voice of the 1980s: Rock Star Cui Jian," *China Information*, vol. 6, no. 1 (Summer 1990).

48. For an interesting account of these new filmmakers, see "Recent Developments in Chinese Cinema: An Interview with Tony Rayns," *China Information*, vol. 7, no. 4 (Spring 1993), pp. 39–47.

Part Six

HISTORICAL NARRATIVES AND KEY WORDS DECONSTRUCTED

For some readers, the last word in the foregoing title is likely to bring to mind the name of Jacques Derrida and other scholars associated with "deconstructionism," but neither of the contributors to this section attempts to link his arguments to that particular school of criticism: Liu does not invoke the name of any leading literary theorists in his chapter; and Wasserstrom draws most heavily upon the work of Northrop Frye, whose formalism is viewed with disdain by many of those who look to Derrida for inspiration. The term "deconstructed" (employed in the looser fashion suggested by Saich in the preceding chapter) is nonetheless an appropriate one to use in the title to this thematic part, since both contributors are concerned with deconstructing (in the literal sense of "taking apart" and examining the workings of) linguistic constructions. The constructions that interest Wasserstrom are texts that describe and analyze the meaning of the events of 1989, while the construction that concerns Liu is a single Chinese political term, *"geming,"* a word for "Revolution" that he argues has acquired sacred properties and has become a dangerous talisman within Chinese politics. Although one author is interested in narratives and the other is concerned with the multiple uses of one key word, both share a common concern with the ways in which an approach to politics that is based on separating all actors into saints and demons distorts our understanding of historical reality. The following supplementary materials list includes works that look at narratives and key words that have figured prominently in other stages of the Chinese Revolution. The list also contains studies that showcase or critique other kinds of approaches to political narratives and sacred symbols, including those that draw upon various types of feminist theory or some form of postmodernist analysis.

Recommended Supplementary Materials for Classroom Use

Scholarship on China: Contemporary Politics

Chow, Rey. "Violence in the Other Country: China as Crisis, Spectacle, and Woman." In Chandra Mohanty et al., eds., *Third World Women and the Politics of Feminism*. Bloomington: Indiana University Press, 1991. An essay that uses media coverage of 1989 as a starting point for a discussion that addresses a variety of issues, including the tendency for Westerners to treat China as a feminized "other" to their own societies.

Schoenhals, Michael. *Doing Things with Words in Chinese Politics*. Berkeley: Institute of East Asian Studies, 1992. A series of essays on CCP rhetoric and propaganda that focus on the way language serves as a mechanism of political control in mainland China.

Solomon, Andrew. "Their Irony, Humor (and Art) Can Save China: Zhang Peili Washes a Chicken, Song Shuangsong Cuts His Hair, and Other Acts of Avant-Garde Terrorism." *New York Times Magazine* (December 18, 1993), pp. 42–51, 66, and 70–72. An essay on the contemporary art scene, which draws attention to the difficulty Westerners often have interpreting the meaning of the performances and creations they come across in China; the work also refers to the doubts some artists have about the official master narrative of the Cultural Revolution as a period when nothing good took place in China; the article includes some interesting illustrations of recent symbol-laden works of art.

Tuohy, Sue. "Cultural Metaphors and Reasoning: Folklore Scholarship and Ideology in Contemporary China." *Asian Folklore Studies*, vol. 50, no. 1 (1991), pp. 189–220. Tuohy looks at the ways in which folklore scholarship is used to reinforce the power of governmentally sanctioned master narratives concerning the Chinese nation; she pays particular attention to official attempts to use images of China's long history as well as its cultural "homogeneity" and "unity" to defuse tensions related to ethnic strife, regional conflicts, and other phenomena associated with diversity.

Unger, Jonathan, ed. *Using the Past to Serve the Present: Historiography and Politics in Contemporary China*. Armonk, N.Y.: M. E. Sharpe, 1993. A multidisciplinary collection of essays that deal with issues ranging from the political implications of contemporary historical dramas, to the ways in which more formal types of historical writing (such as official histories of the CCP) are used to serve factional ends; Unger includes several chapters (by Geremie Barmé, Ralph Crozier, and Rudolph Wagner among others) that could also be read in conjunction with Parts 3, 4, and 5 of this book that focus on issues of artistic creation, the roles of the intelligentsia, and state power.

Scholarship on China: Historical Perspectives

Barlow, Tani. "Theorizing Woman: *Funu, Guojia, Jiating* [Chinese Women, Chinese State, Chinese Family]." *Genders*, vol. 10 (Spring 1990), pp. 132–160.

Duara, Prasenjit. "De-Constructing the Chinese Nation." *Australian Journal of Chinese Affairs*, 30 (July 1993), pp. 1–28.

Fitzgerald, John. "The Irony of the Chinese Revolution: The Nationalists and Chinese Society, 1923–1927." In idem., ed., *The Nationalists and Chinese Society, 1923–1937: A Symposium*. Melbourne: University of Melbourne Press, 1989, pp. 13–43. An essay that uses many of the same concepts discussed by Wasserstrom in Chapter 13 of this volume to analyze the tales told about an earlier series of revolutionary events.

Wasserstrom, Jeffrey N. and Sue Tuohy, eds. *Indiana East Asian Working Paper Series on Language and the Politics in Modern China*. Bloomington: Indiana University East Asian

Studies Center. A multidisciplinary series of studies that presents findings associated with a project on the "Keywords of the Chinese Revolution" that is being funded primarily by the National Endowment for the Humanities; to date, several papers have appeared, including an essay on Cultural Revolution vulgarities by Elizabeth Perry and Li Xun, and a discussion of the perils of translation between Chinese and other languages by Joshua Fogel.

Wolf, Margery. *A Thrice-Told Tale: Feminism, Postmodernism, and Ethnographic Responsibility.* Stanford: Stanford University Press, 1992. This work presents three different types of accounts of a single incident, which Wolf observed while doing fieldwork in Taiwan, as the basis for a critical discussion of a wide range of theoretical issues relating to social-scientific method and textual analysis.

Comparative Works and Case Studies of Other Countries

Anderson, Benedict R. *Language and Power: Exploring Political Cultures in Indonesia.* Ithaca: Cornell University Press, 1990. A study of the linguistic dimensions of political authority; this book has implications for the study of countries very far removed in time and space from contemporary Indonesia.

Hobsbawm, Eric, and Terence Ranger, eds. *The Invention of Tradition.* Cambridge: Cambridge University Press, 1991. A collection of essays by specialists who not only are interested in geographic areas ranging from Africa to Wales but who share a common interest in the uses rulers and their opponents make of symbolically charged public rituals that are "invented" at specific moments in time (often to serve specific nationalist or class-based purposes), and yet derive much of their power from their ability to appear rooted in the distant past.

Hunt, Lynn. *Politics, Culture, and Class in the French Revolution.* Berkeley: University of California Press, 1984. A study of the events leading up to and following 1789, which focuses much of its attention on the changing meanings of political terms and symbols; that includes discussion of the relevance of Northrop Frye's work for historians concerned with revolutionary change.

Scott, Joan W. *Gender and the Politics of History.* New York: Columbia University Press, 1988. A series of interconnected essays, many of which focus on issues relating to political symbolism; some sections argue for the value that some features of Derrida's work has for feminist historians.

Williams, Raymond. *Keywords: A Vocabulary of Culture and Society.* Oxford: Oxford University Press, 1983, revised edition. An influential study by a Marxist literary critic; Williams draws attention to the way in which Western understandings of centrally important terms (such as "democracy") were transformed during the Industrial Revolution.

Primary Sources

Chesneaux, Jean, ed. *The People's Comic Book.* Garden City, N.Y.: Anchor Press, 1973. Translations of People's Republic of China comic books dealing with historical and political themes; Chesneaux's collection gives a clear picture of both the fetishization of revolutionary valor (discussed hereinafter by Liu Xiaobo in Chapter 14) and the "romantic" nature of most CCP historical narratives (referred to hereinafter by Wasserstrom in Chapter 13).

Lu Xun. *Diary of a Madman and Other Stories.* Translated by William Lyell. Honolulu: University of Hawaii Press, 1990. A collection of fictional works by China's most important and iconoclastic modern writer; see especially "Ah Q—The Real Story" (pp.

101–172), which focuses on the events of 1911 and draws attention to the confusion that reigned at that time among many over what exactly it meant to call oneself a "revolutionary."

Zou Rong. *The Revolutionary Army: A Chinese Nationalist Tract of 1903*. Translated and introduced by John Lust. Paris: Mouton, 1968. A work by a famous revolutionary martyr; it is perhaps the first clear attempt to imbue the Chinese word *geming* with talismanic properties; Zou's edition contains useful extended critical footnotes on the meanings of specific Chinese terms at this point in history.

13

HISTORY, MYTH, AND
THE TALES OF TIANANMEN

Jeffrey N. Wasserstrom

During the emotional days that followed June 4, 1989, it seemed as though there were only two ways to tell the story of the Chinese protests and the crackdown that ended them. One could follow the CCP authorities and denigrate the protests as "counterrevolutionary riots," deny that a massacre had taken place, and claim that soldiers were the only martyrs worthy of the name. Alternatively, one could follow the accounts of protesters and foreign eyewitnesses, which told of unarmed innocents whose demands for democracy and dialogue were answered with a brutal assault by tanks and guns. The differences between these two kinds of narratives initially seemed enormous, irreconcilable, and unambiguous to Western observers. The tale the authorities told appeared a cynical fabrication designed to justify an abhorrent act, a myth that should concern us only because it might mislead certain sectors of the Chinese population. The other version, by contrast, appeared a straightforward statement of fact; uncritical acceptance of it laid the groundwork for what one sinologist called a "remarkable and truly moving unanimity on the issue of China."[1]

The question of how the story of 1989 should be told no longer seems so clear-cut. Foreigners concerned with China still tend to agree on certain key points: The protesters had valid grievances; a massacre did indeed take place in Beijing; and many more protesters and bystanders than soldiers were killed on June 4. The initial "unanimity on the issue of China," however, now

I am grateful to Paul Cohen and Henry Rosemont, Jr., for their valuable criticisms of an earlier version of this essay and to Anne Bock for giving the final draft a careful reading. I also want to thank Joe Esherick for getting me to think seriously about the implications of calling 1989 a "tragedy."

appears to have been little more than widespread agreement that the Chinese government's crackdown and subsequent campaign of arrests and disinformation were abhorrent acts. There has certainly been no clear consensus concerning U.S. foreign policy. Writers associated with widely differing points on the political spectrum have attacked attempts by American officials to maintain essentially normal relations with the Beijing authorities as unconscionable.[2] As previous chapters have indicated, China scholars have also disagreed with each other on a variety of interpretive issues, relating to everything from how "democratic" the protesters were to how important factional struggles within the CCP were in shaping the movement.

In retrospect, it has also become obvious that the Chinese authorities were not the only ones to distort or mythologize history in 1989. Western journalists played a key role in getting accurate information out of and back into China, for example, but (as many scholars before me have noted) they also created their own share of myths.[3] Although MacKinnon is right in his chapter to draw attention to the academic training and experience writers like Orville Schell brought to their coverage of the protests, many members of the foreign press corps had only a limited familiarity with the Chinese context and at best a passing knowledge of Chinese history. Western journalists also had limited access to certain kinds of data and locales (even the best were seldom able to develop extensive contacts outside of Beijing), and were hindered by the constraints of time (in the case of broadcasters) and space (in the case of print journalists) that their media imposed. These factors, coupled with a desire to make the situation in China readily intelligible to a mass audience at home, resulted in coverage that was often misleading.

Television commentators tended to concentrate so intently upon protests in and around Tiananmen Square during the weeks leading up to the June Fourth bloodshed, for example, that they obscured the fact that significant (although often unfilmed) demonstrations were taking place simultaneously in other parts of the country. Then, in the immediate aftermath of the massacre, some Western reporters were too quick to give credence to a variety of rumors (that tens of thousands had died in the city center, that Li Peng had been shot, etc.). Foreign media also reinforced the distorted image of the movement as a single-city event by giving very limited attention to the violence in Chengdu and other provincial capitals. As a result of wishful thinking and a desire to find easily graspable analogies for a complex series of events, foreign reporters also tended to leave viewers with an overly simplistic and mythologized picture of the protesters, by acting as if labeling the protests a "democracy movement," a Chinese version of "people power" or "Solidarity," or a modern-day Boston Tea Party said all that needed to be said. That the student activists of 1989, like their predecessors of the Republican period (1911–1949), frequently emphasized different sets of symbols and slogans when appealing to foreign as opposed to domestic audiences, and proved remarkably adept at telling Westerners what they wanted to hear, contributed to this mythmaking process.[4]

The mythologizing did not stop, furthermore, when the camera crews and network anchors left Beijing. Scholars, propagandists, dissidents, pundits, and diplomats have continued to create new myths and perpetuate old ones.

The tendency in the West to reduce the history of the nationwide protests to the story of the (admittedly critical) events that took place in Beijing has if anything intensified since June 1989, and this (rather than my own views) accounts for the use of the phrase "tales of Tiananmen" in the title of this chapter. The Chinese authorities have spent the last two years distributing a wide variety of written and visual treatments of the 1989 "turmoil" that attempt to "prove" the veracity of Deng Xiaoping and Li Peng's fairy-tale version of events. And Chinese dissidents have been guilty at times of passing off hagiography as critical analysis where the martyrs of 1989 are concerned.

Thanks to these and other kinds of mythmaking, there is now no simple way to separate myth from history when dealing with the protests and repression of 1989. This is hardly surprising. The distinction between the two realms is always problematic at best. It becomes especially so when, as Paul Cohen notes in a perceptive essay on treatments of the Boxers, the events in question "resonate with themes of broader historical scope," involve the "most important and controversial unresolved issues" in a nation's past, and touch upon symbols and values that members of a culture prize or fear most fervently.[5] This was certainly the case with the protests of 1989. As earlier chapters by Young and Schwarcz have shown, virtually every major theme in twentieth-century Chinese history reappeared in some form in the rhetoric and action of 1989, as the protesters and the government's spokespersons alike claimed to speak for treasured values such as patriotism, progress, democracy, and revolution and tried to link their opponents to negative images associated with feudalism, despotism, subjugation, and chaos. Foreign journalists, who often presented the protests to the outside world as a simple fight between noble "democrats" and "Communist dictators," ensured that the events would resonate with a somewhat different (but equally potent) set of symbols and ideals.

Historical analogies contributed still further to the mythologization process. Both the students and their opponents insisted from the start that their actions be understood in the light of history. This has made it harder rather than easier, however, to treat the events historically. As Vera Schwarcz suggests, the past actors to whom the students most frequently compared themselves (the heroes of the May Fourth Movement) were already enshrined as mythic figures to be commemorated rather than remembered. And, as Ernest Young shows, the images from the past that the authorities invoked to discredit the students—visions of Qing "feudalism," KMT villainy, and Maoist excesses—were equally mythologized ones. Broadcasts that showed banners inscribed with the words of larger-than-life Western heroes (Patrick Henry, Martin Luther King, Jr., and Abraham Lincoln) and carried narrations that compared the occupation of Tiananmen Square to events like Woodstock and the Prague spring of 1968, meanwhile, led foreign viewers to locate the events within a different (but no less mythic) historical framework.

Mythmaking and Mythbreaking

How, then, should a scholar interested in 1989 deal with the mythic quality of so many of the narratives of Tiananmen? One way to proceed is to try to demythologize the stories of a specific type of mythmaker. In an article defending Bush's China policy, for example, Richard Nixon claims that those opposed to a realpolitik approach have committed the sin of "romanticizing" the realities of Chinese communism. Henry Kissinger has argued in a similar vein that those who disagree with Bush have insisted upon reducing the complex events of 1989 to a "simple morality play" and let "emotion" cloud their judgment. The picture they draw of Deng Xiaoping as a tyrant, he argues, is a "caricature" that does not do justice to the man.[6]

Left-wing and right-wing critics of U.S. foreign policy have used similar language to make the opposite point: that is, that the so-called realpolitik that Nixon and Kissinger defend is itself based on myths and misunderstandings. Fervent anti-Communists have described this policy as one based upon "fantasies," "fictions," and "wishfulness."[7] In her tellingly titled "The Romance of *Realpolitik*," Miriam London expands on this theme, arguing that Western views of Communist China have been distorted for decades by a variety of "illusions" put forth by an unholy alliance of self-proclaimed "China experts" with leftist leanings, liberals like John K. Fairbank (whose sentimentality has led him to underestimate the perfidy of the CCP), and hypocritical anti-Communists like Kissinger (who has been "seduced" by the "charm" of leaders like Zhou Enlai into suspending his principles where China is concerned). Writers of these three types, she claims, have continually obscured the irredeemably evil nature of Dengist as well as Maoist forces, something that only a few clear-sighted analysts such as the Belgian sinologist and former diplomat Simon Leys never lost to view.[8] From the opposite end of the political spectrum, in a powerful recent essay Arif Dirlik and Roxann Prazniak argue that Leys actually has a great deal more in common with both Fairbank and Kissinger than London and others think. Leys and Fairbank share a common sentimental attachment to the Chinese people (as opposed to the Chinese state), Dirlik and Prazniak claim, and both Leys and the defenders of realpolitik share an uncritical conviction that capitalism will inevitably defeat socialism and thus save China, an assumption that leads them to simplify complex events.[9]

A different set of attempts to demythologize the events of 1989 focuses on specific aspects of the protests or the crackdown rather than particular kinds of mythmakers. Sarah Lubman's "The Myth of Tiananmen," for example, was an early effort to show that the actions of the student protesters were often less fully "democratic" than some of their own wall posters and the more enthusiastic Western reporters would have had us believe.[10] Various works (including earlier chapters by Perry and Feigon) have expanded upon this theme, attempting to "strip [the students] of their halos" while leaving them "their humanity," as George Hicks puts it when introducing a piece in this vein by Jane MacCartney.[11] In "Who Died in Beijing, and Why," Robin Munro turns from student actions to those of the government as he looks at one particular episode, the night of June 3 and morning of June 4, that "remains shrouded in myth."[12] This important piece criticizes not only the Chinese government's disinformation campaign but also the myths perpetuated by foreign journalists, such as the idea that most of those who died were students (when most were members of other social classes) and that much of the violence took place in Tiananmen Square itself (when the main killing fields were elsewhere).[13]

Yet a third type of demythologizing work focuses on issues of ethnocentricism. Works such as Harold Isaacs's classic study of perceptions of China and India, *Scratches on Our Minds*, provide one kind of starting point. Isaacs argued that Americans have tended to view the Chinese as either diabolically cruel and clever heathens (the Fu Manchu image) or as hardworking and honest souls who were remarkably like us in many ways (the image popularized in works such as Pearl Buck's *The Good Earth*).[14] Isaacs based his work on interviews with Americans alive in the 1950s, but his main themes have much broader chronological and geographical relevance. European Enlightenment thinkers, after all, were divided over the question whether those who ruled China were perfect rationalists or unrestrained despots. *Scratches on Our Minds* also has contemporary relevance, as the last few decades have witnessed the continuation of what Bill Brugger aptly describes as the Western "sunshine-horror" syndrome in respect to China: Foreign observers begin with unrealistic hopes for each new regime, then in time come to view this same regime as utterly despotic.[15] Western views of individual Chinese leaders and the Chinese populace (as opposed to Chinese regimes) have veered between equally extreme poles. Miriam London's satirical comment that, on the eve of Nixon's first visit to China, "experts" often treated the Cultural Revolution-scarred PRC as if it were a land filled with "happy, relaxed and motivated people, somewhat like our Pennsylvania Amish, only better," indicates that Pearl Buck-style imagery lives on. The language she uses to describe Mao Zedong (a "cruel despot," an "executioner of millions," a "merciless dictator" reigning over a "dark age" of "oppression and despair") and Zhou Enlai (Mao's "wily supporter," whom Simon Leys claimed could tell "blatant lies with angelic suavity" and "stick a knife in your back [with] disarming grace"), meanwhile, is uncomfortably reminiscent of pulp novelist Sax Rohmer, the creator of Fu Manchu.

These positive and negative stereotypes were alive and well before 1989, but (as others have noted) the events of April through June breathed new life into them. In the wake of June Fourth, the same Western analysts who had once treated Deng Xiaoping as a hardworking modernizer began to recast him into a contemporary version of Fu Manchu. "Sunshine"-filled pictures of Deng's China—as a land in which a billion Chinese were being converted to capitalism as smoothly as missionaries had once hoped they could be converted to Christianity—gave way to images colored by "horror." In spite of this new pessimism, however, the images of China as a land filled with honest souls waiting to be converted to our ideals did not disappear. The burden of fulfilling Western hopes was simply shifted to the shoulders of a new generation: the protesters.[16]

Some of those concerned with ethnocentrism and 1989 have been less interested in Western views of China per se than with Western treatments of radically "other" cultures in general. For them, Edward Said's work rather than Isaacs's provides the critical starting point. Said's theory of "Orientalism" is based on the premise that what those in the United States and Europe have called the "Orient" is in fact a Western construction imposed upon the East. Adopting a position of cultural superiority, Western specialists have treated Asia as a reverse mirror image of the "Occident" and attributed to it a series of exotic and usually negative values.[17] Some sinologists have argued that Said's work (the main focus of which is the Middle East) is either overly schematic or needs at least to be modified to have relevance for China. As recent events have reminded us, there has always been much less "sunshine" and more "horror" in Western views of the Middle East as opposed to China. What Edward Graham has referred to as China's own highly developed ideology of "barbarianism" (a view of other cultures as inferior, dangerous, and lewd, which Feigon alludes to in his chapter when discussing official attempts to discredit Wuer Kaixi) also makes it something of a special case.[18] Many sinologists have found Said's general arguments compelling, nonetheless, and some have used his concept to examine Western treatments of 1989. In a provocative recent essay, for example, Rey Chow insightfully combines Said's ideas with concepts derived from recent work in feminist literary theory and a discussion of the colonialist imagery of films such as *King Kong*, to explore the assumptions and implications of foreign press coverage of Tiananmen.[19]

The various kinds of demythologizing efforts outlined above all have their merits. My approach below is somewhat different, however, for I try to cast my net wider than previous writers—including even Dirlik and Prazniak, whose essay attacks not only the myopia of those with "an obdurate conviction in the evilness of communism" but also the short-sightedness of those who see the students as pure democrats or invoke Fu Manchu–style imagery to criticize the CCP.[20] My working assumption is that there are bound to be mythic elements to all of the narratives of Tiananmen, from the most blatantly propagandistic pamphlets issued by the Chinese government to the most carefully documented works of scholarship—the preceding chapters in this volume by no means excepted.

Rather than set out to demythologize one set of texts and present another as opaquely "realistic" accounts, therefore, my aim is to see how a wide range of myths created and perpetuated by a variety of very different kinds of authors work. As a result, in the pages that follow, I treat all of the accounts of what took place in China in 1989 as though they were works of fiction. This premise frees me to use ideas derived from literary criticism to look at how these stories are structured, paying particular attention to the distinction between tragedy and romance that Northrop Frye develops in his classic *Anatomy of Criticism*.

Tragedy, Romance, and Northrop Frye

Frye's work is particularly attractive here for several reasons. First, in his discussion of the different "generic plots" of tragic, romantic, comic, and ironic narratives, he is primarily concerned with forms of literature that are either explicitly mythological (Homeric odes, the Wagnerian *Ring* cycle), have heroes imbued with mythic qualities (Shakespeare's historical plays), or involve quests of mythic proportions (like that of Don Quixote).[21] The events of 1989 certainly involved figures who had already attained mythic stature (Deng Xiaoping was twice named *Time's* "man of the year" and Fang Lizhi had been called "China's Tom Paine"), and Western journalists (such as the two who subtitled their book on the events "An Eyewitness Account of the Chinese People's Passionate Quest for Democracy") also tended to present the protests as an epic struggle.[22]

Another attraction is that Lynn Hunt and Hayden White, two leading proponents of what Elizabeth Perry refers to in her Introduction as "neoculturalist" analysis, have recently demonstrated that Frye's work on generic plots can be applied usefully not only to literary works but also to the kinds of narrative texts that concern me here. Hunt uses Frye's concepts to elucidate the changing rhetorical stances of French revolutionaries as they continually redefined the goals of their quest. White argues that the works of major figures in European historiography (such as Jules Michelet and Leopold Ranke) can be understood as texts that followed one or another type of generic plot.[23]

One possible objection to using Frye's work to look at a Chinese event is that his main concern is with European and American literature, and the scholars such as Hunt and White who have applied his ideas to other kinds of texts have likewise tended to focus upon the work of Western authors. There may indeed be limits to how well some features of Frye's theory translate to the Chinese case; making sense of the Chinese literary tradition may require that his description of specific genres be modified or his schema expanded to include additional genres. For my purposes, however, all that is important is to ask whether his categories can help us make sense of Chinese as well as Western tales of Tiananmen, and I believe there is good reason to think that they can.

My basis for saying this is that accounts of 1989 are usually treated as part of a larger story, that of the Chinese Revolution, and both Chinese and Western metanarratives of this event tend to fit easily into the romantic or tragic categories Frye outlines. He defines romantic quests as myths in which the "essential plot element is adventure" (often the killing of a monster) and the contrasts between heroes (who represent "spring, dawn, order, fertility, vigor, and youth") and villains (who represent "winter, darkness, confusion, sterility, moribund life, and old age") are clear-cut.[24] Chinese Communist historians have taken great pains to create an image of the revolution as just such an epic struggle between good (brave cadres, loyal peasants, valiant soldiers, and patriotic workers) and evil (imperial rulers, warlords, and corrupt KMT officials), in which the forces of youth and spring win victory after victory over the forces of age and winter.[25]

This image of the revolutionary change resonates with long-standing tendencies in Chinese oral, literary, and historiographic traditions. Popular storytellers in China have always been fond of tales of brave and virtuous men who are forced to step outside of the established order to fight unjust officials and then end up in positions of power. Such romantic tales form the core of some of the most famous Chinese historical novels and operas, such as *The Water Margin* and *The Romance of the Three Kingdoms*. The clear division Communist historians make between heroes and villains is also reminiscent of the dynastic histories of imperial times, with their biographical sections devoted to life stories of models of Confucian rectitude, on the one hand, and wicked officials, on the other. By heroicizing the epic struggles the CCP waged to build a "New China" freed from the hold of old forces (the anciens régimes Young describes in his chapter), Communist historians have created a tale that fits in well with enduring cultural myths. It is also one filled with episodes whose very names (the Long March, the war against Japanese aggression, the Great Leap Forward) are quintessentially romantic.

Many Westerners have been drawn toward similarly romantic narrative stances. Some have subscribed to the CCP's brand of romanticism. Others have created an equally romantic vision of the quest but (following KMT historians) have claimed that since 1949 villains have temporarily prevailed. Still others, finally, have viewed the Chinese Revolution as a more morally ambiguous event, a valiant effort that somehow went astray. This third kind of narrative has all of the qualities that Frye associates with tragic myths. Tragic heroes, he argues, must be capable of great deeds yet in some ways all too human; their quests must be noble but ultimately doomed to failure, either because of flaws within the heroes themselves (the element of tragedy that Aristotle stressed) or natural forces beyond their control (what Frye terms a "conspiracy of fate").[26]

Western authors give varying reasons for the "failure" of this tragic quest. Some cite Soviet conspiracies, ideological shortcomings, tactical mistakes, or individual acts of betrayal, whereas others highlight natural forces (such as the economic backwardness of the Chinese nation) and historical contingencies (such as the Japanese invasion). They also differ on the question whether the leaders of the KMT, the heads of the CCP, or the Chinese people as a whole are the tragic figures most deserving of sympathy. What they share is a view of the Chinese Revolution as the work of heroes who (to borrow phrases Hunt uses to describe the tragic phase of the French Revolution) had "an extraordinary destiny within [their] grasp" only to have it slip away, whose "goal was so right" but whose "quest for it inevitably failed."[27]

Accounts of 1989, like these metanarratives of the Chinese Revolution, have tended to take either romantic or tragic turns. Later in this essay, I delineate eight different standard ways of presenting the story of Tiananmen, half of which treat 1989 as a romance and half of which present it as a tragedy. Individual writers often incorporate elements from several of these versions into their own particular narrative of 1989, and in some cases one finds the same author presenting the events as a romance in one context and as a tragedy in another. I do not intend, therefore, to try to pigeonhole everyone who has written about Tiananmen or to place each narrative neatly in one of eight categories. Nonetheless, I hope to show that looking at how these four romances and four tragedies work as stories can help us to put the mythologizing and fictionalizing into perspective.

Myth and Fiction: Preliminary Definitions

Before beginning this process, I must clarify what I mean by saying that all accounts of 1989 can be treated as "mythic" or "fictional" texts. By claiming that all are "mythic," I do not mean they are equally persuasive or equally truthful. The weight of available evidence leaves me with no doubt, for example, that the Chinese government's story of what happened on June 4 deserves to be called part of a "big lie" campaign and is much less accurate than, say, Robin Munro's account. My assumption is simply that, to borrow once more from Cohen's discussion of the Boxers, myth and history are best viewed not as oppositional black-and-white categories but rather as end points on a continuum, and that most texts fall somewhere in the middle. Even careful works of historical scholarship gain narrative power by resonating with the myths of a culture's oral and literary traditions. Conversely, those whose interest in events of the past is solely to use them to serve their own political purposes generally go to great lengths to ensure that their version of history seems at least plausible and attempt to bathe their myths in an aura of facticity.[28]

Even when it is possible to assess the relative accuracy of two different historical accounts, moreover, this does not always tell us all that is worth knowing about the narratives. The stories concerning George Washington that every U.S. schoolchild learns illustrates this. As adults we come to see that some of these tales are much less factual than others. Just because the story of the cherry tree is probably pure fabrication whereas that of the winter at Valley Forge is based on a genuine event, however, does not mean that the former is any less an important part of our national historical memory than the latter. In addition, because the tales of that famous winter survivors told were probably exaggerated at times and each new generation of popular historians has embellished the story of Valley Forge in its own way, it seems foolish to say that only the cherry tree is shrouded in "myth."

It is also dangerous to ignore issues other than accuracy where Chinese history is concerned, as Cohen's essay on the Boxers and Perry Link's recent discussion of the functions of propaganda in the PRC make clear. Link argues persuasively that CCP slogans, pronouncements, editorials, and histories of political events are all part of an esoteric but crucially important language "game"—in which the veracity of a statement is largely irrelevant to both the party spokespeople and their audiences. When Chinese citizens pay attention to this "official language," Link claims, it is not because they expect to hear accurate information but rather because they seek clues concerning how they are expected to behave. Words are not bearers of truth, in this game, but chess pieces: One is well served both to watch how officials use them (to avoid danger) and to study their properties (so that one can manipulate the language to one's own advantage).[29] In light of Link's insightful discussion, it seems foolish to dismiss official tales of Tiananmen simply because they are based on a "big lie." Just as patently false slogans can still tell Chinese citizens how it is safest to act, these obviously mythic stories help us understand the mentality of the CCP.

Throughout the pages that follow, I do try at times to distinguish between accounts on the basis of accuracy. I use information and arguments presented in earlier chapters, as well as other scholarly works, to highlight the weaknesses (including factual errors and faulty logic) of specific types of romantic and tragic treatments of Tiananmen. I conclude the piece by arguing that it is possible to use the contributions in this volume to create a more satisfying tragic version of the events of 1989. I do not deny, however, that this narrative stance is itself mythic: My only claim is that this myth has greater explanatory power than most prevalent ones. My main interest overall, moreover, is not with demythologizing. It is with seeing what different kinds of myths reveal about the language "games" of which they are part.

My earlier use of the term *fiction* also needs to be clarified. I do not wish to imply that everything written about 1989 thus far has been "untrue." We commonly use the term *fictional* as an antonym for *factual*, but (as James Clifford points out) the main thrust of the Latin root, *fingere* is to describe "something made or fashioned." Clifford goes on to claim that ethnographies are therefore best approached as "fictions." Historians interested in the way linguistic models and literary theory can sharpen our perception and representation of past events have made similar arguments for historiography. For them, as for Clifford, the main point is that the supposedly clear line between novels and objective recitations of "facts" is in reality fuzzy at best and that it may be better to treat ethnographic and historical writings as aesthetic rather than scientific texts.[30]

Michel Foucault's seminal studies of the history of asylums, prisons, and sexuality provide a starting point for many who take what is now being called a "linguistic turn." Particularly influential are Foucault's arguments that many of the seemingly "natural" categories social scientists routinely claimed to be using as neutral descriptive terms—madness, deviance, gender, ethnicity—are in fact social constructions, the definitions of which have as much to do with relations of dominance as with unambiguous, observable "facts." These arguments provide much of the basis for Said's discussion of the "Orient" as a social construct as opposed to a geographically defined place.[31]

The merits and shortcomings of taking a linguistic turn is currently a subject of intense debate within anthropology, history, and other fields.[32] Many of those who do not want to follow this turn to its logical conclusion have, however, come to accept the idea that the differences between the texts social scientists and novelists create are not as unambiguous as the former have often liked to think. When I say that narratives of Tiananmen by scholars, journalists, Chinese propagandists, and historical novelists (at least one of whom has already used the events of 1989 as a backdrop for his storytelling) can all be treated as works of "fiction," I do so simply to highlight this point.[33] I wish to draw attention to the similar kinds of decisions that all four kinds of authors have to make concerning which characters, demonstrations, acts of repression, and locations to emphasize and which to downplay or ignore; in every case the choices they make concerning plot, theme, and characterization affect the meaning and plausibility of their texts.

Romantic Myths of Tiananmen

Romantic Version Number 1:
The Students as New May Fourth Heroes

Although the last paragraphs have focused primarily upon the mythic and fictional properties of scholarly works and official propaganda, the most fitting place to start a discussion of the narratives of 1989 is with the words of the protesters themselves. It might seem odd at first to claim that their versions of what took place between April and June tend to be "romantic" as opposed to "tragic" in nature. As George Steiner argues, definitions of tragedy "must start from the fact of catastrophe," and the events of June 4 were clearly catastrophic for the movement.[34] In addition, the terms (such as *canan, canshi, canju, xuelei,* and *beiju*) that Chinese authors sympathetic to the demonstrators routinely use to refer to the events of June Fourth are all commonly translated into English as "tragic" or "tragedy" and are all associated with catastrophic occurrences.[35]

This said, the protesters' narratives of Tiananmen were seldom tragic in the Western sense of the word. As Joseph Esherick and I point out in a note to Chapter 2, the operatic performances known as *beiju* are often more similar to what Westerners think of as melodrama than they are to Greek or Shakespearean tragedy, leading some literary scholars to argue that China "lacks" a tragic tradition. Neither the veracity of this argument (which other literary specialists have disputed) nor the Orientalist assumptions of some of its proponents (i.e., that Western traditions represent a norm and that other cultures are not simply different but inferior in some way) need concern us here.[36] What is important is that when protesters called the events of June 4 part of a *beiju*, they did not mean that there was anything morally ambiguous about the events in question. Nor did they mean that the victims were defeated by either their own tragic flaws or a conspiracy of fate. In the narratives of the protesters, the villains are not mysterious forces at all but savage despots— one meaning of the character *can,* which serves as the root for several Chinese terms for tragedy, is "cruel" or "savage"—and those who died are not noble sinners but heroic innocents.

This makes the protesters' version of June Fourth romantic as opposed to tragic. In their narratives, as in all true romances, attention is directed to the "conflict between a hero and his enemy" and "all the reader's values are bound up with the hero," who possesses the various qualities related to youth and rebirth discussed earlier. The conflict in romances is always between good and evil, according to Frye, and the "nearer the romance is to myth, the more attributes of divinity will cling to the hero and the more the enemy will take on demonic . . . qualities."[37] A fully developed romantic myth will end with virtue triumphing over wickedness, but individual romantic episodes can end with mourning exercises for a hero or heroine who has died for the good of the cause. This "exaltation of the hero" is less a finale than a call to arms aimed at those who survive, a ceremony that launches a new attempt to carry the original quest through to its intended conclusion.[38]

The themes Frye associates with romance began to appear in the movement's rhetoric early on. As Elizabeth Perry has argued in Chapter 3, students began in mid-April to transform the deceased Hu Yaobang into a more heroic figure than he had ever been in life, simultaneously valorizing their own role as patriotic protesters. The new Hu Yaobang celebrated in protest poems was "a star of hope," one of "the people's most glorious heroes," in short, a martyr to a noble cause. He was also somebody who, like all of the romantic deliverers Frye describes, had by his very death helped to further the quest he led. In the outpouring of grief that accompanied the popular mourning for Hu, one writer claimed, one could "see a hundred million living souls awakening the heroic spirit of China." The new generation of awakened heroes destined to carry on his "behest" and "advance the cause of freedom" would be youths determined to serve as the "vanguard of history." They would "bravely bear high the banner of democracy" and battle "villains" and "devils" so that a "new sun" could rise in the sky.[39]

The romanticism of student imagery reached new heights at the time of the May Fourth anniversary. In our discussion of political theater, Esherick and I describe various attempts protesters made to appropriate the official symbolism associated with the May Fourth Movement, and Schwarcz's essay has shown that in contemporary China simply to invoke the year 1919 was to conjure up a series of images with romantic implications. As these and other chapters have suggested, when students spoke of their actions as part of a "New May Fourth Movement," they instantly located themselves within an ongoing tradition of youthful patriotic engagement and linked themselves to an event that the CCP authorities had helped to turn into a sacred national myth. Communist educators and propagandists have spent the last decades treating May Fourth figures much as Western Sunday school teachers and evangelical ministers handle the characters in Biblical parables, hoping to instill a similar familiarity colored by reverence in their charges. Ironically, these efforts ensured that many Chinese would see the "New May Fourth" students of 1989 in romantic terms: as youths attempting to finish the quest to establish a truly "new" and democratic China that the protesters of 1919 had begun and those of 1935, 1976, and other years had continued.[40]

References to 1919 did more than simply link the protesters to positive images of youth, democracy, new cultural values, and revolutionary progress: Such comments also implied that the current CCP leadership was made up of men who were not only old in chronological terms but the representatives of old ideas and practices as well. To call the 1989 protests a "New May Fourth Movement" was to associate figures such as Deng Xiaoping and Li Peng with the anciens régimes of imperial despots and corrupt warlords. When the students argued that they were also carrying on in the tradition of the April Fifth Movement of 1976, they added a third ancien régime to this list.[41] The official CCP line on the protests of 1976 is that they were a revolutionary event that aided Deng's rise to power. Student references to April Fifth implied that Deng was now acting more like a successor to than a true opponent of the former Gang of Four regime.

Throughout the middle and end of May, students used various techniques to embellish their romantic image of 1989 as a sharply defined battle between progressive youth and oppressive age. The "Statement of the May Thirteenth Hunger Strikers" began by reminding readers that the protesters ready to die for the nation were in "the full bloom of youth." Wall posters in late May castigated Deng Xiaoping as an "invalid" leading a "group of elders" and described him as a "last emperor." Some presented him as a modern-day empress dowager.[42] And on May 23 a coalition of protest groups issued perhaps the most romantically titled of all 1989 manifestos: "The Final Battle Between Light and Darkness." This "statement on the current condition" claimed that the newest social movement had "surpassed" those of 1919 and 1976 and launched a "new historical epoch." Victory would be certain as long as the people persevered in their just fight for freedom, despite the attempts of people like Li Peng to "stop the progress of history."[43]

The image of 1989 as a battle between good and evil took on new meaning in the wake of June Fourth, as Wuer Kaixi's famous videotape broadcast from Hong Kong on June 28 (which presents an almost perfectly romantic vision of events) illustrates. On the one side are the "martyrs" who were "innocent" and hoped for peace but who eventually "gave their lifeblood in an effort to keep the sinking ship of China away from dangerous shoals and lead her toward the bright and open ocean." On the other side are "the reactionary warlords" who "revealed themselves" to be "cruelly bestial fascists."[44] Tragic deaths are important primarily for how they affect our emotions or for the lessons they teach us about what we can do to avoid suffering a similar fate.[45] Wuer implicitly rejects such an approach and demands that the deaths of June Fourth be seen in romantic terms—that is, as violence that in some way ensures the final victory of the forces of virtue. The fight against the "beasts" who rule China now continues, he insists, and those who survive are certain to win, thanks to the strength they will gain (through a vaguely defined process of spiritual communion) from the deaths of their fallen comrades. "Their lives [those of the martyrs] have been melded together with ours," he says, so that his life and those of other survivors "no longer belong to us alone."[46]

Other statements protesters issued in June and July 1989 were often more restrained in their imagery than Wuer's rousing call to arms, but many harped on similar themes. His presentation of the authorities as demons in human form, for example, was far from exceptional. Posters in which hardliners appeared as beasts, modern-day Hitlers, or other kinds of incarnations of evil had become common as soon as martial law was declared in late May, and a June 4 report by Beijing's leading student organization said that in carrying out the massacre, the "fascist government [had] lifted its hypocritical veil and the dictators [had] revealed their disgusting intentions."[47]

Wuer's vision of the deaths at Tiananmen Square serving to guarantee final victory also has many counterparts. The idea that the blood of martyrs can have regenerative and cleansing (as well as polluting) powers was a common one in 1925 and 1926, when police forces under the control of foreigners and native warlords fired on unarmed crowds of protesters in a series of massacres.[48] This same theme resurfaced in 1989. April and May wall posters bearing sanguinary poems (with titles such as "Bloodstains") and essays (which argued that blood could "wash clean the disgrace of autocracy") were followed by post-June Fourth banners that spoke of the blood of martyrs' enriching China's soil.[49] Even if the occupation of Tiananmen Square had ended in catastrophe, the proponents of the New May Fourth romance maintained, this was not the end of the quest but merely a temporary setback, the prelude to a more lasting future victory for the forces of progress, youth, and freedom.

Romantic Version Number 2: *The Students as Anti-Communist Heroes*

Protesters have not been the only ones to treat the events of 1989 as an epic battle between heroic students (representing the forces of light) and monstrous hard-liners (symbolizing the powers of darkness). Many scholars, politicians, and journalists in Taiwan, Hong Kong, and the West have also created romances of this sort. Some of these have essentially echoed the students' own New May Fourth story, and these need not concern us here. Of more interest are two variations on the theme, beginning with one I label the "end-of-history myth."

This label is taken from a controversial essay by Francis Fukuyama, which argued that Western liberalism was in the process of winning a well-earned and definitive victory over Communist tyrannies throughout the world, a process he described as ushering in the "end of history" (at least in the Hegelian sense of dialectical change).[50] Critics of this article have argued that almost all of its premises are questionable at best—particularly its assumption that all former Communist regimes will inevitably be replaced by Western liberal democracies.[51] The essay remains important both because of its direct influence and because it is representative of the quasi-millenarian expectations that recent events (such as the fall of the Berlin Wall) have triggered, which often find expression in academic and journalistic discussions of the "new world order."

Chinese events would seem at first to pose a problem for the Fukuyama thesis. If the massacres of June are treated as merely a temporary setback, however, anti-Communists can see the protests of 1989 as a prelude to the "end" of Chinese history. This is clearly the implication of works by some Western sinologists (such as those by Simon Leys and his supporters alluded to above), as well as of anti-Communist Chinese partisans of the KMT.[52] Their story of the events goes roughly as follows. The massive demonstrations of 1989 showed that the Chinese people had finally become aware of the venality of the CCP and the bankruptcy of Marxist and Maoist theory. Inspired by Western democratic ideas and emboldened by decades of chafing under the yoke of Communist oppression, the protesters valiantly struggled to free their country from the hold of a repressive ideology and Party apparatus. The protesters may have lost the battle in 1989, but they are destined to win the war and lead China down the same kind of path toward a market economy and democratic institutions that Eastern Europe has begun to follow. The savagery of the government's actions on June 4 was a temporary setback to the cause of freedom, but by offering unforgettable proof of the monstrousness of even so-called moderate Communists like Deng Xiaoping, it actually made the final victory of anti-Communist forces more certain.

Romantic Version Number 3:
The Students as Maoist Heroes

There is one other kind of romantic tale, which I call the New Cultural Revolution myth, that presents the protesters as messianic figures and the authorities as devils incarnate. This account is in most ways the exact inverse of the end-of-history myth, for instead of treating the students as anti-Communists, it presents them as Marxists trying to carry out the Communist Revolution's original vision. Deng Xiaoping's cardinal sin, in this romance, ceases to be his failure to instigate comprehensive enough economic and political reforms and becomes instead his abandonment of egalitarian socialist ideals. The New Cultural Revolution myth has more in common with the New May Fourth one, which also stresses that students were angered by the regime's failure to live up to long-standing revolutionary goals. The key difference is that instead of interpreting the new struggle as a continuation of that of 1919, the New Cultural Revolution myth argues that the students of 1989 were emulating the positive aspects of the Red Guard Movement of the 1960s.

Accounts of this sort are often overlooked because they have been much less central a part of mainstream discourse than the other two kinds of romances described above. Virtually the only authors outside of China who have celebrated (as opposed to criticized) continuities between the Cultural Revolution and 1989 have been those writing for explicitly Maoist publications such as the *Revolutionary Worker*, an organ of the Revolutionary Communist Party (RCP). Their arguments, furthermore, have often been fairly simplistic—that is, they act at times as if the mere fact that some protesters carried portraits of Mao validates the RCP line.

This said, the New Cultural Revolution myth deserves to be treated as more than just a fringe idea, as at least one careful attempt to argue its merits exists: Mark Hager's "Roots of Repression in Deng's China." Hager views the use of Mao portraits as revealing and presents Deng's flirtation with market economy capitalism as a negative development. He breaks with RCP purists on other points, however, when he criticizes the "romanticism" of Western leftists who insist upon treating Mao as a "pure revolutionary hero," and he argues that the Great Helmsman's mistakes were largely responsible for the Cultural Revolution's having ultimately "yielded incalculable mayhem and suffering." He claims, nonetheless, that the image of Mao simply as a "quintessentially authoritarian dictator" is also deeply flawed, as are treatments of the Cultural Revolution that ignore its roots in an effort to "democratize abusive power structures."

His argument about 1989 then unfolds as follows. If one focuses on the early goals of the Red Guards rather than upon "vicious petty intrigues and wars" and the growth of the Mao cult that followed, the protesters of 1989 seem to have a great deal in common with those of the 1960s. Both were concerned with official corruption and despotic tendencies. The Cultural Revolution left a complex legacy, and the protesters of 1989 were certainly not trying to revive all of its features. Nevertheless, one part of that legacy was the "experience of active democracy and dreams of its restoration in more adequate form, which has persisted as a force in Chinese life." The Democracy Wall Movement of the 1970s (in which many former Red Guards took part) and the protests of the late 1980s (in which many former Red Guards served as advisers or inspirational figures) need to be understood as "manifestations" of this force.[53]

Romantic Version Number 4:
The Soldiers as Revolutionary Martyrs

The last kind of romantic myth that deserves consideration is the official account of the protests as counterrevolutionary riots. The hard-line story draws in one way or another from each of the preceding three versions of events but ultimately reverses the implications of each by inverting the positions of heroes and villains. Like New May Fourth accounts, official propaganda argues that in 1989 China faced the same threat it had faced in 1919. The difference is that, for the officials, the familiar danger was not government corruption but foreign attempts to subjugate China. Like the proponents of the end-of-history myth, official propaganda argues that the protests were inspired by anti-Communist forces seeking to overthrow the CCP and turn China into a capitalist country. But according to the official literature, this would have destroyed rather than saved the nation. Like the New Cultural Revolution myth, finally, official propagandists stress the parallels between the Red Guards and the students of 1989. The key distinction here is that the government literature takes it for granted that every aspect of the Cultural Revolution should be repudiated. Like all three previous romances, the story is presented as a clear-cut battle between light and darkness (or in this case "red" patriots and "black" hands) in which the heroes are almost divine, the villains less than fully human.[54] The casting is, however, radically different from that of any other romance: The monsters whose humanity is called into question are not Deng Xiaoping and Li Peng but "troublemakers" like the dissident Liu Xiaobo (the author of the following chapter) and "conspirators" like Zhao Ziyang.[55]

It may seem strange at first to term the government's story a "romantic myth," as Frye stresses that romances always involve battles between noble youth and ignoble age. Given that the students were generations younger than those responsible for the crackdown, it may appear farfetched to claim that government spokespeople present Deng Xiaoping's forces as fighting for progressive values of regeneration and try to link the protesters with backwardness and decay. This is, however, precisely what official propaganda pieces—ranging from English-language pictorial histories of PLA actions to compilations of speeches by key government leaders—attempt to do.[56]

Official narratives use three main techniques to associate their cause with romantic forces representing progress, youth, and order. First, they portray the demonstrations as acts of *luan* or *dongluan*. Young has already discussed the potency these terms had to conjure up negative memories of the "chaos" and "turmoil" of the warlord and Cultural Revolution eras. These words have a long history within Chinese political discourse: Long before the cataclysmic events that those alive today lived through, the terms for chaos were already enshrined as pejorative descriptions for anything that threatened the stability and security of the community.[57] To say that the protesters were creating *luan*, therefore, was to suggest that anyone who could bring an end to the movement would be saving the nation by restoring order. Moreover, because the Deng regime has continually stressed that the post-1978 reforms can only succeed if the political environment remains stable, to put an end to turmoil also accomplishes the romantic goal of defending progress toward a long-term goal.

Second, official narratives go beyond simply treating the task of pacification as a heroic one to personally valorize the soldiers assigned to carry out this romantic quest. All of these young patriots performed "immortal feats," according to Beijing's mayor, and various government spokespeople have singled out for special praise those soldiers who died in action. Along with describing the bravery of these soldiers (and drawing attention to the youthfulness of these heroes), officials have honored fallen members of the PLA with all of the rituals traditionally accorded other kinds of "revolutionary martyrs" (such as the student protesters who died in the "good" student movements of the pre-1949 era): Young Pioneers (the CCP's equivalent to Boy Scouts) have laid wreaths honoring their memory at Tiananmen Square, top government figures have paid highly publicized visits to their families, and hagiographic memoirs by former comrades in arms have been published.[58]

The third way official authors have romanticized the crackdown has been by insisting that the Deng regime is composed of revolutionaries and that all those who oppose it are by definition counterrevolutionaries. This terminology is crucial, as it implies that no matter how youthful many of the protesters were in chronological terms, the demonstrations were somehow linked to one or more of the revolution's anciens régimes. Young has insightfully analyzed the implications of such a linkage in his chapter, so only the briefest reminder is needed here. When officials continually connected the 1989 protests to such discredited phases of the Chinese past as the Nationalist era (the students would turn China into "a bourgeois republic subordinate to the West"), they not only associated their opponents with old values, but they made the crackdown seem just one more stage in an ongoing revolutionary quest to create a "new" China. This imagery continued into 1991, with CCP leaders presenting their policies as part of a "New Long March," a heroic effort to overcome the obstacles (including the activities of reactionary dissidents) that have prevented China from becoming a socialist paradise.

Tragic Myths of Tiananmen

If most Chinese accounts of 1989 can be classified as romances of one sort or another, foreign narratives have more often presented the events in tragic terms. Writing in July 1989, Orville Schell noted the prevalence of the word *tragic* in early attempts observers made to "articulate their feelings in the [immediate] aftermath of the June Fourth massacre," and this word has continued to appear in virtually all of the scholarly and popular accounts of the events published in Western languages, including the preceding chapters in this volume.[59] Words like *tragedy* and *tragic* are employed so loosely in English that their appearance can be misleading at times. For example, even writers with views similar to those of Leys (who I have argued present essentially romantic narratives of 1989) refer in passing to "tragic" features of specific events. This said, most Western accounts (and a few Chinese ones) contain all of the elements that Frye says must be present in fully realized tragic myths: They have heroes who seem both part divine and all too human. The stories begin with heroes "on the top of the wheel of fortune," with their goals seemingly within their grasp. The tales end with nemesis inexorably overtaking and vanquishing the heroes, proving that the quest (though noble) was doomed from the start to fail, because of either the natures of the heroes, the immutable laws of the environment in which the quest was attempted, or some combination of the two.[60]

Although most foreign narratives share this tragic view of 1989, there is a great deal of variety when it comes to exactly how the plot is shaped. I divide foreign tragic accounts, therefore, into four categories, largely on the basis of which political actors are cast in the roles of heroes and villains. In contrast to the four kinds of romance described above, however, it is not always easy to find specific works that exemplify each tragic variation; most texts in fact combine elements from at least two categories. The categories are thus primarily intended to serve as heuristic devices, and the same is true of the titles I give them—each of which is either the name of a Shakespearean tragedy or a classical Greek myth. As artificial as these categories admittedly are, they are useful in that they give a sense of the main themes that shape tragic accounts of 1989, as well as the issues that differentiate these accounts from each other. I would also argue that there is nothing inappropriate about using Elizabethan and Athenian analogies in a discussion of events that occurred in China, as most of the tragic accounts that concern me here were written by Westerners.

Tragic Version Number 1: 1989 as King Lear

Shakespeare's famous rendition of the story of this legendary British monarch seems at first far removed from the events of Tiananmen Square. Upon reflection, however, it is not so hard to understand why some writers have come to treat Deng Xiaoping as a kind of modern equivalent to Lear: a once proud ruler whose body and mind are suffering the infirmities of age. It is also worth remembering that Shakespeare's tragedy centers on the harm that comes from a father's inability to distinguish between loyal and unworthy children. We are meant to feel some compassion for the father: Lear is certainly to blame for much of his own suffering, but the inexorable force of age and the false words of those he mistakenly trusts also play a role in his fall. Our greatest sympathy is directed elsewhere, however. The primary victim in *King Lear* is Cordelia, the faithful daughter who earns her father's wrath by telling him the truth rather than simply what he wants to hear, much as

Zhao Ziyang is seen by some as having lost Deng's patronage by insisting (after May 4, 1989) that the popular movement would aid the cause of reform.[61]

The *Time* magazine publication *Massacre in Beijing*, one of the first book-length narratives of 1989 to appear in print, is perhaps the best example of a work that treats Deng's condemnation of Zhao as comparable to Lear's treatment of Cordelia. Writing of the elderly Chinese ruler's former greatness, the authors state that in "the summer of 1986, Deng Xiaoping appeared to be on the verge of accomplishing a feat unprecedented in modern Chinese history [having] put his country firmly on the path to modernization [and] secured what seemed to be a firm guarantee of political stability." They then describe his rapid descent from the top of the wheel of fortune, attributing his transformation into a petty tyrant to forces at least partially beyond his control (a worsening economy, the aging process) as well as character flaws (his erroneous belief that China could import Western technology without being affected by foreign ideas). The authors of *Massacre in Beijing* admit that Deng should be held accountable for the crackdown of 1989, and they present Zhao as a heroic figure to be pitied. They stress, however, that opposition figures were not the only victims of this tragic event. Just as Cordelia's death broke Lear's spirit, the massacres destroyed Deng's "hopes for the kind of political stability and economic progress that would make China a world power in the next century."[62]

The analogy between Cordelia's death and the massacre goes further in some texts, for the protesters (as well as Zhao Ziyang) can be presented as loyal children whose filiality is misinterpreted. Westerners who thought of the pre-1989 Deng Xiaoping as a courageous ruler working to transform China from a socialist dictatorship into a capitalist democracy held onto the hope through April and May that he would realize in time that the students were anxious to achieve this same goal. That Deng ultimately sided with hardliners like Li Peng and Yang Shangkun (who fill the roles of Cordelia's two evil sisters) and rejected both Zhao Ziyang and the protesters became for them a tragic error similar to Lear's mistaken favoring of Goneril and Regan instead of his one truly filial child. According to this narrative, Deng's vision was clouded by bad advice (given by a "clutch of elderly and semi-retired leaders . . . suspicious of any sweeping innovations") and the haunting power of old memories (of his own "humiliation and banishment" during the Cultural Revolution). These two factors combined to produce a kind of madness similar to Lear's, under the spell of which Deng failed to recognize the loyal students for what they were ("the model of peaceful idealism") and viewed them instead as traitors ("old enemies in new guises returning to pursue the unfinished anti-Socialist battles of decades past").[63]

Tragic Version Number 2: 1989 as Julius Caesar

This alternative version of the tragedy of 1989 also asks its audience to feel compassion for both Zhao Ziyang and Deng Xiaoping. When people who encountered Shakespeare's *Julius Caesar* in school think back upon the play, the line that most often comes to mind is the stricken ruler's comment that

Brutus has betrayed him. As various scholars note, however, a close textual reading of the play reveals that Brutus is far from a villain: Caesar may be a victim, but Brutus is actually the true tragic hero of the drama. It is he whom Shakespeare has Antony refer to as the "noblest Roman of them all," and his decision to side with the evil Cassius against Caesar (although it proves his undoing) is treated less as an act of wickedness than as what one Shakespeare scholar calls a "noble error." Even his stabbing of Caesar is motivated by pure (if misguided) impulses: He is trying to prevent his beloved Rome from falling prey once more to political ills (personal as opposed to oligarchic rule) that plagued it in the past.[64]

There are obvious problems with using this plotline to understand tales of Tiananmen. Most importantly, perhaps, China's supreme leader, Deng Xiaoping, was not killed or even purged in 1989, and popular demonstrations do not figure in Shakespeare's political drama set in ancient Rome. Nonetheless, with a little imagination, it is possible to see some Western accounts of the Chinese crisis as reworkings of the tale of Brutus and Julius Caesar, with Deng Xiaoping cast in the role of the former and Zhao Ziyang cast in that of the latter.

Henry Kissinger's August 1, 1989, *Washington Post* opinion piece, "Caricatures of Deng as Tyrant Unfair," is an important example. Just as literary scholars argue that focusing on Brutus as a simplistic betrayer obscures the nobility and complexity of his character, Kissinger wants us to see Deng Xiaoping not as a villain but as a hero who erred when faced with a difficult choice. The brutality of the crackdown should be condemned, Kissinger claims, but we should remember that most (if not all) regimes in other parts of the world would have used some form of violence if dissidents had occupied and refused to leave their nation's major political center. We should also remember that Deng Xiaoping has long been the noblest of all Chinese, at least when it came to normalizing relations with the United States and introducing capitalist economic reforms. According to Kissinger, he is a flawed figure—he listens to the wrong advice, misinterprets situations, and has failed to see that sweeping political reforms must accompany economic ones—but he is much more than simply a power-hungry tyrant. Even in June 1989, according to Kissinger, Deng saw himself (as Brutus did when stabbing Caesar) as protecting the nation from a familiar danger: in this case a resurgence of the kind of mob action that accompanied the Cultural Revolution.

Tragic Version Number 3: 1989 as Romeo and Juliet

The two kinds of tragedies sketched above have centered on high politics and emphasized the actions of top officials. Other kinds of tragic narratives of Tiananmen focus instead upon the character and behavior of the student protesters. The course of events in Shakespeare's *Romeo and Juliet* provides a useful outline for one such student-centered version of the events. In this play, the quest of the hero and heroine is presented as a noble one that is nonetheless destined to fail. Despite the purity of their love, a variety of factors—some, but by no means all, of which are within their control—conspire to ensure that they will not succeed in marrying and living happily as husband

and wife.[65] Similarly, various Chinese and Western authors imply that, as virtuous as the goals of the 1989 protests may have been, the inexperience of the students and the intractability of the obstacles they encountered meant that these goals, too, were unattainable.[66]

There are several more specific parallels between some portrayals of the Chinese students and Shakespeare's treatment of the Italian lovers. In both cases, doubts are raised as to how well the heroes really understood their causes. The protesters of 1989 were certainly passionate about the cause of "democracy," but some authors argue that the youths had at best a limited sense of just what the word entailed and that the students' attitude toward figures such as Hu Yaobang and Zhao Ziyang was fickle to say the least. Similarly, although Romeo is often thought of as true love personified, Shakespeare reminds us that he was just as ardent a suitor of Rosaline before Juliet appeared on the scene. In addition, in both cases, the heroes and heroines are portrayed as being able to realize their dreams temporarily within an artificial environment, but they prove unable to carry this small-scale paradise into the real world: Just as the love that blossoms on the balcony and is nurtured by the light of the moon withers in the city in the cruel light of day, the island of pure democracy that the students create in Tiananmen Square remains an isolated phenomenon.

In at least some variations upon the theme of 1989 as *Romeo and Juliet*, yet another parallel appears: Certain Chinese dissidents and Western analysts suggest that impatience may have played as great a role in the Chinese tragedy as it did in the Shakespearean one. If only the students had been less determined to carry the occupation of Tiananmen Square through to the end, these authors imply, the outcome might have been very different. It is hard to say how Romeo and Juliet would have fared if they had each waited a bit longer to get all of the facts before committing suicide, but their chances for happiness would certainly have been greater. Similarly, had the students exercised more caution, Hu Ping and other veterans of events such as the Democracy Wall Movement have argued, the crackdown might have been avoided or at least have been less severe.[67]

Tragic Version Number 4: 1989 as Oedipus

The final kind of tragic presentation that needs to be examined here is Greek rather than Shakespearean. To quote W. H. Auden, who has written insightfully on the main difference between these two distinctive forms of Western tragedy, the former leaves one saying, "What a pity it had to be this way," whereas the latter leaves one saying, "What a pity it was this way when it might have been otherwise."[68] Shakespeare gives more credence to notions of free will than did his Greek predecessors. Even in *Romeo and Juliet* (in which fate is accorded a strong role as nemesis), the audience retains some hope that the young lovers will not commit suicide, and when they do die their own folly as well as forces beyond their control are to blame. The Greeks, by contrast, seldom left any room for hope. The audience knew from the start that if the gods or the furies were intent upon thwarting a hero, there was no way that he would escape a dreadful fate. The heroes of Greek tragedies frequently suffer from delusions of grandeur, a prideful conceit that they will be able to escape their destiny, and this is shown as contributing to their ruin. Neither hubris of this sort nor the other kinds of sins against the gods that Greek heroes commit (often unwittingly), are of much real consequence in determining the outcome when compared to fate itself. In most Greek trage- dies, in short, "the fall lurks behind every word" and the coming of a predes- tined catastrophe is always imminent.[69]

Lucian Pye's recent essay "Tiananmen and Chinese Political Culture" pre- sents June Fourth as just such a foreordained calamity. There "was an inevita- bility in the escalating confrontation," he writes, that made the events of April through June "a Chinese version of a Greek tragedy."[70] The massacre should not have surprised anyone, he insists, and the only Western China specialists who should have been shocked by it were those who had romanti- cized the nature of the Deng regime and the CCP.

Pye's vision of Chinese communism as an inherently evil force resistant to any kind of fundamental change links him to Leys and other authors who treat 1989 as an anti-Communist romance. What sets Pye apart is his refusal to see the Party's ideology, institutions, and leaders as the only villains. For him, nemesis takes the form of an intransigent, authoritarian political culture whose roots go back much farther than 1949 or even the founding of the CCP and that he claims has continually frustrated all nineteenth- and twentieth- century attempts to transform China into a freer and more modern nation. This vision of Chinese political culture, which he spells out in much more detail in the earlier works that Perry discusses in her Introduction, leads him to be anything but sanguine about the future prospects for a democratic China. The bloodshed of June Fourth will neither cleanse the nation nor change the basic rules of Chinese politics, he predicts, but will only lead to more violence "driven by the dictates of revenge."[71]

In a sense, Pye's essay goes beyond tragedy when he tries to place the events at Tiananmen Square into a broader historical framework that fits Frye's definition of ironic myth. According to Frye, such myths frequently take the form of a "parody of romance: the application of romantic mythical forms to a more realistic content that fits them in unexpected ways."[72] This is precisely what Pye does when he shifts his attention away from 1989 to the modern period as a whole and claims that the very notion that China has ever experienced a true "revolution" (a central starting point for most ro- mantic interpretations of 1989) is nonsensical. If one focuses on real transfor- mations in mentality and social life, as opposed to "wishful dreams" and hopeful rhetoric, he claims, little has changed in China in the last century and a half. Each successive effort to create a new China has merely led to the rep- lication of old patterns of authoritarian rule; whereas romance depends upon forward motion, modern China has been stalled in a vicious cycle.

Although his vision of modern Chinese history veers toward irony, Pye treats the protesters much as Greek playwrights treated tragic heroes. The very circumstances of their birth (in this case within a political environ- ment fundamentally inhospitable to the growth of democratic or egalitarian thought and action) plays a role in sealing their doom, as it does for Oedipus.

In contrast to the Oedipus trilogy, in 1989 it was the fathers who slew the sons (and daughters) rather than the other way around. Nonetheless, one comes away from Pye's essay with a sense that China's history has left it under the same kind of long-standing curse, with the power to punish the innocent as well as the guilty, that haunted the family of Oedipus. And for Pye, the protesters' main sin (like that of Oedipus) was a kind of hubris. A "blind confidence that virtue should conquer all" led them to believe that they could succeed where "revolutionaries" of the past had failed, and this led them "vulnerable to the realities of Chinese authoritarianism."[73]

A Critique of Eight Straw Men

Earlier I described my four tragic categories as ones created to serve "heuristic purposes," but perhaps a blunter (and fairer) statement would be that in the eight versions of the tale of Tiananmen sketched out above I have created straw men. Even some of the writers whose works I have used to illustrate specific plots make use of more sophisticated lines of argumentation than my bare-bones sketches of their texts would suggest, and it would be impossible to place many other accounts of 1989 into a single category without doing an even greater disservice to their authors. Neither analyses of 1989 that Andrew Nathan, Lowell Dittmer, and Andrew Walder offered in an early symposium on Tiananmen, for example, nor most of the chapters in works such as *Perspectives on the Chinese People's Movement*, a collection edited by Tony Saich, fit cleanly into any of my eight narrative categories.[74] The same is true of Jonathan Spence's discussions of Tiananmen: These should be easier to classify (because they have taken the fairly straightforward narrative forms of textbook chapters and introductions to sourcebooks), but his nuanced, historically grounded interpretations of the events incorporate both romantic and tragic elements. The Chinese accounts published to date have generally been simpler to categorize, though there are signs that this situation is beginning to change (at least where former protesters and their supporters, if not CCP officials, are concerned). Shen Tong's autobiography, with its mixture of personal and movement history and its ambiguous assessments of various issues, is difficult to place in any of my eight categories.[75] Similarly, conversations with Su Xiaokang have convinced me that if he ever writes an extended narrative of 1989, the work will be hard indeed to pigeonhole.

Although the categories I have offered are best treated as straw men, analyzing their weak spots seems a useful first step toward constructing a more satisfying mythology of 1989. Straw men may be easy to knock down, but we can still learn something from the exercise. In addition, examining texts that readily fit into my categories can indirectly help us see how hybrid narratives (that combine elements from two or more plotlines) work. To take but one example, John Fincher's essay entitled "Zhao's Fall, China's Loss" presents a considerably more complex interpretation of 1989 than *Massacre in Beijing*. Fincher incorporates elements from various kinds of tragic and romantic tales of Tiananmen to create a narrative hard to categorize.[76] He also introduces important new arguments into the debate on the causes and consequences of the crisis, such as a claim that the spread of cities and the growth of a semi-urbanized population have made obsolete our (and the CCP hard-liners') vision of an overwhelmingly "peasant" China (i.e., as a country with 80 percent of its populace living essentially untouched by metropolitan culture). Nonetheless, the title he gives his piece positions Zhao as a central tragic figure in his narrative and thus suggests that a critique of the *King Lear* approach may provide some insight into his line of reasoning as well as that of the authors of *Massacre in Beijing*.

What, then, are the primary weaknesses of the eight plotlines outlined above? It is easiest to begin with the four romances, as most of the preceding chapters have tried (in one way or another) to suggest that any vision of 1989 as an unambiguous struggle between pure good and unadulterated evil is extremely problematic. For example, although sympathetic to the protesters' goals, Elizabeth Perry and Lee Feigon have stressed that the students who occupied Tiananmen Square often replicated features of the ideology and Party structure they opposed. Their chapters argue that, despite the wall posters heralding the students as the creators of a completely "new" and enlightened China, the protesters were influenced by a variety of decidedly "old" ideas relating to social class and gender. Vera Schwarcz has also suggested that student claims to represent the May Fourth legacy, as opposed to that of the Cultural Revolution, need to be balanced against the reemergence during the movement of patterns of crowd politics reminiscent of Red Guardism. In a provocative law review article, William Alford also reminds us that members of the same generation of students who took to the streets in the name of enlightenment in spring 1989 had been involved in anti-African riots six months before. And in a powerful recent essay, Geremie Barmé discusses the extent to which the protesters of 1989 fell prey to the same kind of "movement mentality" that permeates the CCP's official campaigns.[77]

None of the contributors to this volume presents as extensive a critique of the end-of-history myth as the one Dirlik and Prazniak have recently published.[78] Various chapters do, however, point to some of the key problems with the image of students as romantic heroes striving to free their nation from the hold of an evil Communist ideology. Daniel Chirot suggests that the end-of-history concept needs at least to be modified, arguing that anger inspired by governmental corruption and a general sense of "moral rot," as opposed to disgust with the formal ideology of Marxism, played the fundamental role in leading protesters in various countries to challenge ruling Communist parties in 1989. Ernest Young, who stresses that the protesters and their opponents shared many similar viewpoints concerning the anciens régimes plaguing China, goes further by suggesting that the demonstrators may not have been repudiating the CCP's "revolution" as much as they were simply trying to get it back on course. Moreover, Timothy Cheek argues that right up to June Fourth intellectual dissidents still tended to see themselves as loyal critics, trying to radically reform rather than overthrow the Communist system.

Joseph Esherick and I criticize efforts to present the students as enlightened

May Fourth democrats and committed antiCommunists in our chapter, which also addresses some of the shortcomings of the New Cultural Revolution myth. In this last regard, we stress that treating the use of Mao posters as "proof" that the students identified with the goals of the Cultural Revolution is problematic at best. Mark Hager is right in claiming that the Western media underestimated the continuing influence Marxist ideology has had for Chinese dissidents and that they often overlooked or obscured the tactical and ideological continuities between the Red Guards and the protesters of 1989. Nonetheless, as various contributors argue, the students took great pains to distance themselves from the legacy of the Cultural Revolution, and many of the similarities with Red Guard activism that emerged were inadvertent, not intentional. There were pragmatic reasons for the students to repudiate all features of the Cultural Revolution to be sure, as memories of the chaos of the "ten bad years" continue to haunt many Chinese. The extant evidence makes it hard to believe, however, that all student repudiations of the Red Guard legacy stemmed from strategic calculations as opposed to genuine convictions.

So much has been said about the inconsistencies and inaccuracies of the Chinese government's interpretation of 1989, both in the preceding chapters and in a wide range of works by eyewitness observers, that it may seem that little comment needs to be made about the shortcomings of the fourth romantic tale of Tiananmen I describe.[79] As obviously unfounded as many of its claims are, however, the hard-line version of events should be taken seriously, if for no other reason than that the CCP has gone to such great lengths to try to make its myth seem credible. Chinese television has shown carefully edited documentaries in which violence against soldiers is highlighted and the lone protester's famous confrontation with a tank is presented as "proof" of the enormous restraint that the military showed under stress. Official publications (including works intended for foreign readers, such as a PLA-sponsored pictorial history of the events that provides English-language captions for each picture) exploit errors made by the Western press, citing tales of rivers of blood flowing in Tiananmen Square as evidence that nothing the capitalist media said should be believed.[80] Propagandists and academics have also published collections of source materials, the "documents" in which range from photographs of crowd violence to reprints of the writings of noted "counterrevolutionaries."[81] No matter what form official narratives take, in sum, close attention is often paid to providing "proof" of one sort or another to back up the government's claims. Even the Beijing mayor's report on the protests (which Young discusses in his chapter) contains fairly precise references to specific foreign newspapers to back up its claim that the protests were manipulated from abroad.[82]

One clear sign of the bankruptcy of the regime's romance, however, is that this very concern with facticity has often undermined the official line. The government has had to ban at least two major official publications because they could too easily be "misinterpreted" as contradicting rather than reinforcing the orthodox version of events. One was a detailed chronology of protest activities in cities throughout China prepared for limited circulation

to school officials. Eventually this was deemed too sensitive for even this select audience, apparently because the impression it gave of a truly national
(and largely spontaneous) outburst made the government's insistence that a
small group of malcontents was behind the "turmoil" harder to believe.[83] The
other banned work was a massive two-volume collection of memoirs by
close to two hundred soldiers who took part in the crackdown. This fascinating compilation—the chapters of which have titles such as "Knocking Down
the 'Goddess' Statue" (vol. 1, pp. 259–262), "The Last Four Hours of Six [Sol-
dier] Martyrs" (vol. 2, pp. 58–63), and "The People's Liberation Army: OK!"
(vol. 2, pp. 429–431)—was quickly removed from open circulation, in part
because of the frequent references contributors made to being spat at and
cursed by ordinary citizens. This was seen as undermining official attempts
to present the soldiers as delivering the masses from the threat posed by a
few "bad elements" and "enemies of the people."[84]

The tragic myths of Tiananmen stand up better to scrutiny, on the whole,
than do their romantic counterparts. Here too, however, earlier chapters
point to key weaknesses. The comments that Esherick and I make about the
limitations of factional explanations are a case in point. The best discussions
of intra-Party struggle certainly help us understand a great deal about how
the movement evolved.[85] Nonetheless, treatments of 1989 as contemporary
versions of *King Lear* or *Julius Caesar* put too much emphasis upon the actions
of high officials and draw our attention away from the primary arenas of action (such as the streets) and the broader forces that precipitated conflict
(such as intractable economic difficulties that would have posed dilemmas
for any leadership group).[86]

Previous chapters and other scholarly works also suggest that these first
two tragic versions of the tale of Tiananmen are based upon a variety of
overly simplistic or fallacious assumptions. Did age, bad advisers, and
maybe a touch of Lear-like madness really transform a noble leader into a
completely new person in 1989, or were there continuities between "Deng the
Reformer" (whom foreign opinionmakers of the mid-1980s had valorized as
a brave pragmatist intent upon using "Western-style capitalism" to save
China) and his tyrannical successor, "Deng the Repressor"? Was the behavior
of the latter (and his regime) really based on a determination to maintain
power that had nothing to do with a continuing ideological commitment to
some vision of socialism and revolution? Was Zhao Ziyang's behavior in
1989 as unambiguously heroic and self-sacrificing as Cordelia's in *King Lear*,
or was Zhao too prone to the kinds of vices (greed, nepotism, corruption, an
interest in maintaining his own power) usually attributed to his rivals, such
as Li Peng? And were the protests the result of frustration triggered by the
leadership's failure to introduce political reforms fast enough to keep pace
with generally successful economic ones (Deng's great tragic mistake, in
Kissinger's view), or rather were the very "successes" of the economic reforms a cause of considerable popular dissatisfaction (as Huang Yasheng argues in a convincing essay on the reforms and 1989)? These are the questions
that the contributors to this volume and other scholars have been asking, and

the answers they have given raise significant doubts about the explanatory power of the *King Lear* and *Julius Caesar* plotlines.[87] The authors of earlier chapters also tend to agree on one basic failing of these two versions of the tale of Tiananmen: The tragic figures most deserving of our sympathy are not Deng Xiaoping or Zhao Ziyang but the protesters.

What, then, of the tale of Tiananmen that I compare to *Romeo and Juliet*, a version of events that *does* treat the protesters as the central tragic figures in the plot? This narrative looks fairly good in light of the preceding chapters. The main problem with it is that, like the New May Fourth romance, it presents too hagiographic an image of the students. Not only were the protesters fickle in their devotion to leaders like Hu Yaobang and Zhao Ziyang, Perry and others remind us, they were also capable of elitist behavior that cut them off from social forces that might have helped them transform more than just isolated spots such as Tiananmen Square. Youthful naiveté and impetuosity may have contributed to the tragedy of 1989, but authoritarian and elitist follies more frequently associated with age than with youth also played a role.

Some participants in the movement were clearly aware of the dangers these more "mature" vices posed for the protests. For example, the author of an article that appeared in the May 25, 1989, issue of the dissident journal *Democracy Forum* warned that "the outmoded ideas and sentiments of the dying order [were] invading the cradle of our democratic order [i.e., Tiananmen Square] in a new form." If protesters did not take heed of the lingering influence of a "master-slave framework" imbued by centuries of "autocratic rule," the author continued, "the student movement [would] simply become another autocratic and bureaucratic stratum."[88] The "June 2 Hunger Strike Declaration," issued by three prominent intellectuals and artists (including Liu Xiaobo and the rock singer Hou Dejian), is a second important case in point. Its authors begin with a call for the "birth of a new political culture" based on an egalitarian sense of citizenship, in which everyone is "first and foremost a citizen and only second a student, a professor, a cadre, a soldier, and so forth." The declaration harshly criticizes the regime for bringing "shame to the Communist Party" by using martial law to suppress "democratic ways of expressing the popular will." The authors also point out, however, that those who supported the movement still "lacked a sense of themselves as citizens," and that it was time for the protesters to spend less energy on "sloganeering" and "begin turning our talk into democratic practice."[89]

One might have expected that I would save my harshest words for the fourth tragic narrative of Tiananmen, as Perry's Introduction explicitly distances our approach to political culture in this book from that of Pye. Although I agree with her arguments, however, it is worth stressing here that Pye's version of events in fact has a good deal in common with many of those presented in earlier chapters. Like Pye, most contributors to this volume have highlighted the continuities linking the imperial, Nationalist, and Communist periods of Chinese history. Like Pye, many of us have focused our attention on the way in which cultural factors—patterns of interaction, rituals, beliefs inculcated through education, ideas concerning how the world should work and how one finds one's place in it—shape acts of protest and repression. And, like Pye, many of us have emphasized the need to take the symbolism of the movement very seriously.

This said, the contributors to this volume generally break company with Pye on at least two crucially important issues. The first relates to historical change. The differences between pre- and post-1949 are often overstated, but the previous chapters show that the China of 1989 is in fundamental ways quite different from that in which the May Fourth Movement or even the Cultural Revolution took place. Continuities relating to such things as repertoires of collective action and definitions of the role of intellectuals have been stressed throughout the preceding pages. Authors of earlier chapters have also insisted, however, that even when seemingly familiar slogans (such as "Science and Democracy") and tactics (such as the carrying of Mao posters) have been revived in recent years, these "old" symbols and forms have often been handled in new ways and invested with novel meanings. In short, when taken as a whole, the chapters in this volume contradict Pye's claim that no revolution worthy of the name has taken place in China. They suggest instead that we need to think in terms of not one but several Chinese "revolutions," each of which has tried to present itself as part of an ongoing quest, but each of which has also subtly changed the rules of Chinese politics. Each revolution has transformed the ideological concerns of both the powerful and the powerless and even the relationship between these two groups, leaving rulers and their opponents with new configurations of anciens régimes against which to define their quests.

A second and related way in which most or all of the contributors part company from Pye is that they tend to treat culture as a more fluid and less deterministic force. Although Perry is the only one who explicitly states what she means by the term, most contributors have shared her assumption that culture needs to be treated as something that people create and recreate rather than as an externally imposed set of belief structures and patterns of behavior, that is, as something that creates as well as circumscribes choices. Contributors to this volume have certainly drawn attention to ways in which features of China's cultural inheritance (authoritarian and patriarchal traditions, an orientation toward ritual-based politics, a tendency of intellectuals to think in terms of loyal service to the state, and so forth) helped limit the achievements of the protesters of 1989. They have stopped far short, however, of treating political culture as a curse condemning each new generation to replicate the mistakes of the past, implying instead that though old patterns may be hard to break, they can and in practice continually are being broken.

Toward History: 1989 as a Promethean Myth

It is much easier to use the preceding chapters to highlight the shortcomings of straw men than it is to use them to construct if not a purely "historical" account of 1989, than at least a more satisfying myth of Tiananmen. One essential problem is simply that the contributors, who work in different disciplines and have different orientations, not surprisingly do not agree with each other on a variety of substantive and interpretive issues.

It is possible, however, to use this collection to begin to sketch out the general contours of a tale of Tiananmen that would have greater explanatory power than the eight versions discussed above. The central characters in this narrative would be the protesters themselves, but attention would also be paid to a variety of other actors, beginning with the high officials whose factional struggles affected the growth of the movement, the soldiers who were ordered to suppress the protests, and the journalists who covered the events. It would also have to make room for the contributions made by many who took no direct part in the events and yet fulfilled a crucial role: that of the audience for whom acts of street theater and acts of repression were performed, and to whom competing versions of the story of Tiananmen were told.

This myth would definitely be more tragic than romantic; references to the "tragedy of 1989" appear in many of the preceding chapters, as does an insistence that the students be treated as flawed heroes rather than paragons of virtue. Whether it would be more like a Shakespearean or Greek tragedy is harder to say. The failure of the movement would be attributed in part to factors beyond the control of the protesters. It would, however, stop short of treating June Fourth as a foreordained catastrophe, leaving considerable room for the role of free will. The intractability of forces of repression and traditions of authoritarianism would be seen as helping to seal the fate of the protesters, but so, too, would the behavior of student leaders and the decisions that activists made when creating their own politics and culture within the movement. As far as historical precedents are concerned, the events of 1989 would be seen as related to but also significantly different from earlier PRC struggles.

What kind of implications for China's future does this new mythology have? Given the visions of catastrophe the term *tragedy* conjures up, one might imagine that following this kind of narrative leads only to gloomy predictions. Some of the foregoing essays reinforce this assumption by stressing the enormity of the cultural and political obstacles that future generations of protesters will have to overcome in order to succeed where the demonstrators of 1989 failed. I would like to end this essay, however, by suggesting that adopting this sort of tragic plotline does not necessarily require one to abandon all hope.

The main potential source of optimism lies in the idea that political culture is a fluid rather than static force, and that just as cataclysmic events change individual psyches, they also leave their mark on political cultures. The protesters may not have succeeded in creating the kind of "new political culture" the authors of the "June 2 Hunger Strike Declaration" envisioned, but the demonstrations and the violence that followed certainly did not leave the old political culture unscathed. The China of today, in short, is different in important ways from that of 1989. Its population (at least in the cities) is now more cynical of all claims made in official language. Its young workers and students are more experienced in staging impressive acts of street theater.

And its dissidents are much readier to accept the possibility that saving the nation may require overthrowing, as opposed to merely reforming, the CCP. Differences such as these create room for hope: To leave open the possibility that the events of 1989 may have fundamentally altered Chinese political arrangements, and perhaps even Chinese political culture itself, is to suggest that those who died on June 4 may not have sacrificed their lives in vain.

It may seem that my language has now moved from pure tragedy toward romance. It is worth remembering, however, that historical and mythological traditions are filled with examples of tragic heroes who through their own failure destroyed obstacles that would otherwise have thwarted those who followed. The classic tale of Prometheus is perhaps the best example of this: By giving fire to humans he doomed himself to a bitter fate, but this heroic act changed forever the rules by which mortals and immortals interacted. I would argue that the tragic heroism of people like Wang Dan, Chai Ling, and those who died in the massacres of early June may someday be viewed in a Promethean light. Like Prometheus, their sacrifices may prove to have transformed a power relationship that had hitherto seemed impervious to change: the relationship between China's twentieth-century rulers and those they rule. It is perhaps fitting, therefore, that one slogan of the protesters at Tiananmen Square was: "Seeds of fire cannot be extinguished."

Notes

1. Simon Leys, "The Curse of the Man Who Could See the Little Fish at the Bottom of the Ocean," *New York Review of Books*, July 20, 1989, p. 29.

2. Stephen I. Solarz, "Kissinger's Kowtow," *Washington Post*, August 6, 1989, p. B7; Thomas Oliphant, "A China Lesson Bush Misses," *Boston Globe*, August 13, 1989, p. A30; Miles Kahler, "The Myopic New China Lobby," *New York Times*, August 26, 1989, p. 15; Chalmers Johnson, foreword to George Hicks, ed., *The Broken Mirror: China After Tiananmen* (London: Longman, 1990), pp. vii–xiv.

3. For an insightful sample critique of foreign media coverage of 1989, see William P. Alford, "'Seek Truth from Facts'—Especially When They Are Unpleasant: America's Understanding of China's Efforts at Legal Reform," *UCLA Pacific Basin Law Journal*, 8, 2 (1990), pp. 177–196, esp. pp. 188–189.

4. Student attempts to adapt their communication to appeal to specific audiences are dealt with in detail in Jeffrey N. Wasserstrom, *Student Protests in Twentieth-Century China: The View from Shanghai* (Stanford: Stanford University Press, 1991), ch. 8 and epilogue. Perhaps the clearest example in 1989 relates to the role of nationalism. Whereas English-language student propaganda made few references to the "patriotic" side of the protests and instead highlighted almost exclusively their "democratic" aspects, in Chinese-language texts references to *aiguo* (love of country) were almost as frequent as those to *minzhu* (democracy); for examples, see the documents translated in *Chinese Sociology and Anthropology*, 23,1 (1990), a special issue edited by James Tong and Elaine Chan entitled *Fire and Fury: The Democracy Movement in Beijing, April–June*, esp. pp. 51–52, 83, and 88.

5. Paul Cohen, "The Contested Past: The Boxers as History and Myth," *Journal of Asian Studies*, vol. 51, no. 1 (1992), pp. 82–113. A perceptive general discussion of the distinction (or lack thereof) between mythical and historical narratives, which takes a more

extreme view than Cohen's is Hayden White, *The Content of the Form: Narrative Discourse and Historical Representation* (Baltimore: Johns Hopkins University Press, 1987).

6. Richard Nixon, "Rapproachement and Democracy," *New Perspectives Quarterly*, 6, 2 (1989), pp. 57–58; Henry Kissinger, "The Caricature of Deng as a Tyrant Is Unfair," *Washington Post*, August 1,1989, p. A21.

7. William Pfaff, "The Myth of China," *Baltimore Sun*, June 8, 1989, p. A17; Johnson, foreword to Hicks, *Broken Mirror,* and William McGurn, "The U.S. and China: Sanctioning Tiananmen Square," in Hicks, *Broken Mirror*, pp. 233–245.

8. Miriam London, "The Romance of *Realpolitik,*" in Hicks, *Broken Mirror*, pp. 246–256; see also Leys's own contribution to that volume, "After the Massacres," pp. 155–161.

9. Arif Dirlik and Roxann Prazniak, "Socialism Is Dead, So Why Must We Talk About It?" *Asian Studies Review*, 14, 1 (1990), pp. 3–25. This article is the opening piece to a symposium edited by Nick Knight, *Looking at China After Tiananmen*, which contains other pieces that present similar criticisms of those who champion Simon Leys and his views. See, for example, Michael Dutton, "The Massacre and Method," pp. 30–35. For still another insightful critique of the realpolitik school, see Marie Gottschalk, "The Failure of American Policy," *World Policy Journal*, 6, 4 (1989), pp. 667–684, which argues that the "realism" of Bush's China policy is based on a variety of "unrealistic assumptions."

10. Sarah Lubman, "The Myth of Tiananmen," *Washington Post*, July 30, 1989.

11. Hicks, *Broken Mirror,* p. xviii; Jane MacCartney, "The Students: Heroes, Pawns, or Power-Brokers?" in ibid., pp. 3–23.

12. Robin Munro, "Who Died In Beijing, and Why," *Nation*, June 11, 1990, pp. 811–822.

13. Not all of Munro's conclusions have gone unchallenged by Westerners who were in Beijing at the time; see, for example, the comments concerning the events in Tiananmen Square in Michael Duke, *The Iron House* (Salt Lake City: Peregrine Smith Books, 1990).

14. Harold Isaacs, *Scratches on Our Minds* (New York: John Day, 1958); Pearl Buck, *The Good Earth* (New York: Triangle Books, 1931).

15. Bill Brugger, "Do We Need to Reassess the Chinese Regime After the Events of Mid-1989?" in Knight, *Looking at China*, pp. 36–40.

16. None of the contributors to *Looking at China* mentions *Scratches on Our Minds,* but many of its contributors present arguments that complement those Isaacs makes. See also the opening sentences of the important essay by Henry Rosemont, Jr., "China: The Mourning After," *Z Magazine* (March 1990), pp. 85–96.

17. Edward Said, *Orientalism* (New York: Vintage Books, 1979).

18. Edward Graham, "The 'Imaginative Geography' of China," in Warren Cohen, ed., *Reflections on Orientalism* (East Lansing: Michigan State Center for Asian Studies, 1983), pp. 31–44. For other relevant responses to Said's work, see the other contributions to Cohen's *Reflections;* the symposium in *Journal of Asian Studies*, 39, 3 (1980), pp. 481–517; Paul Cohen, *Discovering History in China* (New York: Columbia University Press, 1984), p. 150; and Jonathan Spence, "Western Perceptions of China from the Late Sixteenth Century to the Present," in Paul S. Ropp, ed., *Heritage of China* (Berkeley: University of California Press, 1990), pp. 1–14, which also refers to the enduring relevance of *Scratches on Our Minds.*

19. "Violence in the Other Country: China as Crisis, Spectacle, and Woman," in Chandra Mohanty et al., eds., *Third World Women and the Politics of Feminism* (Bloomington: Indiana University Press, 1991). See also Nick Knight, "Guest Editor's Introduction," in Knight, *Looking at China*, pp. 1–2; and Dutton, "Massacre and Method," p. 32.

20. Dirlik and Prazniak, "Socialism Is Dead," pp. 6–9, 14, and passim.

21. Northrop Frye, *Anatomy of Criticism* (Princeton: Princeton University Press, 1957), pp. 158–238.

22. Scott Simmie and Bob Nixon, *Tiananmen Square* (Seattle: University of Washington Press, 1989).

23. Lynn Hunt, *Politics, Culture, and Class in the French Revolution* (Berkeley: University of California Press, 1984), pp. 34–39; Hayden White, *Metahistory* (Baltimore: Johns Hopkins University Press, 1973), esp. pp. 1–42. See also, Lynn Hunt, "Introduction: History, Culture, and Text," in Hunt, ed., *The New Cultural History* (Berkeley: University of California Press, 1989), pp. 1–24.

24. Frye, *Anatomy*, pp. 186–206, esp. pp. 187–188.

25. Two of many illustrative works are: Hu Sheng, *Cong yapianzhanzheng dao wusiyundong* (From the Opium War until the May Fourth Movement) (Beijing: Renmin, 1982); and Shandong Province High School Party History Lecture Group, Zhonggong gongchandang lishi jiangyi (Lectures on the history of the Chinese Communist Party) (Jinan: Shandong renmin, 1980). For an example of seasonal imagery of the sort Frye has in mind, see Wang Min et al., eds., *Chuntian de yaolan* (The cradle of spring) (Beijing: Gongqingtuan, 1984), which contains memoirs by student protesters who worked to turn the "winter" of KMT rule into the "spring" of the CCP's "liberation" of the nation.

26. Frye, *Anatomy*, pp. 206–223.

27. Hunt, *Politics, Culture, and Class*, p. 37. A good discussion of the tendency to present the Chinese Revolution in tragic terms can be found in John Fitzgerald, "The Misconceived Revolution," *Journal of Asian Studies*, 49, 2 (1990), pp. 323–343.

28. Cohen, "The Contested Past."

29. Perry Link, *Evening Chats in Beijing: Probing China's Predicament* (New York: Norton, 1992), pp. 3–9, 177–181, and passim.

30. James Clifford, "Introductions: Partial Truths," in James Clifford and George Marcus, eds., *Writing Culture: The Poetics and Politics of Ethnography* (Berkeley: University of California Press, 1986), p. 6, quoted in Aletta Biersack, "Local Knowledge, Local History: Geertz and Beyond," in Hunt, *New Cultural History*, pp. 72–96; Hayden White, The Question of Narrative in Contemporary Historical Theory," *History and Theory*, 23, 1 (1984), pp. 1–33; Lynn Hunt, "Introduction," p. 21.

31. Said, *Orientalism*, pp. 3 and 22. A useful introduction to Foucault's thought is Hubert L. Dreyfus and Paul Rabinow, *Michel Foucault: Beyond Structuralism and Hermeneutics* (Chicago: University of Chicago Press, 1982).

32. See Gabrielle Spiegel, "History, Historicism, and the Social Logic of the Text in the Middle Ages," *Speculum*, 64 (1989); and Biersack, "Local Knowledge, Local History."

33. William Bell, *Forbidden City: A Novel of Modern China* (New York: Bantam, 1990).

34. Steiner, *The Death of Tragedy* (New York: Knopf, 1961), p. 8.

35. Chen Ping, "Shinian gaige weihe daozhi zhengzhi beiju?" (Why have ten years of reform led to political tragedy?), *Zhongguo lun* 30, 5 (1990), pp. 9–13; Ding Chu, *Minzhu yundong de Sunzi bingfa* (Sunzi's military strategy in the democracy movement) (San Francisco: Minzhu Zhongguo shulin chubanshe, 1989), p. 1; Wu Mouren et al., *Bajiu Zhongguo minyun jishi* (Annals of the 1989 Chinese democracy movement) (New York: privately published, 1989), pp. 656, 782, 789, and passim; *Beiping datusha* (The great slaughter in Beijing) (Taipei, 1979), preface. See also the Hong Kong newspapers *Dagongbao* and *Wenhuibao*, June 4, 1989.

36. For an extended discussion of the idea that China has no tragic tradition, the implications of this claim, and citations to works that argue that one or another particular Chinese drama should indeed be called a "tragedy," see Yun-tong Luk, "The Concept of Tragedy as Genre and Its Applicability to Classical Chinese Drama," in Ying-hsiung Chou, ed., *The Chinese Text: Studies in Comparative Literature* (Hong Kong: Chinese University Press, 1986), pp. 14–27. Two important recent discussions of the lesser impor-

tance of tragedy in Chinese as opposed to Western mythic and literary traditions, which avoid the Orientalist assumption that this difference makes China in any sense inferior to the West, are David N. Keightley, "Early Civilization in China: Reflections on How It Became Chinese," and Paul Ropp, "The Distinctive Art of Chinese Fiction," in Ropp, *Heritage of China*, pp. 13–54 and 309–334, esp. pp. 20–21 and 311–315.

37. Frye, *Anatomy*, pp. 187–188.
38. Frye, *Anatomy*, p. 187.
39. Han Minzhu, ed., *Cries for Democracy* (Princeton: Princeton University Press, 1990), pp. 5–8, 39, 43–45.
40. The first calls for a "New May Fourth Movement" came about a month before the anniversary itself. See "Xinwusi xuanyan" (New May Fourth proclamation), as reprinted in *Shiyue Pinglun* (October review), ed., *Zhongguo minyun yuanziliao qingxuan* (A critical selection of original materials from the Chinese democracy movement) (hereafter ZMYQ) (Hong Kong: Shiyue Pinglun, 1989), vol. 2, p. 185. For sample later evocations of May Fourth, see ZMYQ, vol. 1, p. 82, and vol. 2, p. 191; Tong and Chan, *Fire and Fury*, pp. 15–17, 76–77, and 82–83; and Han, *Cries*, pp. 134–140.
41. For a detailed comparison of 1976 and 1989 by protesters, see the wall poster in ZMYQ, vol. 1, p. 65, an English-language translation of which appears in Mok Chiu Yu and J. Frank Harrison, eds., *Voices from Tiananmen Square* (New York: Black Rose Books, 1989), pp. 54–55. See also the documents in Han, *Cries*, pp. 121–124 and 321.
42. See Yu and Harrison, *Voices*, pp. 95–97; and Han, *Cries*, pp. 199–201, 310, and 335–337.
43. ZMYQ, vol. 2, p. 27; trans. in Tong and Chan, *Fire and Fury*, pp. 49–51.
44. For Wuer's speech, see Han, *Cries*, pp. 376–377.
45. White, *Metahistory*, p. 9.
46. Wuer in Han, *Cries*, pp. 376–377.
47. Yu and Harrison, *Voices*, p. 191, and see also pp. 176–200; Han, *Cries*, p. 359, and the picture of a wall poster presenting Li Peng as a man-eating monster in Wasserstrom, *Student Protests*, photographic section.
48. For the events themselves, and the "fetishization of blood" that followed, see Vera Schwarcz, *The Chinese Enlightenment* (Berkeley: University of California Press, 1986), pp. 158–163; and Wasserstrom, *Student Protests*, ch. 4.
49. Han, *Cries*, pp. 44–45; Human Rights in China, ed., *Children of the Dragon* (New York: Macmillan, 1990), p. 181; Wu, *Bajiu Zhongguo minyun jishi*, p. 788.
50. Francis Fukuyama, "The End of History," *National Interest* (Summer 1989), pp. 3–18.
51. Stanley Hoffman, "A New World and Its Troubles," *Foreign Affairs* (Fall 1990), pp. 115–122; see also Dirlik and Prazniak, "Socialism Is Dead."
52. Two English-language examples of works by these kinds of Chinese authors are Maria Hsia Chang, "The Meaning of the Tiananmen Incident," and Lin Yu-siang, "China's Reunification and Tiananmen," both of which appear in *Global Affairs* (Fall 1989). For examples of more simplistic versions of the "New Cultural Revolution myth," see *Revolutionary Worker*, May 22 and June 19, 1989.
53. Mark Hager, "Roots of Dissent," *UCLA Pacific Basin Law Journal*, 8, 2 (1990), pp. 197–266; quotes are from pp. 204, 209, and 214.
54. The best example of official color symbolism appears in a work on 1989 entitled *Hong yu Hei de Jishi* (A true account of the red and the black) (Shanghai: Renyaojian, 1989).
55. Two key documents that spell out the hard-line romance appear in Wu, *Bajiu Zhongguo minyun jishi*, pp. 52–53 and 301–305; for translations of these and related works, see the appendixes to Yi Mu and Mark V. Thompson, Crisis at *Tiananmen*, (San Francisco: China Books, 1989), pp. 155–236. At least one entire work devoted to "prov-

ing" Liu's villainy has been issued: Zheng Wangli, ed., *Liu Xiaobo Qiren Qishi* (Liu Xiaobo and his troublemaking) (Beijing: Beijing qingnian chubanshe, 1989).

56. A valuable general introduction to official publications on 1989 (as well as other kinds of materials), can be found in James Tong's introduction in *Chinese Law and Government*, 23, 1 (1990), pp. 3–9. This special issue of the journal is devoted to Tiananmen and contains translations of important speeches by several top government officials defending the hard-line story.

57. I am grateful to Paul Cohen for reminding me (in a personal communication) of the pre-warlord-era roots of concern with and fear of *luan*.

58. For examples, see the newspaper reports reprinted in *Xuechao, dongluan, baoluan* (Student storms, turmoil, disturbances) (Sichuan: Sichuan renmin chubanshe, 1989); see also the PLA pictorial work and memoir collection discussed later in this essay.

59. Orville Schell, introduction to David C. Turnley and Peter Turnley, *Beijing Spring* (New York: Stewart, Tabori, and Chang, 1989), p. 19.

60. Frye, *Anatomy*, pp. 206–223.

61. My interpretation of *King Lear* has been influenced by Harriet Honigmann, "Dramatic Judgement in *King Lear*," in Robert B. Heilman, ed., *Shakespeare: The Tragedies— New Perspectives* (Englewood Cliffs, N.J.: Prentice-Hall, 1984), pp. 163–174; Kenneth Muir, *Shakespeare's Tragic Sequence* (London: Hutchinson, 1972), pp. 117–141; and James C. Bulman, *The Heroic Idiom of Shakespearean Tragedy* (Newark: University of Delaware Press, 1985). My general understanding of this and other Shakespearean tragedies has also been shaped by Northrop Frye, *Fools of Time: Studies in Shakespearean Tragedy* (Toronto: University of Toronto Press, 1967).

62. Donald Morrison, ed., *Massacre in Beijing* (New York: Warner, 1989), pp. 235–250, esp. pp. 235 and 236.

63. Michael Fathers and Andrew Higgins, *Tiananmen: The Rape of Peking* (New York: Independent, 1989), quotes from pp. 1 and 9.

64. My reading of *Julius Caesar* has been most heavily influenced by Nicholas Brooke, "On *Julius Caesar*," in Heilman, *Shakespeare*, pp. 50–63; quotes taken from pp. 61 and 62. See also Bulman, *Heroic Idiom*, pp. 51–55; Muir, *Shakespeare's Tragic Sequence*, pp. 42–54; and H. B. Charlton, *Shakespearean Tragedy* (Cambridge: Cambridge University Press, 1949), pp. 74–78.

65. James L. Calderwood, "Romeo and Juliet: A Formal Dwelling," in Heilman, *Shakespeare*, pp. 37–49. See also Charlton, *Shakespearean Tragedy*, pp. 53–56, which addresses the question why Shakespeare gives "fate" a more decisive role in this play than in most of his other tragedies; and Muir, *Shakespeare's Tragic Sequence*, pp. 34–41.

66. This is the sense one gets from many journalistic treatments of the events; one of the best remains Simmie and Nixon, *Tiananmen Square*.

67. See Hu's statement in Human Rights in China, *Children*, pp. 210–211; see also Frank Viviano, "Dissidents Criticize Pre-Tiananmen Protests," *San Francisco Chronicle*, August 21, 1989.

68. W. H. Auden, "The Christian Tragic Hero: Contrasting Captain Ahab's Doom and Its Classic Greek Prototype," in Lionel Abel, ed., *Moderns on Tragedy* (Greenwich, Conn.: Fawcett, 1967), pp. 40–44.

69. Karl J. Reinhardt, "Oedipus Tyrannus," in Abel, *Moderns on Tragedy*, p. 188. See also Albin Lesky, *Greek Tragedy* (New York: Barnes and Noble, 1965), pp. 63–64 and passim; and Charlton, *Shakespearean Tragedy*, p. 10.

70. Lucian Pye, "Tiananmen and Chinese Political Culture," *Asian Survey*, 30, 4 (1990), pp. 331–347, quote from p. 347.

71. Pye, "Tiananmen," p. 345; for his general interpretation of Chinese political culture, see *The Spirit of Chinese Politics* (Cambridge: Cambridge University Press, 1968).

72. Frye, *Anatomy*, p. 223.

73. Pye, "Tiananmen," p. 331.

74. Andrew Nathan, Lowell Dittmer, and Andrew Walder, "Tiananmen 1989: A Symposium," *Problems of Communism* (September–October 1989); Tony Saich, *Perspectives on the Chinese People's Movement: Spring 1989* (Armonk, N.Y.: M. E. Sharpe, 1990). Two chapters in the latter volume do, however, follow what I have called the "New May Fourth Movement" plotline quite closely: Lawrence Sullivan's "The Emergence of Civil Society in China, Spring 1989" (pp. 126–144) and my own essay on "Student Protests and the Chinese Tradition, 1919–1989" (pp. 3–24). The comparatively romantic vision of 1989 I present in that piece, as opposed to the more tragic spin I put on events in the present volume, illustrates a general point: A wide variety of factors (the intended audience, the amount of information available when writing, and so forth) have led individual authors to follow differing plotlines in differing texts dealing with Tiananmen. Because I am aware of this, my goal in this essay is not to associate specific writers with particular generic plots (as White's is in *Metahistory*), but rather to highlight the romantic and tragic elements in designated texts.

75. Jonathan Spence, *The Search for Modern China* (New York: Norton, 1990), and introduction to Han, *Cries*, pp. xi–xvi; Shen Tong and Marriane Ye, *Almost a Revolution* (Boston: Houghton Mifflin, 1990).

76. Fincher, "Zhao's Fall, China's Loss," *Foreign Policy*, 76 (Fall 1989), pp. 3–25.

77. Alford, "'Seek Truth from Facts,'" p. 188 and accompanying note; Geremie Barmé, "Traveling Heavy: The Intellectual Baggage of the Chinese Diaspora," *Problems of Communism* (January–April 1991), pp. 94–112, esp. pp. 104–105. Although the racist behavior Alford cites clearly contradicts the implications of the new May Fourth myth, neither this racism nor the elitism of the 1989 protesters necessarily distances them from their flesh-and-blood counterparts of 1919. As I argue in *Student Protests*, ch. 2 and epilogue, a variety of features of the May Fourth Movement that do not fit in with idealized visions of that event (such as outbursts of anti-Japanese violence and the creation of highly bureaucratic and hierarchical protest organizations) have too often been ignored or downplayed by historians in China and the West.

78. Dirlik and Prazniak, "Socialism Is Dead."

79. Sample refutations of the "big lie" by eyewitness accounts can be found in Fathers and Higgins, *Tiananmen: The Rape of Peking*, pp. 134–145; Simmie and Nixon, *Tiananmen Square*, pp. 197–206; Lee Feigon, *China Rising: The Meaning of Tiananmen* (Chicago: Ivan R. Dee, 1990), pp. 244–258; and Munro, "Who Died in Beijing, and Why." For an important (though brief) scholarly critique of the "big lie," see Helmut Martin, *Origins and Consequence of China's Democracy Movement 1989* (Cologne: Bundesinstitut für Ostwissenschaftliche und Internationale Studien, 1990), pp. 29–31.

80. People's Liberation Army, *Quelling Counter-revolutionary Rebellion in Beijing* (Beijing: PLA, 1989), a copy of which can be found in the New York Public Library's Tiananmen Collection. A work in Chinese that is clearly intended for foreign as well as domestic readers is *Beijing Fengbo 50 Wen* (Fifty questions about the Beijing unrest) (Beijing: Huayi Chubanshe, 1989), a catechism of the official line that uses the old-style (or complex) characters usually eschewed in the PRC but favored in Taiwan and Hong Kong.

81. Along with previously cited works, see Guangming ribao, eds., *Pingbao yingyong pu* (A guide to the heroic quelling of the violent disturbances) (Beijing: Guangming ribao chubanshe, 1989).

82. Translated in Yi and Thompson, *Crisis at Tiananmen*, pp. 194–233. This report is a good deal more carefully documented than were many explicitly scholarly works published in the People's Republic prior to the early 1980s, though the use of evidence is cavalier to say the least.

83. *Jingxin dongpade 56 tian* (A soul-stirring 56 days) (Beijing: Dadi chubanshe, 1989).

84. PLA Zongzheng wenhuabu zhengwen bangongshi (Central Political and Cultural Bureau, Essay Solicitation Department), eds., *Jieyan yiri* (One day of martial law) (Beijing: Jiefangjun wenyi chubanshe, 1989). I am grateful to Eugene Wu for alerting me to the existence (and fate) of this work.

85. See, for example, Tony Saich, "When Worlds Collide: The Beijing People's Movement of 1989," in Saich, *Chinese People's Movement,* pp. 25–49.

86. On this second point, see Kathleen Hartford, "The Political Economy Behind Beijing Spring," in Saich, *Chinese People's Movement,* pp. 50–82.

87. One or more of these issues is dealt with in other contributions to this volume and in works such as the following: Huang Yasheng, "The Origins of China's Prodemocracy Movement: A Tale of Two Reforms," *Fletcher Forum of World Affairs* (Winter 1990), pp. 30–39; London, "Romance," and other contributions to Hicks, *Broken Mirror;* and Dirlik and Prazniak, "Socialism Is Dead."

88. "Reflections Under the Monument to the People's Heroes," trans. in Tong and Chan, *Fire and Fury,* pp. 88–90.

89. Wu, *Bajiu,* vol. 1, pp. 550–553; for a partial translation, see Human Rights in China, *Children,* pp. 122–123. See also Barmé, "Traveling Heavy," for discussion of other dissenting views within the movement, as well as background information on Hou Dejian and Liu Xiaobo.

14

THAT HOLY WORD,
"REVOLUTION"

Liu Xiaobo

In Communist China, there is no word more sacred or richer in righteous indignation and moral force than "revolution." In the name of revolution, one-party despotism and individual autocracy have been carried out. Again and again, in the name of "revolution, inhumane political movements have been launched. In the name of revolution, individuals have been stripped of all the rights that they ought to enjoy. In the name of revolution, the economy has been destroyed and historic culture has been extinguished. The name of revolution has even been used in the service of hygiene—in the elimination of the "four pests," which sacrificed flies and sparrows at the altar of revolution. Contemporary Chinese are too enthusiastic about revolution, too worshipful of revolution. Each and every one of us is both victim and carrier of that word, revolution: "The Paris Commune Revolution"; "The October Revolution"; "The Revolution of 1911"; "The Old Democratic Revolution"; "The New Democratic Revolution"; "The Socialist Revolution"; "The Communist Revolution"; "Continual Revolution Under the Dictatorship of the Proletariat"; "The Great Cultural Revolution"; "Reform is a profound revolution." Contemporary Chinese call every social change either a "revolution" or a "counterrevolution." (For example, the 1989 protest movement was referred to by the students as "The Great Revolution For Democracy and Against Dictatorship"; the government, however, referred to it as a "counterrevolutionary rebellion.") Whether to express gratitude or resentment, everyone borrows the name of revolution to speak with the force of justice. It has even reached the point where people will say: "the family revolution," "the marriage revolution," "revolution erupting in the depth of one's soul," as well as "revolutionary heroism," "revolutionary romanticism," "revolutionary realism," "revolutionary writing," "revolutionary couple," "revolutionary descendants," "revolutionary successor." Revolutionary righteousness of itself requires no precondition; on the contrary, revolution is a precondition for the righteousness of any other thing. Whoever the person or whatever the thing, all that is necessary is to give it the name "revolution" and it becomes progressive and full of righteous sentiment. No one suspects or even asks: What in fact is revolution? There is no use in asking and no need to ask. All that we do and all that we think is for the sake of "carrying forth revolution to the very end!"

Regardless of whether we consider its etymological root and modern meaning or the sociological, cultural, and mass-psychological relevance of its practical, concrete application, *geming* (revolution) cannot be translated, as a complete equivalent, into the English "revolution." In English, "revolution" has three levels of meaning: (1) revolve; (2) a large, fundamental social change; and (3) the use of violence to effect a transfer of political rights.[1] It is noteworthy that, in English, the word "revolution" does not carry much of its Chinese counterpart's connotation of sacred righteousness. In Chinese, however, "revolution" in its original ancient sense is the mandate of heaven that a sovereign borrowed or accepted in order to usher in a new dynasty; the word carries a sense of the sacredness and justification associated with carrying out the will of heaven. In the modern era, whether in Sun Yatsen's "the revolution has yet to be completed" or in Mao Zedong's "carry the revolution through to the end," the term "revolution" connotes a supreme sense of the sacred and an exaggerated righteousness. Particularly since the Communist Party took power, "revolution" has become a pure, holy word. For example, "the proletarian revolution was the greatest, most profound, most just socialist revolution in human history." "Revolution" possesses an inherent justice, as sacrosanct as "natural rights" in recent Western history. When we examine the composition of the word, we find that *geming* is a verb-object combination. "Ge" is the verb, meaning "change, eliminate, revoke, strip." As for "ming," it means "heavenly mandate, law, life." Together, "ge-ming" has the sense of "social transformation" or "taking a man's life." For example, "ge-zhi" implies "revoking an occupational duty" or "stripping away rights." Thus, the word "revolution" in Chinese, even when one merely examines the component characters, possesses a not-to-be-doubted quality of righteousness and a not-to-be-blasphemed sacredness. It is one of the most frequently used words in the Communist Party lexicon.

The term "revolution," considered from its sociological, cultural, and mass-psychological angles, has in post-1949 China implied justice, correctness, kindness, virtue, good fortune, and holiness. It also has implied supreme authority; to lay claim to it is to make a bid for what Tony Saich refers to (Chapter 12) as "symbolic capital." It is not possible to express suspicion or opposition to "revolution." "Revolution" implies devotion, sacrifice, daring, fearlessness, idealism, and romantic feelings. It implies longevity and flourishing vitality. All you have to do is say "for the revolution. . . ." It always indicates an iron will, a willingness to "die nine deaths without regret." "Revolution" implies the justice and reasonableness of "profound hatred from great bitterness," violent bloodshed, and cruel struggle. Hatred and poverty are driven by "revolution." If there is to be revolution, there must be hatred. Whoever is the poorest is also the most revolutionary. All members of the working class are the most revolutionary. That is why Mao Zedong called the revolution that he led "a movement of ruffians." "Revolution" implies unyielding, uncompromising, intolerant, uncooperative qualities—a radical justice that shows no forgiveness; the more radical, the more extreme; the more absolute, the more revolutionary. It is not possible for one's faith to be shaken in any way. "Revolution" implies that to rebel is just; that individual actions pale in the sight of heaven compared to actions done in the name of revolution. No matter how cruel the behavior, how blind and unconsidered the action, how absurd the movement—if it can be termed "revolutionary," it becomes reasonable and can be carried out unscrupulously.

In the education system of the Communist Party, an obsession with "revolution" caused us to lose our humanity and rationality, to lose our social conscience and tolerance, to lose the most basic standards of right and wrong, and even to lose the distinction between good and evil. We have been driven mad by "revolution." We have been suffocated by "revolution." We have been spoiled by "revolution" so that we have lost any capacity for feeling awe, fear, or humility. The 1989 protest movement once again showed that "revolution" prevailed. The venom of "revolution" is too deep within us, with the result that we continually become unconscious sacrificial items for the cause of revolutionary justice. We still are infatuated with "revolution."

Revolutions Are the Festivals
of the Oppressed and the Exploited

Although we have experienced the unprecedented cruelty of the "Anti-Rightist Movement" and the "Great Cultural Revolution," we still are not truly aware of the horror and cruelty of "revolution." Although ten years of reform have attenuated the sacred quality of "revolution" and weakened the political culture built upon class struggle, we still worship "revolution" in our bones. We are still the "revolutionary successors." As soon as we meet with a large-scale political movement, our enthusiasm for "revolution" swells; as soon as the kindling of revolution is lit, it burns—the fire rapidly becoming flames that reach to heaven, consuming everything. It does not matter whether the movement is of the extreme Right or the extreme Left, autocratic or democratic, progressive or regressive; "revolution" supersedes all. From within any tendency, it is possible to excite our frenzied worship of "revolution." The 1989 protest movement was once again the "great revolution" of the army advancing toward democracy. In spite of its tragic, bloody end, the revolutionary enthusiasm that had lain dormant for nearly ten years once again ruled us; finally, it again revealed its vigor and dynamism. It was an earthshaking opportunity. Everyone wanted to take advantage of this opportunity to perform a great deed, a great achievement to impress the generations that would follow.

The events in May 1989 in Tiananmen Square were a reminder of that famous statement of Lenin's: "Revolutions are the festivals of the oppressed and the exploited."[2] The crowds that came to Tiananmen Square to demonstrate and parade at first arrived on foot; later they came in squadrons of bicycles, three-wheeled vehicles, and finally motorcycles and cars. The roar of the motors, the unfurled flags, the banners raised in great numbers, the slogans chanted one after another, the ubiquious "V" (for "victory") signs, and the wide smiles on the faces of the people—all of these elements created a celebratory atmosphere as though it was a show. The gigantic banner, several dozen meters long, that hung from the Revolutionary History Museum, displayed but one word: "Awake." The fasting students kept on collapsing; doctors in white uniforms shuttled back and forth, and the sirens of the ambulances wailed. The tragic sense of a righteous advance to death heightened the already intense, showlike atmosphere of the Square. The celebratory events on the Square, in which the university students were the principal actors, attracted farmers, workers, soldiers, cadres, merchants, entrepreneurs, intellectuals, and even a silver-haired old professor making his way with a walking stick past the ranks of people expressing their support for the students. An old retired woman, her face all wrinkled, rode on a three-wheeled vehicle pulled by her son. She, too, made the "V"-for-victory sign. High-school and elementary students carried banners supporting their elder brothers and sisters and raised their fists in show of support. Innocent kindergarteners, waving colored triangular flags, led by the teachers they called "aunties," joined the celebration. There were also robed, shaven-headed monks, chanting their prayers amidst the sounds of their "wooden fish." All of these diverse elements joining together gave people the mistaken impression that this was a revolution that was about to succeed. All of this deepened the atmosphere of celebration. It was like the joyous Square on every National Day or May Day—even more like a square where exuberant crowds throng in the midst of "revolution." The 1989 protest movement did really make every participant dance with joy in high-spirited celebration. Beginning on October 1, 1949, when Mao Zedong led the state-founding ceremony, every year similar events have taken place at Tiananmen Square. Forty years ago, Mao Zedong, brimming with confidence, announced the success of the revolution; forty years later, young university student leaders and prominent intellectuals, too, full of confidence, awaited the success of the "newest" revolution.

We thought that Deng Xiaoping's dictatorship could really come to an end in the midst of this earthshaking revolution; a government of one-party despotism really could fall among that "forest" of arms. How many heroes of the moment set their hearts on the roles they wanted to play after they attained fame? The celebratory, revolutionary atmosphere made it impossible for us to face China's political reality and the stability of Communist Party rule. It was not simply that the Communist Party held in its grip all of the national government machinery as well as an army of several million men; it was also the case that Deng Xiaoping had, through ten years of reform and liberalization, won popular support. We mistook the popular dissatisfaction over some problems associated with reform for a complete loss of hope in the

Deng Xiaoping regime. We were of the opinion that—with the support of the masses—Zhao Ziyang would replace Deng Xiaoping. However, we were unable to reasonably assess the successes and failures of ten years of reform and liberalization. We prominent intellectuals, based on our own interests (the depreciation of knowledge in the rising tide of commodities; the relative decline in living standards of intellectuals, and so forth), took popular rejection of the regime's "eliminate corruption" and "antiliberalization" campaigns and exaggerated its significance so that it seemed a rejection of all of Deng Xiaoping's administrative policies. In reality, although people were dissatisfied with some problems related to reform and although the "eliminate corruption" and "antiliberalization" campaigns somewhat lessened the credibility of Deng Xiaoping, the people nevertheless recognized that in the Deng Xiaoping era (in contrast to the Mao Zedong era of class struggle) every effort was being made to develop the economy and raise the standard of living. This resulted in widespread and deep popular support and a solid, practical legitimacy. The weakening of this popular base and practical legitimacy due to the "eliminate corruption" and "antiliberalization" campaigns was mainly limited to intellectuals. The masses demanded only that there be money to earn and that their standard of living be gradually raised. With these demands being met, the masses were unwilling either to completely abandon the current administration or to thoroughly reject the governing policies of Deng Xiaoping. Objectively speaking, compared to the Mao Zedong era, the changes in Deng Xiaoping's China—the progress of the ruling Party itself and the awakening of the consciousness of the masses—have amazed the world. The enormous changes and progress that ten years of Deng Xiaoping rule have brought to China are greater than those that ten Mao Zedongs could have produced. We cannot, just because of Deng Xiaoping's dictatorship, completely deny the achievements of reform. The despotism of the Party, gunning down people, dictatorship—all of these are evils that must be rectified, but when we face the realities of China, we recognize that this rectification must be gradual, peaceful, and long term. We must not only rely on political pressure from the people but also rely even more on the self-reform of the Communist Party. If the popular political pressure exceeds the actual capacity of those in power to bear this pressure, the reaction that it will cause will not speed up the Communist Party's self-reform and democratization process. To the contrary, it will interrupt or delay this process. The lesson from the blood of June 4 has made this clear already. Moreover, after June 4, Deng Xiaoping rapidly restored social order. The Communist Party again gained solid control of the situation. This shows that Deng Xiaoping's authority does not rely only on violent oppression and bloody terror. It also depends on the accumulated popular support of ten years of reform. The blood of June 4 by no means completely undid this popular support. Deng Xiaoping need only continue to persist in the reforms and develop the economy. If the Communist Party persists in improving itself, Deng Xiaoping's rule will not topple overnight. The pre-June 4 reality, the fact of the June Fourth Massacre, and the fact of the steadfast implementation of post-June 4 reforms all manifest a truth that we participants in the June Fourth movement are emotionally unwilling to accept but that intellectually we must accept: In today's China, the least costly way to democratization and modernization is self-reform of the Communist Party. Political pressure from civil society can only moderately promote this kind of self-reform. A little imprudence could even lead to a greater tragedy than that of June Fourth.

Now that we have seen the Chinese political reality for what it is, let us return to the 1989 protest movement. We have come to see how, tempted by revolutionary righteousness, we abandoned our rationality. We have no way of objectively knowing how many of the nearly one million who gathered in Tiananmen Square were completely dissatisfied with the reforms. How many knew that these forty years of tragedy in China were because of the wild excesses of despotism? How many participated guided by a clear and certain concept of democracy? The illusion created by the dynamism of the moment caused us to ignore the horrible consequences that would result from the continual escalation of the movement and caused our confidence in democratic righteousness to grow far from political reality into a wild presumption that was on the verge of dominating China.

The June Fourth Movement found itself in an environment that, created by ten years of reform, was the most liberal since 1949, and the movement was both inspired by the global democratization trend and thought itself protected by the human rights demands of the Western democratic nations; it opposed despotism and called for democracy in an excessively righteous way. The tragedy lay in the fact that we were only aware of the pursuit of democratic righteousness, aware of the fact that democratization was a global trend and was the future direction of China, aware of the popular opinion expressed by the tumultuous crowds in the Square, aware that our encirclement by countless foreign journalists demonstrated the entire globe's support for us; we were once again overwhelmed by the righteousness of our romantic idealism. We were too righteous, too bold, and too assured. We were completely intoxicated. Therefore, we completely overlooked the fact that Chinese reality lacks the conditions for putting in place overnight a democratic society. We were not aware that, although political democratization is a prerequisite to China's modernization, it is by no means the only prerequisite. Without political democratization, the current reforms in China cannot be carried forward and deepened. But if the focus is skewed too much toward only political democratization, it is not possible to effect a change in direction toward reform and modernization. In the China of today, democratization is not a miraculous prescription, for China lacks the appropriate conditions. Not only is it the case that the Communist Party, which has a firm grasp on political power, is unable to accept a political system that involves multiparty rule (or pluralism, for that matter); it is also the case that the masses still do not understand democratic rights well enough and are incapable of using legal measures to protect themselves in their struggle for individual rights. What is even more telling as to the failure of the movement is that we university students and intellectuals, who have been called "soldiers of democracy," and "stars of democracy" only understand democracy on paper and in theory and do not have a "working" knowledge of real, operating democracy. We do not understand how to establish and implement democracy as a political system or as a comprehensive set of legal procedures. Professor Fang Lizhi, who has been called China's Sakharov, abandoned a great opportunity to use legal measures to protect his own basic human rights even before the 1989 protest movement. The incident—in which he was prevented from attending a banquet to which he had been invited by U.S. President Bush—passed almost completely unnoticed. The famous Liu Binyan, who has been called China's conscience, holds different political views from those of the movement. Prior to the 1989 protest movement, he still persisted in upholding Marxism and socialism and continued to champion the concept of "A Second Kind of Loyalty."[3] Therefore, the chance that there would arise—from this mixture of intellectuals who still needed to learn the ABC's of democracy—the force of popular opposition was extremely slight. The 1989 protest movement produced by these combined factors could only be the symbolic representation of a formalized consciousness. The democracy that we sought during the movement was too empty, too emotional, and did not go beyond the exciting, romantic stage of hollow slogans and idealism of our newly formed consciousness. Most of the resources and methods we made use of to mobilize the masses were ones that the Communist Party itself had used many times before. We were pursuing a large-scale, yet hollow, sensational effect and were unwilling to make point-by-point, concrete requests as well as unprepared to actually implement the vision. This is to say that we still did not understand that democratization is not only an ideal, not only a grand spectacle; it is also the actual, concrete, detailed, even tedious process of setting up and applying democratic procedures. With respect to the specific task of actually creating a functioning democratically governed society, we are just like the Communist Party: We both must begin from scratch.

The revolutionary celebration, which shook the world and which was supported by our great yet empty democratic righteousness, led us down the wrong path. To us, the prominent intellectuals on whose lips is always found democracy, it was discovered to be a more complex undertaking than we had anticipated.

Altar of Righteousness—Sacrifice

The pursuit of spectacular, astonishing effects necessarily leads to a radical stirring of the emotions. The climax of radical emotional excitement is the collective giving up of lives to heroic undertakings. For the race, for democracy, for freedom, we were willing to march to the altar of righteousness—and consequently of sacrifice. In May 1989, the students organized a period of collective fasting involving more than one thousand persons. The movement was not led by the ideals of any one person but by an emotional radicalism. Whoever was radical became the object of everyone's attention. Everywhere—in the pronouncements of the fasting students and in the pronouncements of each group supporting the fast, in the "forest" of banners and in the slogans, on the T-shirts of the students wearing the white cloth headbands of the fast—one could see these words: "We are making history with our lives"; "We are using our fresh blood to launch a new era for the Chinese people"; "I will have no regrets with respect to future generations"; "Blood spattered on the gate of the nation, tears sprinkled on the fertile earth"; "Without freedom, I prefer to die." At the students' command headquarters in the Square, they again and again broadcast the oath: "Heads may be chopped off, blood may flow, but democratic liberty may not be lost." The sad strains of the official song of the Chinese Communist Party, the "Internationale"; the increasingly heavy atmosphere of martyrdom; and the spirit of sacrifice blended together perfectly. Writing letters in their own blood and writing wills, the students evaluated their own commitment to the cause by means of fabricated deaths. This image of giving one's life for righteousness infected everyone on the Square. The mournful wailing of the ambulances cut through the sky, indicating that at any moment a death might occur. By way of the "lifeline" that was maintained by members of the public order squads (their hands linked), the ambulance hurried, red lights flashing, never stopping for a moment. The faces of those near death on the stretchers, doctors in white overcoats, nurses shouting and gesticulating for the crowd to "clear the way"—all demonstrated the tragedy of the collective sacrifice of lives. The pathos of the twelve students from the Central Drama College who abstained from water exceeded that of even the fasters, and the twelve, as a matter of course, became idols on the Square. Through every means of propaganda, and by the watching crowds, they were raised high and placed on the altar of righteous sacrifice to highlight this scene of martyrdom. This most majestic and most moving image of China at the end of the twentieth century satisfied the people's long-quiescent martyrdom complex. If those several students who demanded self-immolation had not been persuaded against such an act, the fires of martyrdom would really have been lighted on the Square, and the ancient Confucian morality of "killing oneself to attain virtue" would have had its contemporary expression.

This fanaticism of giving lives and this spirit of sacrifice came from the lofty sense of mission that society bestowed on the students. Young scholars, supported by what they perceived to be the entire society, felt themselves to be incarnations of righteousness. Moreover, people of every level of society revered them as incarnations of righteousness. As this sense of righteousness became more and more radicalized, no one, except for the heartless government, rationally asked: what will be the result of this radicalism? It was as if the whole society had, by means of their actions, affirmed that the young students should bear upon their collective shoulders the enormous, heaven-sent responsibility of saving China from the grip of despotism. The exaggerated sense of mission and the grandiose sense of history-in-the-making caused the students to lose their ability to control themselves and to know themselves. They did not know that their young shoulders were simply incapable of bearing such a heavy burden. Drawn by the increasingly strong attraction of righteousness, the students, putting their lives on the line, engaged in a continually escalating and futile resistance against the government. It was as though only by giving up one's life could one move the government, only by

sacrificing could one awaken the masses, and only by dying could one accomplish righteousness or become qualified to represent righteousness. No
wonder that Chai Ling, who was commander in chief of the Square and who
successfully fled overseas, replied in a matter-of-fact manner to some people
who criticized the students for being overly passionate and brave at the expense of wisdom and reason: "On the Square at the time, courage was simply
the standard." That is, do not consider reality; abandon reason, we need only
be brave, need only be willing to devote and sacrifice ourselves; we are the
heroes of the 1989 protest movement. What is regrettable is that, after the
1989 protest movement was repressed with bayonets and tanks, the people
scanned the list of the leading persons in June Fourth and failed to find a
single contemporary Tan Sitong. Those who were regarded as heroes during
the climactic moments of the movement as well as those leading persons who
regarded themselves as heroes were, following June Fourth, one after another
tried in the court of morality and justice. The people cannot bear the fact that
the entire nation awaited a martyr and yet not a single one was produced.
Our passion was wasted. Our blood was shed in vain.

In this pursuit of sacrificing lives and in the mass-psychology of awaiting a
martyr, one can see the enormous success of Communist Party socialization.
Seeing the heroic bearing of those walking in the tracks of martyrs, people
could not help thinking of those Communist Party members who, for
the birth of the new China, remained underground for long periods. The de-
fenses written in jail by Wang Juntao and Chen Ziming both mention that the
awe-inspiring acts in the cause of justice that the previous generation of the
Communist Party carried out before the executioner's knife might be called
models for this generation. Beginning from the time we enter elementary
school, we hear the stories of Liu Hulan and Dong Cunrui;[4] we know Mao
Zedong's statement: "Born great, died glorious." The team song of the avant-
garde youth is titled "Always Preparing." Preparing for what? Preparing to
give one's life for the Communist Party. Altogether, too much teaching that
warm blood be willingly spilled for the revolution has caused us to believe
that one need only be willing to give one's life and bravely sacrifice oneself
and then justice can be accomplished (and it is this justice that can ensure
immortality). We simply have not considered that all that this fresh blood
and death have established is a barbarian, despotic government. Mao Zedong, who promoted the spirit of sacrifice and who made everyone "first, not
to fear hardship, second not to fear death," was none other than a murderous
despot. We have not become aware that this righteousness—formed precisely from rashly giving one's life and fearlessly sacrificing oneself—has
caused us to believe that to carry out a revolution, all that is needed is courage and not wisdom; all that is needed is passion and not reason; radicality
and not compromise; a majestic spectacle and not attention to the mundane
facts. Chai Ling's remark that "courage is the standard" can be understood as
meaning that bravery is righteousness or, more exactly, that it is the kind of
self-righteousness that causes us to believe that we can carry forth democracy without understanding the attendant responsibilities of democracy;
that we can demand freedom without understanding the responsibilities of

freedom. In other words, it causes us to understand democracy as the passion for giving one's life and the bravery of sacrifice; to understand it as a lot of soaring passion, a grand spectacle of large crowds, a profusion of slogans. We simply were not wont to know that democracy is the design, implementation, and operation of a rational system. Democracy has its cold side. Democracy is not at all romantic like the ideal we extol; democracy is mundane, even mediocre. Perhaps only by having learned the lesson of blood can we be aware that courage is not righteousness and resistance is not democracy.

The Righteousness of Doing as One Pleases

For forty years, we have not had any democratic political experience; our eyes and ears have been full of nothing but the cruel struggles and devious plots of despotic government. As soon as we began our revolution, we became extremely conceited—just as if we had reverted to the time of the Cultural Revolution and felt ourselves to be the most revolutionary. As soon as we joined into the 1989 protest movement, we considered ourselves to be the most democratic. After all, had we not fasted for democracy and devoted ourselves to it and made sacrifices for it? This made us even more certain that our conduct was of the highest righteousness. Our voice became the only truth. We felt as though we possessed absolute power. Truth became an absolute that would tolerate no questioning; righteousness became doing as one pleases; democracy became privilege; the Square became a miraculous place in which truth was judged, commitment was tested, sentiment was tempered, justice was extended, and rights were exercised. Whoever did not come to the Square or criticized the Square was an antidemocratic, unjust coward. The movement transformed the Square into a touchstone by which everyone was judged. "I spent some time at the Square" and "I've been to the Square" became passwords of a democratic consciousness and of a social conscience.

"There's been a revolution; now there's democracy." So now we can do as we please. Student management replaced the social order of a political party. The public order squads became traffic police. The student identification card became an all-purpose card—with it, we could ride without paying any fare, eat a meal without paying, intercept a vehicle as we pleased, frisk or interrogate any suspicious pedestrian, arbitrarily squander and waste the money that citizens donated, disregard hygiene, spit anywhere, litter at will, defecate or urinate anywhere, even smear feces on the windows of public buses and ignore legal procedures. With only the seal of the Square headquarters, we could declare ourselves married—this was called a "democratic wedding on the Square." We could arbitrarily destroy public property, release the air from the tires of public buses, and self-assuredly declare that this was to smash the government's plots. The Democratic Square was the Square of doing as one pleased. It was a Square from which the odor of feces and urine rose and spread; it was the Square where garbage was piled sky high.

"There's been a revolution; there's now democracy." So now we cannot compromise or cooperate but can form factions as we please, create organizations, anoint ourselves kings, dub our groupings as the Supreme Autonomous Federation, the Fasting Group, the Dialogue Group, the Foreign Supreme Federation, the Federation of Autonomous Unions, the Federated Association of Intellectuals, the Journalists' Alliance, the Dare-to-Die Squad, the Flying Tigers Squad, the West Route Army, the Children's Army, and so on. No one gave into anyone else, and no one could manage anyone else. The ancient saying "Everyone can become Yao Shun" became "Everyone can become a politician." Everyone had a different political philosophy. The Square, which on the surface seemed to be where the multitudes were united as one, was in fact the scene of many divisions, where everyone regarded themselves as separate, sovereign governments. Even if an agreement was reached, it could be abrogated at will. Even if one raised his hand and cast a vote to approve a policy decision, he could personally reject it just as soon as he left the meeting site and then, in the name of righteousness, carry out the decision after all. Between schools and between organizations, there were impassable walls. This frame of mind—in which one thinks oneself the wisest in the world—made everyone in the movement extremely conceited. A right-of-way permit became a mark of privilege. Those who had the right to distribute right-of-way permits seemed to have the right to decide who could join the revolution and who was qualified to participate in democracy. Our movement mobilized so many people and excited passions to such heights, yet we could not make reasonable policy decisions; we found ourselves in a policymaking limbo. If it had not been for the fact that the government repeatedly made incorrect policy decisions, which provided us with points to rally around, we might really have become a directionless, blind crowd.

"There's been a revolution; now there's democracy." So now we could fill our hearts with hatred, holding a bloody shirt and denouncing the wicked Communist Party; gnashing our teeth and berating them; mocking the character of others; engaging in unscrupulous personal attacks. We could berate so-and-so as an idiot, so-and-so as a dwarf, so-and-so as a fool. We could announce the execution of so-and-so, that so-and-so was to be boiled in oil, so-and-so was to be buried alive, so-and-so was to be made to commit suicide, so-and-so was to be made to return home to his family; we could speak even more nastily of those who did not belong to our race. Our attitude was rude and unreasonable, even to the point that we came to blows; we could borrow the name of righteousness to give expression to our personal gripes; we could choose not to accept any mediating force; regardless of the place or the person, we could adopt a hard-line attitude of noncompromise, intolerance, and noncooperation—blindly radical, blindly antagonistic—with the result that the protest movement escalated from concrete demands for redress to an antagonism that sought to bring down the government and throw out Deng Xiaoping. At the same time that we forced ourselves into a situation from which there was no backing out, we forced the government, whose position was at first one of dialogue and compromise, into the predicament of suppressing the peaceful movement with military force. In addition to the government, which has responsibility for the crime of opening fire and killing people, was it not also we, the "warriors of democracy" who were so sure of our righteousness, who had moral responsibility for the making of the final bloody tragedy? Hatred, radicalism, intolerance—these are precisely the revolutionary qualities that Mao Zedong had boldly called for; these were precisely where the essence of the political culture of class struggle is located. Revolution must be unwaveringly carried out to the end. Whoever argues for eliminating hatred or reaching agreements by means of compromise and tolerance is a coward, a traitor, or an academic bandit. The result is that our oath to die defending Tiananmen—our resolve to live or die with the Square— became the final negotiation, compromise, and peaceful retreat when the threat of death actually arrived.

"There's been a revolution; now there's democracy." Now we could, with our eyes open, speak lies; in broad daylight, manufacture rumors; face those concerned and claim that our lying was justified; irresponsibly announce: "Deng Xiaoping has died"; "Li Peng has fled"; "Yang Shangkun was injured"; "Zhao Ziyang has returned"; "Wan Li organized a new government in Canada"; "Twelve cadres of the State Council have declared their departure from the current government"; "Guangzhou and the minority autonomous regions have declared independence"; "The Twenty-seventh and Thirty-eighth Armies have started fighting"; and so on. Tiananmen Square, the symbol of the democratic movement, became a place where lies and rumors were gathered and dispersed. Lies that grew larger the more they were told and rumors whose sources grew increasingly uncertain suddenly became a driving force of the movement. They made radicalism seem more reasonable, raised people's unrealistic hopes of victory, and made it impossible for us to know what, in fact, was happening in China. After June 4, the "warriors for democracy" who fled overseas wantonly twisted the facts so as to exaggerate the cruelty and wickedness of the Communist Party and form the heroic image of themselves as having climbed out of a bloodbath; they stained the bloody surface of Tiananmen Square and misled international opinion. The ebb and flow of time has gradually returned the original scene to history, and after people are able to rationally understand the 1989 protest movement, the evil consequences and tragedy created by the lies and rumors will dissipate.

"There's been a revolution; now there's democracy." We could choose to value only our own freedom of speech, while stripping this freedom of speech from others. We were like Mao Zedong used to be, not permitting any different opinions to exist. As for our own actions, we could only envision support for them on the part of others; our actions could not be criticized. We were like the Communist Party police, forcing journalists not to take pictures that were not to our advantage or that might damage our image. When the journalists shouted out "freedom of the press" and still took pictures, we savagely grabbed the cameras from the journalists' hands, opened them, and exposed the film to light. We sometimes even smashed the journalists' photographic equipment to pieces. We only considered our own rights and safety. Any behavior that threatened our safety and rights, regardless of whether it was justified or legal, was determinedly put to an end by us. In order to keep the government from using an act of vandalism as an excuse for crushing our movements, we escorted the men who defiled Mao Zedong's portrait to the public security bureau, with the result that they were sentenced by the Communist Party to imprisonment for 20 years, 18 years, and 15 years. Were they not exercising their own rights? Should they really remain in prison?

What is even more tragic is that the self-righteousness of the 1989 protest movement was a kind of threat to everyone. People with different opinions fell silent under the pressure of this self-righteousness. Those who did not dare to speak differently and did not want to participate in the movement took to the streets because they feared being called a coward or a scab. The fast transformed the university students into revolutionary saints who could not be criticized. It might be said that, to a certain degree, the students' fast not only presented the government with a difficult issue; it presented society with a difficult issue. When people saw young students paying the price of their lives to oppose the government, who could say the word "no"? Whoever could have said "no," whoever's heart was not moved by such a commitment, did not have a conscience. Whoever doubted the absolute sincerity of the students was an accomplice of the despotic government. The fast caused most people to temporarily forsake their reason and caused the very small minority who retained their reason to fall silent. The rational few even suspected that their own calmness might show a lack of basic sympathy.

The democracy that was extolled during the 1989 protest movement possessed only the smallest amount of realistic, rational righteousness. During the movement, we madly sought blind, abstract righteousness and abandoned actual, rational righteousness.

Would That June Fourth Were
the Last of Blind "Righteousness"

The failure of the 1989 protest movement lay not only in the shedding of blood, the consequent deaths, and the violent suppression of a large-scale, spontaneous mass movement; the failure lay also in the fierce antagonisms that grew out of the continual escalation of the movement. This escalation led to the delay of the reform process and weakened the people's trust in Deng Xiaoping's rule. It also interrupted the process by which the ruling Party was gradually democratizing and reforming itself, thereby causing China to suffer a total reversal of the Party's self-reform. The relaxed atmosphere of early 1989 was gone, replaced by an atmosphere of antagonism, tension, and terror. After June 4, 1989, the reorganization of political rule caused the economy to stagnate. The return to an emphasis on the concept of class struggle made political reform a highly sensitive issue. The murderous air of the Mao Zedong era once again hovered over the vast land of China. The hatred buried in the hearts of the masses as a result of this bloody event will erupt as soon as the opportunity arises. Although Deng Xiaoping still upholds the reform line and his Southern Tour gave rise to an upsurge in economic development, the tight political control in the wake of the events of June 4 has resulted in abnormal development of the Chinese modernization process, and Zhao Ziyang's fall from power has ensured that the power struggle after Deng Xiaoping's death will be most dangerous. Because of the fall from power of Zhao Ziyang—a man with a strong conscience—crisis has emerged around what should have been a smooth and stable transfer of power. A kind of crazed "end of the century" psychology has driven people to think of nothing but getting the most that they can (out of the remaining reform) before calamity strikes. The masses are acutely aware that in Deng Xiaoping's health lies the last chance. If it is missed, they will become meaningless sacrificial pawns in the chaotic world that will follow Deng Xiaoping's death. This "end of the century" phobia cannot be eliminated simply through economic development. At the same time, dispelling the political fears of the ruling Party itself and assuaging the hatred of the masses cannot be accomplished through social stability or a prosperous economy or by raising the standard of living. The political fears of the ruling Party and the "end of the century" phobia of the masses have made it very unlikely that China can move smoothly and steadily toward a modernized, democratic society. Unless the ruling Party and all the people end their antagonism right now and attain social cooperation,[5] it will be impossible to dispel the hatreds and fears on both sides. As the date of Deng Xiaoping's death approaches, those hatreds and fears will become more and more intense, leading to social upheaval sooner rather than later.

Therefore, ending the hostility, dispelling fears, attaining social cooperation, and smoothly and steadily leading China to a modern, democratic society cannot simply depend on the ruling Party resolutely carrying out self-reform and revising its public image; realizing these goals also depends on the cooperation of opposition groups among the people. With this cooperation, self-reform can be gradually accomplished. The current stability in China is perhaps our last chance. The ruling Party must recognize that (1) its own political democratization is not only the direction favored by popular conscience but also by the general trend of world events and that (2) rather than be forced by external factors, it is best to consciously make the changes oneself. The only one who can save the Communist Party is the Communist Party itself. If it gradually, step by step, reforms itself and moves toward democratization, the Communist Party will survive. But if it continues to uphold one-party despotism, the Communist Party will perish. At the same time, opposition groups among the people should not drive the Communist Party from its ruling position; instead, while the Communist Party is carrying out self-reform, these groups should encourage changes under Party rule. For the ruling Party and for the masses, this would be China's wisest choice during a period of rapid transformation.

During this process, the ruling Party should seriously consider playing a political card—the June Fourth card. No one can avoid a re-evaluation of the June Fourth Massacre. The June Fourth card must be played. The critical question is—how is it to be played? And when should it be played? As a sudden redress following the death of Deng Xiaoping? Or by the ruling Party, beginning now, gradually relieving the accumulated dissatisfactions and hatreds of June Fourth? Should the investigation into criminal responsibility for the bloodshed be pursued urgently? Or should the investigation be put off? I think that the wise choice would be the latter. There is no need to make social commentaries, no need to hold a big meeting, and no need to make public proclamations. All that needs to be done is to privately compensate the kin of the June Fourth victims; release all June Fourth political prisoners; restore to their former positions those who, because of June Fourth, were unfairly treated; gradually remove and demote those who rose to power on the blood of June Fourth; and allow those who fled overseas because of June Fourth to safely return. All of this is, I believe, a necessary part of the changing of the ruling Party's image, part of its democratization, part of what will win the hearts of the people. If the ruling Party does not begin now, if after Deng Xiaoping's death some politician relies on a sudden redress of June Fourth wrongs to gain power, it will likely be a catastrophe not only for this politician, but for China. The explosive consequences of a sudden redress are beyond anyone's control. The flood of hatred will drown all who want to have a piece of the June Fourth pie. In the China of the future, those people who, as it were, come to the battlefield with the flash of cold steel might, for the sake of righting the wrongs of the June Fourth bloodshed, cause an even larger scale, even crueler bloodshed. It might even be a bloodbath.

In today's China, five years after the June Fourth bloodshed (and after nearly three continuous years of June fourth–inspired retrenchment throughout China), in a China filled with the fear of the end of the century—much remains to be reconciled. I don't know if we university students and intellectuals who played the role of revolutionary saints and democratic stars for two months can reasonably, calmly, justly, and realistically reevaluate what we did and thought in 1989; I don't know if we can face the Chinese reality of crises emerging on all sides and find within ourselves the courage and wisdom to pursue patiently a feasible plan for lasting reform beginning with the smallest details. If we can, then even if we have only the slightest strength, the blood of June Fourth will not have flowed in vain—it will still be thicker than water. If we can't, then the blood of June Fourth will at most be able to nurture those shameless bloodsuckers.

Would that June Fourth were China's last government by the people in which every person believes himself a politician.

Would that June Fourth were China's last grand spectacle of blind revolutionary self-righteousness.

Notes

1. Very insightful but quite differently structured accounts to Western understandings of the term "revolution," and the way these understandings have changed over time, are provided in Raymond Williams, *Keywords: A Vocabulary of Culture and Society* (Oxford: Oxford University Press, 1983), revised edition, pp. 270–274; Mona Ozouf, "Revolution," in François Furet and Mona Ozouf, eds., *A Critical Dictionary of the French*

Revolution (Cambridge: Harvard University Press, 1989), pp. 806–817; and John Dunn, "Revolution," in Terrence Ball et al., eds., *Political Innovation and Conceptual Change* (Cambridge: Cambridge University Press, 1989), pp. 333–351. *Ed.*

2. Stephan T. Possony, ed., *The Lenin Reader* (Chicago: Henry Regnery, 1966), p. 349. *Ed.*

3. See Jonathan D. Spence, *The Search for Modern China* (New York: Norton, 1990), p. 726, for a concise description of Liu Binyan's notion of loyalty. Its main feature is a belief that supporters of the Party should be able to criticize specific acts of official misbehavior without being branded disloyal; such criticisms, the journalist claimed, actually served to strengthen rather than weaken the CCP. *Ed.*

4. Liu Hulan was a 14-year-old girl. The KMT executed her prior to 1949. She died in quite a heroic manner. Mao Zedong said of her, "A great life, a glorious death," thereby calling all of the nation's people to learn the spirit of revolution from her. Dong Cunrui was a young soldier in the Liberation Army. During the War of Liberation, he used his body as a supporting frame for explosives in an attack on the KMT army positions. He destroyed himself as well as a KMT army pillbox. After 1949, the movie *Dong Cunrui* proclaimed his revolutionary heroism.

5. The one who called for social cooperation was my friend, Zhou Duo. In 1989, when we jointly drafted "The June Second Fasting Manifesto," he pointed out that one of the main points of the manifesto was a call for an end to hostilities and for total social cooperation.

POSTSCRIPT: APRIL 1994

Jeffrey N. Wasserstrom

My preceding chapter was written three years ago, at a time when televised images of the protests of 1989 and the crackdown that followed were still fresh in the minds of many Americans and serious attempts to make sense of the events leading up to June Fourth were just starting to appear. So much new material has come to light since then that, if I had given in to the temptation of revising the piece for the second edition, I would have ended up making a great many changes relating to both style and substance. Some of these revisions would have reflected shifts in my own understanding of specific aspects of the movement.[1] Other revisions would have addressed new issues raised in recent publications that analyze the meaning of the events of 1989 in Chinese and world history.[2] Still other revisions would have been influenced by works on narrative theory that I have read since 1991 that have suggested ways in which my use of Northrop Frye's categories could have been refined. Most notably, I would have looked for some way to combine Frye's genre-centered approach with other sorts of formalistic analytical strategies (such as those employed by Vladimir Propp in his classic study *Morphology of the Folktale*) that use different methods to highlight the varying effects that are achieved when a common set of plot elements are combined in varying ways.[3]

In the end, I decided that it would have been inappropriate for me to update my piece in any kind of comprehensive fashion, since (for reasons spelled out in the Preface) other contributors to the first edition were not

In writing this epilogue, I have benefited from comments made by audiences who attended talks I gave on related subjects at the University of Chicago, Harvard University, Duke University, and Indiana University. I am grateful to Prasenjit Duara, Merle Goldman, and Arif Dirlik for inviting me to make presentations at the first three of these institutions, respectively. I would also like to express my gratitude to Paul Strohm for taking the time to go over the original version of this essay with me and making a variety of suggestions for improvement, a few of which I have incorporated into this postscript.

given the option of revising their chapters. Nevertheless, since being an editor carries added burdens, it seems only right that it should come with a few privileges. Thus, I have decided that it is legitimate for me to add a few comments here concerning four specific things I would have done differently—if I *were to* revise the piece for this edition.

Coming to Terms with New Publications

To do justice to the widely varying ways that recent publications have treated the events of 1989, a "revised" version would have had to contain an even stronger statement than the original concerning the need to view the eight basic plotlines (the four romantic and four tragic myths of Tiananmen detailed in Chapter 13) as "straw men."[4] This is true even though the plotlines continue to have a good deal of heuristic value. Not only can they still help us make sense of the first wave of publications relating to the occupation of Tiananmen Square, but a variety of recent texts (including films, journalistic accounts, historical novels, and textbook chapters) continue to follow one or another of the romantic or tragic narrative routes identified and critiqued in the preceding pages.[5]

Nevertheless, a trend toward telling the tale of Tiananmen in more complex ways was already under way in 1991, and it has continued to gain force in the last couple of years. As a result, many recent works are difficult or impossible to associate with any one of the eight plotlines. Two recent anthologies of primary sources, *China's Search for Democracy* and *New Ghosts, Old Dreams*, are important cases in point. These collections differ from each other in a variety of ways, thanks in part to the fact that the former focuses exclusively on the protests leading up to June 4, while the latter ranges more widely in considering China's contemporary political and cultural predicaments. One of the things that these two disparate works have in common, however, is that each is formatted in such a way that classification in terms of a single generic plot becomes impossible. This is because, in each case, one finds groups of translated documents interspersed with brief analytical essays by the editors that approach the events of 1989 from a series of different angles.[6]

Coming to Terms with Postmodernism

A second change that I would have made in revising Chapter 13 concerns my somewhat tortured effort, in the original version, to stake out a theoretical position that would allow me to treat all stories of the past as "fictions" of a sort, while at the same time retaining the ability to claim that some of these fictions get closer to the truth than others. Thankfully, it is much easier to articulate such an intermediary position now than it was in 1991, since recently published works by a variety of different kinds of scholars, ranging from ethnographers (such as Margery Wolf) to literary specialists (such as

Paul Strohm), are exemplary in showing how one can draw upon some of the
more attractive features of structuralist or poststructuralist analysis, without
embracing the more extreme forms of postmodern relativism.[7] A revised version of my essay would have used references to some of these works to clarify and reinforce my approach to the complex question of the overlaps and
differences between facts and fictions, events and texts.

The work that would have proved most helpful in this regard is Joyce
Appleby et al.'s recently published *Telling the Truth About History*. This work
encourages historians to be skeptical about the fragmentary and biased nature of all versions of the past that they encounter in contemporary and historical texts as well as to constantly remind themselves that their own narratives are the work of people who are by necessity "situated," that is, writing
from and "embedded in a [particular] cultural perspective."[8] Nonetheless,
the authors argue, history is not (as some postmodernists would have us believe) "a mere discourse on other discourses," in which there is no "truth" to
be found but only "truth-effects" to be achieved through narrative tricks.[9]
Nor, they claim, does an interest in the way narratives work preclude a concern with trying to use texts to get a clearer sense of what actually happened
in the past—through a careful sifting of all available evidence.

One of the later passages in *Telling the Truth About History* does a particularly good job of summarizing the advantages of taking what the authors describe as a "practical realist" stance to scholarship. Building on the oft-used
metaphor of historians inevitably having to view history through lenses that
are somehow distorted, the authors write:

> The telescope of an enquiring mind [that historians] train on objects may later
> seem concave or convex, at moments fogged, even cracked, in constant need of
> repair, but it remains an operational tool. Knowing that there are objects out there
> turns scholars into practical realists. They can admit their cultural fixity, their par-
> tial grasp of truth, and still think that in trying to know the world it's best not to
> divert the lens from the object—as the relativist suggests—but to leave it on and try
> to keep it clean.[10]

If I had revised my essay, I would have cited this passage and enlarged upon
it to make two specific claims. First, that analyzing the tales of Tiananmen is
a useful way to keep the "lens" used for viewing contemporary China as
"clean" as possible; and second, that the extant evidence should leave us
with little doubt that Chinese government spokesmen have looked at (or at
least asked their audience to view) the protests of 1989 through a telescope so
"cracked" that it barely qualifies as an "operational tool" at all.

Defending the Use of Imported Categories

A third change in the piece I would have made would have been to take more
time in explaining why I felt that, even though Frye's theories were devel-

oped primarily through analysis of Western literature, it was appropriate to use them to interpret Chinese texts dealing with 1989. I still believe that, in this particular case, the importing of analytical categories is relatively unproblematic, but my decision to do so should have been defended with more care.[11] A recent article by Grant Hardy, which focuses on the narratives of Sima Qian (ca. 145–86 B.C.), one of China's most famous historians, brought this point home to me with particular force. This is because one of Hardy's arguments is that Hayden White's reliance on Frye's categories creates problems where the study of Chinese historiography is concerned. According to Hardy, China specialists can find much in White's approach that is interesting and "suggestive," but in the end it is "too dependent on Western genres to be truly useful in evaluating Chinese narratives."[12]

The case Hardy makes for this position in regard to Sima Qian is impressive, but his arguments have considerably less validity where late twentieth-century texts are concerned. This is because, by this point, most of the Chinese authors in question are people who have been heavily influenced by imported romantic metanarratives of linear progress and social evolution—of the sort which (as Peter Brooks and others have noted) began to play increasingly prominent roles in Western thought and writing during the nineteenth century, at precisely the time that Chinese reformers and revolutionaries became interested in foreign ideologies.[13] This means that, while Hardy may be right when he says that it is problematic to speak of Sima Qian's narratives as veering between "romance" and "tragedy," it may still be perfectly sensible to use these categories to highlight certain features of the stories about the past constructed by contemporary Chinese writers. The tales of Tiananmen constructed by Chinese authors (protesters as well as officials, Communists as well as Nationalists) are, after all, the work of people who have been shaped not only by indigenous historiographic traditions but also by foreign ones that have entered mainstream discourse through the syncretic ideologies espoused by Sun Yatsen and Mao Zedong. It is also worth remembering that, in the case of younger writers, we are also dealing with people who first learned of the Chinese Revolution by reading official textbooks that presented this struggle as a quintessentially romantic quest for renewal.

Lest the preceding paragraph seem to privilege the role of the West as a provider of models for historical understanding, it is worth noting in passing that influences can (and sometimes have) run in the opposite direction as well. Most notably, the image of dynastic cycles (in which a change in regime is presented as masking a deeper continuity) typically associated with Chinese philosophers and historians of the imperial era has periodically exerted a powerful hold on China specialists in the West. Elizabeth Perry draws attention to one famous example of this in the section of her Introduction devoted to the work of C. P. Fitzgerald. There is currently a revival of interest in this kind of approach, moreover, with Harrison Salisbury's 1991 popular history of contemporary China (which is tellingly titled *The New Emperors*) perhaps the best known case in point.[14]

Narratives and Metaphors

Finally, in analyzing the similarities and differences between varying types of authors, a revised version of my essay would have combined an interest in formal narrative structures and plotlines with a concern for other types of literary conventions. More specifically, because I have spent the last three years participating in a collaborative study of the shifting meanings of Chinese political terms sponsored by the National Endowment for the Humanities (NEH), much closer attention would have been paid to the specific metaphors and words used by different groups in describing the events of 1989.[15] One advantage of expanding discussion to include imagery and terminology as well as plotlines as subjects for scrutiny is that it would have allowed me to flesh out my original claim that there is something to be learned from the interesting (and at times surprising) parallels between the tales of Tiananmen told by students, on the one hand, and those told by the regime, on the other.

Since the topic I have worked on most recently for the NEH project has been the political uses of familial metaphors, one of the things I would have focused on to illustrate this point would have been kinship terminology. This choice might seem like an obvious one to Americans who watched television reports transmitted from Beijing in 1989, since as the protests were unfolding newscasters occasionally commented in passing that China's old guard seemed to be acting like angry fathers confronted by disobedient children. Western scholars writing in the aftermath of June Fourth have also occasionally used these kinds of analogies in a casual fashion, as I do in my discussion of the myth of 1989 as a King Lear-like tragedy.

The topic becomes a much more interesting one, however, if we shift our gaze away from Western commentators and focus on Chinese texts. Here we find kinship terms taking on much more prominent and significant roles, and we see protesters and their opponents using the same kinds of metaphors to make opposing points. Thus, some students wore T-shirts bearing the slogan "Mama, We're Not Wrong," which was meant both as a response to all mothers who pleaded with their sons and daughters not to risk their lives by taking militant action and as a reminder that loyalty to the national family and *zuguo* (ancestral homeland) must sometimes take precedence over filiality to one's parents. The regime countered by blasting songs over loudspeakers that included lines such as the following: "I will love you from a distant valley, the Party is your mother and she loves you dearly." When factory workers and journalists carried banners expressing support for their "younger brothers" on hunger strike, official organizations such as the Chinese Women's Association countered by appealing to the nation's "children" not to endanger their health by fasting, and also on occasion invoked the same image alluded to above of the Party as a "mother who loved them deeply." A 1989 student handbill criticized a government official for giving a "father's lecture" to student representatives whom he should have treated as equals, while in a 1993 biography of Deng Xiaoping, a daughter of China's most powerful political figure suggests that the violence of 1989 has done nothing to desanctify her father in the eyes of ordinary Chinese, many of whom (she claims) still place statues of him beside statues of Chairman Mao atop familial altars that were once reserved for representations of revered ancestors. Examples such as these could easily be multiplied, but it is enough for now simply to call attention to the fact that Chinese texts coming from both sides of the political divide share a common concern with either supporting or debunking the image of regime leaders and the CCP itself as good parents to the people of the nation.[16]

These references to kinship metaphors are not meant to revive old stereotypes of China as a peculiarly "clannish" nation, in which political and familial concerns are intertwined in a way that Westerners are bound to find strange. China is undeniably a land where kinship terms often have political meanings, a phenomenon attested to by everything from the prominent place accorded family metaphors within many canonical Confucian texts to the more recent promulgation of the notion that Sun Yatsen should be referred to as the *Guofu* (National Father). There is nothing peculiarly "Chinese," however, about either this general phenomenon (since references to "brotherhood" and "sisterhood" have played important roles in many American political struggles) or the more particular case of radicals claiming that leaders should be deposed for failing to act like good political parents (since just this kind of imagery was employed to justify attacks on Louis XVI and Marie Antoinette during the French Revolution).[17] When Chinese protesters and officials invoked familial metaphors in 1989, they were thus both carrying on in a long-standing indigenous tradition (which is in some ways quite different from that of many Western countries) and engaging in a type of political discourse that has foreign counterparts.[18] For the purposes of a revised version of this piece, however, the main thing worth underlining about the use of kinship imagery in 1989 would have been simply that it draws attention to yet another way in which protesters and their opponents tended to rely upon a common (though by no means immutably fixed) cultural repertoire—a theme that is highlighted by many of the other contributors to this volume.

Notes

1. I discuss some changes in my attitude toward the events leading up to June Fourth in Jeffrey N. Wasserstrom, "Putting 1989 in Historical Perspective: Pitfalls and Possibilities," *Duke Working Papers in Asian/Pacific Studies*, 93-03 (1993); and idem., "Mass Media and Revolutionary Mass Actions in China, 1919–1989," in Jeremy Popkin and Jack Censer, eds., *Media and Revolution: Historical and Comparative Perspectives* (Lexington: University of Kentucky Press, forthcoming).

2. To cite but one example, a revised version of this essay would have had to include a discussion of the scholarly debate triggered by George Bush's claim that a "new world order" has begun to take shape, thanks to the effects that the crises of 1989–1991 had on state socialist systems in various parts of the world. For a fascinating look at this debate, which pays particular attention to the difficulty of placing Chinese events within a "new world order" framework, see Steven I. Levine's review essay on "China's Fuzzy Transition: Leninism to Post-Leninism," *China Quarterly*, 136 (December 1993), pp. 972–983.

3. Vladimir Propp, *Morphology of the Folktale* (Austin: University of Texas, 1968), second edition, translated by Laurence Scott. My attention was drawn to Propp's relevance for this project by conversations with Paul Strohm and comments in Peter Brooks, *Reading for the Plot: Design and Intention in Narrative* (Cambridge: Harvard University Press, 1992), pp. 14–17.

4. Some of the most significant recent publications dealing with 1989 are cited in this volume's lists of suggested readings as well as in the endnotes to the newly included pieces by Calhoun (Chapter 4), Jones (Chapter 7), and Saich (Chapter 12). Three additional works, which focus on media coverage of 1989 as opposed to the events themselves, are also worth mentioning here: James Lull, *China Turned On: Television, Reform, and Resistance* (London: Routledge, 1991), especially pp. 182–207; He Zhou, "The Role of the Chinese National News Media and the Voice of America in the 1989 Chinese Pro-Democracy Movement" (unpublished dissertation, Indiana University, School of Journalism, 1991); and Michael J. Berlin et al., *Turmoil at Tiananmen: A Study of U.S. Press Coverage of the Beijing Spring of 1989* (Cambridge: Harvard University, John F. Kennedy School of Government, 1992).

5. For example, if one focuses on its treatment of the 1989 movement (as opposed to its presentation of the personal travails of student leader Zhang Boli), the recent documentary "Escape from China" (directed by Iris Kung) can be classified as following what I have labeled "The Students as New May Fourth Heroes" plotline. This version of events is also showcased in a fascinating document entitled "In Mourning for the Perished Nation," which (though written in 1989) has only recently become available in the West, thanks to its appearance in an appendix to Tong Boqiao (compiler) and Robin Munro (editor), *Anthems of Defeat: Crackdown in Hunan Province, 1989–92* (New York: Asia Watch, 1992), pp. 193–196. Identified as an oration given at a mass remembrance meeting held in Changsha on June 8, 1989, "In Mourning for the Perished Nation" is very similar in tone and narrative form to the speech by Wuer Kaixi cited in note 44 of Chapter 13.

6. Suzanne Ogden et al., eds., *China's Search for Democracy: The Student and Mass Movement of 1989* (Armonk, N.Y.: M. E. Sharpe, 1992); and Geremie Barmé and Linda Jaivin, eds., *New Ghosts, Old Dreams: Chinese Rebel Voices* (New York: Random House, 1992). The approach to 1989 taken in these texts (and the latter in particular), ends up bearing an interesting resemblance to what Grant Hardy, "Can an Ancient Chinese Historian Contribute to Modern Western Theory?—The Multiple Narratives of Ssu-ma Ch'ien," *History and Theory*, vol. 33, no. 1 (1994), pp. 20–38, describes as the classical historian Sima Qian's emplotment of individual events within "multiple narratives" that vary in formal construction and narrative genre.

7. Margery Wolf, *A Thrice-Told Tale: Feminism, Postmodernism, and Ethnographic Responsibility* (Stanford: Stanford University Press, 1993); Paul Strohm, *Hochon's Arrow: The Social Imagination of Fourteenth-Century Texts* (Princeton: Princeton University Press, 1992). See also various contributions to Saul Friedlander, ed., *Probing the Limits of Representation: Nazism and the Final Solution* (Cambridge: Harvard University Press, 1992).

8. Joyce Appleby, Lynn Hunt, and Margaret Jacob, *Telling the Truth About History* (New York: Norton, 1994), p. 268.

9. Ibid., pp. 227 and 250.

10. Ibid., p. 269.

11. For a thoughtful discussion of the dilemmas involved in using Hayden White's approach to look at Japanese phenomena—a discussion that grapples with many of the same issues that I dealt with, see George M. Wilson, *Patriots and Redeemers in Japan: Motives in the Meiji Restoration* (Chicago: University of Chicago Press, 1992), pp. 43–75.

12. Hardy, "Ancient Chinese Historian," p. 32, note 4.

13. Brooks, *Reading for the Plot*, pp. 6–7.

14. Harrison Salisbury, *The New Emperors: China in the Era of Mao and Deng* (Boston: Little, Brown, 1991).

15. The collaborative study referred to here is being funded by the National Endowment for the Humanities, the Spencer Foundation, and the Pacific Cultural Foundation and is titled "Keywords of the Chinese Revolution: The Language of Politics and the Politics of Language in Modern China." Along with holding workshops on the topic, members of the project have begun to publish their findings in the working paper series cited in the list of suggested readings that precedes this chapter (see Wasserstrom and Tuohy, eds.). The term "keywords" is borrowed from Raymond Williams, *Keywords: A Vocabulary of Culture and Society* (Oxford: Oxford University Press, 1976).

16. For the specific illustrations given, see Han Minzhu, ed., *Cries for Democracy* (Princeton: Princeton University Press, 1990), pp. 113, 126–128, 212–218, and passim; Rudolph Wagner, "Political Institutions, Discourse and Imagination in China at Tiananmen," in James Manor, ed., *Rethinking Third World Politics* (New York: Longman, 1991), pp. 121–144 (esp. pp. 138–141), which contains an insightful discussion of the general phenomenon sketched out here; and Mao Mao, *Wode Fuqin, Deng Xiaoping* [My Father, Deng Xiaoping] (Beijing: Zhongyang wenxian chubanshe, 1993), p. 652.

17. For a detailed and innovative analysis of the French case, see Lynn Hunt, *The Family Romance of the French Revolution* (Berkeley: University of California Press, 1992). The perils and possibilities of applying some of the ideas Hunt develops to the Chinese case are explored in Jeffrey N. Wasserstrom, "Gender and Revolution in Europe and Asia: A Review Essay," *Journal of Women's History* (forthcoming, 1994); and idem., "Was There a 'Family Romance' of the Chinese Revolution?" (An unpublished paper presented at the 1994 meetings of the American Historical Association.)

18. One key difference between the Chinese and French or American traditions, where kinship terminology is concerned, is that words describing sibling ties are typically used to refer to hierarchical rather than purely egalitarian relations in the former case. This is true of ordinary family situations, where older sisters and younger sisters, for example, use different terms of address to refer to one another. It is also true of political cases: The Chinese sworn brotherhoods that played crucial roles in many late imperial uprisings were not bands of fully equal generic brothers, but rather groups made up of dyads composed of *di* (younger brothers deserving of protection) and *xiong* (elder brothers deserving of respect).

ABOUT THE BOOK

This innovative and widely praised volume uses the dramatic occupation of Tiananmen Square as the foundation for rethinking the cultural dimensions of Chinese politics. Now in a revised and expanded second edition, the book includes enhanced coverage of key issues, such as the political dimensions of popular culture (addressed in a new chapter on Chinese rock-and-roll by Andrew Jones) and the struggle for control of public discourse in the post-1989 era (discussed in a new chapter by Tony Saich). Two especially valuable additions to the second edition are art historian Tsao Tsing-yuan's eyewitness account of the making of the Goddess of Democracy, and an exposition of Chinese understandings of the term "revolution" contributed by Liu Xiaobo, one of China's most controversial dissident intellectuals. The volume also includes an analysis (by noted social theorist and historical sociologist Craig C. Calhoun) of the similarities and differences between the "new" social movements of recent decades and the "old" social movements of earlier eras.

ABOUT THE EDITORS
AND CONTRIBUTORS

Jeffrey N. Wasserstrom is associate professor of history and of East Asian languages and cultures at Indiana University. The author of *Student Protests in Twentieth-Century China: The View from Shanghai* (1991), he has also written a variety of articles and book chapters on subjects ranging from the historiography of the Boxer Uprising, to China's one-child family policy, to comparative theories of revolution.

Elizabeth J. Perry is professor of political science at the University of California at Berkeley. She is the author of *Shanghai on Strike: The Politics of Chinese Labor* (Stanford, 1993) and co-editor of *Urban Spaces: Autonomy and Community in Chinese Cities* (Cambridge, forthcoming).

Craig C. Calhoun is professor of sociology and history and director of the Center for International Studies at the University of North Carolina. His major publications include *The Question of Class Struggle: The Social Foundations of Popular Radicalism in the Industrial Revolution* (1982) and an edited volume on *Habermas and the Public Sphere* (1992). An eyewitness to the Chinese events of 1989, his essays on China have appeared in *Dissent* and *Public Culture*, as well as other journals.

Timothy Cheek is associate professor of history at The Colorado College and editor of the *CCP Research Newsletter*. His research and publications focus on the role of intellectuals in the Chinese Communist Party and on propaganda systems.

Daniel Chirot is professor of international studies and of sociology at the Jackson School of International Studies, University of Washington, Seattle. His most recent books are *Modern Tyrants: The Power and Prevalence of Evil in Our Age* (Free Press, 1994) and *How Societies Change* (Pine Forge Press, 1994).

Joseph W. Esherick is professor of history and Hsiu professor of Chinese studies at the University of California at San Diego. Author of *Reform and Revolution: The 1911 Revolution in Hunan and Hubei* and *The Origins of the Boxer Uprising*, he is now writing on the Communist movement of the Shaan-Gan-Ning Border Region in the 1930s and 1940s.

Lee Feigon is professor of history and East Asian languages at Colby College. Author of *China Rising*, an eyewitness account and analysis of the events of 1989, and *Chen*

Duxiu: Founder of the Chinese Communist Party, shorter pieces by Feigon have appeared in the *Atlantic,* the *Chicago Tribune,* and various academic journals.

Andrew F. Jones is a doctoral candidate in East Asian languages at the University of California at Berkeley and the author of *Like a Knife: Ideology and Genre in Contemporary Chinese Popular Music* (Cornell East Asia Series, 1992).

Liu Xiaobo, a literary critic based in Beijing, is one of China's most important and controversial young intellectuals. Singled out by the CCP as one of the "black hands" behind the protests of 1989, his writings have also been harshly criticized by some members of the Chinese dissident community. Aside from several pieces included in the anthology *New Ghosts, Old Dreams: Chinese Rebel Voices* (1992), very little of Liu's work has thus far been available in English.

Stephen R. MacKinnon is professor of history and director of the Center for Asian Studies at Arizona State University. Recent books include *China Reporting: An Oral History of American Journalism in the 1930s and 1940s* (1987) and *Agnes Smedley: The Life and Times of an American Radical* (1988).

Tony Saich is professor with reference to contemporary Chinese politics and organization at the Sinologisch Instituut, Leiden, and a senior research fellow at the International Institute of Social History, Amsterdam. His publications include a two-volume study of the role of Sneevliet (alias "Maring") in *The Origins of the First United Front in China* (1991).

Vera Schwarcz holds the Freeman Chair of East Asian Studies at Wesleyan University. Author of *The Chinese Enlightenment,* a study of the May Fourth Movement, and *Time for Telling the Truth Is Running Out,* an oral history biography of Zhang Shenfu, Ms. Schwartz has recently completed a book manuscript on similarities and differences between Chinese and Jewish approaches to the topic of historical memory.

Tsao Tsing-yuan is an artist and art historian from China who received her M.A. in the Art History program at the Central Academy of Fine Arts in Beijing in 1988. She is presently completing a Ph.D. at Stanford University, with a dissertation on the paintings of the Liao (Khitan) dynasty.

Ernest P. Young is professor of history at the University of Michigan–Ann Arbor. He is currently doing research on late Qing foreign relations and Catholic missions in China. He is the author of *The Presidency of Yuan Shir-k'ai: Liberalism and Dictatorship in Early Republican China* (1977).

Index

Qing dynasty (1644–1911)
    Deng's ancien régime and, 21, 23–24
    New Policies/civil society, 49, 58, 88
    and 1989 protesters, 27
    public contact, 47, 48
Qinghua University, 50
Qiu Jin, 115
Qiushi (journal), 190
Quao Guanhua, 209
Qu Yuan, 55–56

Radio Free Europe, 231
Rand, Peter, 209
Ranke, Leopold, 279
Rankin, Mary, 59
RCP. *See* Revolutionary Communist Party
Red Guards, 33, 287, 288
"Red Sorghum" (*Hong gaoliang*) (Mao Yan), 267(n41)
Reform
    communist systems and economic, 220, 224
    Deng's program for, 18–19, 20–24, 25–26, 107, 313
    and dissent, 87–88, 96, 225, 298
    effect on legitimacy, 247–248, 252–256, 264(n2)
    1989 protests as delaying, 321–322
    See also Change; Modernization
Reform Institute and Rural Development Center, 203(n17)
Relativism, 327
Religion
    and Chinese intellectuals, 195
    folk, 81, 87
"Report to the National People's Congress" (1989), 23
Repression
    closing public spaces, 258
    Communists and popular protests, 54, 59
    and Deng Xiaoping, 76
    as eroding legitimacy, 75
    of history, 170–171
    neoculturalist approach and, 6
    and 1989 protests, 301
    during Republican era, 52–53
    and rock music, 157, 266(n37)
    See also Censorship
Republican era
    nationalism during, 98

political theater during, 51–53, 58, 86–87
    rituals and symbols borrowed from, 37
"Requiem March" (Wang Yong), 158, 159
Resistance, 6. *See also* Criticism; Popular protest
Revolution
    ancien régime and ideology of, 20
    Chinese reverence for, 309–312
    communism established through, 75
    moral decay as cause of, 224–225, 236–237
    progression of 1989 protest towards, 173–174
    versus reform, 18, 88
    role of political culture, 5
    symbolic struggles in producing, 215
    theory on, 218–219, 243(n44), 244(nn 48, 50, 51, 52)
    types of modern, 234–235, 245(n55)
    See also Eastern Europe, collapse of communism
Revolutionary Communist Party (RCP), 287
Revolutionary Worker (RCP organ), 287
Righteousness, 317–321, 323
Ritual
    characteristics of, 42–46, 64(n44)
    and Chinese protest movements, 45–46, 53, 54
    Chinese state and official, 37, 46–49, 52
    defining, 41–42, 60
    divination, 65(n54)
    in neoculturalist approach, 5, 6
    and Taiwan student protest, 11
    in Tiananmen Square occupation, 36, 38, 39–40, 63(n31), 77
    and U.S. politics, 66(n62)
River Elegy. *See* He Shang
Rohmer, Sax, 277
Romance, 279–280, 283–289, 296–298, 328
Romania, 232, 234, 242(n41)
    and Ceausescu, 222, 224, 230–231
    economy, 219, 233
Ruan Chongwu, 85–86
Rural politics, xiii. *See also* Peasantry
Russian Revolution, 235, 245(n57)
Ru Xin, 190–192
Ryzhkov, Nicolai, 239(n12)

Sacrificed Youth (film), 129
Saich, Tony, 9, 295
Said, Edward, 277–278, 282